Post-structuralist readings of
English poetry

Post-structuralist readings of English poetry

EDITED BY
RICHARD MACHIN
AND
CHRISTOPHER NORRIS

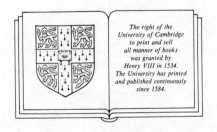

The right of the
University of Cambridge
to print and sell
all manner of books
was granted by
Henry VIII in 1534.
The University has printed
and published continuously
since 1584.

CAMBRIDGE UNIVERSITY PRESS

Cambridge
London   New York   New Rochelle
Melbourne   Sydney

Published by the Press Syndicate of the University of Cambridge
The Pitt Building, Trumpington Street, Cambridge CB2 1RP
32 East 57th Street, New York, NY 10022, USA
10 Stamford Road, Oakleigh, Melbourne 3166, Australia

© Cambridge University Press 1987

First published 1987

Printed in Great Britain at
the University Press, Cambridge

British Library cataloguing in publication data

Post-structuralist readings of English poetry.
1. English poetry – History and criticism
I. Machin, Richard II. Norris, Christopher
821'.009 PR502

Library of Congress cataloguing in publication data

Post-structuralist readings of English poetry.
1. English poetry – History and criticism.
I. Machin, Richard. II. Norris, Christopher.
PR503.P67 1987 821'.009 86–12962
PR503.P67 1987 821'.009 86–12962

ISBN 0 521 30605 1 hard covers
ISBN 0 521 31583 2 paperback

Contents

Contents

Notes on contributors

JONATHAN ARAC is Professor in the Program of Literature at Duke University. Author of *Commissioned Spirits* (1979) and *Critical Genealogies* (Columbia University Press, forthcoming), he has coedited *The Yale Critics* (1983) and *Postmodernism and Politics* (1986). Currently his work focuses on nineteenth-century American prose narrative.

CATHERINE BELSEY is Lecturer in English at University College, Cardiff. She is the author of *Critical Practice* (1980) and *The Subject of Tragedy* (1985). Her main interests are in Renaissance drama and poetry, critical theory and feminist studies. At present she is writing a short book on Milton for Blackwell's "Re-Reading Literature" series.

HAROLD BLOOM is Professor of English at Yale University. He is the author of numerous books and articles on aspects of Romantic and post-Romantic poetry. His work has been highly controversial, partly through its strong revisionist reading of this canon, and partly through Bloom's radically antinomian concepts of poetic influence, authority and tradition.

STEPHEN BYGRAVE is currently Lecturer in English at the University of Leeds. He has written on various topics in the fields of critical theory, nineteenth-century aesthetics and the history of ideas. Macmillan have recently published his book, *Coleridge and the Self: Romantic egotism*. At present he is at work on several projects, including a study of Kenneth Burke for the Croom Helm series "Critics Of The Twentieth Century".

THOMAS DOCHERTY teaches English at Corpus Christi College, Oxford. His *Reading (Absent) Character* was published in 1983 by Oxford University Press; *On Modern Authority: the condition of writing from 1500 to the present* is forthcoming from Harvester. His essay in this volume is from work-in-progress toward a study of Donne, to be published by Methuen. His other main interest at present is in "postmodern" theory and culture, especially as related to the various "modernisms" in Europe from the Renaissance to the twentieth century.

JOHN DRAKAKIS is Lecturer in English Studies at the University of Stirling. He has published books on *Othello* and *Much Ado about Nothing*; has edited volumes of essays on Shakespeare and British radio drama; and is General Editor of a new series, "Methuen English Texts", commencing publication in 1986. He has written widely on Elizabethan and Jacobean drama, and is currently preparing a new edition of Marlowe's *Doctor Faustus*.

ANTONY EASTHOPE teaches English and Cultural Studies at Manchester Polytechnic. In addition to *Poetry as Discourse* (1983) his published work includes *The Masculine Myth*, a study of representations of masculinity in popular culture. His latest book *Poetry and Phantasy* – on aspects of psychoanalysis and ideological critique – should be published during 1986. At present he is writing a critical survey of developments in British post-structuralist theory.

MAUD ELLMANN is Lecturer in English at the University of Southampton. She has also taught and lectured at various North American universities. Her publications include essays from a feminist and post-structuralist standpoint on a wide range of authors, from Chaucer to T. S. Eliot and Joyce. She is closely involved with the journal *Oxford Literary Review*, and has recently completed a book entitled *Modernist Writing and the Problem of the Subject*, soon to be published by Harvester.

FRANCES FERGUSON is Professor of English at the University of California, Berkeley. She has published widely on various aspects of romantic poetry, and her book *Wordsworth: language as counter-spirit* appeared from Yale University Press in 1977. At present she is completing a study of education and its ideological dimensions in the eighteenth and nineteenth centuries.

JONATHAN GOLDBERG is Professor of English at John Hopkins University, Baltimore. He is the author of *Endlesse Worke: Spenser and the structures of discourse* (1981), *James I and the Politics Of Literature* (1983) and *Voice Terminal Echo: postmodernism and English Renaissance texts* (1986). He is currently engaged in research on Shakespeare and cultural graphology.

GEOFFREY HARTMAN is Professor of English and Comparative Literature at Yale University. His many published works include books on Wordsworth, on Derrida (*Saving the Text*, 1981) and on various issues in present-day cultural and critical theory. Since the essays collected in *Beyond Formalism* (1971), it has always been his aim to broaden the scope and enliven the style of literary criticism, drawing on Continental sources (from Hegel to Benjamin and Derrida) as a means of resisting the "teetotal" ethos of the dominant Anglo-American tradition. His most recent book, *Easy Pieces* (1985), sets out to present these issues at a somewhat more accessible level of debate.

ROB JOHNSON is a Reader in English at the University of Adelaide. His publications include *Walter Pater as Critic* (1981), *Aestheticism* (1969) and a volume of poems, *Caught on the Hop* (1984). He hopes to publish a second collection within the next year. His current main interests – in Victorian poetry and critical theory – reflect his belief that these new ways of reading are at once more adventurous and more subtly responsive than traditional approaches.

MURRAY KRIEGER is University Professor of English at the University of California, Irvine. He was the founding Director, and is presently an Honorary Senior Fellow, of the School of Criticism and Theory. The author of many books, among them, most recently, *Theory of Criticism, Poetic Presence and Illusion* and *Arts on the Level*, he is currently at work on *Ekphrasis: space, time and illusion in literary theory.*

RICHARD MACHIN has written on various topics in modern criticism and literary theory. At present he is completing a book on Paul de Man, to be published by Croom Helm in 1987. His other interests extend to Artificial Intelligence, machine translation and the history of science in its textual or rhetorical aspects. He taught for two years in the Department of English at UWIST, Cardiff, before taking up his present work in the field of computer research.

WALLACE MARTIN teaches at the University of Toledo (Ohio). His essays on critical theory have appeared in *Comparative Literature, Critical Inquiry,* and *Diacritics.* He is the author of *"The New Age" under Orage: chapters in English cultural history* and coeditor (with Jonathan Arac and Wlad Godzich) of *The Yale Critics: deconstruction in America.* His latest book *Recent Theories of Narrative* was published by Cornell University Press in 1985.

J. HILLIS MILLER is Frederick W. Hilles Professor of English and Comparative Literature at Yale University. He has published many books and articles on nineteenth- and twentieth-century English and American literature. Most recent of these are *Fiction and Repetition: seven English novels* (1983) and *The Linguistic Moment: from Wordsworth to Stevens* (1985). He is currently at work on a book whose main concern is the ethics of reading.

CHRISTOPHER NORRIS is Reader in English at the University of Wales in Cardiff. His books include *William Empson* (1978), *Deconstruction: theory and practice* (1982), *The Deconstructive Turn* (1983) and *The Contest of Faculties* (1985). He has also published widely in British and American literary journals, and has edited two volumes of essays, on Shostakovich (1982) and George Orwell (1984). At present he is writing a book on Jacques Derrida for the "Modern Masters" series.

DANIEL T. O'HARA is Professor of English at Temple University, Philadelphia. An editor of the journal *boundary 2*, he is also the author of two books from Columbia University Press: *Tragic Knowledge: Yeats's autobiography and hermeneutics* (1981) and *The Romance of Interpretation: visionary criticism from Pater to de Man* (1985). In addition, he has published many essays on nineteenth- and twentieth-century literature and has edited two collections of essays on critical theory. He is currently completing a book on Lionel Trilling and American culture during the Cold War period.

RICHARD RAND is currently a Visiting Professor of English at Trinity College, Hartford, Connecticut. He has contributed essays to various journals and anthologies of criticism, mainly on English Romantic poetry. His translation of Derrida's *Signéponge/Signsponge* was published by Columbia University Press in 1984, and he is now at work (with John P. Leavey) on the yet more extraordinary task of Englishing Derrida's *Glas*.

GAYATRI CHAKRAVORTY SPIVAK is Longstreet Professor of English, Emory University, Atlanta, Georgia, having lectured widely and taught at several American universities during the past few years. She has written numerous articles on feminism, politics and critical theory, and is known as one of the chief exponents of "left" deconstruction in America. In 1977 Johns Hopkins published her elaborately annotated translation of Derrida's *Of Grammatology*, probably the single most influential text in recent critical debate. Her main interests at present are in the uses of deconstruction as a means to resist various forms of racial, political and sexual oppression.

Introduction

RICHARD MACHIN AND
CHRISTOPHER NORRIS

I *"Post-" what, exactly?*

We begin by sorting through just a few points from the critical debate raised by this collection. This should not suggest that the essays have been completely understood and then set out in précis, with the intention of drawing the reader on into the pages that follow. But as it is customary for introductions at least to pretend omniscience, the reader is quite entitled to ask of this introduction two relatively straightforward questions: "What do the essays have to say about English poetry?", and "What do they have to say about literary criticism?" By way of a reply, the introduction asks another question: "Why is it so hard to provide an answer?"

First of all, these authors are not united in any common theoretical pursuit. "Post-structuralist" is a non- or even anti-name, drawing attention to what the essays are *not*, rather than to any shared critical system that characterizes them. In fact many of the contributors evinced anxiety when asked to stand beneath, if not to go ahead and wave, the post-structuralist banner. Essays such as these exhibit a diversity which threatens the tradition of institutionalized criticism; in response, that tradition is ever willing to assimilate them by means of just such a collective name. The name pins the writer down, makes it possible to speak species, and offers a bootstrap by which talk about the new theory can raise itself above talk about the old. But this name also begs the immediate question of another, previous name: what is it about "structuralism" that prevents these essays from being post- anything else? We are already implicitly adding a "Speaking post-structurally . . ." qualifier to each of them which, when made explicit, seems ludicrously uninformative. In view of these objections, why use the term at all?

Structuralism offered criticism its last chance to make a science out of theorizing literature. Fortunately enough, it resulted in a cross-fertilization of disciplines that spawned this latest and spectacularly impotent offspring. Criticism after structuralism is impotent in so far as

1

it is unable to produce further and greater structuralisms. There's not much science of the kind favoured by structuralism to be found nowadays. It is as though the literary structuralists represented the culmination and the grand finale of all previous attempts to produce a scientific theory of literature; in this case, no "new structuralism" was possible. Perhaps "fitz-structuralism" more usefully describes what happened next; it hints, among other things, at both the dangerously over-productive parent and the contentiously illegitimate offspring. But even this seems too closely to confine, or even to exclude its subject. In the event we have the equally graphic "post-structuralism", a term that seems not to name what we do in the present at all, but rather to re-name structuralism itself, as what we used to do in the past. It provides a post to which structuralism is then hitched, confining it by means of the shortest tether the language has to offer.

If the terminology doesn't seem to tell us much about the writers, neither can it have a lot to say about any new critical context that they provide for the poems. Perhaps that is a good thing. After all, the ambition to escape the jargon, the prejudice, and the restriction of formalized theory is not without precedent in literary studies. "Literary theory" seems as indigestible today as it must have been in Leavis's time; literature, then, was strictly non-theory. To this way of thinking, it is not literature's place to be theoretical. And it couldn't be theory if it sounded like literature: each should know its allotted place. But this view founders on the recognition that any talk about literature presupposes a theoretical ground for the discussion, while theoretical discussion inevitably strikes literary poses during the course of argument. Clearly, the distinction is blurred and cannot be rigorously maintained; the impulse suggested by the "post-" seems to be to leave these misleading categories behind. But it also reintroduces the questions with which we began: in the light of post-structuralism's indeterminacy as to what literature and theory *are*, and therefore what it (post-structuralism) might be capable of doing, what does this collection of essays have to say about English poetry? And how are we to view criticism? As theory? Or as non-theory – that is to say literature?

Fixed and mounted by the great tradition, these poems should by now be known inside out. Especially by professional readers, who must be quite familiar with the sort of literary taxidermy still to be found in the academy. But no less than their precursive colleagues, modern readers articulate a continued and persistent need to come to an understanding of these poems. Though the readings are new, strange and different, the occasion of the discussion remains the same. Many professional readers of literature regard the upsurge of literary theory with a fair degree of apprehension; the canon is threatened by inter-disciplinary onslaughts which seem not to play the literary game (at least, not by the familiar rules). Nevertheless, the poems emerge from their ordeal intact – even revitalized. We, the onlookers, complete a triangle in which readers stand alongside poets in an endless struggle with language.

Throughout this struggle, the importance and the necessity of the poetry is unquestionable on two counts: first, the subject of each essay is taken "as read"; that is to say, both as having been read before, and as presenting us with a legacy of interpretative problems which still, as a matter of course, demand a solution. Second, and perhaps more importantly, each new act of criticism questions, rather than enhances, the critical tradition. In the process, it implicitly casts doubt on the relevance of previous readings. Our understanding of the text is renewed, alongside the recognition that any understanding to which we are brought can only be partial and incomplete.

The present essays seem to owe as much to the archaeological as they do to the literary-critical tradition. The dead letters of canonized texts are reorganized even as the readings preserve them; a new context is offered, and the poem appears in startling relief. This process tells us as much about the context as it does about the poems, and writing about literature begins to merge with writing about the changing cir-cumstances in which literature is both written and read. As the poems are translated into this alien context, readers new to post-structuralist criticism might justifiably feel that, on occasions, they are faced with a different language. But as they work to interpret it the process of translation itself reveals new and revised significance for the poems; they seem to speak strangely, and about unfamiliar things.

No, they don't; surely it can't really be the poems that are speaking. Another characteristic of these (and other) post-structuralist readings is their tendency to feature the text as an active subject. Where once the author was, now shall the text be. Strictly speaking, texts cannot do anything. They don't affect anything or anyone until they are read. And yet, the process of reading seems inevitably to employ agents to work on its behalf, be they personal (the name of an author, "this reader", or an implied ideal recipient) or more purely grammatical (an impersonal "it"). The source of meaning always used to be an author. But it might be the reader (just another author), language (the medium as the message), or ideology (a mixture of all three). We do always re-quire a source, a centre around which we can coordinate strategies to "make sense" of a piece of writing – much as we require the subject for a verb. (In this sense, "It's great", said of a poem, is akin to "It's raining", said of the weather.) Within the ensuing discourse a new subjectivity emerges, which the text then claims and reproduces as its own. Since, without enlisting the help of powerful rhetoric, we can't attribute will to an (often departed) author, and since we get the feeling that, no matter how partisan we are, significance within the text is not solely our own responsibility, on many occasions the text's usurpation of a strictly human capacity to make meaning takes place by default. There is certainly a sort of floating subjectivity around when we talk about literature, an "it" waiting to seize its chance to become an "I". (It just did it again.) Such texts, and the autonomy with which they speak, have become the prerequisite source of the power that we ascribe to authors, to readers, to language and to ideology. This turns out to be the transcendental proof, if any sort of proof were needed, of the permanence of the canon.

But if language seems to cover its tracks, in this case by transforming a structural effect (the grammatical third person) into subjective agency, then the same must be said for the critic. Barthes took structuralism to its limits, applying highly systematized but entirely fictitious codes in a mixture of certitude and inspired mythmaking. The present essays, too, owe much to the fact that language always tends to look the same, whether it is used in literature or theory, fact or fiction. The critic is free to borrow from a limitless number of different registers, providing a fluid context into which the poem enters at successive turns of the argument. Indeed, it is often hard to distinguish the reading as context for the poem, and the poem as context for a discourse which seems at odds with the conventions of critical argument. Why should this be?

In part, these readers implicitly reserve the right not to talk about the poem in question. Or rather, to present the poem in tandem with issues which seem alien to it, about which we might have thought it had little to say. In these cases the reading is less an exposition, or an interpretation, than a dialogue. And the poem's part in the dialogue, the statements it makes and the meanings it introduces, can be far from conventional in the impression they create of the "personality" of the poem. Perhaps this is the most authentic way in which these poems can be said to "speak" at all in the present day. Meaning, and the sense of an underlying "intention to mean" that is produced, now arises from the poems' structure rather than from their more overt statement. We are invited to consider how the functional aspect of poetry, its manifest task to make meaning, combines with a more apologetic justification of its success: the language itself remains, after a poem has been read, as the mute foundation of its elegant speech. The language must be accounted for, its rudeness overcome; it must be either hidden, or quaintly featured in the overall architectural scheme. To dismantle this elegant facade is to see the difference between the raw materials, which must claim to be singularly meaningless, and the finished structure, which has a completeness, an identity which is at once appearance and essence. Keats's vocabulary and Lloyd-Wright's bricks have this much in common. The poems haven't changed in all this. They are still the same, and in an important sense they remain the same whatever we say about them. Criticism itself produces and maintains the category "literature", even when it appears to deny principles on which the institutionalized study of literature is founded. Literature is produced, and reproduced, as the site for interpretative contests among competing theories of reading; the changing contexts in which it appears produce an equal and opposite sense of permanence. One of the theorists in this collection demonstrates Yeats's permanent presence within attempts to control, explain and overcome his influential aesthetic. Even as the demonstration unfolds, we see the poetry materialize behind this present struggle to come to terms with powerfully exclusive critical theories. So as change is forced upon convention, convention itself receives an added prop. Stability and change depend on one another, just as post-structuralism reproduces such oppositions even as it appears to prove them groundless.

Nevertheless, it is often when post-structuralism attempts to shift our attention away from "primary" literary texts, and toward the "secondary" works of the critics themselves, that it meets most resistance. Resistance, in this case, often entails fear – fear that something important will be lost, or replaced by an inferior product. There's no doubt that, on the evidence of the present essays, such fears are groundless. Their effect is not to replace study of canonized poetry with study of canonized critics; rather, it is to change those habits of reading with which we approach the work of both the poets and their critics. For example, there is a convention which attaches to poetry a timeless, or more precisely an ahistorical, notion of work. This work is exclusive to "primary" literary texts, and it implicitly excludes whatever it is that critics do. Criticism can still smuggle in its own influential judgments, yet it must do so while claiming merely to provide a service function. But now, this service function is able to reflect on its own history; criticism not only serves, but uses literature as a benchmark against which it can measure its own progress. These poems exist, for us, on the far side of a whole critical history of attempts to read them, a series of attempts to theorize the interpretative problems that have arisen in the course of producing a coherent theory of reading. And so there is an important sense in which the present essays cannot but impose upon the poetry their own pre-history of interpretative struggle. Are we reading the poems through the criticism, as convention would have it, or are these poems offered as media for the tensions and the manoeuvrings of modern critical debate? Tension and manoeuvring is certainly in evidence in these essays. It works both to revise our understanding of the poetry, and – in part as a result – to subvert the conventions by which the poems are fitted into a history of literary interpretation.

We are asked to consider the complex and largely unspoken notion of subjectivity which structures our appraisal of "metaphysical" poetry. This notion sustains, and is in turn sustained by, the sort of subjectivity that we then repeatedly find among the metaphysical poets. The means by which we come to understand the poems, and the poems that we subsequently feel we understand, are inextricably interwined: when we are now asked to question our view of one metaphysical writer's expression of subjectivity, we are immediately led to relativize the position from which we speak, as interpreting subjects in the present. And just as the developmental history of the subject is defined by developmental changes in what the subject knows, so our notion of subjectivity is itself produced, and threatened, by what we know and by how we account for our knowledge. In a subject-centred universe knowledge, understanding and personal identity are held in a disconcertingly fine balance. This is perhaps why it seems so important for us to maintain a coherent picture of literary history, with a firm if diffuse basis in the past and a sharp relevance in the present. Take away that coherence, and we are in danger of falling off the top of the pyramid.

This is one respect in which it makes sense for post-structuralists to insist on the crucial importance of interpretation – sometimes over and above the assumed primacy of real, historical events. Interpretation is not the medium through which the stark immediacy of historical events is made visible; to read is to reproduce images with which we have become familiar, in contexts whose diversity merely serves to increase an accompanying sense of inevitability. In this way a narrative is produced, from which processes of interpretation can make innumerable versions of "the real". Great historical texts make history, and great critical texts make literature. Critical readings of history-texts and historicizing readings of critical texts are, in this respect, similar. They each look for traces of production, marks of the struggle to come to terms with, or find terminology for, experience. Close readings, the sort that do justice to the effort of writing, seek to trace this struggle; it follows that they should best look for it in the *terminology*, rather than in the experience that the terminology seeks to produce. They lead us to examine intricate rhetorical crossings and reversals by which language demonstrates, in order to confess, its ability to get something for nothing, to produce meaning and understanding where formerly there was none. These are points at which the narrative structure of the text, that which provides the support for conventional interpretations, breaks down. It betrays a need to account for its success; moments when language seems to offer an apology for its triumph over the real can be teased out from the text, rather as an analyst unravels the neuroses that are the key to the real within a dream. What emerges is not the meaning of the texts, which would be merely one more misleading version of the real, but the complex mix of ways in which meaning is produced − historical, psychological, and rhetorical. Hence the strangeness of many modern readings in the light of conventional critical response. They seem wilfully offbeat; they leave the rails, disrespecting the norms of literary debate and seeming somehow to miss the point in an unsettling way, often by pushing the poems into issues from which poetry has in the past been excluded. And since the productively unfamiliar tone of this discourse is not easily reduced to conventional terms, convention is often forced to use its last-ditch charge − irrationality − by which it is able to normalize any discourse by excluding it.

However, these essays are clearly far from irrational. Indeed, the very rigour with which they are conducted, collectively and individually, is perhaps their most unsettling characteristic. Each reading develops an insistent coherence of its own that drives toward conclusive and irrefutable assertions. But it does this while holding open the possibility of a multiplicity of competing meanings, each of which denies the primacy of the others. This can be viewed as a self-defeating undecidability at the very foundation of the entire post-structuralist enterprise. But it is also, and more usefully, the practical demonstration of a fundamental insight that the readings bring to light.

Interpretation begins with two kinds of intention: the intention of the interpreter when constructing text, and the intention that is produced from within the structure of language, once its grammatical system gets under way. Just as we can never write exactly what we intend, so we can never write and intend nothing at all. Language has its own inbuilt intention to mean, which we can at best only attempt to harness in a way that seems to suit our present needs. In the past, personal intention when discussing literature has been suppressed −

often in favour of claims to neutrality of motive and universality of judgment. This leads to a corresponding necessity to claim access to the "real" meaning of words on the page, by treating them as transparent carriers of author-to-reader communication. Upon this base is constructed a whole superstructure of literary taste, discrimination and classification, and the skill of the author becomes a function of the degree to which the reading cares to demonstrate his or her control of the wayward tendencies of language. Such demonstration is more a case of carefully restricting the text, rather than respecting it.

Present-day readers are fortunate enough to have this history of repression against which to work. These essays are deliberately, and explicitly, partisan. They arrive on the scene of literary debate with the clear aim of revising the way in which we read the poems – not in order to bring us closer to the author's intention, but to exploit the potential of the text to support arguments that are radically at odds with, and sometimes alien to conventional interpretations. This has two effects. It alerts us to the readers' interests – political, literary, philosophical or whatever. But these essays also collectively draw attention to the failure of previous criticism to make explicit its own interest, on the basis of which the literary canon has been established. They stress the relativity of meaning; that is to say, they deny that any text is able to contain a meaning or set of meanings effectively enough to gain an established identity from them. Meanings overstep boundaries, change and merge, do not obey the orderly rules of time that structure canonical literary history. For this reason, these readers favour a sort of interpretative opportunism: the importance of the text lies primarily in the way that it is made to enter current theoretical debate. Each reader makes quite clear the issues which she or he wishes to address. A new reading in philosophy, for example, might produce interpretative questions which, when turned on a Romantic poem (and its associated interpretative convention), provide a new and revised relevance. Issues raised by contemporary feminist theory are illustrated, and developed, even as they enlighten our view of Wordsworth's programmatic autobiographical poem.

This is an important characteristic of these readings: they offer us new ways of discussing familiar texts, or, more usefully, they offer means of entering the discussion in ways which are relevant in the present day. If theory seems to have been stressed in the last few pages, then it is theory in a particularly utilitarian sense. Perhaps the overriding aspect of these readings is their practical, rather than their theoretical effect. Reading is, and has always been, primarily a practical activity, oriented toward varyingly well-defined goals. Moreover, when this activity seems most transparent, natural and free of effort, it is correspondingly suspect. So in the work that follows, the going is often pretty tough. "Theory" and "criticism" do not, in themselves, hold much interest for any of these essays; what is important is the *practice* of reading and writing, the ways in which the fruits of that practice are consumed, and their more broadly social and historical effects.

When we see the problematics of contemporary theory read into a text from which it seems quite far removed, we are already drawn into a struggle to continue to "know" well-read texts in the light of new knowledge, often derived from a completely different discipline of study. This new knowledge doesn't make reading in itself difficult, but rather it complicates reading in proportion to our familiarity with the text in question. What gets increasingly difficult is the task of maintaining our received impressions of what the text is "about"; it is hard to accept a new, strange and uncanny version of a text which we once thought we recognized. These new essays seek out canonized poems as their most fruitful subjects, the most productive point of greatest resistance to their revisionary practice.

But if practice is the keynote, theory is always about to return, to unsettle and to complicate practice time and time again. Literary criticism has as its goal the production of critical readings, but for as long as it is locked in the complexities of theoretical debate it cannot turn attention to the "primary" texts of literature. Theory upsets the otherwise smooth and uncomplicated process of reading, and so to read must be temporarily to forget the unavoidable incursion of theory (which would otherwise prevent the reading ever from getting started). The only way to do this is to merge theory and practice, letting theory structure, rather than deconstruct, the critical discourse. In this way the practice of reading becomes a demonstration, and therefore an at least partial defeat, of its own limitations. Harold Bloom's readings provide a spectacular example of the way in which theory can be placed in the service of a practice which it would otherwise overwhelm: his complex scheme of correspondence and continuity is above all else a powerful critical practice. Indeed, so powerful is his practice (and his alternative tradition of influential texts) that it seems to rise above the combined potential of its constituent turns of theory.

The upsetting of any firm distinction between theory and practice is characteristic of the collection as a whole. Any call to theory which the essays make transforms that theory into prior practice, and we are left to ponder its significance over and above its truth, or even its coherence. Discussion of modern criticism often uses the sort of terminology, and makes the sorts of assumption, from which the criticism is attempting to escape. This collection demands judgment of a different kind, starting out from radically different premises. We should ask what its effect is on the English poetic canon, on institutionalized literary study and, above all, on our own practices of reading. What does it mean – outside of strictly "literary" interpretation – to suggest that our view of seventeenth-century poetry has been dictated by opinions which have become so deeply entrenched that they are now practically instinctive? What is the effect of linking contemporary semiology, its problematizing of the relation between signifiers and signifieds, and the failure of sixteenth-century poets to trap their Gods within language? And what are the consequences of writing a criticism whose rhetoric renders it indistinguishable from "literature"? Where does reading end, and writing begin? This anthology produces far more questions than ever it could answer – each one related to the questions with which we began. After all, solutions are best provided by engineers, not readers. We are offered what one of the contributors ironically lampoons as "insane adulterations" of texts with meaning. The phrase admirably characterizes the view that sees post-structuralists as mad, and their work as somehow immoral. It includes the sense that there is an almost sacrilegious disrespect for binding professional vows, and that the readings break the norms of commonsense literary talk. It even allows one (and only one) excuse; temporary loss of sanity is the only explanation for this unsanctioned, albeit pleasurable, action. "Post-structuralist", "fitz-structuralist" – so what about "Insane adulterer"? Though equally imprecise, it is certainly more colourful.

Each of the essays that follow is an individual example of modern critical theory "in action". And the effect of the collection as a whole is to demonstrate the impact of theory on texts which can already be considered familiar to students of English literature. It should thus help to close the gap which in recent years has divided practical criticism and critical theory. These readings also hint at the vast amount of work that we have yet to do before we begin to understand the processes at work behind the formation of the canon and the construction of literary history.

II The uses of theory: some historical bearings

The resistance to theory goes deep and far back in the history of English criticism. It has typically taken its sharpest, most aggressive form at times of ideological stress when the values of a native "commonsense" tradition were felt to be threatened by alien modes of philosophical and political thought. The response – clearly visible in a line of conservative thinkers from Burke to T. S. Eliot and the current New Right – was to set up a mystified concept of tradition as guard against theory and its radical claims. What had to be resisted at all costs was the idea that thought could get a critical vantage-point outside the given context of values and assumptions that made up the national culture. A large role here was played by those dominant organicist metaphors which served critics like Coleridge, Arnold and Eliot as a substitute for actively thinking through the issues raised by a nascent sociology of art. Raymond Williams's *Culture and Society* (1957) set out to show how these metaphors developed and how deep was their hold on subsequent thinking, notably in the case of Leavis. What they chiefly worked to promote was a notion of timeless human good divorced from all practical dealing with history, politics or any kind of *theory* that criticized existing relations of power. The "organic community" of these thinkers' imagining was a transposition of aesthetic values into the sphere of historical myth. It begins with the Romantic ideal of poetry (or "aesthetic education") as the means of regaining a long-lost equilibrium between thought and sensibility, intellect and emotion.

In philosophers like Schiller this idea possesses a genuine utopian dimension, aimed at a future state of society where instinct and desire would no longer be shackled by the dictates of repressive rationality. But this aesthetic ideology takes a very different turn when Coleridge – like Eliot after him – conceives of society itself in terms of the organicist metaphor. It then becomes impossible to think of social change except as brought about by that long slow process of organic development whose causes and effects mere critical reason can scarcely grasp in retrospect, let alone hope to predict or actively promote. Theory is deluded if it seeks to comprehend this process on terms more radical or historically far-seeing than anything provided from within its own cultural tradition. And this for the reason that any such knowledge simply wouldn't *count* as genuine understanding in the light of those same values and assumptions that make up the relevant background of debate. Disaffected intellectuals (or critical theorists) would find no place in this tradition where the limits of reason are implicitly equated with the self-understanding of a national culture.

These are some of the motives that seem to be at work in the current round of hostilities. What perhaps needs accounting for is why such battles should so often be fought on the specialized ground of aesthetics and literary theory. I have already suggested the outline of an answer, one that might begin (taking a lead from Paul de Man) precisely by questioning the assumed identity of interests between "aesthetics" and "theory". In his late essays on Kant and Hegel, de Man lays the ground for a reading of modern intellectual history that centres on the uses of aesthetic ideology to evade certain issues of cultural politics.[1] His argument can be summarized roughly as follows (though the summary will hardly do justice to the subtlety and rigour of de Man's critical thought). Since Kant, it has been the role of aesthetic philosophy not merely to carry on a marginal discourse about questions of artistic "taste", but to occupy a certain crucial position in the philosophical enterprise at large. This came about (so de Man argues) through the problems thrown up in Kant's attempt to drive off the demons of sceptical doubt by providing experience with a solid groundwork of *a priori* concepts and categories. Where philosophers like Hume had gone wrong, Kant believed, was in raising ontological problems, i.e. questions as to how things must stand *in reality* if thought was to make intelligible sense of them according to its own commonsense assumptions. Hence the notorious difficulties that Hume encountered in trying to explain how concepts like that of cause-and-effect could possibly possess any kind of necessary truth, given that they rested on facts-of-observation rather than analytic reasoning. Kant's "Copernican revolution" in philosophy consisted of turning this problem round, of asking what deep regularities govern our ways of understanding the world, given that we *do*, in practice, share a great number of fundamental concepts and beliefs. Rather than confess oneself baffled, like Hume, by the lack of any cogent "philosophical" grounds for accepting these deep-laid assumptions, why not take the more sensible course of redefining the powers and proper interests of philosophy? It would then be a matter of showing precisely what limits could be drawn, and what capacities ascribed, to the *a priori* structures of human cognitive grasp.

So much – in drastically simplified form – for the major shift of philosophical perspective brought about by Kant's revolution. It was *not*, he insisted, just another species of idealist argument, abandoning the claims of real-world experience for the sake of preserving some edifice of abstract mental representations. "Concepts without intuitions are empty; intuitions without concepts are blind." This two-way dependence was Kant's guarantee that thinking on the *a priori* structures of mind could still keep in touch with a sensory life-world sufficiently "real" to assure the whole enterprise of philosophical reason. Otherwise thought would be free to run wild in speculative puzzles of its own groundless inventing, a danger of which Kant provides various warning examples in the so-called "Antinomies of Pure Reason". But the imperative that concepts be matched with intuitions remained very much a *formal* imperative, a requirement enjoined upon Kant's interpreters rather than built absolutely into the structure of his argument. That he could, in fact, be read as lending support to a variety of subjectivist or idealist creeds is evident enough from the subsequent history of Kantian interpretation.

What is mainly of interest in the present context is the fact that aesthetics had a crucial role to play in establishing the series of conceptual links by which Kant hoped to make good his central claims. Aesthetic understanding is the meeting-ground where concepts are most intimately tied to the sensuous experience which prevents pure reason from becoming lost in the toils of metaphysical abstraction. The *Critique Of Judgement* is no mere appendage to the Kantian enterprise but marks, on the contrary, the problematic point of transition between all its major strategies of argument. Aesthetic experience becomes, in effect, the test-case and exemplary instance of a sensuous activity that also appeals to constitutive laws of its own self-governing nature. What is in question here is not only the passage from concept to experience but also the further – ethical – problem of articulating judgments of value with matters of rational argumentation. Hence Kant's insistence that aesthetic valuation is *not* just an affair of individual "taste" (which would place it beyond all reach of rational debate), but a sphere of judgment where reasons can be given and where there is, indeed, always an implicit appeal to larger, impersonal (or intersubjective) grounds of justification. Such reasoning is therefore closely related to the overarching process of critique by which Kant works his way from "pure" to "practical" reason, or – roughly speaking – from epistemology to the analysis of moral laws and obligations. Aesthetics becomes the indispensable source of arguments and analogies for accomplishing some of Kant's most crucial and difficult passages of reason.

De Man sees the current "resistance to theory" as a refusal, among critics and philosophers alike, to take up the labours of critical thought bequeathed by Kantian aesthetics.[2] More specifically, it involves a series of strategic evasions, a mystified ontology of art and aesthetic experience which in turn provides support for a mystification of language, history and politics. There is no room here to follow out the intricacies of de Man's argument. His point is that aesthetics has effectively been kidnapped by a conservative ideology whose interests entail a will to ignore the crucial problems and antinomies encountered in the Kantian critique of judgment. Art becomes the source of extrapolated metaphors which serve to ease the passage from a simplified (phenomenalist) theory of perception to an equally simplified (organicist) notion of society and cultural politics. One could trace this emergent ideology through the line of conservative critic-philosophers, from Burke to Eliot and present-day spokesmen like Roger Scruton. In each case there is a three-fold strategy at work. *Aesthetics* takes on the privileged role as a mode of understanding where "thought" and "intuition" are reconciled beyond all the hateful antinomies of mere critical reason. *Politics* becomes – in much the same way – a realm of mystified organicist metaphors where thinking harks back to a non-existent past age of unified thought and sensibility. And essential to both these strategies – so de Man would argue – is the move that ignores those anomalous and problematic details of the Kantian *text* which are brought to light by a close deconstructive reading.

This suggests one reason why aesthetics and critical theory should currently occupy such different ground as to seem antagonistic disciplines. For theory has the power to demystify aesthetics precisely by revealing its textual blind-spots and its covert dependence on simplified and question-begging models of thought and perception. Aesthetics has taken refuge in a kind of premature phenomenalist reduction which confuses linguistic and natural reality, and thus short-circuits the difficult labour of reading texts with an adequate attention to their full rhetorical complexity. This habit of taking the word for the deed – of implicitly accepting what poetry says when it claims to hand over sensations bodily – is the chief form of aesthetic mystification which de Man sets out to deconstruct. "Theory" is thus opposed to traditional asethetics in so far as the latter has typically determined to repress or elide these problems in the way of its own enterprise. And the resistance to theory – as de Man reads it – is a product of that same aesthetic ideology whose effects extend into the realm of cultural politics. "By allowing the necessity of a non-phenomenal linguistics, one frees the discourse on literature from naive oppositions between fiction and reality, which are themselves an offspring of an uncritically mimetic conception of art."[3] In which case – as de Man goes on to argue – the work of deconstruction is also a labour of ideological critique. For it is precisely such wholesale categorical confusions – as between the fictive, the real and the natural – that enable aesthetics to pass off its mystified concepts of language and history alike. So those who attack deconstruction on the grounds of its supposed apolitical character are merely (according to de Man) exposing their own theoretical blindness. They are, in short, "very poor readers of Marx's *German Ideology*".

One can see this mystification at work in Eliot's early essays, most notably "Tradition and the Individual Talent".[4] What Eliot achieves is a perfect circularity of argument, using "tradition" to underwrite his claims about the nature of poetic language, and those claims in turn to back up his highly selective view of "tradition". The myth of a long-lost "organic" community was harnessed to the idea that poetry should properly (as once it did) embody the unproblematical union of intellect and emotion, "thought" and "sensibility". Tradition becomes a communion of minds between those privileged moments when poetry is redeemed from the otherwise uniform tale of secular decline. History (in any real sense) drops out of the picture, replaced by a myth whose central event – the famous "dissociation of sensibility" – goes to confirm that mere intellect is powerless to grasp the full extent of its loss. Thus "tradition" (in Eliot's special sense of the word) goes along with a willed suppression of history and a marked aversion to any kind of theory that would complicate relations between thought and language. So far as it involved a philosophical "position", this attitude came down to an uneasy mixture of Bradleian idealism (the mind and its objects in a solipsistic state of preestablished harmony), and the straightforward phenomenalist assumption that mind simply registers sensory impressions in a language of highly charged vividness and detail. This latter coincided with Eliot's commitment to the Imagist ideal of a simple, clear-cut correspondence between the language of poetry and the objects of sensory perception. And the Bradleian metaphysics made it possible to extend this simplified picture of the mind and its workings to a wholesale theory of poetic "tradition" that left no room for awkward questions in the province of history and interpretative theory.

In his essay "The Perfect Critic", Eliot looked to Aristotle as the great exemplar of "intelligence itself, operating the analysis of sensation to the point of principle and definition".[5] This formula is of interest for those stages in the process of "intelligent" reading which it prefers to jump over or to leave unexamined. The sentence swings clean across from a phenomenalist idiom of pure "sensation" to a language of highly abstract "principle and definition". In this respect it mirrors precisely the character of Eliot's critical practice, the constant doubling back and forth (in essays like "Tradition and the Individual Talent") between passages of detailed close-reading and statements of a massively generalized import. What tends to drop out in this "perfect" encounter of mind and text is any sense of the *mediating* processes at work, the checks and resistances – as well as the insights – of responsive understanding. It is here that critical theory holds out against those various forms of premature phenomenalist reduction that mark the discourse of a certain (militantly *un*-theoretical) aesthetics.

Leavis provides the most obvious example of a criticism that flatly refuses to "theorize" and stakes its claims on a direct passage from language to experience. Thus Leavis assumes that there *must* be some inherent, self-evident connection between the sensory or synaesthetic qualities ("muscular enactment", etc.) manifest in a poet's language and the level of creative intelligence or maturity there to be discovered by the fit reader. Where language refuses this proper relationship – as with Shelley or a text like *Finnegans Wake* – Leavis can deplore the intrusion of an overly self-conscious or hypersensitive verbalism that signals a breakdown of true creativity. One of Leavis's objections to Joyce was the way that he afforded such rich opportunities for the band of "knowing exegetes" devoted to his work.[6] Thus Leavis's idea of "mature" creative writing goes along with his principled resistance to literary theory. It is precisely where language disrupts the phenomenalist scheme of things – the economy relating thought, word and poetic truth – that Leavis perceives the dangers of unbridled critical ingenuity. In Shelley's case, one can see how Leavis (like Eliot before him) refused to read the poetry as anything but a failed attempt to put across clear-cut visual and sensory images. It was left to later critics – like Hartman and Bloom – to reject this absurdly simplified account and develop a degree of self-consciousness in their *own* writing that answered to the full complexities of Shelley's style. And of course this revival of interest in Shelley had an ideological dimension. Eliot's charge of poetic "immaturity", though mounted on vaguely technical grounds, went along with an evident distaste for Shelley's left-wing political views. Nor is it a coincidence that the current Romantic revivalists see themselves as pitted against that whole conservative neo-classical "tradition" which Eliot managed to set so firmly in place. What these critics are out to contest is a powerful ideology that would limit the play of self-consciousness in language, whether "creative" or "critical". And the demand for an "answerable style" on the interpreter's part is also a demand that the speculative energies of criticism should not be held subject to rules handed down by a cramping orthodox tradition.

Responses to critics like Hartman and Bloom – especially among British commentators – would indeed suggest that something more is involved than a difference in prose etiquette.[7] What is interesting about these attacks is that they don't all come (though many of them do) from plain-prose pedestrians who merely resent their own inability to rise to the challenge. Thus one finds Christopher Ricks – himself a stylist of impressive subtlety and resource – denouncing those interpreters who want to raise criticism to a level with "genuine" creative writing. And this despite the fact – which he would certainly, on principle, deny – that Ricks is often more interesting to read than the poet or the passage he happens to be writing about. As with Empson, it is sometimes hard – even impossible – to decide how much is "there" in the text under scrutiny, and how much is a product of interpretation. Yet Ricks is fierce in condemning these signs of a growing *rapprochement* between creative and critical writing. A strange obligation would seem to be in force, with interpreters refusing to acknowledge in themselves what they seek out most zealously in literary texts.

According to Hartman, this missed opportunity is just one symptom of a wider (moral and political) failure in the present-day function of criticism. The "conservative reaction", as he terms it, "makes of literary criticism the last refuge of neo-classical admonitions against mixed genres, against quitting the demarcation between criticism and art or criticism and anything else – philosophy, religion, the social sciences".[8] Hence Hartman's tendency to raise the mixing of genres into a high point of principle, a standing rebuke to that tidy "neoclassical" parcelling-out of disciplines and styles. Hence also the offence he gives to critics who – not without reason – associate Hartman's stylistic licence with the claims now advanced on behalf of literary theory. What these opponents won't recognize is the fact that "theory" is not the kind of typecast abstract system that would end up (if only it could) by reducing criticism to a species of applied science. Theory for Hartman – and for all the contributors to this volume – is a speculative venture that mixes disciplines precisely in order to escape such a doctrinaire beating of bounds. The "post-" in poststructuralism is best understood as a signal of criticism having moved beyond any cramping obsession with matters of system and method. As Derrida reminds us – especially in his readings of Freud[9] – to theorize is always to *speculate*, to offer ideas as hostages to fate and risk all manner of "uncanny" after-effects, textual and historical.

In so far as they promote any common cause, these essays all argue for a loosening-up of the limits that once seemed to mark off "poetry" from other kinds of language. The "old" New Critics did everything in their power to enforce those limits and discourage interpreters from straying outside their proper domain. On the one hand criticism was to confine itself decently to the role of rhetorical explication and not – repeat *not* – allow itself those freedoms of language and style that characterized poetry. On the other, it had to keep a careful distance from the various forms of alien discourse (history, philosophy, psychoanalysis) which could only distract the critic from attending to the sacrosanct words on the page. And so there developed that whole elaborate system of protocols and anathematized "heresies", designed to keep criticism firmly in its place and to preserve poetry as a realm of autonomous meanings and values.[10]

Post-structuralism rejects the whole system of assumptions – the implied metaphysics or ontology of form – that lay behind this widely influential movement in criticism. It opens poetry up to a practice of intertextual reading that can take in philosophy, history or psychoanalysis, *not* on the reckoning that these are "meta-languages" or ultimate sources of truth, but in order to see how texts relate and produce new dimensions of sense. No longer is it a question of theory setting up as some kind of ultimate explanatory method that would seek to comprehend literary texts through application of scientific principles. In the case of psychoanalysis – to take what is perhaps the most striking example – it now becomes clear that Freudian readings are themselves preeminently *textual* constructions, narratives which ask to be read with an eye to their rhetorical devices and tell-tale elisions of sense. Indeed there is a strange reversal of roles whereby (as post-structuralists are fond of remarking) "theory" becomes the straight-man or foil of a literary language that everywhere outwits its powers of conceptual command.[11] Ironically enough, this has led some adepts of deconstruction to a point where they seem to be stating – albeit in more advanced rhetorical terms – precisely that distinction between "poetic" and "ordinary" language that once so preoccupied the New Critics. One could easily cite passages from the work of Paul de Man, Geoffrey Hartman or J. Hillis Miller that overtly celebrate this power of literature to show up the blind-spots or deluded claims-to-truth of other, less rhetorically sophisticated texts.

But this is to ignore the more significant point: that these critics have *worked through* the various kinds of intertextual relation and achieved, in the process, a notable extension and refinement of "theory" itself. The essays that follow are offered partly in support of this claim and partly to refute the widespread idea that post-structuralism is a species of "textualist" mystification which ignores – indeed denies – any access through writing to a knowledge of history or the world outside the text. If these new ways of thinking have problematized such access – for instance, by making us look more closely at the narrative tropes that structure historical discourse, or the various rhetorics of political argument – they have also put obstacles in the way of any criticism that wants to keep poetry pure by excluding such alien concerns. Taken altogether, we hope that these essays will indicate something of the range, the subtlety and speculative power of recent post-structuralist criticism.

Notes

1 See Paul de Man, "Phenomenality and Materiality in Kant", in Gary Shapiro and Alan Sica (eds.), *Hermeneutics: questions and prospects* (Amherst: University of Massachusetts Press, 1984), pp. 121–44. Also Paul de Man, "Sign and Symbol in Hegel's *Aesthetics*", *Critical Inquiry*, 8 (1982), 761–75.

2 See especially Paul de Man, "The Resistance to Theory", *Yale French Studies*, 63 (1982), 3–20.

3 de Man, "The Resistance to Theory", p. 11.

4 T. S. Eliot, "Tradition and the Individual Talent", in *Selected Essays* (London: Faber, 1964), pp. 3–11.

5 T. S. Eliot, "The Perfect Critic", in *The Sacred Wood* (London: Faber, 1928), pp. 1–16.

6 F. R. Leavis, "Joyce and the 'Revolution of the Word' ", *Scrutiny*, 6 (1937), 193–201.

7 See for instance Christopher Ricks, "In Theory", *The London Review of Books*, 16 May 1981, pp. 3–6. For some other recent British responses to "theory", see Laurence Lerner (ed.), *Reconstructing Literature* (Oxford: Blackwell, 1984); Tom Paulin, "English Now", in *Ireland and the English Crisis* (Newcastle: Bloodaxe Books, 1984); and A. D. Nuttall, *A New Mimesis: Shakespeare and the representation of reality* (London: Methuen, 1984).

8 Geoffrey Hartman, *Easy Pieces* (New York: Columbia University Press, 1985).

9 See Jacques Derrida, "Freud and the Scene of Writing", in *Writing and Difference*, trans. Alan Bass (London: Routledge and Kegan Paul, 1978), pp. 196–231; also Derrida's "The Purveyor of Truth", *Yale French Studies*, 52 (1975), 31–113; and "Speculations – On Freud", *Oxford Literary Review*, 3 (1978), 78–97.

10 For the classic statement of this formalist position, see W. K. Wimsatt, *The Verbal Icon: studies in the meaning of poetry* (Lexington: Kentucky University Press, 1954).

11 For virtuoso performances in this vein, see Barbara Johnson, *The Critical Difference: essays in the contemporary rhetoric of reading* (Baltimore: Johns Hopkins University Press, 1981) and Shoshana Felman, "Turning the Screw of Interpretation", *Yale French Studies*, 55–6 (1977), 94–207.

Presentation and representation in the Renaissance lyric: the net of words and the escape of the gods

MURRAY KRIEGER

I begin by trying to convey some idea of the exhilaration I feel as I respond to the dynamics within the linguistic forces set and maintained in motion by the English Renaissance lyric at its best. Let me suggest two rather different, if not opposed, modes of verbal behavior.

Here is the first movement I seek to follow: a word seems about to turn into another word. It is very exciting to watch it happen. But how can the transformation occur? Here is the word in the process of over-running its bounds, destroying its own sense of territorial integrity along with its neighbor's. It is undoing the very notion of "property", whether we relate the term "property" to that which defines an entity or to that which defines a possession, so that it is defying the operational procedures of logic and law – and those as well of language itself. For property is the elementary basis for the differential principle underlying the operation of language, which in turn underlies the operations of both logic and law.

Still, in the face of such impressive resistance, the word seems to pursue its errant career, if we know how to watch it perform. At which moment does a word stop being its own sealed self and begin to merge with its neighbor? Can a system of conventionally accepted meanings continue to function if any of them turns unstable and thus slides into fluidity? All these difficulties are exacerbated if the differences between the terms being transformed into identity are – more than merely different – wholly contradictory: if they are nothing less than binary oppositions that are forced into a fusion. Often, it is through the exploited coincidence of the arbitrary phonetic properties of words that such fusion is apparently achieved. (It would take another essay to deal with the complicated process by which the act of silent hearing is incorporated into the reading habits of the educated reader when confronted by a poem.) Because words, however different in meaning, sound alike – or almost alike – they are forced, as we hear by watching, to become alike. Often it occurs in the coupling act of rhyming or – more extremely – of punning. But often the poet slips from word to word and from sound to sound in a continuing parade of subtle echoes.

We find this extraordinary poetic tactic in many English Renaissance poems. We can begin with an obvious example. In Ralegh's "Poesy to Prove Affection is Not Love" ("Conceit, begotten by the eyes, / Is quickly born and quickly dies"), the poet deals with the death-in-life of affection, the "conceit" that "within the Mother's *womb* / hath his beginning and his *tomb*". This collapsing of the womb–tomb opposition into a womb that is also and at the same moment a tomb becomes an enabling act for the poem's complex claim.

Or a more subtle example. In Ralegh's "Nymph's Reply" to Marlowe's "Passionate Shepherd", in the line "Time drives the flock from *field to fold*", we find a simplicity that should not hide its density. The single alteration of the vowel from "field" to "fold" carries with it the equation within the course of nature's seasons as well as within man's life: from open freedom to coffinlike enclosure, under the driving hand of time, the second ("fold") already implicit (inscribed) in the first ("field") – in its very letters. And, a bit later, the line, "Is fancy's spring, but sorrow's fall" – following "A honey-tongue, a heart of gall" – uses its chiastic pattern of alliteration ("fancy's" and "fall" on the outside, "spring" and "sorrows" on the inside) to hold its oppositions and yet convert them into the sameness of echo.

Let me cite one last quotation from Ralegh, this one at a desperately and conclusively late moment in the magnificent "Nature, that washed her hands in milk". Having created an elegantly balanced ideal mistress at the behest of love, nature must suffer her delicately wrought creature to be undone by time, which "Turns snow and silk and milk to dust". The sequence of alliteration and internal rhyme leads to the crumbling of language into a negative, universal equation. Nature earlier turned away from earth, using snow and silk instead, as she propagated the moist by excluding the dry, but the moistness of snow and silk and milk ends with the alliterative equivalent of the *dry*ing that is a *dy*ing: ends, like earth, in *d*ust with the collapse of all distinctions. (Pages could be written on the destructive power that Ralegh – in more poems than this one – imposes on the alliterative extension of words beginnng with the letter *d*.)

Shakespeare everywhere reminds us of the transformational power of words, their appearing to defy their own distinctness by overlapping and changing places with one another. As he suggests in Sonnet 105, his verse, "One thing expressing, leaves out difference". The sonnets are full of examples. I'll cite just a few, choosing almost at random. I have dealt with some of these, often at length, in other places, so that it should be enough for me to do barely more than mention them here.

There is the obvious collapse of the line between truth and falsity, as well as the multiplication of the meanings of those terms *true* and *false*, in the lines from Sonnet 72, "O, lest your *true love* may seem *false* in this, / That you for *love* speak well of me *untrue*." Or there is the collapse of the line between opposition and advocacy in Sonnet 35: "For to thy *sensual* fault I bring in *sense* − / Thy *adverse* party is thy *advocate*." In Sonnets 6 and 9 we find a verbal play that muddies distinctions among use, interest, waste, and abuse: "That *use* is not forbidden *usury*" (Sonnet 6, line 5) and, later, "But beauty's waste hath in the world an end, / And kept, *unused*, the *user* so destroys it" (Sonnet 9, lines 11–12). In Sonnet 71, the calculating world of material self-interest, in its concern to feed the body, is quickly identified with the feeding *off* the body by those most materialistic inheritors of the grave: "that I am fled / From this *vile world*, with *vilest worms* to dwell". The vileness of the world is totally realized only in the superlatively consistent activity of the vilest worms, which correct the spelling (*world* to *worms*) and extend vileness to the ultimate degree.

Opposites are turned into one another even more extremely in the fully realized pun, in which two words − violently at odds with one another − share a single phonetic entity. Thus, in Sonnet 87, "Farewell! thou art too dear for my possessing", "dear" must embrace and identify that which is dear in the marketplace with that which is dear in our unworldly affections. The mixed argument that follows springs from both sides of this doubleness of "dear". We find in a good number of sonnets a similar use of puns to bring together into a phonetic identity meanings that are normally differentiated or even opposed − for example, in "state" in Sonnet 124 ("If my dear love were but the child of state") and in "refigured" in Sonnet 6 ("Then let not winter's ragged hand deface"): "Ten times thyself were happier than thou art, / If ten of thine ten times refigured thee." The device of having one word turn into another, under the pressure of the poem's dynamics, is only exaggerated in the pun that forces at least two words to be one another at the same time. Words seem to undermine themselves and the way they are supposed to function, as if they insist on reminding us that their meanings, with oppositions flowing into one another, must be as inconstant as the experience they would record. Most of my examples, from Ralegh onward, have related the inconstancy of these words (despite their pretense to be fixed entities) to the inconstancy of time, so that words as fixed entities would be an inaccurate representation of experience under the fickleness of time. The purely poetic device cannot escape having thematic consequences − indeed must be seen as the consequence itself of a thematic cause. The thematic and the poetic are circularly related, like the chicken and the egg. The words, as a conceit, may seem to be a fixed or static formula of meaning, but Sonnet 15, furnishing me my final example of the movement from one word into another, indicates how unfixed the verbal formula becomes after all: the sonnet refers to "the *conceit* of this *inconstant* stay" (line 9), forcing the conceit itself to collapse into inconstancy.

But I mentioned at the start that I would point out two rather different, if not opposed, modes of verbal behavior, and so far I have spoken of one only. Now for the second. Instead of our watching as meanings come together in violation of the law of differentiation or even binary opposition, we may find what seems to be the reverse operation occurring. As we watch, a word finds itself at odds with itself, falls out with itself, indeed negates itself, in effect canceling itself out; it undoes the integrity of words upon which the operation of language depends. A stunning example occurs in Shakespeare's Sonnet 116 ("Let me not to the marriage of true minds"): "love is not love / Which alters when it alteration finds / Or bends with the remover to remove." The negative repetition ("love" to "not love") is indeed a self-denial of language, a self-cancellation. Language in effect wipes itself out as everything is made relative, contingent, arbitrary. The poet must protest at a language that operates this way, though it seems to be an inevitable consequence of the function of language.

A similar expunging of the word occurs in Thomas Campion's song, "Thou art not fair", when the poet threatens the beloved to take away her nature (that is, change his mind about her) if she is less than constant: "thou shalt prove / That *beauty* is *no beauty* without love." Or Ben Jonson's "Slow, slow, fresh fount", in which time forces the acknowledgment, "*Our* beauties are *not ours*." If, in the first poetic manipulation of language that I have described, differences collapse into apparent identity in a way that violates the notion of verbal boundaries and property, in this second operation we find the most immediate linguistic entity losing identity, falling itself into difference – now at a distance from itself, so that there is no single, undifferentiated verbal self.

Perhaps the most striking example of this second device is found in "The Phoenix and Turtle" in the climactic cry of reason, which, in its admiring acknowledgment of the impossible union it has witnessed, in effect denies its own name: "Love hath reason, reason none, / If what parts can so remain." The miraculous destruction of number in love is a violation of the operation of reason, and love's very existence changes what reason must be as it changes the way in which language can work – in effect, by insisting that, in the way we usually understand it, language cannot work at all.

But this final example should indicate to us that our two seemingly opposed modes of poetic devices are themselves in the end identical and mutually reenforcing. The line "Love hath reason, reason none", emphasized both the falling apart of a verbal entity ("reason none") and the growing together of opposed entities ("love hath reason"). Despite my separating these two devices, it should have been clear throughout that there is a similar, if reverse, duplicity operating in both, a duplicity that forces our observation to see every movement of words toward identity as accompanied by an equally urgent movement in them toward differentiation, each from itself as well as from every other. It is precisely this need to hold both awarenesses at once – the identifying and the differentiating – that makes these movements we have been observing so exciting in their stretching of the resources of linguistic operation.

Probably no example can serve more forcefully to reflect this duplicity than those lines I have already quoted from Ralegh's "Nymph's Reply": "A honey tongue, a heart of gall, / Is fancy's spring, but sorrow's fall." The mingling of the move to identity with the move to differentiation among fancy and fall, spring and sorrow, or rather spring and fall, fancy and sorrow (echoing the cross-relations within the parallels of the preceding line) is only the more forceful when we remind ourselves that these lines are preceded by the lines, "The flowers do fade, and *wanton* fields / To *wayward* winter reckoning yields." The unpredictability and indiscriminacy of unlimited fertility turn into the unpredictability and indiscriminacy of unlimited death, the "wanton" into the "wayward", words that overlap as much as they are distinguished, as they are applied to "fields" and the alliterated "winter". Hence, in "honey", "heart", "tongue", "gall", or "fancy", "fall", "sorrow", "spring", the interlacings of parallelism and chiasmus, of meaning and sound, join opposition to dissolution.

These duplicitous manipulations of words, as they are made either to move outward to interanimate one another or to move inward to cut off from themselves – or to manage somehow to do both at once – such manipulations arise from the poet's struggle to win from language a representational power that he does not trust words normally to provide. By exploiting the sensory side of words – their sound, which is their only material aspect – the poet tries to invoke the illusion of their presence. This is for him to use the sensible to transform the intelligible. It is his way to overcome our impression of verbal absence – inspired by an exclusive interest in the merely intelligible aspect of words – our impression of words whose object is elsewhere as they mean, often vainly, to point to it. Thus their auditory character, normally most arbitrary in that it has no relation to their meaning, seems – by means of devices such as those I have suggested – to turn words substantive, in effect allowing them to take on the illusion of body. So, apparently acknowledging normal language to be a verbal parade of arbitrary meanings, of empty, bodiless counters, the poet seeks to turn the arbitrary into the necessary and the functional – into the materially present. It is as if he uses the sound of words as the most extreme symbol of their arbitrary character, forcing those apparently insignificant phonetic elements to prove the poem's power to break through arbitrariness to substantive inevitability, to transform our awareness of words' absent, though intelligible, objects to their own material, fully sensible presence.

I can point to Sir Philip Sidney's Sonnet 35 ("What may words say, or what may words not say"), which I might refer to as his semiotic sonnet in that it deals explicitly with the problem of representation and the futile contribution made by our usual words to solving it. The poet is worried that even our noblest words – names of our most glorious abstractions – can have no meaning because the living reality of Stella forces them to contradict and hence negate themselves. In the sonnet we find example after example of the second of the two devices I described earlier, the self-denial by words of their own entityhood ("Love is not love . . ." or "Love hath reason, reason none"):

> What may words say, or what may words not say,
> Where truth itself must speak like flattery?
> Within what bounds can one his liking stay,
> Where Nature doth with infinite agree?
>   What Nestor's counsel can my flames ally,
> Since Reason's self doth blow the coal in me?
> And ah what hope, that hope should once see day,
> Where Cupid is sworn page to Chastity?

How can words have meaning if Stella's very being forces truth to speak like flattery, forces nature to be one with infinity, forces reason to be the sponsor of desire, forces Cupid to be "sworn page" to chastity? And then the climactic inversion: instead of a person growing rich through achieving fame, "Fame / Doth even grow rich, naming my Stella's name." The invocation of the one true name, the one word in the language that encloses its own essential value, is the only act that authenticates language, gives it a reality. Fame can grow rich in the act of naming Stella's name; and the poem itself guarantees the claim by at that moment naming Stella's actual name, Rich, following it with her mythical name, Stella. (Is the double name the reason for the poet's repeating the word "name"?) So fame has aggrandized itself; it becomes "rich", in effect becomes Stella. The one way for other verbal names (truth, nature, reason, chastity, fame) to have substance is for them to share the substantive magic of the one true name, the name that *is* its meaning (thanks to a fortuitous pun). Otherwise words are without substance, empty. And the sonnet's conclusion follows: it is she who teaches wit what perfection is, and it is she who raises praise to the level of being itself praised in the moment of being praised herself: "Not thou by praise, but praise in thee is raised: / It is a praise to praise, when thou art praised." Once Stella herself has entered the poem by way of her name to en-rich fame, she is able, similarly, to convert the incapacities of words ("wit", "praise") to a new power, although she licenses them only for the single act of serving her own reality, her being finally bestowing meaning upon them.

The poet has in this sonnet indulged – and in this sonnet sequence freely indulges – the magical act of invoking Stella's name to convert all other names, those unmagical nouns that fill both our language and our empty poetic conventions, from nonsense to meaning, a living meaning attached to her living being. In sonnet after sonnet we find the magic word *Stella* incanted and then watch the transformations that follow from that incantation. From the first sonnet in the sequence (and the first sonnet itself is a splendid example), the poet is struggling with a halting, recalcitrant, and inoperative language that will not do the job of representation, and resolves his struggle by breaking through to the substantive image of Stella, a reality carried in the image and usually invoked by the name, the latter being the one signifier that suffers no separation from its signfied. Stella, her being as well as her name, must be made by the poet to invade the unreal net of words – and to invest it with substance. In this one case, the nominal reality becomes the fleshly reality, a language that enables this poetry to speak as man otherwise cannot. Thus, in Sonnet 74 ("I never drank of Aganippe well"), the poet, a "layman" forsaken by the antique, figurative muses and unfit "for sacred rites", has his mouth inspired by the mouth of Stella, a fleshly muse who gives speech through oral embrace: "My lips are sweet, inspired with Stella's kiss." The introduction of Stella's kiss, in the final couplet, is an invocation of a present and literal muse indeed. The poet's invocation is an act that puts the sonnet in the present tense, and, since her name alone is substantive, she is to enter the poem with her name.

It is as if the poet has discovered the built-in futility of our usual attempt at verbal representation. That futility is carried in the prefix, the *re* of *re*present. Words are empty and belated counters because it is their nature to seek to refer to what is elsewhere and has occurred earlier. Any pretension by them to present reality is frustrated by the *re*, which requires that what they would represent – what has already presented itself in person – has had its presence, its presentness, elsewhere and earlier. But the poet would dabble in verbal magic, calling upon a sacred name that would overcome belatedness and introduce a living, bodily hereness that would make language more than properly representational, that would make it nothing less than presentational.

What, in Sidney's enraptured fiction, makes Stella's name so special in its powers, at once exempted from the empty inconstancies of words and able to reendow language with a vital function? The name is to remind us that the language around it has long been deactivated, even as it creates for us a new dispensation under which words can be reactivated, given substance, *her* substance, once again. But what permits the name to function in this remarkable way? Clearly, as in much Renaissance lyric poetry that reaches ambitiously toward presence, what is paramount is the analogy to Christian paradox, with its insistence on the participatory magic by which spirit partakes of, and becomes one with, body. Unlike the now-absent gods that once inhabited verbal abstractions often represented by the gods in Classical mythology (truth, reason, love, and so on), Stella *is* her name and constantly remains so, just as that name actively intrudes upon, and participates in, these poems, both as name, with its heavenly trappings, and as the physically present lady herself.

In Sonnet 28 ("You that with allegory's curious fame"), the poet rejects the use of allegorical structures and references in favor of the plain and literal statement, in favor of "pure simplicity". Though he speaks extravagance enough in the poem, it is – because he speaks of Stella, because he speaks the name *Stella* and speaks under its aegis – to be taken as literal simplicity. Thus, "When I say Stella, I do mean the same / Princess of Beauty . . ." And the conclusion: "But know that I in pure simplicity, / Breathe out the flames which burn within my heart, / Love only reading unto me this art." That direct speech should be so apparently metaphorical and simplicity so apparently extravagant is attributable – as in other sonnets – to Stella and the poet's invocation of her rather than to any empty appeal to "allegory's curious frame". But, guided by her powers, the speech remains direct and simple, whatever it may seem; for it is literal speech. After all, the invoked name, Stella, like the lady herself, is at once her name and an *apparently* allegorical reference to the star (thus qualifying her poet-lover as an Astrophil, or star-lover). But, the sonnet is insisting, this too is no allegory; it is simply what she is (and what, consequently, she makes him). Again he would have her participate in, and become consubstantial with, these meanings (as he did with the abstractions in Sonnet 35), claiming a new dispensation for language, not unlike the typological identities being claimed for a semiotic controlled by the Christian paradox.

But, with Stella enacting the role of his goddess, why not this claim? It *is* an outrageous joke for the poet to deny using allegory at the very moment he is speaking her apparently allegorical name ("When I say, Stella, I do mean . . ." and mean nothing more; but what he says he means is more than enough – "princess of beauty" and the rest). Still, his very point is that all that he says is what, simply and literally, she *is*. Whatever he has given away is won back through her; whatever he has given away in language is won back through her name. It all pours into her and out of her – *as* her name. And, as this new dispensation for language, that name is the only language he speaks – and really the only word, since all other words are to be read – or rather reread – in light of it. No wonder, then, that, as he tells us in Sonnet 19, no matter what he tries to write, "My very ink turns straight to Stella's name." And Stella, with all that name means and is, is captured in the poem and, once in it, reconstructs its meaning and its action.

On the other side, in the cynical poem by Fulke Greville, one of Sidney's close contemporaries (Ralegh was another), "Away with these self-loving lads", there are the following lines:

> My songs they be of Cynthia's praise,
> I wear her rings on holy-days,
> On every tree I write her name,
> And every day I read the same.
> > Where Honor, Cupid's rival, is
> > There miracles are seen of his.
>
> If Cynthia crave her ring of me,
> I blot her name out of the tree.

Where there is inconstancy, a failure to overcome the ways of the world under the sway of time, there no name is sacred; a name cannot replenish the emptiness or arbitrariness of language but only shares in it. Names, like all words, come and go, are written and subsequently erased, are interchangeable. Honor is the rival of Cupid and, so long as Honor holds out, justifies the miracle of the lady's name written and each day ritualistically adored. But the eventual victory of Cupid and inconstancy leads to erasure and substitution.

One can look upon such apparently light, if bitter, love poems as serious attempts to treat man's desire as the extreme emblem of the earthly, of the absolutely arbitrary, with the interchange of names representative of the interchangeability of words within a failed and impotent language. Sidney himself is in some sonnets expressing failure, aware of the failure of his magic, of his attempt to invoke the sacred name and, with it, Stella's presence. Nowhere is the invocation of the name more explicit, or the failure − and Stella's continued absence − more starkly acknowledged than in Sonnet 106:

> O absent presence Stella is not here;
> False flattering hope, that with so fair a face,
> Bare me in hand, that in this orphan place,
> Stella, I say my Stella, should appear.

The lack of response leaves the poet, his world, and his language, untransformed as, in the balance of the sonnet, he comes close to (but resists) the temptations of Greville's fickle world of change.

It is the poet's double awareness that concerns me here: he knows, as a result of his impatience with language's representational − to say nothing of its presentational − failures, that he must indulge the pious attempt to use the poem to invoke and contain its object, its goddess; but he knows also the illusory nature of his attempt, the recalcitrance of language, together with its refusal, after all, really to give way. So he knows also the transcendence of the gods, their abandonment of the world and of the world of language. But he continues to try and to cultivate his (sometimes ironic) poetic illusions.

The sonneteer's invocation of the poem's object, bringing her into the poem as an active presence through the use of verbal devices such as those I have examined, returns me to a theme that has been central to all my writings on Renaissance poetry and especially on the English Petrarchan sonnet: the phonetic struggle for an illusion of presence that we find in it reflects the poet's effort to force into the network of language the elusive object that words − his words of love − have not been able to capture. Here is what I have referred to as the poet's quest for a representational power or − more extremely − a directly presentational power that he finds words normally lack. The referent − as the beloved, the poet's goddess, his Platonic heaven − insists on remaining transcendental to the poet's words that would enclose her in order to transform her state from one of absence to one of presence. After all, the fictional given of the Petrarchan sonnet is precisely that which demands such an effort on the part of the poet-lover. He writes his poem out of his lack, his want, of his beloved, who is − and threatens to remain − at a distance from him, like the absent god from the supplicant. But, as we have seen with Sidney, in his poem the poet can do more than complain of this absence, though complain he surely does; he can seek to use the poem to close the breach between his sacred object and himself, to make her responsive and hence present by having her enter the poem by way of her invoked name. So the poem can be as much an entreaty as a lamentation, as much an act – and a call to action in return – as a sorrowful recitation.

What the poet is trying to bring about – whatever his skepticism about the chances for his literal success – is a miracle of linguistic presence as much as a miracle of quasi-religious presence. His task, and the breakthrough he hopes to accomplish, partake of the realm of semiology as well as that of love's theology. The beloved goddess, who is absent from him and who is beseeched by his poem, must be brought bodily into it by having her name break through the emptiness of words to fill them with itself and – through name magic – with herself. As Sidney's Sonnet 35 ("What may words say, or what may words not say") has shown us, it is the language process itself, with all its unmagical incapacities, which must be reconstituted in the act of naming the beloved. To the extent that the poem would succeed, it must transform the naming process of language in order to retain the present goddess trapped within it. Thus, as I earlier pointed out, in Sonnet 74 ("I never drank of Aganippe well"), we see the actual kiss of Stella's lips by the poet's lips replace the empty allusions to the muses with the actual consequences of physical presence.

So the absent goddess sought by the Petrarchan poet is one among the absent signifieds to which the normally dualistic process of language testifies. It is for this reason that I have claimed the poet's trial to be at once semiological and theological, if – indeed – love's theology is not being reduced to a problem in semiology. The world of references stands outside the network of words that seeks in vain to capture it. As the Petrarchan poet conceives the problem, chief within that world, the all-dominating transcendental signified among a host of transcendental signifieds, is the beloved-as-goddess. If the poet can work the magical breakthrough into presence for her, the others will follow within a remade language process.

I see the poet, then, as setting himself the objective of capturing the absent god (or goddess) within a verbal network that he knows cannot hold him (or her). The poet works his magic, changes lamentation to invocation, sometimes claims success; but we see him start the next poem anew as if the task has to be performed all over again. This is a Sisyphus-like concession to the failure of his word-magic to produce more than the momentary illusion of a breakthrough to presence. The absent goddess and the world of being that she dominates are out there still, still resisting capture by his words, whatever he may momentarily have appeared to bring about with his phonetic word play and the invocations that it permits.

The path I have been traveling has led us back to my title, which usefully condenses the theme of this essay: "Presentation and representation: the net of words and the escape of the gods". My reference there was to the language of Ben Jonson's "Why I Write Not of Love", which I now print in full:

> Some act of Love's bound to rehearse,
> I thought to bind him in my verse;
> Which when he felt, Away, quoth he,
> Can poets hope to fetter me?
> It is enough they once did get
> Mars and my mother in their net;
> I wear not these my wings in vain.
> With which he fled me, and again
> Into my rhymes could ne'er be got
> By any art. Then wonder not
> That since, my numbers are so cold,
> When Love is fled, and I grow old.

The poet has set himself the task of binding Cupid in his verse, and Cupid is equally determined to evade capture. And, of course, momentarily the poet does have him – indeed has him as a speaking character. The god reminds the poet of Homer's earlier capture, in *his* net of words, of Venus and Mars in their lovemaking. It is significant that Cupid is attributing the act of binding to the poet rather than to the irate Hephaestus, who in the narrative forges the net (of metal and not of words) to display the lovers. The responsibility, so far as Cupid is concerned, is Homer's: Cupid is looking beyond the narrative cause in the jealous god to the ultimate metapoetic cause in the poet. He is looking, then, to the net of words that, for Cupid's purposes on the present occasion, is more substantive and threatening than the net forged within the frame of the story. Cupid's escape from the present poet follows, and the poet's verse must do without the erotic god.

But the god is referred to in the poem, not as Cupid, but as Love. And what makes the poem work so brilliantly is the gradual movement – anticipated in the poem's title ("Why I Write Not of Love") – that allows Love also to take on all the roles of love as it functions in the poet's life. When the god Love is fled, so is love, leaving an old, cold poet, with his verses emptied of the god – and of desire. If he does not have Love (the god) in his verse, he cannot have love, consequently cannot write of love. Presentation must accompany representation. The language of myth is given life by being made participatory, as literary allusion and living immediacy are made one. Isn't this very much the unified doubleness we saw in Stella as she functioned in her several ways in Sidney's Sonnet 28, with its denial of allegory? Stella's function as star, goddess, and beloved is similar to Cupid's function as erotic god and the poet's desire. The god is both the mythological creature and the existential force that the mythic name represents, so that she or he forces herself or himself into presence and beyond allegory, beyond *re*presentation.

Still, despite the entry into experience by myth, as the poet describes it the mythic god himself struggles against the poet to maintain his absence, to remain transcendental to the words, to keep them from filling themselves with divine presence. So once again, as with Sidney's Sonnet 35, Jonson's poem is concerned with its subject and theme by virtue of its being concerned with semiotics, with what its words – or what words in general as signs – can mean and can enclose, as well as with what escapes words to remain unreachably outside discourse, godlike and transcendent.

In his well-known song, "Drink to me only with thine eyes", Jonson explicitly raises the question of the divinity of the object of desire, prefers her fleshly humanity, and then – if only ironically – suggests the divine consequences of her earthly powers. Early in the poem, the rhyming words "wine", "divine", and "thine" carry the contrast and permit the inversion.

> Or leave a kiss but in the cup,
> And I'll not look for wine.
> The thirst that from the soul doth rise
> Doth ask a drink divine;
> But might I of Jove's nectar sup,
> I would not change for thine.

The lady's kiss is preferred as a substitute for the sacrament of wine, the "drink divine", as the speaker seems – in an anti-Petrarchan vein – to insist upon her as an antithesis to divinity. It is this un-divine nature that is for him precisely the source of her power. But, in the second half of the song, the speaker attributes the transubstantiating power to the lady's effect on the flowers, which, if we are to believe him (he says, "I swear"), can be nothing less than miraculously divine, even though that effect is restricted to the world of sense (how the flowers smell).

> I sent thee late a rosy wreath,
> Not so much honoring thee,
> As giving it a hope that there
> It could not withered be.

> But thou thereon didst only breathe,
> And sent'st it back to me,
> Since when it grows and smells, I swear,
> Not of itself, but thee.

The poem is utterly good-humored about its insistence upon the ungodly, sensual appeal of the lady: it halfheartedly seeks to make her his goddess by virtue of that appeal, and, having found the words that − through a rhyming exchange − could effect her transformation, it relaxes its pressure in order to keep itself within the realm of the sublimity of human limitations. In the contrast and exchange between the wine and the kiss, I am reminded of Sidney's "I never drank of Aganippe well" (Sonnet 74), in which the kiss functions as the earthly substitute for the muse − literal inspiration (mouth to mouth) for empty figurative inspiration. The bodily world of sense is accepted through the exalted metaphors of myth, although those metaphors now appear in their literal nakedness, as deconstructed equivalents of transcendental signifieds brought inside human language for the purpose of functioning in a thoroughly human experience. The poet's lofty language, for all its reductions, does not fail, because his application of it, accompanied by a wink, is restricted to a world from which transcendence has been excluded. The creatures and the actions he has constructed are verbal only, since he implicitly acknowledges the incapacity of his words to do more, though we may − for the occasion − rest in the satisfactions and momentary persuasions of the fusions and transformations his language seems to have worked upon us.

I return to Ralegh's "Nature, that washed her hands in milk" for a final observation about the attempt of a poem to construct an artful object of idolatry within its verbal bounds, and its confessed failure to do so. But, I must insist, if it is thematically about failure, it is a failure that only supports the poem's confidence in its own artifice, which is to say, in its own illusionary success.

> Nature, that washed her hands in milk,
> And had forgot to dry them,
> Instead of earth took snow and silk,
> At love's request to try them,
> If she a mistress could compose
> To please love's fancy out of those.
>
> Her eyes he would should be of light,
> A violet breath, and lips of jelly;
> Her hair not black, nor overbright,
> And of the softest down her belly;
> As for her inside he 'ld have it
> Only of wantonness and wit.

At love's entreaty such a one
Nature made, but with her beauty
She hath framed a heart of stone;
So as love, by ill destiny,
Must die for her whom nature gave him,
Because her darling would not save him.

But time (which nature doth despise
And rudely gives her love the lie,
Makes hope a fool, and sorrow wise)
His hands do neither wash nor dry;
But being made of steel and rust,
Turns snow and silk and milk to dust.

The light, the belly, lips, and breath,
He dims, discolors, and destroys;
With those he feeds but fills not death,
Which sometimes were the food of joys.
Yea, time doth dull each lively wit,
And dries all wantonness with it.

Oh, cruel time! which takes in trust
Our youth, our joys, and all we have,
And pays us but with age and dust;
Who in the dark and silent grave
When we have wandered all our ways
Shuts up the story of our days.

This poem may serve as an allegory of what I have tried to describe
in this essay – and, *pace* Sidney's sonneteer, critics may resort to
allegory and its transparencies even if poets should not. Speaking about
this poem, I commented earlier on the rejection of earth for the moist-
smooth-whiteness of milk and snow and silk as materials to be used in
nature's attempt – in response to "love's request" – to "compose" an
ideal mistress for the pleasure of "love's fancy". But this mistress,
which nature – with whatever self-contradiction – has composed
artificially, is a perfect Petrarchan creation since with her beauty nature
has given her an unnatural "heart of stone" (unnatural though conventional – that is, thoroughly in accord with Petrarchan convention).
The consequences for love and his ideal mistress are controlled within
a "real" world that runs in accordance with enmity and its spite.
Nature's cold creature kills love, for whom she was created, and time
– nature's enemy – in turn destroys nature's prized creation: "His
hands do neither wash nor dry; / But being made of steel and rust, /
Turns snow and silk and milk to dust." Even worse, time's destructive
action is not even a special damnation, specially enjoyed, contrived for

a most precious creation slated for extinction. It is no uniquely prized victory. Instead, the action is, like time itself, automatic in its application: he feeds her specially created parts to death indiscriminately, like any of nature's less endowed creatures, so that death is fed but hardly filled by her.

> The light, the belly, lips, and breath,
> He *d*ims, *d*iscolors, and *d*estroys;
> With those he fee*d*s but fills not *d*eath,
> Which sometimes were the foo*d* of joys.
> Yea, time *d*oth *d*ull each lively wit,
> And *d*ries all wantonness with it.

The poem preciously and delicately composes nature's creature, an absolute poetic creation supposedly responsive to love's poetically conventional desires. That her "heart of stone" is unresponsive to love's actual needs is in accord with the convention that dictates her creation and is a result of nature's forgoing of earth for more delicate, if cool, materials. As a creature of artifice, there is no earth in her, and so no earthiness in her response to love. But the creature, this superb work of art, is reduced – with all of earth – to dust (and I recall my observation about Ralegh's deadly use of the alliterated "d", each instance of which I have italicized in the above quotation). The extravagant metaphor invented by nature to constitute the creature, with all its substitutions of milk and snow and silk for earth, collapses; it dissipates, with the rest of us, into a negative residue. With the metaphoric attempt thus shown to be only a fragile illusion, no more than an aesthetic construct, time takes the stage to give us the sense of an ending that converts the deconstruction it has traced into a narrative that finds formal closure. The metaphor may have failed to sustain itself, since the creature is no more than earth after all, but the illusion it permitted before its deflation is one of the most glorious of the stories that, at the end, time closes off. Which is why the poet has chronicled it.

By the final stanza the characters have been eliminated, one by one: love, the mistress, and – by implication – nature itself. Only time is left at the end to tell the story by ending all stories, supplying the closure for all our stories:

> Oh, cruel time! which takes in trust
> Our youth, our joys, and all we have,
> And pays us but with age and dust;
> Who in the dark and silent grave
> When we have wandered all our ways
> Shuts up the story of our days.

"Shuts up the story of our days" – an echo of "Time drives the flock from field to fold" in "The Nymph's Reply": it sees the flock of all of us shut up by time in the "fold", the universal coffin. In effect, then, time brings even itself to a close in that, although still standing onstage, beyond the last line even it must cease to exist. For the closure, the shutting up the story of our days, is absolute. Ultimately – which is to say beyond the last line – it is only the final negating character, death, time's agent, that remains. Only death remains – together, of course, with the words of the poem ("the story") that seems to have eliminated everyone but itself, now emptied of all it has created narratively and metaphorically, though insistent upon its own verbal presence as testament of what is lost.

I have tried here to center our concern upon English Renaissance poets wrestling with the problem of verbal representation. They see that it is the nature of signifieds – gods and beloveds among less glorious ones – to continue to be transcendental, as it is the struggle of poets to use their specially wrought net of words to capture them and to keep them trapped within discourse. All things that come before the poet's present, belated discourse – whether in language or outside it – stand like elusive gods I beyond it and its attempt to name them. In Sidney's Stella, Jonson's Love, and Ralegh's creature, we have seen various methods by which the poet both closes and reopens the gap between transcendence and participation, between stand-off and breakthrough – in other words, between failed representation and satisfying presentation.

Renaissance poets seemed capable of giving themselves a secular mission that was to demystify language as language operates outside the theological realm. When they were most self-conscious, which was not infrequently, they were aware of the deceptive tendency of all language to deify its would-be objects. Their own obligation was to expose this deception and confess the abandonment of language by the gods. But at the same time they had, themselves, to undertake to create a language that could truly tame the gods and bring them inside. So the poet had to acknowledge what language normally cannot do, what words may not say. He had to manipulate them, in hope of turning them into *his* words, magic words, so that, in spite of their usual incapacities, he could enrich them, endow them with the power to speak after all, the power that attested to a present signified, a captured god within.

But the transcendent god is never caught, after all, however well the verbal net seems to be forged. The poet has sought to open up that net in order to seize and return with his would-be signifieds; to open it up and then, as with "the story of our days", to shut it down. He tries to display them and succeeds in giving us an awareness of the semiotic exhilaration that would accompany such an entrapment. He may even give us a momentary sense that he has them and that we have caught a glimpse of them. But a higher linguistic reality is there too, one that the poet uses to remind us of his sleight of hand, as he shuts up his own story, picks up his verbal magic, and walks off, leaving our gods intact and far away, as we return to our babbling. Fortunately, however, we may still be rescued from time to time; for the poems remain, a permanent presence, ready to perform.

Speculations: *Macbeth* and source

JONATHAN GOLDBERG

This essay (or so its title suggests) poses a plurality of speculations against a presumed singleness of source; it glimpses, thereby, at a dispersal of origins. Source – in its heterogeneity – is its concern, aimed ultimately at locating Shakespeare's relation to *Macbeth*. But, it can be assumed, there is no immediate path to the author as source of the text except through a relay of mediations, and, by the end, even the supposed ultimate source – the author – must be considered within a heterogeneous dispersal.[1]

That dispersal might be termed *history*, and this essay aims at a description of the place of *Macbeth* within some familiar historical determinations – its sources in Holinshed's *Chronicles*, its relation to the rule and rhetoric of James I, its proximity to Jonson's *Masque of Queens*. Yet, in alluding to such historical determinations as heterogeneous, determinations become indeterminate. It is with the openings within the hegemonic that this essay is concerned, and its trope for such situations is specular and speculative: to imagine that within the language of hegemonic imposition and superimposition, duplication opens a spectre of uncontrolled resemblance rendering difference problematic, rendering, that is, determinate differences indeterminate.

Like others in the field – Jonathan Dollimore and Stephen Greenblatt, for example – I am interested in examining the limits of subversion, the modes of representing officially discountenanced positions. The argument that I make depends upon the notion that dominant discourses allow their own subversion precisely because hegemonic control is an impossible dream, a self-defeating fantasy. That fantasy, I will argue, attaches itself to source, to the belief in an ultimate, and ultimately authoritative, origin. What I trace is an absolutist fantasy, and one that not only kings indulge. For literary critics, of various kinds, are prone to its lure as well, when they suppose, for example, that there are certain unquestionable facts, rather than allowing that what counts as factual is itself a discursive formation; or when they imagine for the text and its author some autonomy

38

of intention. I mean to call into question the methods of such critics, and the practices of textual, historical, and formalistic criticism. The method that I offer instead owes much to post-structuralism and, in this essay, to the work of Jacques Derrida. For it is his inquiry into questions of origin that informs my own.[2]

To invoke the name of Derrida in support of an argument that seeks to recover history – even history as a discursive formation – points to the central methodological problem of this essay. Derrida has far too easily been dismissed as unconcerned with history, whereas history is for him a problematic matter precisely because it has been tied to certain metaphysical notions that will not bear close scrutiny. These include the idea of the present moment as one of complete self-presence, the idea of a past moment as one of sheer literality, and the idea of the future as the necessary outcome of such prior moments. He sums up these concerns in *Positions*, in exasperation with certain Marxist critics: "Must I recall that from the first texts I published, I have attempted to systematize a deconstructive critique precisely against the authority of meaning, as the *transcendental signified* or as *telos*, in other words history determined in the last analysis as the history of meaning, history in its logocentric, metaphysical, idealistic . . . representation . . ."[3]

To think of history as heterogeneous dispersal, as I attempt to do in this essay, is to call into question those modes of "logocentric, metaphysical, idealistic . . . representation" that ascribe determinate force to hegemonic rhetoric and that assume that ideological inscriptions really have the power they claim. It is instead the argument of this essay that ideology is haunted by what it excludes, subverted by what it subordinates. Yet the argument does not assume the possibility of some other mode of discourse, for to do so would be to replace one form of idealism with another. And thus, in this essay, the terms which must be used – referring to texts and authors and events – can only be taken as tropes, speculations with counters that discourse fills, but which cannot be contained. Halls of mirrors in which resemblance does not halt. In that respect, this essay might be called "The Mirror of Kings". Although the argument I make seems to me congruent with the thesis of *James I and the Politics of Literature*, there is a shift of emphasis in this paper. In my book I was interested in mapping strategies of representation shared by Jacobean authors and their monarch. This essay looks at the dark side of representation. The emphasis now is on the *re* in representation, the haunting spectre of duplication that unmoors texts and events from a positivistic view of history or literature. What is *real*, then, is the *re*, perhaps itself a recovery of the nothing into which things slide. Latin *rem* lies behind French *rien*.

"Shakespeare deals freely with his source", so Frank Kermode writes, considering the relationship of *Macbeth* to Holinshed. "The actual words of Holinshed are closely followed, notably in IV.ii [*sic*], but Shakespeare deals freely with his source, making Duncan old and venerable, instead of a young and weak-willed man. This is part of the general blackening of Macbeth's character."[4] Geoffrey Bullough marvels at "Shakespeare, with that wonderful memory ever ready to float up, albeit unconsciously, associations from reading or hearsay".[5] Thus, these critics affirm, Shakespeare moves freely in Holinshed, drawing on many narratives to fashion his "composite picture", as Bullough calls it;[6] and whereas, in Holinshed, Duncan is both a good king and a weak one, and Macbeth is at first loyal and then traitorous, Shakespeare − so the common line has it − recombines and simplifies his materials to offer a saintly king and his villainous murderer, and thereby makes differences clear-cut. Holinshed's narrative, because it motivates Macbeth's rebellion by allowing for defects in Duncan's rule − Duncan bars Macbeth's right to succeed to the throne, after all − takes an about-face when Macbeth turns tyrant; his earlier service to the king is labelled "counterfet" (498). Shakespeare, according to Kermode, does not have Holinshed's problem; his Macbeth is "blackened" from the start. The start? What is the source of a "composite" text?

Such a question, I would argue, must be raised, and with it the common assumptions about Shakespeare, implicit in these descriptions of the relationship of *Macbeth* to Holinshed, can begin to be investigated. For the assumption about the autonomous imagination of the author is allied to a description of a text remarkable for its moral clarity and its political conservatism − a description that may reveal more about the critics than about the play.

To test these commonplaces, let us take as an example Duncan's musing on the treacherous Thane of Cawdor:

> There's no art
> To find the mind's construction in the face:
> He was a gentleman on whom I built
> An absolute trust.   (I.iv.11–14)[7]

These lines, cut short by the entrance of Macbeth, are generally seen as an index to the innocence of Duncan's mind. What is their source? In Holinshed, Duncan's words are spoken by a witch. She prophesies that the "trustie servant" of King Natholocus, who has come to her on his ruler's behalf, will murder his monarch. The king, she says, will be killed by one "in whome he had reposed an especiall trust" (478). Duncan's lines, especially as they have been read most usually, suggest clear-cut moral differences. Yet that other habit of Shakespearean composition, its "free" association, might lead one to ask if it is significant that Duncan voices lines spoken elsewhere by a witch. The question resonates if one allows another echo to sound, the reverberations of the witches' greeting of Macbeth – "All hail, Macbeth! hail to thee, Thane of Cawdor! / All hail, Macbeth! that shall be King hereafter" (I.iii.49–50) – that come to occupy Duncan's mouth. Just a few lines after the witches' all-hailing, messengers from the king arrive, bid to "call" Macbeth "Thane of Cawdor: / In which addition, hail, most worthy Thane" (105–6); a scene later, Duncan names the king to be, "Our eldest, Malcolm; whom we name king hereafter" (I.iv.38). The text of *Macbeth* is itself "composite", redistributing the witches' lines.

Is it to be accounted to the *free* dealing of the author's mind that Duncan's lines have their source – in Holinshed, in the play – in the mouths of witches? We might notice, too, that where Duncan swerves from the lines in Holinshed describing a king *reposing* his *special* trust, he substitutes the *activity* of *building* an *absolute* trust, and recall that Shakespeare drops Holinshed's description of Macbeth as master-builder of Dunsinane, virtually the only incident from Macbeth's career not duplicated in the play, and allows Duncan instead to comment on the architecture of Inverness, thus permitting Duncan's to be the constructing mind. In short, the absolute differences and moral clarity that critics have found to be Shakespeare's are, at least in these instances, Duncan's. Monarch of the *absolute*, Duncan constructs differences against the demonic source of his lines, spoken by a witch and to a figure that serves as a model for Macbeth. Duncan's musings on the betrayal of the Thane of Cawdor have always been allowed the ironic echo that extends to the newly named Thane, Macbeth; the lines, I would suggest, might also be thought of as self-reflective. "There's no art / To find the mind's construction in the face"; has not criticism – with scarcely an exception – succumbed to Duncan's glassy surface?[8]

That surface is cut into again if we return to the source of Duncan's lines in Holinshed. For Holinshed also describes King Duff as one "having a speciall trust in Donwald" (481), the loyal retainer that slays him. Holinshed's King Duff is a haunted and sleepless figure who sends his trusty servant to try to discover the cause of his disease. Donwald finds a witch "rosting upon a woodden broch an image of wax at the fier, resembling in each feature the kings person" (480). The king's illness is the result of this demonic voodooism, spectral identification, and he is restored to health as soon as Donwald destroys the waxen image. It scarcely needs mention that Holinshed's King Duff is – except for the line that Duncan speaks – a version of Macbeth. Does the spectre of identification drawn from the composition of Holinshed in *Macbeth* signify in the play? Both Duff and Donwald are versions of Macbeth. Duncan is a further spectral emanation of a source less intent on *absolute difference* than on resemblance. After King Duff is cured, he celebrates his recovery by making a "spectacle" (481) of hanged rebels. Among them are Donwald's kin, and the loyal retainer who cured the king by destroying his spectre turns on the king who has made the spectacle. So, *Macbeth* opens with reports of Macbeth fixing a rebel head upon the battlements (I.ii.23) and closes with his severed head displayed by Macduff (V.ix.20); a plot inscribed and generated within specularity: in each instance, a supposedly saintly king has let another do his dirty work.

As another example of specular contamination, consider this episode from Holinshed: King Kenneth, successor to King Duff and murderer of his son and heir, suffers guilt and sleeplessness; he is told by prophetic voices that he will die and that the heir he has named will not succeed to the throne. His murder is accomplished by Fenella, avenging the death of her son, another child killed by the guilty monarch. Knowing "that the king delighted above measure in goodlie buildings" (486), she constructs an elaborate tower covered with engraved flowers and other images. "In the middest of the house there was a goodlie brasen image also, resembling the figure of king Kenneth" (487) holding in his hands a golden apple which, if plucked, activates crossbows aimed at the taker. The king succumbs to the lure and is killed. Whose career is this in *Macbeth*, Macbeth's – or Duncan's?

Macbeth looks in his conscience, torn by demonic representations and by Duncan's furthering of their designs; in soliloquy, he produces the saintly king – as a mirror. "This Duncan / Hath borne his faculties so meek, hath been / So clear in his great office, that his virtues / Will plead like angels" (I.vii.16–19). Duncan's polished surface: the representation of an absolute power or the mirror of resemblance?

Duncan articulates, constructs, absolute difference, but equivocation arises from the source. "People wished", Holinshed writes,

the inclinations and maners of these two cousins to have beene so tempered and enterchangeablie bestowed betwixt them, that where the one had too much of clemencie, and the other of crueltie, the meane virtue betwixt these two extremities might have reigned by indifferent partition in them both.   (488)

So, Lady Macbeth fears her husband "is too full o' th' milk of human kindness" (I.v.17); so, as Harry Berger has persuasively argued, the opening scenes of the play enact an elaborately concealed hostility between Duncan and Macbeth, scenes, that is, of rivalry between characters who represent (in Holinshed's words) the "indifferent partition" that "reign[s]" in *Macbeth*.[9] "Have we eaten on the insane root, / That takes the reason prisoner?" (I.iii.84–5), Banquo asks after the witches appear. The "insane root" lies in the source; in Holinshed, Duncan disables the rebels by feeding them a poisoned brew that puts them to sleep. "Look up clear", Lady Macbeth counsels her husband (I.v.71), and he looks in a mirror, to find Duncan, "clear in his great office" (I.vii.18). Succession in the play can never take place except in a mirror. Macbeth invents the sainted king; he is not visible in the lines he speaks. After Macbeth kills him, he reports that Duncan's silver skin was laced with golden blood (II.iii.110).[10] Such images are the obstacles that Macbeth finds in his path; they are also the source of his own legitimation when he comes to occupy Duncan's place. Macbeth succeeds as the king of the image-repertoire in *Macbeth*.

Thus, when one looks to the most apparently straightforward scene of the transmission of source − the recasting of Holinshed's conversation between Macduff and Malcolm in IV.iii, what one discovers is that something has come between the source and the scene. What blocks the way of transmission is the text of *Macbeth* itself; Malcolm and Macduff repeatedly echo words and phrases that have come before, words most often heard in Macbeth's mouth. Resemblance, not difference, dominates the text; Macbeth attempts unpartnered to occupy alone what occupies him, to the end "wrought / With things forgotten" (I.iii.151).

"People wished the inclinations and maners of these two cousins to have beene so tempered and enterchangeablie bestowed betwixt them", so Holinshed writes; is that desire, articulated in the source, also Shakespeare's? The chance and wayward associations of his "wonderful memory"? The floating of his unconscious? A conscious design? To consider these questions, another source must be considered, the occasion of the play, for it is equally a critical commonplace to see the author of *Macbeth* succumbing to the exigencies of history, and to regard the play as a royal compliment: Edward the Confessor touches for the King's Evil as James, reluctantly, did; Banquo fathered James's line.[11] Moreover, the text of *Macbeth* that we have derives from a court performance. Could Shakespeare have represented the contaminations of spectral resemblance before James I? Intentionally? Secretly? These questions about source lead to what Fredric Jameson might call the *political unconscious* of the play, a determined heterogeneity rather than the free play of the mind.[12] What, we need to ask, are the political conditions of representation in which *Macbeth* is located?

The text of *Macbeth* offers one index to these conditions, for it is, as Stephen Orgel has remarked, a palimpsest,[13] combining at least two versions of the play, one dating from the time of the Gunpowder Plot – alluded to, for instance, by the Porter's use of *equivocation* in the play (II.iii; and, at V.v.43, by Macbeth), another several years later, and marked by the additions of songs from Middleton's *The Witch*, a play presumed to postdate Jonson's 1609 *Masque of Queens*. From Act III on, if not before, the text of *Macbeth* shows signs of tampering: transposed scenes, cut lines, wholesale interpolations of songs and dances. The menacing powers of the witches are trivialized, and to reduce the impact of their show of kings they propose to "cheer . . . up" Macbeth:

> Come, sisters, cheer we up his sprites,
> And show the best of our delights.
> I'll charm the air to give a sound,
> While you perform your antick round;
> That this great King may kindly say,
> Our duties did his welcome pay.　　　　　(IV.i.127–32)

Who is "this great King" to whom compliment is paid, if not the monarch in the audience? The text alludes to the presence of King James in this compliment as well as in the formal accommodations that make the text of *Macbeth* masquelike. But even these trivial lines of jaunty welcome to the king enact a curious play of resemblance. The editor of the Arden edition of *Macbeth*, for example, takes "this great King" to refer to Macbeth. One king slides into the other, a type of diffusion that can be remarked elsewhere in the latter half of *Macbeth*, in the withdrawal of Lady Macbeth and her replacement with Lady Macduff, or in the English scenes with their echoes of Scottish horror; we see less of Macbeth as the play proceeds, and hear more of him. The presence of King James in the text of *Macbeth*, however much it disturbs the original and irrecoverable designs of the play, also seems to be written within them. Might we say that the earlier relationship between Macbeth and Duncan is re-enacted between Macbeth and King James? That there is room in the text for only one king? That these two monarchs are haunted by spectral identification? A mirror, literally, provides an answer to these speculations. In the show of kings, Macbeth looks into the mirror in which James I is reflected:

> the eighth appears, who bears a glass,
> Which shows me many more; and some I see,

That two-fold balls and treble sceptres carry.
Horrible sight!   (IV.i.119–22)

Disturbing the notion of clear-cut difference in this confrontation is, once again, the problem of source, for the show of kings is provided by the "filthy hags" (115), and however much their subsequent jauntiness means to diffuse the spectacle, it retains its disturbing power. Steven Mullaney has written wonderfully about this moment, about the alliance of the demonic to a linguistic excess. As he says, in that mirroring moment "genealogy and prophecy are made manifest in a visible display, but there is another genealogy in the air as well, one heard rather than seen. Juxtaposed to the projection of James's line, the witches' riddles complicate its complimentary gesture with what amounts to a genealogy of treason and equivocation."[14] If earlier Duncan spoke witches' words, here the king is transported onstage in the witches' show, caught within speculation. If earlier Duncan bestowed gifts and titles to "name" a "hereafter" already named, here James is asked to "kindly say" that the witches' "duties did his welcome pay". The king lives to bestow, as James indicated when he titled his treatise on kingship the *Basilikon Doron*, the royal gift. His gift was his presence and the heir he produced; presentation that is re-presentation. There is an economy of speculation.

Is the show of kings subversive? Do its spectral identifications implicate Shakespeare in a revolutionary politics? Could such a politics evade the reflections of a mirror that catches the king on stage and off? Is there an autonomous realm available for representation that would not be caught within representation? That realm of autonomy, Franco Moretti suggests, is coincident with sovereignty imagined as "a power . . . having its origin *in itself*".[15] When James represented that power, as in the sonnet prefatory to the *Basilikon Doron*, he declared himself a god by announcing that "God gives not Kings the stile of *Gods* in vaine"; the king who gives all has been given his power as a *style*, and as an echoing name.[16] The king stands *in the place* of the "heavenly King", his "Lieutenant". Duncan dresses Macbeth in borrowed robes as well, making a voodoo version of himself. "Remember", James counseled his son and heir, "the throne is Gods and not yours, that ye sit in" (*BD* 39). Presenting himself, claiming all his kingdom as his own – the kingdom was his body and his wife, he declared on more than one occasion – James also saw himself as representation, a king on stage, whose behavior offered a living "image" of himself. Royal existence is representation. "Let your owne life be a law-booke and a mirrour to your people" (30), James urged his son in the book in which he similarly presented himself, counseling him to present himself as

the "vive image" of his "vertuous disposition" (51). Offering himself
to parliamentary inspection, the king was fond of declaring that his
breast was a crystal mirror, both a reflecting surface and a transparent
one. What could one's "owne life" be in such formulations of identity
– even absolute identity – as reflection? Wouldn't this hall of mirrors
include the notion of "a power . . . having its origin *in itself*" –
whether we were to attach that idea of autonomy to the king or to the
sovereign author of *Macbeth*? Could there be an end to these speculations, or a source?

Ben Jonson's masques for King James frequently depend upon such
absolutist assertions and they are our best guide to the conditions of
absolutist representation in the Jacobean period. When Jonson wrote
a masque celebrating James's birthday in 1620, the king was cast as
Pan, for Pan means "all": "Pan is our all, by him we breathe, we live,
/ We move, we are" (170–1). Yet included in the spectacle that Jonson
offered the king were disturbing reflections of himself and his cour-
tiers, particularly in the figure of a court-ape outrageously parodying
the court. Jonson showed James how to view the attack by reprimand-
ing the parodist in the masque. "Your folly may well deserve pardon
because it hath delighted", he is told; "but beware of presuming, or
how you offer comparisons with persons so near deities. Behold where
they are that have now forgiven you, whom you should provoke again
with the like, they will justly punish that with anger which they now
dismiss with contempt" (131–6). The court and its parodist face each
other in this moment to regard one another within the spectacle of
"comparisons" and resemblances; the derisory spectacle is to be seen
with derision. James must forgive all if all reflects him and if he is the
ultimate source of all representation. In Jonson's masques, the representation of the king's claims to totality offers the possibility of
endless replications within the system of reflecting power in which the
king was placed.[17]

This can be demonstrated, too, in *The Vision of Delight* (1617), a masque, as its title suggests, about vision. For in it, the spectacle of the
king's Arcadia on stage, the image of the realm perfected, is presented
by the antimasque figure of Fant'sy. Fant'sy's realm is, in the antimasque, the suspect terrain of wayward dreams:

> Dreams of the maker and dreams of the teller,
> Dreams of the kitchen and dreams of the cellar;
> Some that are tall, and some that are dwarfs,
> Some that are haltered, and some that wear scarfs;
> Some that are proper and signify o' thing,
> And some another, and some that are nothing.   (55–60)

What sort of dream does Fant'sy present when this antimasquer presents the king, and offers this climactic vision of his realm in the masque proper:

> Behold a king
> Whose presence maketh this perpetual spring,
> The glories of which spring grows in that bower,
> And are the marks and beauties of his power.   (189–92)

Is this vision of majesty a tall dream, too? Are not the confusions of Fant'sy's antimasque speech also to be found in the mirror image of the king and his imagined Arcadian state? What kind of spectacle does he present, one that signifies one thing, or many – or even nothing? The impropriety of making Fant'sy the purveyor of the royal image dallies with double meanings and with the subversions that lurk in the mirror of resemblance.

Pan's Anniversary or *The Vision of Delight* can be offered as examples of the proximity of royal compliment and its subversion that Jonson managed before his monarch's eyes. We can come closer to the source of *Macbeth* if we look at the Jonsonian masque that stands somewhere behind the masquelike movement that the play ultimately takes. *The Masque of Queens* is particularly apt for consideration here because, like *Macbeth*, central to its concerns is a contention between royal and demonic powers and, specifically, the question of the source of power.

Jonson's *Masque of Queens* is palpably dualistic in design. It opens with "a foil or false masque" (12) in which eleven witches invoke their Dame. She arrives and the witches join together as "faithful opposites" (120) to "disturb" the entertainment – and, more frighteningly, to oppose the accomplishments of an "Age of Gold" (129) and return all things to chaos. The Dame proposes their plans in these words:

> Let us disturb it then, and blast the light;
> Mix hell with heaven, and make Nature fight
> Within herself; loose the whole hinge of things,
> And cause the ends run back into their springs.   (134–7)

Gathering together the elements necessary for their powers, the Dame attempts to raise a spirit to accomplish their task. She fails, and in the midst of their frenzied dances, loud music and a sudden change of scene usher in Perseus, the figure of Heroic Virtue, announcing the arrival of Fame; she, in turn, brings on a consort of twelve heroic queens, who end the masque in dancing. Virtue has triumphed over vice; as Jonson notes at the climactic change of scene, the hags vanish "scarce suffering the memory of such a thing" (337).

"Scarce suffering" – barely permitting, but yet not entirely effacing.

For, as is apparent even in a brief summary of the action of the masque, the forces of good and evil bear a striking resemblance – twelve hags, twelve queens – and the structure of the two halves of the masque is also broadly parallel – invocations, arrivals, dances. Dualism would seem to be a mirror effect. In *Queens*, moreover, language passes through the mirror, overriding differences. Although ostensibly the two parts of the masque are related only by opposition, and although the second half of the masque removes all traces of the first, the language of the masque is seamless. Its central trope, in fact, involves sources and origins, suggesting an overriding power. Jonson announces that the argument of the masque is "true fame bred out of virtue" (6); yet breeding, arrival, origination are everywhere apparent in the masque, throwing the relationship between the two parts into question. Does the second come from the first? Has the Dame's unsuccessful attempt to raise a spirit issued in the arrival of Heroic Virtue? Is there a beginning principle?

Here is the seamless thread: the witches arrive, claiming they "come . . . from" a landscape replete with death (45–54), and as they try repeated charms, naming all their instruments (owls, baying dogs, toads, voodoo images, and the like), they raise their Dame. More invocations follow, filled with snatchings, gatherings, pluckings, choosing, biting, sucking, getting and making – a depletion and a dismemberment of nature to reconstitute it in the spectre they would raise. The earth is made a grave, they bury (230) what they have gathered and seek to make it rise again, reconstituted. Here, the language of birth that underlies all these activities is made explicit:

> Dame earth shall quake,
> And the houses shake,
> And her belly shall ache
> As her back were brake
> Such a birth to make . . .   (240–4)

At first they are unsuccessful – "our labor dies! / Our magic feature will not rise" (269–70) – and they attempt again their "magic birth" (298). Instead, the House of Fame rises "in the place of" (338) the witches' hell, as the stage direction indicates. Perseus declares himself the "parent" (356) of Fame; Fame arrives acknowledging her "father" (431) and announcing that she will "draw . . . forth" (439) the twelve queens, who sing in celebration of "Fame that's out of Virtue born" (487) and "this famous birth" (500).

These continuities would seem to confirm the Dame's design, mixing hell with heaven, loosing the "whole hinge of things", and making endings fetch their origins in chaotic beginnings – the scarce remembered, almost vanished traces of a design which the masque replicates even as it replaces it. If we ask why this spectre of resemblance should be in the masque, the answer, we may assume, has to do with absolutist power. Power in the masque is figured as origin-giving. Perseus is both parent and strength (356); like the witches, he makes life from death: "When Virtue cut off Terror, he gat [i.e begat] Fame. / . . . when Fame was gotten Terror died" (351–2). As much as the witches, he needs to dismember to make. Powers of making depend upon depletion – and this, too, is how the masque itself is constructed, "scarce suffering" the memory of the displaced hags, but not entirely effacing them. Jonson's making is thus also in question. Although Perseus points to the columns of the House of Fame as "men-making poets" (362), the poet of the masque is at pains to disavow his powers, telling his reader (Prince Henry) that the masque's invention comes from the queen (9–10); that the decorum of the masque derives from Horace (7–8); that the queens and witches are drawn from the storehouse of classical and contemporary books that he has perused; that even the spectators give life to his designs: "a writer should always trust somewhat to the capacity of the spectator, especially at these spec-tacles" (95–6).

The privileged spectator here is the king, of course, and the spectacle is designed to mirror and bring forth his mind. Hence, when Perseus presents the twelve queens, he ends with the king, and although Bel-Anna (Queen Anne's role in the masque) is the highest of queens, she must submit "all her worth / To him that gave it", the one who has "brought forth / Their names to memory" (402–4). The pronoun may refer to the poet; a few lines later, it means the king, source of all "in-crease" (410), conferring the bounty on all which is "contracted" (413) within himself. The king, Perseus says, will "embrace" the "spec-tacle" (414–15). From a "spectacle of strangeness, producing multipli-city of gesture" (17–18), as Jonson describes the antimasque of witches, arises "the strangeness and beauty of the spectacle" (466), the genuine masque of queens. What the text produces is referred to the king's eye.

What lives in the king's eye here, as in *Macbeth*, is genealogy, what he produces; here, as in *Macbeth*, the king lives to bestow, to give gifts which are contracted within him and which are extended without. Royal absolutism is coincident with full ownership and extension over all so that nothing and no one has autonomy except the king; yet this means that, like Duncan, his absolutism also signifies opacity. The king who gives all is appropriated by what he appropriates. Building and constructing all in his all-embracing view, his power is his blindness. His power lies in a mirror whose reflections cannot be controlled.

Such speculative investments may deplete the all-giver. Duncan and Macbeth meet for the first time in the play, and Duncan voices the depletion involved in giving, the horrific sense that their exchanges are spectral identifications, transfers like the voodoo magic between the king and his replica:

> O worthiest cousin!
> The sin of my ingratitude even now
> Was heavy on me. Thou art so far before,
> That swiftest wing of recompense is slow
> To overtake thee: would thou hadst less deserv'd,
> That the proportion both of thanks and payment
> Might have been mine! Only I have left to say,
> More is thy due than more than all can pay.   (I.iv.14–21)

The more he gives, the less he has; his wish: "would thou hadst less deserv'd". A few lines later, Duncan attempts to name the "hereafter" despite Macbeth's success, "so far before".

On 27 August 1605, in the course of a visit James and his family made to Oxford, they were welcomed at St John's College by a learned show, a Latin entertainment hailing the fulfillment of fate's prophesied genealogy (the line of Banquo) embodied in the king and queen and their heirs. The lines were spoken by three woodland creatures, "quasi Sibyllae", they are called, boys masquerading as numinous female powers, all-hailing their monarch:

> Fame says the fatal Sisters once foretold
> Power without end, great Monarch, to thy stock . . .
> And thus we greet thee: Hail, whom Scotland serves!
> Whom England, Hail! Whom Ireland serves, all hail![18]

So, too, the witches greet Macbeth, so Duncan gives addition to the new Thane of Cawdor. Banquo wonders if the witches can speak true, but the echoes go back further. The witches' all-hailing inaugurates Macbeth's career by appropriating a moment of royal compliment. From the start, the mirror of re-presentation respects no boundaries; the show of kings staged for the mutual benefit of Macbeth and King James occurs *within* these representations. There is no source, not even a sovereign author, outside of representation, no end or beginning to these speculations.

Within *Macbeth*, the menacing heterogeneity of uncontrolled duplication that threatens the autonomy of power is embodied in the witches. In the anxiety about women in the play we might find a further reflection of the disturbing questions raised about the sources of the

Shakespearean imagination.[19] Jonson's *Masque of Queens* is instructive
in that regard as well, for in order to represent sovereign power,
women's control over nature and birth are ascribed to the king. Perseus
declares his power – to give birth – and refers it to the king's bounty.
Yet, what is presented to the monarch's eyes is a pageant of armed
women to replace the army of hags, a haunting version of the king's
declaration of patriarchal appropriations. Questions about a power that
"lies like truth" (V.v.43) menace men's words and their assertions of
authority. Kings and authors, then, are menaced.

In *Macbeth*, the heterogeneity of the female as Other is implicated in
scenes of writing and reading that may reflect on the Shakespearean
signature and its sources. "The King hath happily receiv'd Macbeth /
The news of thy success" (I.iii.89–90), Rosse reports, describing
Duncan as reading:

> and when he reads
> Thy personal venture in the rebels' fight,
> His wonders and his praises do contend,
> Which should be thine, or his.   (90–3)

Contention over ownership of the text, however, is, as Rosse goes on
to say, "silenc'd", rendered undecidable; the text that Duncan attempts to master instead masters him, news of success that cannot be
controlled:

> silenc'd with that,
> In viewing o'er the rest o' th' selfsame day,
> He finds thee in the stout Norweyan ranks,
> Nothing afeard of what thyself didst make,
> Strange images of death.   (93–7)

Within the *selfsame* ("th' selfsame day") a spectre of swallowed difference rises;[20] Duncan discovers Macbeth "in the rebels' fight", "in
the stout Norweyan ranks", and he finds himself implicated in
Macbeth's acts. They meet in "strange images of death" which neither
monarch nor his general fear. And so Rosse's report of the king and
Macbeth locked in contention for the interpretation of a text ends with
Duncan's submission to what "came post with post" (I.iii.98), the
news of Macbeth's success and the spectre of succession passing from
king to rebel: the king impressed with the letter. Two scenes later, the
scene of reading is repeated, literally. Macbeth sends his wife a letter,
which he has "thought good to deliver thee", as if he were giving birth
to the word as his child. "Lay it to thy heart", he orders (I.v.10–14).
Lady Macbeth looks in her heart, and finds Macbeth "too full o' th'
milk of human kindness" (17); whose milk does she find in the word,

hers or his? King James declared that his gifts to the nation were their very "nourish-milke" and that he was the kingdom's "loving nourish-father" (*BD* 24); the patriarch as male mother, greedily sucked dry. Reports of Macbeth's success, Rosse says, were "pour'd . . . down before" (I.iii.100) the king, delivering what they "bear":

> As thick as hail,
> Came post with post; and every one did bear
> Thy praises in his kingdom's great defence,
> And pour'd them down before him.   (I.iii.97–100)

And in his letter to his wife, Macbeth relates and conflates the earlier scene, "came missives from the King, who all-hail'd me, 'Thane of Cawdor'; by which title, before, these Weird Sisters saluted me". Thus the letter is embarked upon its circuit of exchange. (Is the hailstorm a dissemination of the all-hailing?) Male attempts to appropriate power encounter a heterogeneity in their attempted representations: an alliance between women and their words. Macbeth's letter suppresses the success the witches have promised to Banquo, just as the play organizes itself around the conflict between Macbeth and Macduff, and the succession from Duncan to Malcolm. Its mirroring structure represents an absolutist fantasy surpassed by the witches' show.[21]

The hypermasculine world of *Macbeth* is haunted – as is *The Masque of Queens* – by the power represented in the witches; masculinity in the play is directed as an assaultive attempt to secure power, to maintain success and succession, at the expense of women. As is typical of many of Shakespeare's tragedies, the play is largely womanless and family relationships are disturbed; Duncan and Banquo both have heirs, but no wives; Macbeth and Lady Macbeth have no surviving children. The one fully gratuitous act of Macbeth's is the murder of Lady Macduff and her children, an act in which Macduff is fully complicit; he has abandoned his wife, and she accuses him of betrayal. He allies himself with Malcolm in a scene in which the future monarch displays his credentials first by presenting himself as excessively libidinous – and Macduff willingly responds as a virtual procurer to satisfy his lust – and then as excessively chaste; either way, masculinity and power are directed against women. When Macbeth is finally defeated, he is replaced by two men who have secured power in the defeat of women. Indeed, Macduff has not only abandoned his wife and family, his very birth represents a triumph over his mother's womb. To mark the new powers in Scotland, the battle concludes with Siward's celebration of the ritual slaughter of his son. It is not Macbeth alone who opposes generativity or wishes to eradicate its source. Good

and bad Scots alike are bent on securing power, and that means to seize
fully the terrain of women. For Scotland is a bleeding mother in the
play, and their aim is to "bestride our downfall birthdom" (IV.iii.4).
"It cannot / Be call'd our mother, but our grave" (165–6), Rosse goes
on to say. Birth and death are, in these paradigmatic utterances, man's
downfall, the limits of beginning and end; they survive his successes,
unlimited limits. The seizure and defeat of women is a bid for immortality, for a power that will never fade.

The shape of that fantasy is revealed in the mirror scene: a line of
kings propagated in the mirror. Males produce males, just as Banquo
and Duncan seem capable of succession without the interference of
women. "Look in thy glass, and tell the face thou viewest / Now is the
time that face should form another"; so the third sonnet opens on the
prospect of a duplication of images that might be called – if we follow
Luce Irigaray – a determining patriarchal fantasy, the glassy facade of
"the sovereign authority of pretense".[22] Macbeth looks in the mirror
and sees his reflection in the line that extends to James; not in the mirror is Mary Queen of Scots, the figure that haunts the patriarchal
claims of the *Basilikon Doron*, the mother on whom James rested his
claims to the throne of England – and whom he sacrificed to assure
his sovereignty.

Men may look in the mirror, may have their being in the mirror; but
in *Macbeth*, the spectre of duplicates is in other hands. The spectacle
of state here, or in *The Masque of Queens*, is the witches' show. All
masculine attempts at female deprivation – including Lady Macbeth's
desire to unsex herself – are robbed of ultimate success. Mortality cannot be killed. What escapes control is figured in the witches;
emblematically bearded, linguistically ambiguous, they represent, in
Harry Berger's brilliant phrase, the textual "display of withheld
surplus meaning".[23] Their words stretch out "to th' crack of doom"
(IV.i.117), an ultimate fissure in which both Macbeth and Malcolm
have their place hereafter.

Confronting source – and end – the play registers an excess, unsettling in its indifferent and repetitious production, one king after
another, a Malcolm for a Macbeth, raised on the body of woman, embodied in the text. The partnership of indifference begins (and ends)
in rivalry over the letter, Duncan's reading of Macbeth, Lady
Macbeth's reading of Macbeth's letter, or Banquo's confrontation with
the witches:

> You seem to understand me,
> By each at once her choppy fingers laying
> Upon her skinny lips: you should be women,

And yet your beards forbid me to interpret
That you are so.   (I.iii.43–7)

Their beards and their fingers on their lips forbid interpretation and
point beyond an order of words and utterance to an excess at the
source. Generators of the text, they suggest that the male fantasy of
Macbeth may have as its counterpart the fantasy of the autonomy of the
artistic imagination – Prospero's fantasy in *The Tempest*, for instance,
when he displays his power in a masque whose deities are all female
– and they caution the critic who would describe the play as the free
workings of a mind playing with its sources.[24] At the furthest reach of
speculation, they intimate that the mirrors in *Macbeth* represent a
meeting of authority and author swallowed in its source. That textual
situation might be named Volumnia.

Notes

[1] The assumption here is that of Michel Foucault in "What is an Author?"
in *Language, Counter-Memory, Practice*, tr. Donald F. Bouchard and Sherry
Simon (Ithaca: Cornell University Press, 1977), that the author must be
replaced by the "author-function" as limited and made possible by historical
formations. Among the signs of the dispersal of the dramatic author in
Shakespeare's time are his failure to publish his plays and the state of at least
some of the texts gathered in the 1623 folio that shows signs of ongoing revision (rather than a stabilizing of an authoritative authorial text); in the case
of *Macbeth*, as discussed below, the folio text is not entirely Shakespearean,
a condition that did not keep Heminge and Condell from publishing it. For
some incisive probing of this issue, see Stephen Orgel, "What is a Text?",
Research Opportunities in Renaissance Drama, 24 (1981), 3–6.

[2] E.g. see "Qual Quelle: Valery's Sources", in *Margins of Philosophy*, trans.
Alan Bass (Chicago: University of Chicago Press, 1982), pp. 273–306; *Of
Grammatology*, trans. Gayatri Chakravorty Spivak (Baltimore: Johns
Hopkins University Press, 1974, 1976), e.g. "There is *a supplement at the
source*" (304) and the ensuing discussion of representation and supplementarity, or the remarks on auto-affection and mothers (152–7) as original
supplementarity.

[3] *Positions*, trans. Alan Bass (Chicago: University of Chicago Press, 1981),
pp. 49–50. See also pp. 57–60 for a discussion of a new mode of conceiving
history and its difficulties, a discussion I take as exemplary for the tasks of
what Stephen Greenblatt has termed the "new historicism" in his "Introduction" to "The Forms of Power and the Power of Forms in the Renaissance", *Genre*, 15 (1982), 5–6.

[4] Frank Kermode, "Introduction" to *Macbeth* in *The Riverside Shakespeare*
(Boston: Houghton Mifflin, 1974), p. 1308. IV.ii is presumably a misprint
for IV.iii.

[5] Geoffrey Bullough (ed.), *Narrative and Dramatic Sources of Shakespeare*,

vol. 7 (London: Routledge and Kegan Paul, 1973), p. 444. Subsequent quotations from Holinshed's *Chronicles* are taken from this volume.

[6] Bullough, *Sources*, vol. 7, p. 448. Stephen Booth argues for Holinshed's "composite" composition in *The Book Called Holinshed's Chronicles* (Book Club of California, 1968). His thesis is that Holinshed attempts "to contain all accounts in one account" (p. 45) and that "the *Chronicles* are the work in English literature that most fully shares the most peculiarly Shakespearean of Shakespeare's traits – the ability constantly to shift the perception of a reader or audience from one set of principles for judgment to another" (p. 72). There are differences between the authors, however, that Booth fails to register. Holinshed is a relentless explainer; however multiple his perspectives he rationalizes each stage in his story; the explanations may not add up, but they are supplied. Shakespeare, on the other hand, omits such things as Holinshed's explanation of Scottish laws of succession, Lady Macbeth's ambition to be queen, etc.

Booth's description of *Macbeth*'s relationship to Holinshed echoes the commonplaces, adding to them the New-Critical idea of textual complexity as the Shakespearean version of Holinshed's composite complexity: "in *Macbeth* Shakespeare omits all indication that Duncan was ever a bad king or Macbeth a good one. He does, however, create a deeper and more intense conflict in his audience by causing its members to sympathize with and share the consciousness of a moral monster" (p. 80).

For a tabulation of Shakespeare's borrowings from Holinshed see Robert A. Law, "The Composition of *Macbeth* with Reference to Holinshed", *Texas Studies in English*, 31 (1952), 35–41.

[7] All citations from the Arden *Macbeth*, ed. Kenneth Muir (London and New York: Methuen, 1982).

[8] A notable exception is Harry Berger, Jr, "The Early Scenes of *Macbeth*: preface to a new interpretation", *English Literary History* 47 (1980), 1–31, an essay to which I am deeply indebted in this discussion.

[9] Without making anything of it, Dover Wilson notes a version of this in his "Introduction" to *Macbeth* (Cambridge: Cambridge University Press, 1947) when he remarks that Holinshed's phrase for Duncan, "too much of clemencie", "came to be associated in his [Shakespeare's] mind with Macbeth himself". More exactly, Lady Macbeth transfers it to her husband. D. W. Harding notes that the source for Lady Macbeth's milk in Holinshed lies in the rebels' characterization of Duncan as a milksop; see "Women's Fantasy of Manhood", *Shakespeare Quarterly*, 20 (1969), 246–7.

[10] Cf. Berger, *English Literary History*, 47 (1980), 16: "From the moment in 1.7 when Macbeth approaches the murder as a real possibility, we see his attachment to the figure of Duncan increase." Construction continues, too, in Macduff's naming Duncan "The Lord's anointed Temple" (II.iii.67), "a most sainted King" (IV.iii.109). No one speaks about Duncan in these terms before his death, and the king is represented as rebel-besieged; tense in his relations to them – and to those, like Macbeth, dependent upon his generosity; peremptory in naming his heir.

[11] Such connections are noted by Kermode and Muir. They are part of a long tradition of reading *Macbeth* in conjunction with James I fully ex-

emplified by H. N. Paul, *The Royal Play of Macbeth* (New York: Macmillan, 1950) and Arthur Melville Clark, *Murder under Trust or The Topical Macbeth* (Edinburgh: Scottish Academic Press, 1981). Such views are answered forcefully by Michael Hawkins, "History, Politics and *Macbeth*", in *Focus on Macbeth*, ed. John Russell Brown (London: Routledge and Kegan Paul, 1982). Hawkins argues against the notion of the monolithic historical background, suggesting instead that Jacobean society was an ambiguous amalgam of tense political relationships and systems; for him, Banquo, Duncan, Macduff and Malcolm all have political and moral weaknesses, and Macbeth is not entirely a villain. The play is equivocal throughout, as was contemporary politics. Hawkins's sceptical and empirical view does not credit the power of symbolic discourse in political behavior, and the ambiguities he details are perhaps more rational than the equivocations in *Macbeth*.

The choice of reflecting James in Edward the Confessor must be set in the context of James's repeated disgust and sarcasm at the practice of touching; see D. H. Willson, *King James VI and I* (New York: Oxford University Press, 1956), pp. 172–3. That Banquo is hardly innocent in the play has been observed by critics from Bradley on. (See A. C. Bradley, *Shakespearean Tragedy* [London: Macmillan, 1956], pp. 379–87.)

12 At the very least, if we account for the composition of *Macbeth* in terms of the operation of Shakespeare's unconscious associations, we should recognize that the unconscious is an historical phenomenon that never operates freely, and is intimately bound to social structures (e.g. the family, the state) that promote and limit autonomy.

13 Stephen Orgel, "Shakespeare Imagines a Theater", in *Shakespeare, Man of the Theater*, ed. K. Muir, J. Halio and D. J. Palmer (Newark: University of Delaware Press, 1983), p. 43.

14 Steven Mullaney, "Lying Like Truth: riddle, representation and treason in Renaissance England", *English Literary History*, 47 (1980), 41. On the political significance of the witches, see the suggestive essay by Peter Stallybrass, "*Macbeth* and Witchcraft", in Russell Brown (ed.), *Focus on Macbeth*. Stallybrass acutely situates the witches in opposition to patriarchal rule as an anti-state and an anti-family; I am particularly indebted to him for suggesting that the dilemma they pose is "solved" by the attempt to form families without women (p. 198). The "normality" of this patriarchal fantasy, and its historical refigurations, is the subject in Eve Kosofsky Sedgwick's *Between Men: English literature and male homosocial desire* (New York: Columbia University Press, 1985).

15 Franco Moretti, " 'A Huge Eclipse': tragic forms and the deconsecration of sovereignty", *Genre*, 15 (1982), 9.

16 *Basilikon Doron* cited from *The Political Works of James I*, ed. Charles H. McIlwain (Cambridge, Mass.: Harvard University Press, 1918), hereafter referred to as *BD*.

17 I consider this moment in the masque from a slightly different perspective in *James I and the Politics of Literature* (Baltimore: Johns Hopkins University Press, 1983), pp. 130–1. All citations from *Ben Jonson: the complete masques*, ed. Stephen Orgel (New Haven: Yale University Press, 1970). The

trope of this essay, and my treatment of the masque, depend upon Orgel's description of the form as "the mirror of the king's mind" in *The Illusion of Power* (Berkeley and Los Angeles: University of California Press, 1975), p. 77.

18 Bullough, *Sources*, vol. 7, p. 471. The relation of this entertainment to *Macbeth* was noted by E. K. Chambers, *William Shakespeare* (Oxford: At the Clarendon Press, 1930), and is conjectured in John Nichols, *The Progresses of King James I* (London: J. B. Nichols, 1828), vol. 1, p. 543. Bullough's text translates a page appended to Matthew Gwinne's *Vertumnus*; it may not represent the exact form of the entertainment, which is discussed by Nichols, pp. 543–5. In *Rex Platonicus* (Oxford, 1607), Sir Isaac Wake gives his account of the royal visit; his description of the entertainment explicitly mentions Macbeth, whereas Gwinne's text alludes solely to the prophecy to Banquo. Wake introduces his account of the entertainment with the story of "tres olim Sibyllae occurrisse duobus Scotiae proceribus *Macbetho & Banchoni*, & illum praedixisse Regem futurum, sed Regem nullum geniturum, hunc Regem non futurum, sed Reges geniturum multes" (p. 18).

19 The subject of masculinity and femininity in the play has been discussed often; see, e.g. Harding, *Shakespeare Quarterly*, 20 (1969), 245–53; Berger, *English Literary History*, 47 (1980), 26–8, and at greater length in "Text Against Performance in Shakespeare: the example of *Macbeth*", *Genre*, 15 (1982), 49–79, esp. pp. 64–74. Madelon Gohlke argues that the play centers on the eradication of the feminine and male fantasies of self-authorship in " 'I wooed thee with my sword': Shakespeare's tragic paradigms", in *Representing Shakespeare*, ed. Coppelia Kahn and Murray Schwartz (Baltimore: Johns Hopkins University Press, 1980), but she tends to essentialize and sentimentalize the idea of the feminine, a view that can be corrected, as Ann Rosalind Jones argues in "Writing the Body: towards an understanding of *L'Ecriture Féminine*", *Feminist Studies* 7 (1981), 247–63, esp. pp. 255–61, only by attention to the historical particularities that would underlie psychic formations.

20 On the question of same and different in Shakespeare, see Joel Fineman's acute development of René Girard's terms in "Fratricide and Cuckoldry: Shakespeare's doubles", in Kahn and Schwartz (ed.), *Representing Shakespeare*, pp. 70–109, esp. pp. 89, 103–4. For a rather mechanical treatment of doubling and a brief consideration of Macbeth's relationship with his wife as a son–mother pairing, see Robert Rogers, *A Psychoanalytic Study of the Double in Literature* (Detroit: Wayne State University Press, 1970), pp. 48–51.

21 In her study of the limiting aspects of masculinity, " 'Be bloody, bold and resolute': tragic action and sexual stereotyping in *Macbeth*", *Studies in Philology*, 78 (1981), 153–69, Carolyn Asp suggests that Macbeth's inhuman project may be related to the sexually undifferentiated witches (p. 165); she sees the end of the play replicating its initial stereotypes, a view also suggested by Howard Felperin, *Shakespearean Representation* (Princeton: Princeton University Press, 1977). As Richard Horwitch notes in "Integrity in *Macbeth*: the search for the 'single state of man' ", *Shakespeare Quarterly*, 29 (1978), 365–73, Malcolm confesses to Macbeth's crimes in IV.iii and

"may be seen as, potentially, a Macbeth in embryo" (p. 371). It is surely to the point that his ultimate position, replicating Duncan's, as Macduff mirrors Macbeth, is offered as a success that the witches have preordained for the line of Banquo.

22 Luce Irigaray, "Des marchandises entre elles" in *Ce sexe qui n'en est pas un* (Paris: Minuit, 1977), p. 189 ("l'empire de semblant"), trans. Claudia Reeder, in *New French Feminisms*, ed. Elaine Marks and Isabelle de Courtivron (New York: Schocken Books, 1981), p. 107. See also the selection from *Amante marine: de Friedrich Nietzsche* (Paris: Minuit, 1980), "Veiled Lips", *Mississippi Review*, 33 (1983), 93–131, for an extraordinary discussion of patriarchal appropriations of the maternal. My use, like Irigaray's, is Lacanian, not the supportive mother of ego psychology, inflected, I hope, with the historical particularities involved in Renaissance constructions of the feminine.

23 *Genre*, 15 (1982), 52.

24 The question of textual autonomy can be approached from many directions. It is surely no accident that *Macbeth* was early appropriated for the New Criticism by Cleanth Brooks, "The Naked Babe and the Cloak of Manliness", in *The Well-Wrought Urn* (New York: Harcourt, Brace and World, 1947) as a particularly *dense* text apt for close readings; not surprisingly, such readings have been intensely conservative. Valuable along these lines, however, is Arnold Stein's "*Macbeth* and Word Magic", *Sewanee Review*, 59 (1951), 271–84, for its emphasis on Macbeth's linguistic insecurity.

As Franco Moretti argues in *Genre*, 15 (1982), 32–4, soliloquy (particularly in *Macbeth* and *Hamlet*) represents an excessive blockage of political process, the excrescence of ideological mystification that I have called, following Moretti, an absolutist fantasy. Steven Mullaney argues in English Literary History, 47 (1980), 42–5 that the linguistic excess in *Macbeth* imbricates treason − an uncontrollable ambiguity rather than the New Critical kind. Finally Stephen Greenblatt, in "*King Lear* and Harsnett's 'Devil fiction' ", *Genre*, 15 (1982), 239–42, and in subsequent papers, has been seeking to describe Shakespearean autonomy as an improvisatory effect accomplished within the institutional/ideological space determined by social fictions and discourses. In their various ways, these critics move toward a demystification of autonomy and a description of the achievement of an autonomy-effect.

In *Renaissance Self-Fashioning* (Chicago: University of Chicago Press, 1980), Greenblatt studies the *submission* of Desdemona, an absorption of text and role that does not exclude her "downright violence" (I.iii.249). If, as I suggest, Shakespeare represents the textuality of his plays through women, and allies his author-function with them, Greenblatt's description might prove useful in exploring the nature and representation of Shakespeare's authorial autonomy.

Trust and transgression: the discursive practices of *Much Ado about Nothing*

JOHN DRAKAKIS

I

In 1834 Coleridge announced the transformation of Shakespeare from a professional dramatist into an individual consciousness whose plays were the repositories of timeless truths. Hence his assertion that Shakespeare "is of no age – nor, may I add, of any religion, or party, or profession".[1] With very few adjustments, the myth has proved durable, with those truths resurfacing recently as the "eterne mutabilitie" of the human condition, those "perennial, unhistorical variations of temperament" which comprise the irreducible core of "human nature".[2] Coleridge had already laid the foundations for the removal of Shakespeare from history some twenty years earlier, in about 1813, in some notes for a lecture in which he formulated a theory of dramatic character which was to receive its most sophisticated expression less than a century later in A. C. Bradley's *Shakespearean Tragedy* (1904). The subject of those earlier remarks was, ostensibly, the relation between "plot" and "character" in *Much Ado about Nothing* in which he anticipated modern formalist distinctions between *sujet* and *fabula*, and the narratological distinction between *histoire* and *discours*:

> Take away from *Much Ado about Nothing* all that which is not indispensable to the plot, either as having little to do with it, or at best, like Dogberry and his comrades, forced into the service when any other less ingeniously absurd watchmen and night-constables would have answered; take away Benedick, Beatrice, Dogberry, and the reaction of the former on the character of Hero, and what will remain? In other writers the main agent of the plot is always the prominent character. In Shakespeare so or not so, as the character is in itself calculated to form the plot. So Don John, the mainspring of the plot, is merely shown and withdrawn.[3]

Coleridge's comments on *Much Ado about Nothing*, especially his suggestion that Don John, "the mainspring of the plot, is merely shown and withdrawn", betray an uneasiness that once the identifiable elements of *fabula* and *discours* are stripped away, then we may be left with "nothing", implying that what may really be at stake here is an irreducibly essentialist conception of "character". What is at risk for Coleridge is the possibility that the play may not contain that "true idea" of which the dramatic structure itself is but an ancillary support. Indeed, the very title of the play is an affront to any expressive theory of meaning, and is, in many ways, a challenge to those forms of criticism based upon such a theory. If, after analysis, the textual representations of universal truths are to be dismissed as "nothing", then even assuming a Coleridgean intentionalist theory of character, signification will depend upon a trust which we are invited to place in the critic's own perception of a non-material reality whose *essence* is derived in stark opposition to textual appearances but whose ultimate location is beyond the play of *difference* which characterizes the act of signification itself. Thus, beyond that "nothing", that material encounter with textual surfaces, there must be "something" more real, uncomplicated by the play of textual difference, a single meaning which it is the purpose of criticism to detach from the text.

This idealism (which lies at the root of much orthodox interpretation of Shakespearean Comedy) depends for its veracity upon a commitment to what Pierre Macherey has termed "the normative fallacy", whereby a text may be modified, "in order to assimilate it more thoroughly, denying its factual reality as being merely the provisional version of an unfulfilled intention".[4] The recent placements of this critical strategy, along with aesthetics itself, within the purview of *ideology* – that hidden means of producing and reproducing as "natural" and "true" relations upon which particular social formations depend for their existence – has far-reaching consequences for the study of Shakespeare.[5] Above all, it has served to bring sharply into focus the contradictions which lie at the heart of attempts to come to terms with Shakespearean Comedy in general and *Much Ado about Nothing* in particular. A classic example occurs in H. B. Charlton's book, *Shakespearean Comedy* (1938), in which he asserts, on the one hand, that "comedy is social rather than metaphysical or theological", while, on the other, he seeks to locate "Shakespeare's comic idea" as what Charlton calls "his surest clue to the secret of man's common and abiding welfare".[6] At one and the same time history is acknowledged and refused, a seemingly contradictory critical strategy which has proved extraordinarily resilient in the case of *Much Ado about Nothing*.

Recuperative ploys such as this are symptomatic of a tendency which would negotiate away those contradictions which constitute the "factual reality" of the play, reducing drastically its complex discursive structures, smoothing over its complex web of contested significations, in the interests of locating some controlling idea secreted at its core but anterior to its structure – in short, its "transcendental signified". For example, John Russell Brown considers the structure of the play to depend "almost entirely on one central theme . . . that of appearance and reality, outward and inward beauty, words and thoughts – in short, the theme of love's truth".[7] More recent criticism of the play has undertaken to refine this "theme", locating the conflict as being between "right" and "wrong deception" with the latter constituting an obstacle to aesthetic and moral harmony finally being overcome by those "good" values: "with suspicion replaced by trust, and with destructive biting by a marriage feast".[8] This type of treatment of thematic contrast in the play aways culminates in the proposal of the total eclipse of one term by another, and is symptomatic of a more generalized ethical criticism which claims to offer an objective, empirically derived record of the dramatic conflict, but which, in fact, imposes a theological pattern on the play.[9] As such, this kind of criticism is always caught in contradiction by what Fredric Jameson has called "the mirage of an utterly non-theoretical practice".[10]

One of the most recent sustained examples of this kind of criticism is Alexander Leggatt's attempt to blend thematic unity and structural contrast together in his suggestion that the action of *Much Ado about Nothing* is structured around "an interplay of formality and naturalism".[11] Opposed though these structural elements may be, that conflict is ultimately resolved, and indeed dissolved, in the perception "that however individual we are we are ultimately bound by the rhythms of life, and we must follow the leaders". Here textual difference and larger stylistic oppositions are neatly displaced by a meaning which is gently prized free from process to clear a path for the return of familiar essentialist distinctions: appearance/reality, formal/natural, individual/society. Yet in the final analysis these terms are seen as two sides of the same epistemological coin, so that the play can be made, as it were *naturally*, to yield up that truth artfully lodged at its centre: "the idea of human reality at the heart of social convention".[12] This, it need hardly be said, is a bourgeois, liberal humanist "reality" whose intentions are *naturally* expressed through "social convention", though somehow individuals submit to its demands voluntarily through the imposition upon *process* of a mystifying logic: "we are ultimately bound by the rhythms of life and we must follow the leaders". So totalizing a rhetoric of social and political quiescence presupposes an always already constituted bourgeois "subject", but also calls to mind Walter Benjamin's astringent observation that there is "no document of civilization which is not at the same time a document of barbarism".[13]

Leggatt's reading of the play, which conforms to the underlying theory of comedy proposed by Northrop Frye in his *Anatomy of Criticism* (1957), implies that Utopia is the ultimate objective of the comic action, and is realized at the point of the resolution of the action when the "inner" ("the idea of human reality") harmonizes with that which fully expresses it, the "outer" ("social convention"). If we theorize this critical stance, then it becomes clear that the moment of carnivalesque release which brings inner into conflict with outer, and which could be read in terms of a political rupture, is aesthetically necessary as the precondition for clarifying what is really a deep structural unity which exists between the two, and which the comic closure finally confirms. This moment of aesthetic closure, the culminating moment in the process of the production of harmony, marks the erasure of textual difference, and is, according to this problematic, the point at which the human essence achieves self-identity and re-establishes its existence beyond discourse. What this theory suppresses are those irreducibly *dialogic* elements of discursive practice, whose challenge to official ideology is always recoverable from the text, and whose irrepressible presence signifies that meaning is always a site of ideological struggle. This is the carnivalesque discourse that resists domestication, directing us back to the place where meanings are produced. In the words of Valentin Volosinov: "there is nothing in the structure of signification that could be said to transcend the generative process, to be independent of the dialectical expansion of the social purview".[14]

II

The reduction of the material contradictions which permeate the discourses of *Much Ado about Nothing* to an ordered hierarchy of fixed meaning is nowhere more evident than in the attempts to identify the *meaning* of the play's title. Since, apparently "nothing" and "noting" were homophones for the Elizabethans, it has been assumed that the play was about "noting" and "misnoting",[15] but more recent criticism has sought to explore the sexual connotations of "nothing" as a synonym for what E. A. M. Coleman, careful to avoid any suggestion of prurience, calls "the female pudend".[16] "Nothing", we may recall, was what Hamlet thought was "a fair thought to lie between maids' legs" (*Hamlet*, III.ii.127), while in *Antony and Cleopatra* this metonym is made to stand for womankind generally, as Enobarbus, commenting upon Cleopatra's sexual prowess, is made to observe: "Under a compelling occasion let women die: it were pity to cast them away for nothing, though between them and a great cause, they should be esteemed nothing" (I.ii.134–7). The location of gender in an *absence* which is both physical and cerebral, augmented with a language of valuation, reinforces the concept of the gendered female subject not in terms of an object or an essence, but a relation. Moreover, this is also true of "nothing" as it appears in *King Lear*, where Lear's chilling "Nothing will come of nothing" (I.i.92) emphasizes a process of "subjection" which reaches inwards towards a domestic filial relation, and outwards to the promised land which doubles as a marriage dowry and as the material expression of political power. It is, in the circumstances, insufficient to invoke a simple linguistic plenitude, *pace* the New Arden editor of *Much Ado about Nothing*, and to assert vacuously that "The play's title is, in fact, teasingly full of meaning."[17]

Clearly, there are considerable dangers in reducing *Much Ado about Nothing* to a unitary "meaning", just as there are in reducing the conflicts in the play to a resolution between two terms for supremacy in which it can be assumed that ultimately the traces of that conflict will be erased. To the ever-growing list of binary oppositions to which the action of the play has been reduced, could be added "trust" and "transgression", in so far as the preferred term in each equation is the index of a hypostasized meaning which is located beyond the essentially dialectical processes of signification altogether, establishing a permanent and unchanging "truth" about an equally hypostasized "human nature". I propose to argue, drawing upon Saussure, that terms such as "trust" and "transgression" are, in fact, differentially derived, and thus must be "defined not positively, in terms of their content, but negatively, by contrast with other items in the same system. What characterizes each most exactly is being whatever the others are not."[18] Such terms – and they exist within the play – constitute the discourses through whose mechanisms reality is constructed, and it is important that an attentive criticism should do more than simply ventriloquize certain of the differentially constructed elements of these discourses *as if they were* objective truths. But, in addition to Saussure's radical perception, a distinction should be made between the notion of *difference* functioning within an abstract linguistic system and conservatively reinforcing the stability of the system itself (the project of the more domesticated forms of structuralism), and the manner of its operation dialectically within particular historically specific discursive practices at the place where ideology reduces the plurality of possible meanings to singular meaning. To speak of "trust" and "transgression" in this context is not to ventriloquize the text's "secret coherence". Rather, it is to insist that terms are forced into an axiological relation with each other through difference, and that to explore their dialectical relation is to lay bare the text's own ideological processes.

In purely bibliographical terms *Much Ado about Nothing* is already a deeply fissured text. The quarto of 1600, thought to have been printed from Shakespeare's foul papers, retains inconsistent speech-headings and, for the romantic essentialist, at least two puzzling scene-headings. Dogberry is variously referred to in speech-headings as "Const.", "Andrew", and "Kemp", interpellations which traverse social role, dramatic/comic role, and the name of the actor who is behind the illusion. Dogberry is self-evidently the site of a full play of intertextual relations involving history, literary tradition, and professional theatrical practice. Similarly, though not quite to the same extent, Verges is variously referred to as "Headborough" and "Couly". More intriguing, the scene-headings for I.i. and II.i. contain references to the supposed wife of Leonato: "*Innogen his wife*" (I.i.) and "*His wife*" (II.i.). In Spenser's *The Faerie Queene*, Book II, which contains a version of the plot of *Much Ado about Nothing*, the figure of "Inogene" appears as the wife of Brutus, "faire Inogene of Italy" (X.13) but it is generally thought that the references in Shakespeare's play are to an early draft, and since 1733 editors have systematically excised her from editions. Her name appears in Furness's variorum edition of the play,[19] but for A. R. Humphreys she is a disturbingly Pirandellian figure, "an unrealized intention" and he goes on to assert with worrying certainty that "originally" Shakespeare "meant Hero to have a mother . . . but then found no use for her".[20]

In a play in which questions of identity and social role are consistently foregrounded, in which the paternalistic control and "silencing" of female characters is a norm,[21] and in which the one exception to that rule can be metonymically reduced to the appelation "my Lady Tongue" (II.i.252), this reduction of the wifely role to silence − the position towards which Beatrice herself gravitates in the play − which diplomatically constituted texts have been prepared to excise, or banish to footnotes, represents in an unusually explicit form the place of the woman in the play's own network of significations. From the woman silence is expected, or achieved through genial coercion as she submits to the paternalistic power of her "governor"; at the moment of transformation from "shrew" to legitimate object of desire Beatrice internalizes this process: "And Benedick, love on, I will requite thee, / Taming my wildness to thy loving hand" (III.i.111–12). In such circumstances, the relegation of "Innogen" to the status of "an unrealized intention" conceals an essentially romantic theory of composition and is consistent with an empiricist theory of meaning. It rejects implicitly what Catherine Belsey has called the notion of meaning as "inter-individual intelligibility",[22] abstracting meaning *from* the play's network of colliding discourses, and is thus caught in the act of processing "truth".

But abstracting a transcendent "truth" from the discursive practices of *Much Ado about Nothing* is precarious, at best, since unlike most of Shakespeare's other comedies the play contains no identifiable centre in the form of a hero and/or heroine, and therefore contains no metonym for it. *Pace* Charles I, who designated the play "the comedie of Benedick and Betteris", critics have been generally disposed to accord them this central position: "Beatrice and Benedick, resembling stars, but serving as planets, outshine those about whom they revolve."[23] Conversely, much critical effort has been expended in asserting the essential weakness of Hero, and the objectionable character of Claudio.[24] What most critics have had some difficulty in coping with is the structural fact that the "plot" effectively deconstructs itself; the plan to bring Benedick and Beatrice together is undertaken using the same mechanism as that which Don John uses to drive Hero and Claudio apart. This difficulty has been negotiated either by extolling "right deception"[25] or, more usually, by insisting that Beatrice and Benedick (like Petruchio and Katherina in *The Taming of the Shrew*) are *essentially* in love with each other, and always have been.[26] One other feature of the play, which does not appear in any of the versions of the story which were current at the time of performance, is that the obstacle to the attainment of harmony is a villain of a special sort, not a harsh or impersonal social law dividing young and old. Don John's "malevolence and unsociability", marked by "images of sickness, festering poison, and incompatibility (the canker-rose, the thief of love, the muzzled dog, the caged bird) and by themes of resentment and moroseness" are, according to A. R. Humphreys, defined by his being "a rebel and a bastard".[27] In a play concerned with marriage and its impediments a reversal of Humphreys's formula would seem to be nearer the mark: Don John is a rebel *because he is* a bastard.

The question of Don John's bastardy is, in principle, similar to that involving the role of "Innogen" in that it is concerned with the whole issue of the construction of human subjectivity in the play. In general this issue involves what Althusser calls a "Law of Culture", a collective term for those historically specific processes which are "the determinate ideological formations in which the persons inscribed in these structures live their functions".[28] Don John's subjectivity cannot be reduced to a role in an Oedipal drama, nor is it sufficient merely to explain his function in post-structuralist terms as a supplement at the origin which constantly resists the closure of the logocentric oppositions of the text (although at a purely formal level this is precisely what Don John does). Rather, he is to be situated at the very point where "pleasure" and "power" intersect. Don John is not "pleasure" standing in opposition to "power", since, as Michel Foucault has observed: "Pleasure and power do not cancel or turn back against one another; they seek out, overlap, and reinforce one another."[29] Structurally he represents the material consequence of pleasure undertaken in defiance of the constraints of power, and thus, translated into historically specific terms, he is the "other" against which the political economy of Messina defines itself differentially. Don John is controlled by being accorded a "christian" subjectivity (his name is the commonest of Christian names according to the *OED*), but he is, by virtue of his illegitimacy, without a "surname" and therefore without access to the socially accepted political channels of the power/pleasure economy. Paradoxically, the definition of Don John's "subjectivity" involves *exclusion* from the political mechanisms of the social formation within which that definition is inscribed. It is a contradiction which Shakespeare broaches in the later play *King Lear*, in the figure of Gloucester's bastard son, Edmund.

In a provocative, but finally idealistic account of the play, Marilyn French argues that Don John's position is, in structural and epistemological terms, that of the "outlaw feminine", and that his rebellion is "terrifying because it comes out of a sense of powerlessness and seems to want nothing".[30] This is to presuppose the existence of an essential "feminine principle" which will ultimately collapse sexuality into the gendered subject. The play itself inscribes femininity within a powerful masculine discourse, and it is in this context that Don John should be viewed as the product of the very type of violation of an institutionally derived femininity against which Messina's masculine "honour" code is differentially produced. Don John occupies, rather, the place of "transgression", and as such in both historical and social terms he has neither legitimate political position nor self-identity; he is literally "nothing", he does not and cannot signify in any actantial sense within a logocentric scheme of things. It is significant that though he supports Borachio's plot he is not the agent of its execution, and therefore to suggest that "he seems to want nothing" is to misread discursive practice *as though it were* simply an effect of essence. A better way of theorizing Don John's position is to suggest that he is "profanation", in that he refuses to accept that the sacred has meaning, and this places him within Foucault's definition of "transgression" as "profanation in a world which no longer recognizes any positive meaning in the sacred".[31] But it is important to remember that Don John's transgression is emphatically *not* a liberation from ideology; on the contrary, his position in the play is conceptualized as part of an ethical universe – he is "evil" – and his radical freedom must be coerced. In general terms, therefore, we may say that Don John becomes the mechanism in *Much Ado about Nothing* whereby the plurality of possible meanings is ruthlessly reduced to a singular, authoritative meaning; this is performed by the forcible subjugation of the disruptive term "bastard", which always returns and threatens to undo the social formation. It is no accident that the play begins with a military victory in which Don John was an adversary – if not *the* adversary – and it ends in a similar fashion.

In *Much Ado about Nothing* the management of sexual relations, and the construction of gendered subjects, is bound up with questions of power and hence of politics. Far from celebrating a "consonance" of "Head and heart, style and substance, convention and nature"[32] in any naive or essentialist sense, the play's aesthetic presents through the symbolic language of festivity a victory *by force* over a particular threat to Messina's determinate social institutions from a villain who "transgresses" its "ideological formations", profanes its sacred values, and exposes a series of contradictions lying at the heart of its discursive practices. But of course Don John has no existence independent from Messina's institutions; he is a "visitor" certainly, but he is also the brother of the legitimate Don Pedro, "Prince of Arragon". Thus, he represents the point at which relations of power manifest themselves negatively as "refusal, limitation, obstruction, censorship", and as such his challenge to the formally constituted relations in the play appears, to use Foucault's terms, "only as transgression".[33]

What Don John's activities in the play highlight is a contest for "history" itself, opposing an "illegitimate" history that is forced to make itself against a "legitimate" history whose status is both sovereign and privileged. The result, however, is not a radical questioning in any conscious sense of the privileged status of historical narrative as such (a radical scepticism which might be taken to form one strand of post-structuralism in its Nietzschean guise), but a struggle for domination at the level of domestic relations at a time when "legitimate" history is under internal pressure to revise its own practices. The problems arise at the very point where "history" enters "discourse". It is important to realize that we are not here dealing with an object, but with what Fredric Jameson has called an "absent cause", which is only accessible in textual form, and that as such "it passes through its prior textualization, its narrativization, in the political unconscious".[34] The specific significance of this for a play such as *Much Ado about Nothing* is that its concern is never with an object, a transcendental signified, a "something" to which its discourses can ultimately be reduced, but with a series of overlapping class and gender relations which always already exist and which are inscribed within the political unconscious as "prior textualizations". It is disturbance at the level of the play's symbolic language that gives us some purchase upon the text's unconscious processes, those areas of which it cannot expressly speak.

The term which occupies that point at which the full range of the play's interrelated discourses converge is "honour", which can be separated out into its constituent elements; it is preeminently the term which mediates the play's masculine discourse, but it also inscribes within its historical narrativization of repressed social and political fears a feminine (or as Spenser's *Faerie Queene* would have it, a Foemen-ine) discourse of "chastity" or "virginitie". It is in Marlowe's poem *Hero and Leander*, from which Shakespeare may have borrowed at least a name, that the relation between these terms is inadvertently demystified, to expose the whole gamut of masculine political relations as an "absent cause" (i.e. as a *history*) which can only be grasped in discourse. Leander, seeking to persuade Hero to submit, proffers the following argument:

> This idoll which you terme Virginitie,
> Is neither essence subject to the eye,
> Nor to any one exteriour sence,
> Nor hath it any place of residence,
> Nor is it of earth or mold celestiall,
> Or capable of any form at all.
> Of that which hath no being do not boast
> Things which are not at all are never lost.[35]

From the woman's perspective there is a dilemma here between freedom of personal action on the one hand, and on the other the paternalistic constraint of a socio-sexual order in which female "honour" is both determined by, as well as determining, masculine honour. Helena in *All's Well that Ends Well* faces part of this dilemma when she debates the issue of female chastity with the aptly named Parolles: "How might one do, sir, to lose it to her own liking?" (I.i.165–6), and it resembles in its sentiments the position which Beatrice occupies initially in *Much Ado about Nothing* with her potentially subversive advice to Hero to defy her father if necessary and please herself in choosing a husband;

"it is my cousin's duty to make curtsy and say, 'Father, as it please you': but yet for all that, cousin, let him be a handsome fellow, or else make another curtsy and say, 'Father, as it please me' " (II.i.48–52). In *Othello* a segment of "textualized history" is transformed into a material object in an attempt to appropriate it for an alternative discourse; Desdemona's "virginitie" upon which Othello's masculine honour rests, becomes a handkerchief which he can, under guidance from Iago, then re-texualize: "Her honour is an essence that's not seen, / They have it very oft that have it not: / But for the handkerchief –" (IV.i.16–18).

Female "honour" is valued in a paternalistic society only in so far as it accepts inscription in the constellation of discursive practices designed to textualize masculine sexual and political impulses. Marlowe's Leander can introduce his textualization of "virginitie" with a statement about female "imperfection": "Base boullion for the stampes sake we allow, / Euen so for mens impression do we you, / By which alone, our reuerend fathers say, / Wome receaue perfection euerie way" (lines 265–8). Within the Christian tradition these discourses converge in the heavily symbolic institution of marriage, within which the woman is simultaneously interpellated as the *cause* of man's fall and of his salvation; it is no accident that the etymology of Beatrice's name is "She who blesses", while that of Benedick's is "He who is blessed". In material terms marriage is also the institution through which possession and power are legitimized and consolidated, offering "subjectivity" in the form of a social identity, and a range of discursive practices for internalizing these objective social relations at a symbolic level of emotions and affections. But differentially these positivities are defined against a constellation of anarchic "others" which collectively threaten to undo this symbolic order: the female refusal of paternal control; shrewishness, or the refusal to accept "silence"; infidelity and cuckoldry (the sexual expressions of a political anarchy); whoredom; suspicion; and – the consequence (significantly) of female promiscuity in an age without effective contraception – bastardy, that term which in the play's discursive economies opposes "honour".

III

It may be argued that this is too heavy a burden of seriousness for a play such as *Much Ado about Nothing* to bear. But far from dealing with human abstractions which can be conveniently transported from one epoch to another, it is concerned with a series of historically specific social issues which collectively resist any idealizing critical gestures, and which Elizabethan society coped with by a form of marginalization through laughter. It is worth pausing briefly to suggest some of the ways in which these contested issues enter Elizabethan discursivities as "prior textualizations".

The Second Tome of Homilies (1595) makes it very clear that female sexuality was conceived as part of a totalizing biblical narrative, although recently attempts have been made to suggest that this narrative was in the process of undergoing revision in favour of women during this period.[36] Such revisionist claims, while not wholly inaccurate, present a polar alternative to the dominant ideology, and thus neglect to point out the contradictions which reside at the core of at least some of these revisionary texts. For the homilist in "A Homilie of the State of Matimonie", authority in marriage rests firmly with the husband who "ought to be the leader and author of love, in cherishing and increasing concord, which then shall take place, if he will use measurablenes and not tyranny, and if he yeeld some thing to the woman".[37] The woman still requires to be controlled, however, since she is regarded as man's inferior in every way:

For the woman is a weake creature, not indued with the like strength and constancy of minde, therefore they bee the sooner disquieted, and they be the more prone to all weake affections and dispositions of minde, more then men bee, and lighter they bee, and more vaine in their fantisies and opinions.[38]

A little earlier, in 1592, the Puritan Henry Smith had shifted the emphasis slightly in favour of women in his sermon "A Preparative to Marriage", in which he explained the divine origins of the institution in the following way: "In the contract Christ was conceived, and in the marriage Christ was borne, that he might honor both estates: virginitie with his conception, and marriage with his birth."[39] But Smith then went on to point out that the bearing of children in marriage reflected "honour" on the woman, but, "for the children which are borne out of marriage, are the dishonor of women, and called by the shamefull name of Bastards".[40] A little later he condemned adulterers whom he "likened to the divell, which sowed other mens ground", inscribing the woman within a discourse of property, and he cited scripture to demonstrate that for bastards "no inheritance did belong to them in heaven, they had no inheritance in earth".[41]

Some six years later in 1598, probably the year in which *Much Ado about Nothing* was first acted, another Puritan, Robert Cleaver, building on Smith, could take the definition of marriage a stage further, not only "spiritualizing the household", to use Christopher Hill's phrase, but rendering its relations explicitly political. In his *A Godly Form of Householde Government*, he noted:

A householde is as it were a little commonwealth, by the good government whereof, God's glorie may bee aduanced, the commonwealth which standeth of seueral families benefited, and all that live in that familie may receiue much comfort and commoditie.[42]

Both Smith and Cleaver are caught in contradiction as each makes a liberal gesture towards the woman's position, while preserving a vocabulary of social control which has its roots in a now seriously troubled biblical narrative. But it is on the question of sexuality that Puritan and homilist alike are at one. In the "Third Part of the Sermon Against Adultery" in the *Second Tome of Homilies* the pleasure/power axis is negotiated through the suggestion that sexual pleasure itself has its origins in Satan: "how filthy, beastly, & short that pleasure is, whereunto Satan continually stirreth us and moveth us".[43] St Paul's wry concession that "It is better to marrie then to burne" is here seized upon by the homilist as a desperate spiritual justification for what he, and later Cleaver, expresses as, in essence, the political management of sexual activity *internalized* as a structure of religious feeling containing its own tension between the world of the flesh and that of the spirit.[44] These are, of course, strands in a much larger body of discursive practices which, at a purely secular level, amalgamates neo-platonic, courtly, and romantic/poetic discourses, all of which are found in contemporary Elizabethan fiction, epic poems such as *The Faerie Queene*, the sonnet tradition, and courtier manuals such as Castiglione's *The Book of the Courtier* (1588).

It is this whole precarious discursive edifice which produces Don John's subjectivity that is threatened in the play. That subjectivity is more than simply a marker of "plot", however, in that Don John internalizes a range of related discursive positions which function from an ethical standpoint to contain his disruptive potential. In his essay "Of Friendship" Francis Bacon argued that "a natural and secret hatred and aversion towards society, in any man, hath somewhat of the savage beast",[45] and it is therefore not surprising to find Don John associated with images of bestiality; he is prepared to "claw no man in his humour", and he asserts: "If I had my mouth I would bite, if I had my liberty I would do my liking:" (I.ii.17 and 32–4). Moreover, in the essay "Of Envy" Bacon observes that "Deformed persons, and eunuchs, and old men, and bastards, are envious", and he concludes that this characteristic is "the proper attribute of the devil, who is called *The envious man, that soweth tares among the wheat by night:*".[46] Don John is also, as Hero informs us, "of a very melancholy disposition" (II.i.5), and therefore suffers from what, in the words of Timothy Bright's *A Treatise of Melancholy* (1586), is called "an unnaturall temper & bastard spirite". Moreover, given the discursive practices within which "love" is textualized, Timothy Bright's designation of the related areas which are the grounds for Don John's challenge as "the primitive emotions", is shown to be nothing more than an empirical reading of what we have seen is an objective social formation: in Bright's terms these are "love mixed with hope" which, we are told, "breedeth trust", and "love mixed with fear", which breeds "distrust".[47] Behind Bright's curiously untheoretical practice lie the twin discourses of salvation and possession. Thus, to adapt Foucault's remarks in relation to "madness", Don John may be said to represent "an area of unforeseeable freedom" where sexual impulse is in danger of becoming unchained from those discourses which would hold it in place, and like the madman's frenzy Don John's bastardy represents "the secret danger of an animality that lies in wait", which "undoes reason in violence" and truth through its violation of social norms.[48]

It is here, however, that we encounter historically a mixture of fact and illusion. Peter Laslett has suggested that during the decade 1590–1600, while the population of England was a little over 4 million, bastardy accounted for just over 3 per cent of all births.[49] But he also argues that while bastardy was an issue among the dominant elite, in actual fact "The engendering of children on a scale which might threaten the social structure, was never, or almost never, a present possibility."[50] Lawrence Stone argues that there is tentative evidence to suggest that on a national scale the specific pressures applied in local communities within the sphere of sexual morality resulted in low illegitimacy ratios, and that when such community pressure failed, then "any constable was empowered to break into any house in which he suspected fornication or adultery to be in progress and, if his supicions were confirmed, to carry the offender to jail or before a Justice of the Peace".[51] The role which Dogberry and Verges play in *Much Ado about Nothing* serves, therefore, to combine political and moral surveillance.

The picture which we get from *The Homilies* is, however, very different in emphasis: a difference, perhaps, between the "imaginary" and the "real", which has come to designate for us the terrain of ideology. It would not be surprising to find both the political and domestic values which constitute the lived relations within ideology inscribed in the letter of the Law itself, especially in relation to the question of bastardy. In his *Commentaries on the Laws of England* the eighteenth-century lawyer Blackstone outlined explicitly the legal rights attaching to the state of bastardy. For the bastard:

The rights are very few, being only such as he can acquire for he can inherit nothing, being looked upon as the son of nobody, and sometimes called *filius nulius*, sometimes *filius populi*. Yet he may gain a surname by reputation, though he has none by inheritance.[52]

Excluded from all forms of inheritance, Don John is precluded from asking the question that Claudio asks Don Pedro concerning Leonato's possible "heirs", since he has no name to promulgate. Legitimate marriage, Blackstone states, gives the husband access to all of the wife's property, though he does not suggest openly that the wife is property herself.[53] Thus, while marriage itself legitimizes the transfer of property (the currency of power), reinforces a social and political identity through the sustaining of a family "name", and is, to use Foucault's terms, that "deployment of alliance"[54] whereby sexual activity enters into discourse, the bastard is without property, without identity, and stands as a defiant reminder of the underside of the pleasure/power axis as an anarchy consequent upon the transgression of its economies.[55] In the legal and juridical sense of the term, and in a manner directly pertinent to Shakespeare's play, the bastard is therefore *nothing*, non-identity in a society caught in the contradictory process of "naming" as the step towards "self-identity" but forced to confront, time and time again, the differential mechanisms of its own signifying practices.

IV

Thus far I have been concerned, selectively, with areas of what might be called "the political unconscious" of *Much Ado about Nothing*, and I have tried to show briefly how historically specific discursive formations "mythologize" a concrete history. In specific terms, faced with either formulating a concept of female sexuality or obliterating it by hiding it, the discourse itself "transforms history into nature", to use Roland Barthes's terminology, naturalizing it as part of a totalizing theological narrative. This is not, of course, to collapse sexuality into the irreducibly metaphysical concept of "power", but rather to suggest that these related discourses ensure the placing of individual subjects in relation to a state apparatus, one which masks, but which would by no means exclude the issue of the exploitation of one class by another. Thus marriage, which in *Much Ado about Nothing* is formulated as a "natural" occurrence ("In time the savage bull doth bear the yoke"

(I.i.241–2)), becomes the domestic bulwark in the fight against "evil" waged on the terrain of "Christian faith". "Faith" and "Trust" are important elements in this discourse, as the homily "A Short Declaration of The True and Lively Christian Faith" indicates. Here "inward faith" is described as being: "not without hope and trust in God, nor without the love of God and of our neighbours, nor without the feare of God, nor without the desire to heare God's worde, and to follow the same in eschewing evill, and doing gladly all good workes."[56] Those who perform "evill workes" and who "lead their life in disobedience and transgression or breaking of God's commandments without repentance" inherit, says the homilist, "not everlasting life but everlasting death, as Christ sayeth".[57] By reading these discursive practices "against the grain", so to speak, we can begin to see how, through "naturalization" of the contradictions of their material history, they conspire to reduce plurality of meaning to a single totalizing narrative which has as its *desideratum* political quiescence. Don John is a threat because he would return this discourse to the place where its writ of privilege does not run, but in the attempt to "recuperate" him (through physical coercion) the contradictions residing at the heart of the whole ideological apparatus of Messina are laid bare.

Everywhere in *Much Ado about Nothing*, from the Messenger's initial communication of Claudio's uncle's expression of joy, which "could not show itself without a badge of bitterness" (I.i.21–2) through to Benedick's final utterances in the play, the linguistic sign itself gapes to reveal the material process of its own production. Deception both *does* and *undoes*; it can destroy, but at the same time it can produce "honest slanders" which, as Hero ironically observes, "may empoison liking" (III.i.84–6). Moreover, by the time that Hero is in a position to generalize that "Some Cupid kills with arrows, some with traps" (III.i.106), she herself is caught proleptically in the articulation of her own "death". But analeptically her comment recalls Benedick's earlier encoding of the figure of "blind Cupid" as the sign on "the door of a brothel-house" (I.i.234–5). For Benedick, liking is already "empoisoned" since the institution which Don Pedro assumes will transform the "savage bull" into a willing husband produces also an animal of a very different complexion: "pluck off the bull's horns and set them in my forehead . . . let them signify under my sign 'Here you may see Benedick the married man' " (I.i.244–8).[58] After the failure of the first Don John plot it is Benedick's female counterpart in "apprehension" who can point to the canker of possessiveness, the "suspicion" or lack of "trust" enshrined at the heart of the notion of civility:

The count is neither sad, nor sick, merry, nor well; but civil Count, civil as an orange, and something of that jealous complexion. (II.i.275–7)

Thus, at the heart of marriage in this play is a *difference* along whose axis of signification the gendered human subject is constructed; the woman is a "subject" *and* she "subjects herself" to the authority of father and husband, while her "virginitie", textualized as "no thing" becomes, not a signifier of female essence, but rather of *masculine* honour. That woman in the play is positioned in masculine discourse is made clear in Borachio's chilling account of the purpose of the second Don John plot; the "poison" which the villain will temper will make it possible for him "to misuse the Prince, to vex Claudio, to undo Hero, and kill Leonato" (II.ii.28–9). Hero is here, literally, embedded in a masculine discourse, which will be *undone* when she is *undone* and which will be reinstated only when her "honour" is re-inscribed.

Against Hero's "subject" positions as daughter to Leonato, and as legitimate object of male affection, we must set Claudio's own constructed subjectivity. He has no independent autonomous "character" as many of his detractors mistakenly assume; rather, he moves through the play from one textual position to another. His military prowess, like that of Benedick, is already inscribed within the "prior textualization" of a masculine honour code, whose domestic inter-subjective manifestation is the discourse of formal courtship within whose boundaries Hero is herself inscribed. Don Pedro locates the smooth transition from soldier to lover: "Thou wilt be like a lover presently, / And tire the hearer with a book of words" (I.i.286–7). By contrast Benedick occupies a contradictory position, accepting the public militaristic discourse of masculine honour but rejecting its domestic intersubjective analogue; faced with the prospect of encountering Beatrice, he expostulates to Don Pedro:

Will your Grace command me any service to the world's end? I will go on the slightest errand now to the Antipodes that you can devise to send me on; I will fetch you a toothpicker now from the furthest inch of Asia; bring you the length of Prester John's foot; fetch you the hair of the great Cham's beard; do you any embassage to the Pygmies, rather than hold three words' conference with this harpy. You have no employment for me? (II.i.247–55)

This frivolous articulation of the discourse of courtly honour will be re-constituted in much heavier circumstances later in the play, when having been persuaded through a deception to negotiate the contradiction in his own position, Benedick's (I believe) now serious expostulations: "I will swear by it (my sword) that you love me, and I will make him eat it that says I love not you" (IV.i.275–6), and "Come bid me do anything for thee", are both met with Beatrice's stony imperative: "Kill Claudio!" (IV.i.286–7). Benedick's reluctance to defend "female honour" to the death makes him less than a man, as the now fully "subjected" Beatrice comes to realize:

> Princes and counties! Surely a princely testimony, a goodly count, Count Comfect, a sweet gallant, surely! O that I were a man for his sake, or that I had a friend that would be a man for my sake! But manhood is melted into curtsies, valour into compliment, and men are only turned into tongue, and trim ones too: he is now as valiant as Hercules that only tells a lie and swears it. I cannot be a man with wishing, therefore I will die a woman with grieving.
>
> (IV.i.314–23)

The alleged loss of Hero's honour marks the point of Beatrice's entry into the very discursive formation that she had before resisted, while its re-constitution at the end marks the re-inscription at different levels of ideological practice of the masculine honour of both Claudio and Benedick. The latter's attempted resolution of the inconsistency of his position at the end: "for man's a giddy thing and this is my conclusion" (V.iv.106–7), effects the transformation from "history" into "nature" so characteristic of myth, but by this time the narrative has become a severely troubled one.

We need only to go back a little to find out precisely how troubled the narrative has become. From Claudio's articulation of "prior textualizations" of female beauty as: "a witch / Against whose charms faith melteth into blood" (II.i.169–70), through to Benedick's cynical jibes at cuckoldry, and his mischievous suggestion that Don Pedro may have stolen Claudio's "bird's nest", it becomes clear that "virginitie" is really a reification of the discourse of an authoritative and paternalist honour. Don Pedro interprets the issue as being one of "trust", and responds indignantly to Benedick's allegation of theft with: "Wilt thou make a trust a transgression? The transgression is in the stealer" (II.i.210–11). The violation of "trust" – the ideological catalyst which guarantees political quiescence – through Don John's persistent questioning of Hero's chastity, raises the disturbing spectre of a plurality of meaning which threatens the whole social order, and which renders Hero a plural object: "Even she – Leonato's Hero, your Hero, every man's Hero" (III.ii.95–6). The drama is played out, literally, over the *undone* body of Hero, which becomes the plural text upon whose surface is inscribed a range of competing meanings that jostle for supremacy. During the relentless deconstruction of the marriage ceremony Hero becomes for Claudio "this rotten orange" who is "but the sign and semblance of her honour" (IV.i.31–2), whose "blush is guiltiness, not modesty" (IV.i.41), and who is translated from a human subject into one of "those pamper'd animals / That rage in savage sensuality" (IV.i.60–1). For Don Pedro the whole issue reflects upon his "honour": "I stand dishonour'd that have gone about / To link my dear friend to a common stale" (IV.i.64–5), while instead of the legitimate re-naming of Hero as Claudio's possession, her female subjectivity is ruthlessly cancelled: "Hero itself can blot out Hero's virtue" (IV.i.82) leaving her the site of contradiction: "most foul most fair", and "Thou pure impiety and impious purity!" (IV.i.103–4).

This is a narrativization to which Leonato himself subscribes, as he transforms Hero's body into a "writing": "Could she here deny / The story that is printed in her blood?" (IV.i.121–2), lamenting her *loss of value* as a signifier in the masculine discourse of possession:

> But mine, and mine, I lov'd, and mine I praised,
> And mine that I was proud on – mine so much
> That I myself was to myself not mine,
> Valuing of her – why, she, O she is fall'n
> Into a pit of ink, that the wide sea
> Hath drops too few to wash her clean again,
> And salt too little which may season give
> To her foul-tainted flesh!   (IV.i.136–43)

Here, in Messina we are offered a glimpse of a society inscribing a body in discourse, constructing a sexuality in historically specific ethical terms. It is because of the inscription of Hero's body within the ethical axis of "good" and "evil" that it can be subjected to an alternative reading; her blushes can be interpreted as marks of "innocence" and "maiden truth", whose full meaning depends upon another sort of "trust" which can recuperate her body for a theological discourse. Significantly, this reading rests with the Friar:

> Trust not my reading nor my observations,
> Which with experimental seal doth warrant
> The tenor of my book; trust not my age,
> My reverence, calling, nor divinity,
> If this sweet lady lie not guiltless here
> Under some biting error.   (IV.i.165–71)

It is this recuperative gesture which serves both to foreclose and provoke subversive questioning of the play's discursive structures, thus permitting a thoroughly "interrogative" reading of the conditions of their formation. As if aware of the Pandora's box of discursive possibilities which it has opened up, beyond the text's own powers of conceptualization, a truly dialogic voice is stifled in the play's retreat from those "real questions" of which Pierre Macherey speaks, which would seriously subvert its dominant ideology, proving the closure of the action "always adequate to itself as a reply".[59]

Heavily implicated in the whole textual process, while at the same time providing a class perspective on the action are Dogberry and the Watch. Dogberry and his colleagues are the instruments of government in Messina, but their collective inversion of sign and meaning represents an habituation of those self-cancelling devices which mark the discursive strategies of the "dishonour'd" Claudio. For Dogberry goodness and truth are punishable, with the victims having to "suffer salvation, body and soul" (III.iii.1–3), while allegiance and responsibility are the rewards of "desartlessness" (III.iii.9); also, the duty of the Watch is defined negatively: "We will rather sleep than talk; we know what belongs to a watch" (III.iii.37–8), while among the manifestations of Dogberry's "merciful" disposition is his willingness to let the "thief" banish himself: "The most peaceable way for you, if you do take a thief, is to let him show himself what he is, and steal out of your company" (III.iii.56–9). Inscribed in such apparently delightful ineptitude is the sense of an imperfectly learned system of values which are imposed from above. In this respect Dogberry and his colleagues are not unlike Beatrice and Benedick who later ape imperfectly the discourse of romantic love, succumbing as they do to its imperatives but failing to internalize slavishly its discursive practices:

Marry, I cannot show it in rhyme; I have tried. I can find out no rhyme to "lady" but "baby" – an innocent rhyme; for "scorn", "horn" – a hard rhyme; for "school", "fool" – a babbling rhyme; very ominous endings! No, I was not born under a rhyming planet, nor I cannot woo in festival terms.
(V.ii.34–40)

In this respect, though on a smaller scale than that of Beatrice and Benedick, Dogberry and the Watch elicit both ridicule and sympathetic laughter: as representatives of the Law on the one hand, but also as repositories of a popular resistance to its demands on the other. The one is inscribed primarily in the discourse of sexuality, while the other is inscribed in the discourse of class. But they overlap in a surprising way with Dogberry's insistence that as Messina's "subjects" he and his colleagues must be "suspected": "I am a wise fellow, and which is more, an officer, and which is more, a householder, and which is more, as pretty a piece of flesh as any is in Messina . . ." (IV.ii.77–9). Here social position and gendered subject are glimpsed through a defensive gesture which asserts hierarchy *at the same time* as it undermines it. It is upon this precarious balance that the discursive formations of Messina rest. The "flesh", a metonymy of Man's inheritance after Adam's "transgression" is textualized as a narrative which reproduces its own discursive practices, and it is no accident that the "prior textualizations" which drive Benedick and Beatrice together are, in the conflation of Dogberry's "tediousness" and Leonato's impatient paternalism, the efficient cause of Hero's undoing.

Structurally Dogberry and the Watch occupy a potentially subversive position in the play, seeming to invert the letter of the Law. But even so they, like Benedick and Beatrice, can hardly be said to represent the "other" of official ideology in any Bakhtinian sense. Indeed, they are shown here to be the repository of values which are ultimately re-affirmed in the court of Messina itself. Borachio makes the point bluntly to Claudio and Don Pedro: "I have deceived even your very eyes: what your wisdoms could not discover, these shallow fools have brought to light . . ." (V.ii.226–9). The result is not a fragmenting, but a *universalizing* of Messina's ethical and discursive practices, while at the same time acknowledging local social antagonisms within this unified structure. Here, momentarily, the text gapes to reveal a glimpse of hegemony in the making.

V

It is this unity which Don John challenges, and into whose precariously balanced structures he must be coerced and held as the mark of "transgression". But we should distinguish the manner of his marginalization from the recuperation, for the play's dominant discourses, of the seemingly independent figures of Benedick and Beatrice. Their admission coincides with the resurrection of Hero, her re-union with Claudio, and the capture of Don John; but even this process of re-inscription cannot be effected without recalling to mind the "other" of discourse itself irrepressibly lodged at the source of meaning as excess. To enter into discourse is to enter into a *political* semiosis, in which all communicative gestures are harnessed to the process of the production of meaning. In a potentially subversive gesture the merry-hearted Beatrice of Act II counsels Hero to "speak" to the silent (but, we recall, "civil") Claudio, "or if you cannot, stop his mouth with a kiss, and let him not speak neither" (II.i.292–3).

But this proves no solution to the problem. Indeed, at the end of the play, and now constrained to accept herself the silence which is the *modus operandi* of the "wife" Innogen, the fully "subjected" Beatrice becomes the victim of her own strategy, as Benedick *suppresses* her former persona into "silence": "Peace, I will stop your mouth"

(V.iv.97). The gesture is, surely, intended to transcend the treachery of language itself, but Don John, the man who is himself "of few words" has got there before the lovers, drawing this gesture back into the material world of difference where meanings have to be contested. Benedick's gesture both unites *and* splits the lovers, as evidenced in Count Bembo's disquisition on kissing in Castiglione's *The Book of the Courtier*:

> For since a kisse is a knitting together both of bodie and soule, it is to be feared, lest the sensuall lover will be more enclined to the part of the bodie, than of the soul: but the reasonable lover wotteth well, that although the mouth be a parcell of the bodie, yet it is an issue of wordes, that be the interpreters of the soule, and for the inward breath which is also called the soule.[60]

This gesture of uniting two "soules" in spiritual bliss is also, paradoxically, a reminder of Man's "transgression". Thus, Benedick's words of advice to Don Pedro to "get thee a wife! There is no staff more reverend than one tipped with horn" (V.iv.121–2) both extols marriage and at the same time seeks to hold in place through laughter the "transgression" that threatens to deconstruct its "transcendental signified". Thus, the platonic ideas of unity and harmony based upon a "trust" are defined only in terms of the proximity of their "other", a "transgression" whose "author" is Don John, and whose image is variously the cuckold, the whore and, most politically subversive of all, the bastard.

At the end of the play it is the "whore", that signifier of the defamatory "writing" on the body of Hero, who dies. Similarly, it is the bastard, Don John, who is rigorously coerced into the ritual affirmation of a collective solidarity which is aesthetic closure, by exclusion. Indeed, Don John's body will become the site of another "writing", this time of a promissory and spectacular nature, connected with what Francis Barker has called "the . . . pageant of sacramental violence".[61] Benedick's final words incorporate this "pageant" into the festive context of the ending itself with his exhortation to: "Think not on him till tomorrow; I'll devise thee brave punishments for him. Strike up, pipers!" (V.iv.125–6). But that process does not clear the path for a progress "through release to clarification"; rather, it constitutes a driving back down into the "political unconscious" of a force that, dispossessed from power, silenced by coercion, and re-inscribed in the pageant of Elizabethan juridical practice, seeks its revenge through the temporary colonization of those discursive practices which struggle to suppress it. Thus, the ending of *Much Ado about Nothing* offers no momentary perception of Utopia through the mechanism of carnival release; rather, it offers us an insight into a politics of comedy in which those strands which constitute the complex economy of power and pleasure are exposed, only to be concealed again within the naturalizing process of "myth". The need for such mythologizing would have been rendered still more necessary for an Elizabethan audience when it is remembered that on the throne of England was a monarch who was both the public epitome of virgin "honour" and who, in the view of religious subversives, was the bastard child of Henry VIII.[62]

Notes

[1] Terence Hawkes (ed.), *Coleridge on Shakespeare* (Harmondsworth: Penguin, 1969), p. 122.

[2] A. D. Nuttall, *A New Mimesis: Shakespeare and the representation of reality* (London: Methuen, 1984), p. 167.

[3] Hawkes, *Coleridge on Shakespeare*, p. 115.

[4] Pierre Macherey, *A Theory of Literary Production* (London: Routledge and Kegan Paul, 1978), p. 19.

[5] See James Kavanagh, "Shakespeare in Ideology", in *Alternative Shakespeares*, ed. John Drakakis (London: Methuen, 1985), pp. 144-65.

[6] H. B. Charlton, *Shakespearean Comedy* (London: Cambridge University Press, 1938), p. 226.

[7] John Russell Brown, *Shakespeare and his Comedies* (London: Methuen, 1957), p. 121.

[8] Richard Henze, "Deception in *Much Ado about Nothing*", *Studies in English Literature*, 11 (1971), 201.

[9] See David Ormerod, "Faith and Fashion in *Much Ado about Nothing*", *Shakespeare Survey*, 25 (1971), 104.

[10] Fredric Jameson, *The Political Unconscious: narrative as a socially symbolic act* (London: Methuen, 1981), p. 58.

[11] Alexander Leggatt, *Shakespeare's Comedy of Love* (London: Methuen, 1974), p. 152.

[12] Ibid., p. 183.

[13] Walter Benjamin, *Illuminations* (London: Collins/Fontana, 1973), p. 258.

[14] V. N. Volosinov, *Marxism and the Philosophy of Language* (New York and London: Seminar Press, 1973), p. 106.

[15] Dorothy Hockey, "Notes, notes, forsooth . . .", *Shakespeare Quarterly*, 8 (1957), 355.

[16] E. A. M. Coleman, *The Dramatic Use of Shakespeare's Bawdy* (London: Methuen, 1974), p. 18.

[17] A. R. Humphreys (ed.), *Much Ado about Nothing* (London: Methuen [Arden], 1981), p. 5.

[18] Ferdinand de Saussure, *Course in General Linguistics*, trans. Roy Harris (London: Duckworth, 1983), p. 115.

[19] H. H. Furness (ed.), *Much Ado about Nothing* (London: Lippincott, 1899), p. 2 and p. 58.

[20] Humphreys, *Much Ado*, p. 77. The figure of "Inogene" the wife of Brutus

appears in Spenser, *The Faerie Queene*, Book II, Canto X, the book in which a version of the story of *Much Ado about Nothing* appears. See *Edmund Spenser: The Faerie Queene*, ed. A. C. Hamilton (London: Longman, 1977), p. 261.

21 See *The Faerie Queene*, Book IV, Canto X:

> And next to her sate sober *Modestie*,
> Holding her hand vpon her gentle hart;
> And her against sate comely *Curtesie*,
> That vnto euery person knew her part;
> And her before was seated ouerthwart
> Soft *Silence*, and submisse *Obedience*,
> Both linckt together neuer to dispart,
> Both gifts of God not gotten but from thence,
> Both girlonds of his Saints against their foes offence.
>
> (Ibid. p. 505)

22 Catherine Belsey, *Critical Practice* (London: Methuen ["New Accents"], 1980), p. 42.

23 Bertrand Evans, *Shakespeare's Comedies* (Oxford: Clarendon Press, 1963), p. 73.

24 See J. R. Mulryne, *Much Ado about Nothing*, Studies in English Literature 16 (London: Edward Arnold, 1965), pp. 38ff. See also, Leggatt, *Shakespeare's Comedy of Love*, pp. 155ff.

25 Henze, "Deception", 201.

26 The evidence for this is located usually in Beatrice's reply to Don Pedro's allegation that she has "lost the heart of Signior Benedick":

> Indeed, my lord, he lent it me awhile, and I gave him use for it, a double heart for his single one. Marry once before he won it of me with false dice, therefore your Grace may well say I have lost it.
>
> (II.i.260–4)

(Cf. also Christopher Marlowe's poem, *Hero and Leander*, in *The Works of Christopher Marlowe*, ed. C. F. Tucker-Brooke (reprinted Oxford: Oxford University Press, 1962), p. 500: "*Heroes* lookes yeelded, but her words made warre, / Women are woon when they begin to iarre" (lines 331–2).

27 *Much Ado about Nothing*, p. 52.

28 Louis Althusser, *Lenin and Philosophy* (London: New Left Books, 1971), p. 211.

29 Michel Foucault, *The History of Sexuality*, vol. I (Harmondsworth: Penguin, 1981), p. 49.

30 Marilyn French, *Shakespeare's Division of Experience* (London: Jonathan Cape, 1983), p. 132.

31 Michel Foucault, *Language, Counter-memory, Practice* (Oxford: Blackwell, 1977), p. 30.

32 Ruth Nevo, *Comic Transformations in Shakespeare*, (London: Methuen, 1980), p. 178.

33 Michel Foucault, *Power/Knowledge* (Brighton: Harvester, 1980), pp. 139–40. Dramatically speaking, he occupies a place which is not unlike that

which Jonathan Dollimore ascribes to Marlowe's figure of Faustus who is the stimulus for a subversive questioning which is both foreclosed *and* provoked, although, of course, unlike Faustus, he is never allowed to occupy the central position in the play. See Jonathan Dollimore, *Radical Tragedy: religion, ideology and power in the drama of Shakespeare and his contemporaries* (Brighton: Harvester, 1984), p. 110.

34 *Political Unconscious*, p. 35.

35 *The Works of Christopher Marlowe*, p. 498.

36 See Juliet Dusinberre, *Shakespeare and The Nature of Women* (London: Macmillan, 1975). See also Catherine Belsey, "Disrupting Sexual Difference", in *Alternative Shakespeares*, ed. John Drakakis (London: Methuen, 1985), pp. 168ff.

37 *The Second Tome of Homilies* (London, 1595), sig.Gg5r.

38 Ibid., sig. Gg5v.

39 Henry Smith, *The Sermons of Master H. Smith* (London, 1592), p. 2.

40 Ibid., p. 4.

41 Ibid., p. 12.

42 Robert Cleaver, *A Godly Form of Householde Government* (London, 1598), p. 9.

43 *Homilies*, sig. L5r.

44 See Stephen Greenblatt, *Renaissance Self-Fashioning: from More to Shakespeare* (Chicago and London: University of Chicago Press, 1980), p. 186; see especially his account of the destruction of *The Bower of Blisse* in *The Faerie Queene*, Book II, pp. 183ff.

45 Francis Bacon, *Essays* (reprinted London: Dent [Everyman], 1962), p. 80.

46 Ibid., p. 25.

47 Timothy Bright, *A Treatise on Melancholy* (London, 1586), p. 81.

48 Michel Foucault, *Madness and Civilization: a history of insanity in the Age of Reason* (third impression, London: Tavistock, 1977), pp. 76–7.

49 Peter Laslett, *The World We Have Lost* (reprinted London: Methuen, 1983), p. 59.

50 Ibid., p. 154.

51 Lawrence Stone, *The Family, Sex and Marriage in England: 1500–1800* (Harmondsworth: Penguin, 1979), p. 106. See also pp. 276–7 on the question of infanticide, though Stone makes no mention of *female* infanticide.

52 William Blackstone, *Commentaries on The Laws of England*, 4 vols. (Dublin, 1769), vol. 1, p. 459.

53 Ibid., vol. 3, pp. 433ff.

54 Foucault, *The History of Sexuality*, p. 107.

55 See Louis Montrose, " 'The Place of a Brother' in *As You Like It*: Social Process and Comic Form", *Shakespeare Quarterly*, 32, 1 (Spring, 1981), 28–54; see especially his comments on Shakespeare's exploration of the conditions "in a rigorously hierarchical and patriarchal society, a society in which full social identity tends to be limited to the propertied adult males who are the heads of households" (p. 35). My own conclusions depart radically from Montrose on the question of "subjectivity", and I cannot accept his conclusions concerning Shakespeare's plays as "reflections" of conflict (p. 54).

56 *Homilies*, sig. C8r.

57 Ibid., sig. D3r.

58 Cf. Montrose, "The Place of a Brother", p. 49 on the issue of "Charivari": "traditionally the form of ridicule to which cuckolds and others who offended the community's moral standards were subjected".

59 Macherey, *Literary Production*, p. 131.

60 Baldassare Castiglione, *The Book of the Courtier* (London: Dent [Everyman], 1966), p. 315.

61 Francis Barker, *The Tremulous Private Body: essays on subjection* (London: Methuen, 1984), p. 76.

62 G. R. Elton, *Reform and Reformation: England 1509–1558* (London: Edward Arnold, 1977), p. 255.

Donne's praise of folly

THOMAS DOCHERTY

Mutato nomine de te fabula narratur
> (Horace, *Satires*, Book I, Satire 1;
> cited by Marx, in *Capital*, vol. 1,
> ch. 10, sect. 5, "The struggle for a
> normal working day")

On a huge hill,
Cragged, and steep, Truth stands, and he that will
Reach her, about must, and about must go;
And what the hill's suddenness resists, win so;
Yet strive so, that before age, death's twilight,
Thy soul rest, for none can work in that night,
To will, implies delay, therefore now do.
Hard deeds, the body's pains; hard knowledge too
The mind's endeavours reach, and mysteries
Are like the sun, dazzling, yet plain to all eyes.
> (John Donne, Satire 3, "Kind pity
> chokes my spleen")

This is a disadvantage I am powerless to overcome, unless it be by forewarning and forearming those readers who zealously seek the truth. There is no royal road to science, and only those who do not dread the fatiguing climb of its steep paths have a chance of gaining its luminous summits.
> (Karl Marx, letter to Maurice La
> Châtre; cited in Althusser and
> Balibar, *Reading Capital*)

I

In 1873, Arnold established a distinction between "scientific" and "literary" language which had been latent in theoretical thought for centuries. He posed the distinction in his preface to *Literature and Dogma*, where he suggested that "To understand that the language of the Bible is fluid, passing, and literary, not rigid, fixed, and scientific, is the first step towards a right understanding of the Bible".[1] This problematic of exegesis focusses on the conflict between truth and interpretation. It is a problem which the English church had faced before, most clearly at the moment of its institutionalization in the Reformation. When Henry VIII

85

divorced England from Rome, he inadvertently inaugurated a problem or conflict of "many authorities", and a relativization of truth in scriptural exegesis. The publication of an *Authorized King James' Version* in 1611 did little to alleviate the problem. A *version* (from *vertere*, to turn) is a translation, a turning or *trope* (from *tropos*, a turn); this version, then, comes dangerously close to a rendering from a specific point of view, and thus a variant or interpretation. The *Authorized Version*, in fact, contributed to the outbreak of a Civil War in which one party questioned precisely the "authorization" of the king. The king's "good name", interposing itself as the mediator of the truth in this version/interpretation, had been "wounded" or doubted; and the exegetical problems remained.

For Augustine, biblical exegesis depended upon an initial act of faith, a *credo* which framed the act of reading. Once "inside" this frame of faith, truth could be rendered directly to the heart of the reader, without the intervention of a sceptical, critical consciousness. But this faith, in ridding us of interested intermediaries, also rids us of our own consciousness. Our voices are silenced, *our* readings unheard: we are supposed simply to *hear* the words of scripture, as if they emanated from within, and to make no critical or even conscious response. Such "faithful reading" depends on a notion that the source of the scripture and its guarantee of truth is within us: this Bible preaches to the *converted*, for it depends upon our *turning*, in complete faith, towards it and away from our own thought.

This strangely self-satisfying strategy was taken over to some extent by Renaissance humanists; but among some of these, there was concern about the interposition of their own mediating consciousness or identity (their name) between the truth of the text and its interpretation or reading. Cave points out that Erasmus tries to circumvent this by the adoption of a quasi-phenomenological approach:

Erasmus constructs the model of a dynamic imitation or reproduction of Scripture. The text is to be wholly absorbed by the reader and located in the *pectus*, that intuitive focus of the self which is presumed to guarantee profound understanding and *living* expression. In other words, the scriptural text is made consubstantial with the reader and is then re-uttered in a speech-act grounded in the living presence of the speaker, a process which achieves its end in that vivid penetration of the listener's mind which is in itself a mark of authenticity.[2]

The reader here is afflicted by glottophagia, swallowing her or his tongue as s/he digests the material of the text; the material thus absorbed is then re-produced, but transformed, spoken not in the tongue of the reader but in the tongue of God as ultimate authority. The experience of the listener is not a mark of authenticity, in fact, but is rather a mark of ideology; for this reading-process pretends to eradicate the transforming labour, activity, or medium of the reader's name in the reading-production of the text. The reader, in mediating the word of God, "identifies" her or his voice with that of God; and it is this voice which is supposed to guarantee and authorize the ideology. Such a reader performs two related "impersonations": firstly, an *imitatio Christi* in the conventional sense; and secondly, an *imitatio Mariae*, impersonating the virginal mother in her innocent and "immaculate conception" of the word of God, which she transforms, in her labour, into living flesh. The dangerous mediating identity of the reader now meshes with the incarnation of God in the *pectus*: God, as it were, now inhabits the heart, spirit or personal identity (that is, individuated proper name) of the reader, and there is a mutual recognition (an acknowledgment of truth) in this consubstantiality of the two identities of God and reader.

The self-presence of the reader, this "intuitive focus of the self" is actually informed then as a "scene of recognition" by an "impersonal" self. This kind of reading-activity came to determine secular writing as well. Erasmus prefigures the position adopted by Montaigne whose essayistic attempt at self-portraiture (or self-nomination, fundamentally) becomes one which involves structural change and a form of "impersonality". The portrait constructed in the *Essais* is always grounded in the response to previous writings, including previous *essais*; a degree of sceptical self-criticism is the result. In the *Essais* the self portrayed changes with the writing or production of the text as such, as each new essay adds to, and, significantly, makes a critical response to, previous accumulations of details. Cave detects a similarity in Erasmus: "The name or pseudonym of Erasmus (Desiderius, the loved one) figures in many of his writings – the *Praise of Folly*, the *Ichthyophagia* – as an ironically paraded self, a special instance of that mirror-image which, according to the theory of *oratio* as *speculum animi*, is to be composed by the text." But this involves Erasmus, or that euphemistic pseudonym, Desiderius, in a process of impersonation, and hence in a kind of inauthenticity:

Erasmus purports to write as an evangelical humanist; but the compulsion endlessly to extend his writing reveals, with increasing evidence, the desire to recognize himself (see his face in the mirror) and be recognized. He must become an alien surface in order to constitute himself as an identity, an *apparent* nature, grafted (perhaps) only on the culture of discourse. The Erasmian *sensus* or *sententia*, issuing supposedly from a unique identity, translates itself into words, and thus inevitably betrays itself.[3]

This translation, or *version*, of the self and its name, then, produces not the Augustinian "faithful reading", but rather, precisely the contrary, an act of "betrayal" or *infidelity*. To put this more simply, the self, as an ideological construction in this cultural and historical milieu in and through which Donne lived, always finds itself in a state of differential, structural change; the name of the self is always to be found in its "betrayal" or identification with the name of an Other.

The principle of change, then, which is constitutive of the contruction of a historical selfhood, can perhaps better be described as a principle of exchange; and the fundamental locus of that exchange can be identified as the "proper" name or word (now, clearly, no longer strictly "proper") or individual essential identity. That is to say that at the very moment of constructing a "pure" essential identity the impurities of a mutability or exchangeability appear. In terms of reading and writing, the effect of this is to replace the notion of an essential or grounding truth in a text by a conflict of mutable, critical interpretations; such interpretation is a properly historicized act of reading, a "reading" now always mediated by an "impure" reader who guarantees that there can be no possibility of hygienic "sanity", no sanitization, of the text or of its reading. The name, identity or consciousness of a reader of the Bible or of a poem, say, enters to vitiate the purity or immediacy of truth in the text's reading, giving in its place a "maculate" mediation or critical interpretation of the text. As a corollary, the proper name itself is but another *version* or trope. It is the purpose of this essay not to lay bare the "true name" of Donne (for such a final ground in truth is denied), but rather to reveal some important other versions or tropes of the name of Donne.[4]

II

Erasmus makes some play with proper names, though not specifically in the terms described above, in the Dedication of his *Praise of Folly*. The work is prefaced by its Greek title, *Morias Enkomion*, in its dedication to Erasmus's friend, Thomas More. The text becomes instantly ambiguous as Erasmus plays on the name of More and its near homonym, the Greek *morias*, and the title of the text is ironized:

let me be hanged if I have enjoyed anyone more in my life! Therefore, since I thought that something should be done about it and the time seemed little fit for serious thinking, I decided to have some fun with a praise of folly.

'How did the goddess Pallas put that into my head?' you ask. First of all, there was your family name of More, which is as close to the Greek word for folly as you are from the meaning of the word . . . and besides, you are a sort of Democritus amid the common run of mortals.[5]

More's name is, then, a kernel of the work of Erasmus; and further, this "praise of folly" becomes an oblique or ironic praise of the name of More/*morias*, in whose house Erasmus stayed, recovering from illness, while writing the text.

Folly enters directly to disrupt the stability of truth; the *pectus*, or scene of recognition between the name of More and the word for folly, far from being a locus of truth and authenticity, becomes tainted by the impurities of ideology, hypocrisy, madness or unhygienic insanity. Foucault has made the correlation between madness and truth in a suggestion that "La Folie commence là où se trouble et s'obscurcit le rapport de l'homme à la vérité."[6] Further, madness is linked to the comedy of *quiproquo*, that principle of exchange which mediates between More and *morias*:

La folie, c'est la forme la plus pure, la plus totale du *quiproquo*: elle prend le faux pour le vrai, la mort pour la vie, l'homme pour la femme, l'amoureuse pour l'Erynnie et la victime pour Minos.[7]

This, in fact, is one fundamental value of a comedy based upon the punning *quiproquo*: it suggests that things may be arranged differently from what they seem, and allows for, or even encourages, the possibility of change, of the provisional triumph of one version or trope over other interpretations of the world. A quest for epistemological veracity, on the other hand, is inherently more tragic. The *quiproquo* of Sophocles's *Oedipus Rex* or of Racine's *Iphigénie en Aulide* turns towards tragedy when an essentially "true" identity is revealed or discovered: *quiproquo* resolves into monologue or "mono-logicity". On the other hand, a drama such as Shakespeare's *Comedy of Errors* endorses a comic attitude in which impure identities can be tolerated or modified to suit the "mad" but pragmatic pursuit of pleasure (however ideological that pleasure may be) rather than the dogmatic and nostalgic pursuit of a transcendent, monological version of an Absolute Knowing.[8]

Wilbur Samuel Howell has drawn attention to an opposition in the Renaissance between logic and rhetoric, an opposition which was typically reproduced symbolically (see illustration 1). He writes in explanation of this metaphor of the open and closed hand that:

Over and over again in logical and rhetorical treatises of the English Renaissance, logic is compared to the closed fist and rhetoric to the open hand, this metaphor being borrowed from Zeno through Cicero and Quintilian to explain the preoccupation of logic with the tight discourse of the philosopher, and the preoccupation of rhetoric with the more open discourses of orator and popularizer.[9]

ILLUSTRATION 1

Logic and rhetoric were regarded as two different, but complementary, modes of communication, according to Howell; and poetry was considered to be a third mode, one which was simultaneously closed and open:

poetry was thought to be a form of communication which, because it habitually used the medium of story and characterization, spoke two simultaneous languages . . .[10]

This is a little misleading in its simplification. The separation of the two hands, for a start, is a falsification, for logic is always intertwined with rhetoric, philosophy always mediated stylistically.[11] That is to say, poetry as such is the ground of both rhetoric and logic, and the principle of exchange, of *dialogicity*, is the ground of poetry. Poetry may itself affirm nothing, but it forms the condition of whatever propositions may be made; it may *say* nothing, but it conditions what may be *done*, or at least what may be thought.

Dialogicity is integral and fundamental to Lyly's *Euphues*, a text which was immensely popular in the final decades of the sixteenth century, and which spawned many imitations of its style. The single most insistent device of Lyly's text is antithesis and antithetical chiasmus; and other devices, including rhyme and pun, the radical of antithesis and chiasmus, follow from this. Both rhyme and pun invite the possibility of potentially comic linguistic exchange, *quiproquo* and folly. Appropriately, Lyly's text closes on an act of intertwining of hands, in a formal handshake which operates as a clear symbol of the commerce of exchange, of the interchange of positions on the part of speaker and listener, and of the organization of a certain kind of friend-

ship or social relation which is one of the major organizational principles
in the text. This friendship is constituted precisely on a ground of exchangeability. The relation between Euphues and Philautus is disturbed
only by the intrusion of the woman, Lucilla, who threatens, by the
merest fact of her sexual difference from these characters, to displace
their association. More immediately pertinent here, however, is the
description of the establishment of friendship offered by Euphues:

I have red . . . and well I beleeve it, that a friend is in prosperitie a pleasure,
a solace in adversitie, in griefe a comfort, in joy a merrye companion, at all
other times an other I, in all places the expresse Image of mine owne person[12]

This is precisely in line with the Donnean and Montaignean realization
of identity. The self is always a part of a social relation; that is, it is
constituted by social dialogue and not through a monologue derived
from that social relation with the Other. The self, then, derives from
an anterior community; and the moment of discovery of self-awareness
or of self-nomination is also the moment at which the self discovers her
or his exchangeability, mutability and mutuality.

This is one aspect of Euphuism which Donne takes over to some
extent; but in his hands it becomes more clearly a kind of dialogical
euphemism,[13] in which sacred or taboo words and names are "heard"
without being explicitly said. One extremely important such dialogical
pun is, aptly enough, on the word "mutually" in Elegy 7, a poem
which Donne writes of, and in, the "language of flowers" or
euphemism:

> I had not taught thee then, the alphabet
> Of flowers, how they devisefully being set
> And bound up, might with speechless secrecy
> Deliver errands mutely, and mutually.[14]

This is nothing less than an "apology for poesy" and a kind of advert-
isement for the language of flowers. The play between "mutely" and
"mutually", in which they come together as homonyms, and thus as
euphemisms for each other, makes of these lines an apology for the
dialogical handshake of poetic communication, and suggests that it is
basic or fundamental to any other mode of communication. Further,
this poesy substitutes itself for the historical "posy", the wedding ring
or circle into which Donne wants to break in the poem. The language
of flowers, in Donne as in Shakespeare,[15] allows secret messages to be
understood; more pertinently here, the "posy/poesy" establishes a
parabolic riddle which is understood by an "elect", those within the
hermeneutic circle or "ring". This is essentially modelled on Christian
parabolic teaching. As Kermode has it:

To divine the true, the latent sense, you need to be of the elect, of the institution. Outsiders may content themselves with the manifest, and pay a supreme penalty for doing so. Only those who already know the mysteries – what the stories really mean – can discover what the stories really mean.[16]

The Donnean poetic riddling language is slightly different, inasmuch as it has conceded any notion of privileged access to the true. The "latent sense" in Kermode's definition here is no more "true" for Donne than any other sense. In this poem, what is at stake is simply the exchange of one "posy" for another little ring; the exchange of the historical wedding-posy for the posy/poesy which establishes a ring or circle including Donne and his co-elect, the woman who now understands his language of flowers.

Although the text has given up the notion of making truth-propositions here, history has not been lost.[17] There is a movement from the play of signifiers, from the poesy (language of flowers) towards the establishment of historical action, in the formation of the posy. This posy, proposed in the act of reading the poem, establishes a ring or circle which demarcates an ecclesia of sorts around the poem. But, given the fact that the readers of this poem constitute a numerous group (the poem is not simply a letter to one historical individual woman) the shape and formation of this posy/ecclesia is indeterminate, open. That is to say, the movement from poesy to posy does not simply establish one specific "adulterous" or unfaithful situation in the alignment of Donne and one woman and their consanguinity symbolized in the new posy; rather, this potentially univocal and "private" sense is opened out to a community of elect readers. It is this elect who make the poem legible and who legitimate or authorize its ecclesiastic community. The text, then, is inherently dialogical, if not multilogical.[18]

In the lines cited, further, this possibility of mutuality or relational identity (the establishment of open posies) arises from the interchange of "mutely" and "mutually"; but this is done in a specific way – "with speechless secrecy". What is "mutely" communicated is important in this mutual relation or mutable consciousness; for it is this "mute" aspect of the act of understanding which turns linguistic play into historical action. A relevant example occurs in Satire 2, where we have:

> One would move love by rhymes; but witchcraft's charms
> Bring not now their old fears, nor their old harms:
> Rams, and slings now are silly battery,
> Pistolets are the best artillery.[19]

There is a manuscript variant which gives greater clarity to the concealed pun; there is justification to emend "slings" to "songs". This makes more apparent the pun on "ram/rhyme", giving what may in fact appear to be more coherent: "Rams [rhymes] and songs now are silly battery, / Pistolets are the best artillery". This makes doubly significant the pun on the word "rhyme" itself, suggesting a reading or version in which the power of rhyme does, despite the first two lines quoted, have the historically real power of the "ram". "Rhymes" can be, and are, more than mere rhetorical efflorescence, and can have logical, scientific or, more generally, historical applicability and efficacy.

The "mutism" of such linguistic exchanges is important when the poet wants to write "indecorous" or controversial things, without actually saying them. The pun allows words to be "heard" without their being said. A pertinent example is in "Air and Angels" where we hear of the poet who:

> Whilst thus to ballast love, I thought,
> And so more steadily to have gone,
> With wares which would sink admiration,
> I saw, I had love's pinnace overfraught.[20]

The word "pinnace" is odd in this context: a ship of fools may be one thing, but a ship of love or of lovers is another, even if Shakespeare may have aligned "the lunatic, the lover and the poet" in terms of imagination in *A Midsummer-Night's Dream* (V.i). Drawing attention to itself the word "pinnace" invites the obvious exchange with "penis". The silent reading makes explicit sexual sense of the lines, in which there appears now a revelation of the otherwise unspeakable enormity of Donne's erection, and a notion that it attracts such admiration as to make rival "pinnaces" sink, fall downwards or become detumescent. The euphemistic language of rhetorical flowers is useful as a means of allowing a reader to "hear" texts or voices other than that presented to her or his eyes and ears. It opens the poem to the intrusion of "alien" impurities, ghostly verbal visitations which haunt the reader with the possibility of producing multiple meaning, "dialogical sense", so to speak, from the poetry. The example cited here reveals the operation of euphemism in sexual matters; but precisely the same principle applies in poems (by Donne and many of his censored contemporaries) which make audible the politically unspeakable. The multiplicity of meaning produced in these instances offers the reader, in the now dialectical process of reading, a series of historical and political choices in terms of how s/he will understand and construe the poem, and thus opens up the possibility of historical action and political change.

Fundamental to this is the principle of exchange, through the "friendly" intertwining of logical and rhetorical hands; but in Donne, this seems more readily understood in terms of the clasping of these hands in an attitude of prayer. This enables the possibility of "mute/ mutual" relation between reader and writer, or rather among a community of interpreters, around the focal mirror of the text. The text itself, then, becomes a scene of mutual recognition, the producer of ecclesia. In the ideal, dialogical or poetic reading of poetry, nameable personal identity is lost: the reader discovers or "hears" herself or himself in the voice of the Other, and a corporate identity is produced, in a condition in which a kind of monastic silence allows the voice of a ghostly spirit to be heard. The theological idea is that through this economic ideology of the principle of bartering exchange in language, the reader has a chance to discover her or his own "vocation" in hearing her or his name called out and identified in the ecclesia (where the reader comes to recognize herself or himself). In the hearing of silent puns, the reader is actually hearing/understanding herself or himself speak, "mutely"; and such mutism is precisely the locus, in this theology, of mutuality and ecclesia. The body of the reader becomes the body of the church; but only through the "madness" of mediation, of interpreting these punning exchanges seriously, and through the hearing or understanding of ghostly voices and spirits which haunt the reader in the act of comprehension.[21]

III

The area between two stable certainties, which is precisely the area occupied by the exchange-pun in language, is characterized by Foucault as the locus of folly. Writing of the mad person on the "ship of fools", Foucault suggests:

Et la terre sur laquelle il abordera, on ne la connaît pas, tout comme on ne sait pas, quand il prend pied, de quelle terre il vient. Il n'a sa vérité et sa patrie que dans cette étendue inféconde *entre deux terres* qui ne peuvent lui appartenir.[22]

It is the very quality of alterity and the fact of alienation which constitute Folly as such; the mad person is always an Other, alien to herself or himself. Moreover, another way of expressing the italicized phrase here, *entre deux terres*, is in a classical formulation as *in medias res*: that is, it is "in the middest" or in the act of mediation (interpretation, hearing or reading) that such alterity is discovered, in hearing or even in understanding that folly or madness lies.

Might it be the case, then, that Donne is writing his own version, a comic version or revision of a *Praise of Folly* in his rhetorical poesy? It is apposite at this point to recall two things. First, there is the joint influence of the Reformation and of Ramist logic, in which Protestantism becomes instrumental in raising the voices of individual readers in a quasi-democratic babel of confusion and historical conflict, when conviction means simply the strident and stubborn proclamation of a monological discourse, deaf to all other voices in the babel. Secondly, there is the more particular principle of exchange which makes Erasmus's *Praise of Folly* fundamentally ironic and ambiguous: the "hearing" of More's name in its Greek title, *Morias Enkomion*. In the light of these points, might it also be apposite to suggest that Donne is writing a concealed "praise of More", and, by the slightest of anagrammatical shifts which is startlingly appropriate to the name of More, a praise of *Rome*, or of Roman Catholicism?

It has rightly been stressed that Donne was descended from the family of Thomas More, who was the uncle of Donne's maternal grandmother, Joan Rastell Heywood. If it were indeed the case that Donne was writing a "praise of Folly/More", then he would clearly have to adopt the euphemistic mode of writing described here. Given his historical situation, with the persecution of Roman Catholics and his own subsequent career in the Anglican church, he would have to tread warily if he wanted to produce a "catholic" (universal, though some might say "totalitarian") mode of prayer through his playful "comic" verse. It may, of course, equally be the case that he simply could not erase all traces of his own personal theological history, and that he could not "purge" himself of various Roman Catholic predilections. The ghost of More, as it were, echoes in many "more-more-ings" or murmurings in the verse, alerting critics such as Paul M. Ochojski to the "impurities" which reveal such residual Roman Catholicism in Donne's work.[23]

More Mores than Thomas More, however, played an important part in the personal history of Donne. Not the least of these was his wife, Ann More, and her father, Sir George More. After Donne's hasty clandestine marriage to Ann, George More was instrumental in removing Donne from the service of Sir Thomas Egerton, thus leaving him without patronage and without a source of income, and he finally pursued Donne until he managed to have him imprisoned. From such circumscription, another "posy" of sorts, Donne contrived to discover some comic "poesy", in the linguistic play on his name: "John Donne/Ann Donne/Undone". The covert "praise of (Thomas) More" and of a theological imperative might well be intertwined also with a "praise of (Ann) More" and an imperative which has a greater bearing on sexual and marital matters in the writing.

In the Protestant ideology of Reformation England, questions of spiritual truth and of biblical exegetical interpretation begin to tie in with questions of a more "privatized" domestic nature. In Satire 3, "Kind pity chokes my spleen", Donne ponders the search for one true religion, and finds an interesting way of discerning the true from the heretical:

> unmoved thou
> Of force must one, and forced but one allow;
> And the right; ask thy father which is she,
> Let him ask his; though truth and falsehood be
> Near twins, yet truth a little elder is.[24]

To find the truth, Donne advises some degree of conformity to past or traditional models; more correctly, he suggests that we can learn something of the truth from our familial heritage. This is of special interest in Donne's own case, for it is precisely such a heritage, that of the family of the (Thomas) Mores, which he betrayed in his apostasy.

The argument advanced bears a similarity to the ideological imperatives of primogeniture, which had been a central political issue in Henry VIII's "great matter" in 1527 and after, when Thomas More had questioned Henry's actions, at great cost. Given the law of primogeniture, there is an assumption that truth, essence or veracity, like familial or more precisely patriarchal blood, flows in the veins of the faithful sons of fathers. In the marital arrangement which this produces, women are explicitly variable "counters" or mutable vehicles through whom truth is mediated and represented (as son echoes or represents father). By extension, their names become extremely mutable (as they change the name of a father for that of a husband in marriage), and with this mutability of nomination goes an exchangeability of identity, according to the ideology.

The name of the woman, then, is in some ways analogous to the very springs of poetry based upon the principles of exchange. Women, Ann More among them, become the unnameable mobile counters who derive their identity from appropriative men in this arrangement. But it is through women, and more pertinently through the mobility of their names, that the stability of a masculinist epistemology which claims access to the truth is assured. Male lovers look into the mirror of their lover's eye, or womb, and see the reflection of themselves (or of their sons, as representations of themselves), thus supposedly guaranteeing a stable, transhistorical male identity; and such eternal "sameness", identity, slips into "truth". Yet there is a contradiction here, and one which reveals the logical priority ascribed to woman in the lines from Satire 3 cited above, in which the *father* becomes the vehicle of an anterior *female* church: "ask thy father which is she". It is, in fact, from the name of the woman, understood as the location of a scene in which an act of mute/mutual recognition can occur, that the poetry can be written at all. The exchangeability of the woman's name becomes paradigmatic of the organization of the rhetoric of poetry as such. Woman, or her name, is thus logically prior to the poetic creation (both of the written text, and of a poet's masculinity), and is tantamount to the very condition of the poem's possibility. In Donne's case, the search for the name and stability of truth (in religious terms, equated here with the name of his Roman Catholic heritage in Thomas More) is satisfied with a name that "puns" or exchanges with it that of Ann More. Most importantly, such an exchange reinstates the priority of the woman's name over the demands of the masculinist epistemology which reposes in primogeniture.

The marriage between Donne and Ann More also betrays a father, and it refuses George More the degree of patriarchal control of his family and especially of his primogenitive history, which was the societal and ideological norm. This betrayal, or "infidelity", threatens the stability or control of the family name and identity (really the Name of the Father), and thus also, as a corollary in this arrangement, dissolves transcendent truth into historical interpretation. The writerly equivalent of this "Name of the Woman", which can be identified as the principle of linguistic or rhetorical exchange, similarly threatens the truth-propositionality of any text. If the language of a text is rigidly controlled, in ways which strive to combat the principle of rhetorical mutability and to reinstate the myth of a monological discourse, then the poem approaches the condition which not only stabilizes a (male) identity for the poet, but also establishes a masculinist epistemology. If, on the other hand, a "promiscuity" of linguistic play is indulged the opposite happens: there is a seeming madness or folly in the language which frequently allows two contradictory things to be heard simultaneously, and the individual identity of a voice which makes such poetic statements is threatened. The reader/hearer of such a text is forced to mediate, as an historical activity, and to produce historical meaning. The Name of the Woman, then, which in Satire 3 is identified as the true religion or true church, is that which allows the poet to *escape* from individuated personality; for he here betrays a patriarchal filiation in some way and replaces the stability of an eternizing truth with the mutable and historical or secular discourse of Folly.

Donne's writing is done in the name of more/More; that is to say, it is a writing which, like that of Erasmus or Montaigne, produces or demands "more" writing, more mediation, more interpretation; and this "more" or supplementary excess of writing is "done" and "undone" in the now ambiguous "identity" (really a non-identity) of More (Roman Catholic Thomas, and female Ann). After the model of punning Erasmus, Donne can write his own "praise of Folly"; and it is this folly which allows the interweaving of a metaphysical quest (for truth in theology) with a physical one (for material meaning in secular affairs, or ideology). It also generates the link between the praise of Thomas More (and thus of "true" religion) and that of Ann More (who, with Donne, enacts that religion in an act of betrayal of dogmatic "truth", and an act which threatens the promiscuous dissemination of the name of More). To write in this now dissolute or impure "name of more/More" suggests precisely the "undoing" of the name of Donne in the seemingly incidental joke: "John Donne/Ann Donne/Undone". When George More had Donne imprisoned, and held his own daughter until April 1602, there was an attempt being made to "undo" the name of Donne and to challenge its power to appropriate Ann More. Four months after the marriage, however, the suit between Donne and Ann More was declared legally binding, "legitimate". The attempt to control his familial history, on the part of George More, was, fundamentally, an attempt to "cross" or undo the name of Donne, as Donne himself saw.

IV

I have commented already on the extensive use of chiasmus in the Euphuistic manner of writing which dominated English culture in Donne's early years. The fundamental chiasmus performed in "undoing" Donne's name is of especial interest. The word, *chiasmus*, derives from the Greek letter *chi*, X, the symbol, for us at least, of a cross; and rhetorically, chiasmus is a "trope of crossing" or mirroring. In "crossing" himself, a movement akin to blessing himself, Donne's name is reversed, and becomes precisely the caricatural figure which George More had applied to Donne the libertine: "Don Juan". This "crossing" or crucifixion, in the undoing of Donne, makes him the "lord" or "don" after his Spanish travels; and it also replaces the patriarchal familial name with the perhaps more arbitrary first or given name, John/Juan.

This legend of Don Juan is more than a fortuitous play on names; the legend is important in Donne's "moorish/More-ish" writing. The first literary transcription of the Don Juan legend is usually considered to be Tirso de Molina's *El burlador de Sevilla y Convidado de Piedra*, written some time after Donne had been in Spain. But the legend had existed in many other forms before Tirso or Calderón (in *Tan largo me lo fiáis*) created stage versions of it, and it was of some prominence in Spain. In one form, the myth is simply that of the libertine of masculinist sexual ideology, clear enough as an overt influence on Donne's verse. But the other part of the legend, the address to or from a dead person or statue (often in the form of a skull or skeleton of sorts) is of even more pertinence to Donne. Shakespeare takes the motif over wholesale in *Hamlet's* gravedigger scene; Donne contrives addresses to relics and bones which no longer claim any singular shape or identity. Shakespeare takes on the idea of the living statue in *The Winter's Tale*; Donne puns on the idea of the "living stone" and theologizes it. The church or "true religion", and even truth itself for Donne, is not built upon the stability of a rock or even of the theological Word. "Where the word was, the pun shall be", as Hartman writes in another context.[25] The church of More is built not upon a rock, but upon a pun, operating between the word for "rock" and the proper name "Peter". Donne's folly, then, his existence as a mad figure *entre deux terres* in Foucault's formulation, between (Thomas) More and (Ann) More, between spirit and body, between tradition and independence, between "upright" John Donne and "crossed" Don Juan, is axiomatic to his writing. The "one true church" is precisely the church which is "crossed", bifurcated, undone. It is in the undoing of the patriarchal name, and the undoing of the illusion of truth in that Name of the Father, that ecclesia can be historically found or constructed. That is to say, the act of sexual and social infidelity and promiscuity which is basic to Donne's "self-undoing" in his marriage to Ann More, is precisely what constitutes religious fidelity, or faith, legitimacy, authenticity and "right reading". The one true church here is no dogmatic institution, but is rather, as in Donne's own version of the Don Juan legend, a "living rock" or Christian sepulchre around which ecclesia or community is to be produced.[26] Donne's praise of divinity is also, then, a praise of *morias*/folly; and paradox (itself a term with specific theological connotation) or "madness" is at the root of the writing in this particular sense: faith (as a historical act replacing a transcendent truth) lies in "crossing" oneself, in "infidelities" (paradoxes, heterodoxies) which threaten the sense of personal transcendent individuality.

Folly becomes the medium through which the divinity is revealed or "betrayed". One of Erasmus's ironic presentations of rhetorical exegesis clarifies this, and offers one rationale for the kind of rhetorical criticism which I proffer here. Folly speaks of a fool/scholar who meditated on the name of Jesus, akin to my concentrations on nomenclature

here, and shows that through an adulteration of the name of "Jesus"
lies the "pure" meaning of that figure; through a kind of bastardization
of the names comes legitimacy and right reading:

> The name Jesus was equally divided into two parts with an s left in the middle.
> He then proceeded to point out that this lone letter was Ψ in the Hebrew
> language and was pronounced Schin, or Sin, and that furthermore this Hebrew
> letter was a word in the Scottish dialect that means *peccatum* (Latin for sin).
> From the above premises he declared to his audience that this connection
> showed that Jesus takes away the sins of the world . . . when did the Greek
> Demosthenes or Roman Cicero ever cook up such a rhetorical in*si*nuation as
> that?[27]

The rhetoric may be mad, but there is method in it, and it is productive
of an orthodox truth or belief of the church. Folly may mock the procedure, but it does produce the "sane" proposition, that "Jesus takes
away the sins of the world". What is of consequence here for Erasmus
is "right reading", a hermeneutic productive of faith; and this
hermeneutic is also therapeutic, a hygienic "sanitizing" mode of exegesis. But orthodoxy can only be discovered through paradox, and the
way to therapeutic sanity, for an exegetical manner based on Folly, is
through an "insane" adulteration of the text with meaning.

Donne argues precisely this in "The Triple Fool", whose title is suggestive, as are all "threes in one" in Donne, of the theological Trinity.
The ostensible point of this poem is to validate the proposition that
although love and grief can be "fettered" in verse or poesy, the reading
of that verse works to release or re-activate such feelings historically.
Donne begins by being already "duplicitous", a "double fool":

> I am two fools, I know
> For loving, and for saying so
> In whining poetry[28]

But he immediately sets out to justify his lines by suggesting that
poetry can be cathartic, therapeutic:

> I thought, if I could draw my pains
> Through rhyme's vexation, I should them allay.
> Grief brought to numbers cannot be so fierce,
> For, he tames it, that fetters it in verse.

The paradoxical problem, however, is that this simply produces more
folly, in publication of the original two follies or in the reading of this
"binding" verse:

> But when I have done so,
> Some man, his art and voice to show,
> Doth set and sing my pain,

> And, by delighting many, frees again
> Grief, which verse did restrain.

And so, in the very act of reading the poem, there is a multiplication of folly, and no recovery: "And I, which was two fools, do so grow three." The problem is that the reading of this poem produces folly; but we must read it in order to be able to make the very proposition which the poem seems to be thus making. It is not an apotropaic warding-off of folly at all, not a balm for the grief of love or the posy-ring, but is actually precisely the construction of folly, and the multiplication of this "insanity". Such production, further, is exponential: duplicitous folly becomes triple folly; this triple folly is itself doubled and tripled on subsequent reading of the poem, and so on, potentially indefinitely. This paradox fuels a greater paradox. The production of the triple fool, which is also the rehearsal or production of the text, "The Triple Fool", depends, then, upon a reading of the poem, carried out *before* the poem can be written. Folly is very much the condition of these lines; the writing of the poem, the production of the triple fool, is itself dependent upon the reading of the poem, paradoxically before it has been written at all. The text we have, then, is a *version* of "The Triple Fool". This "insane" proposition, that reading is prior to writing, is in fact the one sound proposal to come from the text. Contrary to what it seems to suggest, that writing fetters grief, it demonstrates that writing, poesy, produces the "insanity" or impurity of historical emotion, the historical fact of the posy-ring which causes the problem in the first place. In these terms, the exponential production of folly, of "more" insane writing, becomes inevitable: the greater one's emotional "insanity", the "more/More/madder" one has to write in order to counter the folly; but such a fettering of the folly of the posy (love) is itself merely productive of even more "insanity" or, one might say, comedy, in the activities of reading and writing.

Folly is aligned not only with love, both sacred and secular, but also with poetry itself. Donne writes in the name of More/Folly, and finds himself in a situation which prefigures a comic Shandean state of affairs. The praise of folly in Donne's circumlocutory writing is in some ways a counter to a primal curse; it is the attempt to exchange the primal biblical curse for another version of that curse, for the "self-crossing" constitutive of blessing. The biblical curse is twofold: Eve (not yet named) is cursed with childbearing and sexual subservience (Genesis 3:16), and Adam is cursed with death and the necessity of physical labour (Genesis 3:19). Donne's "mad" enterprise, then, is an attempt to "cross" the *Authorized Version* with his own authorized tropes (and thus he challenges both church and state: hence the necessity for euphemism). The writing is an attempt to make the tragic "bleeding" into a comic blessing, and to convert labour into pleasure or play. Donne's praise of folly, then, is instrumental in producing what he considers as theologically valid historical *action*, a mode of attaining health through the "sickness" of folly in exegesis or understanding.

If there are such things as truth, health, divine blessing, so this argument would go, then the way towards them is through acts of infidelity and betrayal (revelation), through a "sickness unto death", and through the curse of human existence, a curse of secular history in the form of various "bleedings" (in birth and death). Such, at least, is the Donnean theological praise of folly. Lyly's intertwined hands at the close of *Euphues* are re-worked in Donne, in a version or trope which clasps the hands in prayer; and the intertwined hands and legs and eyes of Donne's "profane" verse are "sanitized" in their final realization as an ascetic theological relation, itself productive of instability and even "insanity": "Those are my best days, when I shake with fear".[29]

Notes

[1] Matthew Arnold, *Literature and Dogma* (London: Thomas Nelson and Sons, n.d.), p. 15.

[2] Terence Cave, *The Cornucopian Text* (Oxford: Clarendon Press, 1979), pp. 85–6.

[3] *Idem*, p. 47, p. 48.

[4] Eugene Goodheart, *The Skeptic Disposition in Contemporary Criticism* (Guildford: Princeton University Press, 1985), pp. 57–8, makes a relevant comparison between Marx and Barthes in terms of the kind of "demystificatory reading" which I am suggesting here. He writes: "in the chapter on commodity fetishism, Marx could penetrate the false pretensions of commodities to an 'existence as independent beings endowed with life, which entered into relations with one another and the human race', because he was confident that behind the illusion the real value of the product was ascertainable: the labor expended in its production. And it is not simply the truth or the conviction of truth that Marx possessed. The reality to which the truth corresponded was substantial and filled with promise, for the labor theory of value becomes the justification for the socialist revolution. Demystification may expose a corrupt reality – for example, the exploitation of the working class concealed in the exchange of commodities in the marketplace – but such a reality is substantial and, moreover, contains within it the dialectical possibility of progress to a condition that restores to the worker the product of his labor." For Barthes, demystification is a word which "is beginning to show signs of wear" (Preface to *Mythologies*), and the reason for this, according to Goodheart, is that Barthes lends credence to the

hypothesis that "there is no reality behind illusion", and so, "to 'penetrate the object', is, as Barthes put it, not to liberate it but to destroy it. Demystification for Barthes shows signs of wear because, necessary as it may be, it cannot satisfy the appetite for wholeness, for substantiality, for presence as it did for Marx." The implication of this distinction between Barthes and Marx seems to be that some kind of epistemological grounding is *necessary* as a justification for Marxian revolution; but this is not the case. The exposure of a *version*, the demystification of a transformation, even if it only reveals another version or trope, with no epistemological ground, can reveal the *fact* of transformation. This revelation can itself be instrumental in the demystification of a mode of production; and that is sufficient, in the Marxian analysis, to produce a critical consciousness. The distance between Barthes and Marx in this respect is not so enormous or fundamental. Demystification can be socially productive, even without a guaranteed epistemological verification of its object.

5   Erasmus, *The Praise of Folly*, in John P. Dolan (ed.), *The Essential Erasmus* (New York: Mentor Books, 1964), p. 99.

6   Michel Foucault, *Folie et Déraison* (Paris: Plon, 1961), p. 292.

7   *Idem*, p. 49.

8   The reference here is to Hegel, *Phenomenology of Spirit* (trans. A. V. Miller; Oxford: Oxford University Press, 1977), p. 493. In these closing comments, Hegel writes of the trajectory of Spirit in terms which recall the tragic Christian myth: "The *goal*, Absolute Knowing, or Spirit that knows itself as Spirit, has for its path the recollection of the Spirits as they are in themselves and as they accomplish the organization of their realm. Their preservation, regarded from the side of their free existence appearing in the form of contingency, is History; but regarded from the side of their [philosophically] comprehended organization, it is the Science of Knowing in the sphere of appearance: the two together, comprehended History, form alike the inwardizing and the Calvary of Absolute Spirit, the actuality, truth, and certainty of his throne, without which he would be lifeless and alone." Cf. a telling comment in a footnote by Kenneth Burke, in his *Language as Symbolic Action* (Berkeley and Los Angeles: University of California Press, 1966), p. 20, note 2: "In his *Parts of Animals*, Chapter X, Aristotle mentions the definition of man as the 'laughing animal', but he does not consider it adequate. Though I would hasten to agree, I obviously have a big investment in it, owing to my conviction that mankind's only hope is a cult of comedy. (The cult of tragedy is too eager to help out with the holocaust . . .)" The point of bringing these two together in this context is to indicate that it is in fact the cult of tragedy which is Optimistic: the apocalypse, religious or secular, is seen as some kind of purgatorial experience, which will leave or produce an ameliorated Edenic realm. In tragedy, the "Calvary" leads to the "throne". The "only hope" which Burke writes of, then, is actually a hope of "no hope"; comedy, as my theoretical position here stands, corrects the tendency to tragedy inherent in Optimistic schemes or organizations of history, and is valuable for that reason.

9   Wilbur Samuel Howell, *Logic and Rhetoric in England, 1500–1700* (New Jersey: Princeton University Press, 1956), p. 4; cf. Geoffrey H. Hartman, *Saving the Text* (Baltimore: Johns Hopkins University Press, 1981), p. 91, on Genet's reaction to Giacometti's sculpture: "What is revealed by these

appropriations is the *hand of a thief*, a particular, peculiar *main-tenant*, writing considered as a Discourse of Theft going back to Prometheus and Jason."

10 Howell, *Logic and Rhetoric*, p. 4.

11 See Jacques Derrida, "La mythologie blanche", in *Marges* (Paris: Minuit, 1972); and cf. Richard Rorty, "Philosophy as a Kind of Writing", in *Consequences of Pragmatism* (Minneapolis: University of Minnesota Press, 1982; also published by Harvester (Brighton) in 1982) and Berel Lang, *Philosophy and the Art of Writing* (Lewisburg: Bucknell University Press, 1983).

12 John Lyly, *Euphues*, in James Winny (ed.), *The Descent of Euphues* (Cambridge: Cambridge University Press, 1957), p. 14.

13 Etymologically, strictly speaking, the words euphuism and euphemism, of course, are not directly related: Euphues derives from *eu* = well, *physis* = nature; Euphemism derives from *eu* = well, *pheme* = speaking. The movement, or slippage, between them effected in Donne's writing, is a movement, then, from the body, from Euphues (well-endowed by nature, well-natured) to the voice, Euphemism (well-speaking).

14 John Donne, Elegy 7, in A. J. Smith (ed.), *John Donne: Complete English Poems* (Harmondsworth: Penguin, 1971; repr. 1973), p. 102.

15 The most obvious instances in Shakespeare are in *Hamlet*, IV.v, and in *The Winter's Tale*, IV.iv. There might indeed be a useful argument in which Ophelia is construed as a mother of sorts to Perdita, thus establishing some kind of matriarchal historical lineage of Shakespeare's plays. For a further development of this argument, see my *On Modern Authority* (forthcoming).

16 Frank Kermode, *The Genesis of Secrecy* (Cambridge, Mass.: Harvard University Press, 1979), p. 3.

17 See, in this context, Paul de Man, *The Rhetoric of Romanticism* (New York, Columbia University Press, 1984), p. 262.

18 The link between legibility and legitimacy is an etymological one.

19 John Donne, Satire 2, in Smith (ed.), *John Donne*, p. 158.

20 John Donne, "Air and Angels", in *ed.cit.*, p. 41.

21 Cf. Geoffrey H. Hartman, *The Fate of Reading* (Chicago, Ill.: University of Chicago Press, 1975), p. 255: "The extinction ... of the personal names of *both* author and readers shows what ideally happens in the act of reading: if there is a sacrifice to the exemplary, it involves the aggrandizement neither of author nor of reader but leads into the recognition that something worthy of perpetuation has occurred."

22 Foucault, *Folie et Déraison*, p. 14; italics mine.

23 Paul M. Ochojski, "Did John Donne Repent his Apostasy?", *American Benedictine Review*, 1 (1950), 535–48.

24 Donne, Satire 3, in *ed. cit.*, pp. 162–3.

25 Hartman, *Saving the Text*, p. 79.

26 See the full study from which this essay is an edited extract for many further examples of Donne's name "graved" and "engraved" in stony texts.

27 Erasmus, *The Praise of Folly*, in Dolan (ed.), pp. 151–2; emphasis on "sin" in "insinuation" added.

28 Donne, "The Triple Fool", in *ed. cit.*, p. 81.

29 Donne, Divine Meditation 19, "Oh, to vex me, contraries meet in one", in *ed. cit.*, p. 317.

Love and death in "To his Coy Mistress"

CATHERINE BELSEY

I

"The omnipotence of nature", Philippe Ariès says in his fascinating history of western mortality, "asserts itself in two areas: sex and death."[1] At the same time, these supremely natural areas of experience do not, at least in their human manifestation, exist outside culture. People have always, we may reasonably assume, made love, and always died. But the meanings of love and death are discursively and historically specific. Marvell's poem, which may well have been drafted in 1649, the year when the execution of Charles I emblematically established the end of the old order of sovereignty and subjection, can be seen as marking the border between two regimes of discourse, bringing into collision two distinct sets of meanings for these terms and for the relationship between them. As a poem about love and death, "To his Coy Mistress" may be read as displaying the cultural relativity and the historical instability of those areas which assert themselves as so self-evidently natural.

Formally the poem promises a certain transparency. This is a persuasion to love which apparently sets out to convince rather than to perplex or to dazzle. The structure, as is widely recognized, is that of a logical argument:

> Had we but World enough, and Time,
> This coyness Lady were no crime. (lines 1–2)

> But at my back I alwaies hear
> Times winged Charriot hurrying near. (lines 21–2)

> Now therefore . . . (line 33)[2]

The octosyllabic couplets effortlessly reproduce the word-order and the rhythm of speech: there are very few inversions. And this, in conjunction with the familiarity of the vocabulary, lends a certain laconic quality to the hyperbole of the first section of the poem and the macabre imagery of the second. The result is a combination of poise and intensity which is hard to resist.

To his Coy Mistress

    Had we but World enough, and Time,
    This coyness Lady were no crime.
    We would sit down, and think which way
    To walk, and pass our long Loves Day.
    Thou by the *Indian Ganges* side
    Should'st Rubies find: I by the Tide
    Of *Humber* would complain. I would
    Love you ten years before the Flood:
    And you should if you please refuse
10 Till the Conversion of the *Jews*.

La patriarche et Le connesta
Guyot de Marchant, 1

    My vegetable Love should grow
    Vaster then Empires, and more slow.
    An hundred years should go to praise
    Thine Eyes, and on thy Forehead Gaze.
    Two hundred to adore each Breast:
    But thirty thousand to the rest.
    An Age at least to every part,
    And the last Age should show your Heart.
    For Lady you deserve this State;
20 Nor would I love at lower rate.
      But at my back I alwaies hear
    Times winged Charriot hurrying near:
    And yonder all before us lye
    Desarts of vast Eternity.
    Thy Beauty shall no more be found;
    Nor, in thy marble Vault, shall sound
    My ecchoing Song: then Worms shall try
    That long preserv'd Virginity:
    And your quaint Honour turn to dust;
30 And into ashes all my Lust.
    The Grave's a fine and private place,
    But none I think do there embrace.
      Now therefore, while the youthful hew

    Sits on thy skin like morning dew,
    And while thy willing Soul transpires
    At every pore with instant Fires,
    Now let us sport us while we may;
    And now, like am'rous birds of prey,
    Rather at once our Time devour,
40 Than languish in his slow-chapt pow'r.

From the *Danse Macabre des Fem*
Paris, 1

    Let us roll all our Strength, and all
    Our sweetness, up into one Ball:
    And tear our Pleasures with rough strife,
    Thorough the Iron gates of Life.
    Thus, though we cannot make our Sun
    Stand still, yet we will make him run.

Like so many Renaissance lyrics, the poem offers itself as a text of performance. It is neither directly addressed to the reader, simulating the spontaneous overflow of powerful feelings, nor yet a fully fledged dramatic monologue, specifying an ironic relationship between speaker and author, speaker and reader. The poem is presented as a speech, or perhaps a rehearsal of a speech, a marshalling of the arguments, addressed to a mistress. The reader is offered a position outside the event as a third person, present and absent, an observer, detached and knowing.

And yet by the end of the poem what precisely is it that we know? Is the text an invitation to savour the rhetoric of seduction (Marvell's control, wit, urbanity), or to celebrate the punishment of feminine coyness (the body of the mistress is anatomized, buried and then desecrated)? Or are we to delight in the triumph of love over time and death, as most critics have assumed? Or alternatively does the relationship identified in the text between love and death call in question, in ways these readings ignore, the system of differences that we, as twentieth-century readers, take for granted?

The argument of the poem depends on a series of oppositions between time and eternity, active and passive, life and death, and also on the transgression of the antitheses between them. The first section defines a world of infinite space and time:

> We would sit down, and think which way
> To walk, and pass our long Loves Day.
> Thou by the *Indian* Ganges side
> Should'st Rubies find: I by the Tide
> Of *Humber* would complain. I would
> Love you ten years before the Flood:
> And you should if you please refuse
> Till the Conversion of the *Jews*.   (lines 3–10)

This rich imaginary world embraces the exotic and the familiar, east and west (the Ganges, the Humber), past and future (the Flood, the Conversion of the Jews), wealth and deprivation (rubies, complaints). It contains everything – everything, that is, except action. To love is to sit down, think, complain, gaze, adore.

> An hundred years should go to praise
> Thine Eyes, and on thy Forehead Gaze.
> Two hundred to adore each Breast:
> But thirty thousand to the rest.   (lines 13–16)

The promise for the lover is "vegetable Love" (line 11), like the Aristotelian vegetable soul, endowed with life but not motion, and for the lady "State", ceremony (line 19). For them both endless courtship and endless refusal, coyness endlessly endorsed.

The absurdity is crucial to the rhetorical project. It depends on the precision of the arithmetic (one hundred years for eyes and forehead, two hundred per breast . . .), and on the vegetable love, a giant plant, "Vaster then Empires" (line 12). The comedy throws into relief the limitations of an imaginary plenitude which is the effect of a gaze moving epoch by epoch across the dissected fragments of a woman's body: "An Age at least to every part" (line 17).

But the poem never doubted the impossibility of its own golden world. The plenitude of the first section is precisely imaginary: "Had we but World enough, and Time . . . we would . . . you should . . ." In the rhetoric of the proposition it is the imminence of death which constitutes the imperative to action:

> yonder all before us lye
> Desarts of vast Eternity.
> Thy Beauty shall no more be found;
> Nor, in thy marble Vault, shall sound
> My ecchoing Song: then Worms shall try
> That long preserv'd Virginity:
> And your quaint Honour turn to dust;
> And into ashes all my Lust.   (lines 23–30)

Death makes a desert of eternity – and of honour, body, lust, poem and all. "Now therefore . . .", the text urges, "let us sport us" (lines 33, 37). Death introduces into the continuous and motionless plenitude of timeless adoration the mortal difference which has the effect of redefining love as action.

Time moves: its hurrying chariot threatens lovers, propels them towards eternal emptiness. Worms act, penetrating virgin cadavers. Death actively pulverizes beauty and coyness and desire to supply the deserts of vast eternity. To stay ahead, the text proposes, the lovers are to construct a counter-sphere, a full and continuous globe of their own, a new world of love in motion, all strength, all sweetness, all states, all princes, complete with its own (pre-Copernican) sun which, in contrast to Donne's in "The Sun Rising", will have to race to keep up with them:

> Let us roll all our Strength, and all
> Our sweetness, up into one Ball:
> And tear our Pleasures with rough strife,
> Thorough the Iron gates of Life.
> Thus, though we cannot make our Sun
> Stand still, yet we will make him run.   (lines 41–6)

The logic of the argument, of course, does not hold. It was a woman, perhaps less impressed than some of her critical predecessors by the display of masculinity they found in the poem, who perceptively pointed out that the argument was not valid. If we had time we should wait; but we don't; so we shouldn't. " 'It does not follow', the lady might have replied."[3]

And if the logic is false so, however erotically enticing, is the rhetoric. It was another woman who suggested that "To his Coy Mistress" was not really a seduction poem at all, "but something much lonelier: it tells, not woos, and what it tells is not encouraging".[4]

> The Grave's a fine and private place,
> But none I think do there embrace.
> Now therefore . . .   (lines 31–3)

And yet in the margins of the difference which it is the apparent project of the poem to cement as opposition, the antithesis between love and death, morning and perpetual night, the sexual act and the passivity of decomposition, a figure steals out of the tomb to haunt the embrace which the grave itself excludes. Love is urgent because death threatens; love is action because time devours. It is the Ovidian commonplace which makes the logical and rhetorical case against delay. But the poem's alternative is that the lovers themselves should supplant time, simultaneously emulating and accelerating time's gradual consuming process: "Rather at once our Time devour, / Than languish in his slow-chapt pow'r" (lines 39–40). To act is to behave like time and death.

But in the economy of the poem to take time's place is to speed towards the desert, and to accelerate the process is to hurtle through the gates of life. An earlier version of the text makes the point more sharply: "Lett us att once our Selves devoure . . ."[5] Love, death's opposite, is also its double in the "rough strife" which identifies the lovers as falcons, tearing their pleasures. The verbs, establishing the antithesis between the first section of the poem and the third, simultaneously indicate a parallel between the third section and the second. Love is like death – as violent and as destructive. As the rhythm drives the text forward, repeatedly eliminating the caesura (lines 35–6, 40, 44), the act of love sweeps the lovers through the gates of life, speeding up the sun and thus propelling them towards death. Love acts like death; sex is deadly; to make love is to die. And so the poem invokes without citing it the seventeenth-century pun which has so delighted generations of students.

II

In the fifteenth and sixteenth centuries the Dance of Death was familiar all over Europe. During the 1420s it was painted, with accompanying verses, round the walls of the Cemetery of the Holy Innocents in Paris, where it formed a backdrop to sermons, social events, commercial exchanges, illicit meetings and prostitution. It was, in other words, part of life. It subsequently decorated the walls of the Pardon Churchyard of St Paul's Cathedral in London, where it remained until the churchyard was demolished in 1549, with verses translated from the French by Lydgate. There is evidence to suggest that the Dance was widely imitated in a number of churches in England and Scotland, including the parish church of Stratford-upon-Avon.[6] Its most famous representation is probably the series of woodcuts designed by Holbein and printed in 1538. It is to be found in miniature in a number of Books of Hours, and in at least one Anglican book of prayers printed in 1578. It survives in seventeenth-century England as a ballad with woodcut illustrations.

In the Dance of Death emaciated cadavers seize as partners living men and women, each representing a specific social position, usually beginning with the Pope and the Emperor and including the Ploughman, the Peasant or perhaps the Beggar. Rhythm and movement are the property of the desiccated figures: the living hang back, reluctant to join the dance, coy. The gestures of the dead are not overtly erotic, but the irony of the Dance of Death depends on the parallel between love and death. In Lydgate's English version Death tells the Lady of Great Estate that she must now learn a new dance step. The Lady acknowledges that there is no remedy. "Dethe hath yn erthe no ladi ne maiestresse / And on his daunce yitte moste I nedes fote."[7] More explicitly, in a sixteenth-century version Death takes hold of a princess with the words, "Content you, I am your mate."[8]

There is no defiance among the living. Death's invitation is recognized as irresistible, inexorable and final. In consequence mortal sexuality is seen to be vain and fleeting in the context of eternity. The parallel between love and death also marks an ironic distance between them. (As another of Marvell's poems reminds us, parallel lines, "though infinite can never meet".[9]) In Guyot Marchant's version of the Dance of Death, printed in 1485, the Squire claims a moment as Death accosts him to bid farewell to earthly pleasures: "Adieu deduis, adieu solas, / Adieu dames". The Knight's boast as he joins the dance that he has been loved by the ladies is no more than a pathetic irrelevance.[10] Lydgate's Baron was accustomed to dance with women, but he finds that Death has made him lame.[11] A ballad version, probably printed in 1625, shows Death in the company of Time, who has wings (but no chariot), an hourglass and a scythe. In this text Death is more specific than some of his predecessors about the pleasures he destroys:

> And you that lean on your Ladies laps,
>   and lay your heads upon their knee,
> Think you for to play with beautious paps
>   and not to come and dance with me:
> No, fair Lords and Ladies all,
> I will make you come when I do call,
> And find you a Pipe to dance withal.[12]

In a French book of hours dating from the mid sixteenth century (MS. Douce, 135) a miniature Dance of Death decorates the Office of the Dead. At the foot of the pages depicting Death and the Emperor a lover shows his mistress her face in a glass. No sooner are they married than Death, in a grim parody of the god of love, aims his dart at them as they stroll together in the fields. Death is equally indifferent to the youth and beauty of Lydgate's Amorous Gentlewoman. Polixena, Penelope and Helen were just as handsome, and they all joined the dance.[13]

Love is momentary, death eternal. But the Dance of Death also exposes the instability of other earthly values – glory, wealth and power. Death releases the soul from its temporal and temporary alliance with the body, leaving the corruptible flesh to inevitable decay. The project of the Dance of Death is to invite the spectator to see the world and flesh in their transience, and to view them in consequence with a proper contempt, choosing instead the spiritual values which promise eternal life. Death itself is an affair of the body.

Medieval asceticism leaves its mark on "To his Coy Mistress". The body devoured by worms was a common warning against worldly pride. The image of a beautiful woman attacked by worms in the grave served as a reminder of the mutability of the flesh.[14]

> Thy Beauty shall no more be found;
> Nor, in thy marble Vault, shall sound
> My ecchoing Song: then Worms shall try
> That long preserv'd Virginity.   (lines 25–8)

In medieval representations of the punishment of lechery, sin of the flesh, serpents twined themselves round the body of a woman, sucking at her breasts and entering her vagina.

It is not necessary to argue that Marvell was personally familiar with these images, or with the Dance of Death, though he may have been. Lydgate's text of the Dance of Death was reprinted by Tottel in 1554, and new versions appeared in ballad form with graphic woodcuts in 1569, 1580(?), 1625(?) and 1631. "To his Coy Mistress" itself makes clear that the images, and the contempt of the world which they urge on the spectator, were wholly intelligible in the first half of the seventeenth century.

But there intervenes between the Dance and Marvell's poem the Renaissance discovery of the *carpe diem* tradition of Latin poetry, which recognizes a similar network of differences between love and death, but reverses the values. In innumerable Renaissance poems daffodils, roses, dew, snow, spring and all of nature conspire to demonstrate the worth of things that perish. The imminence and the eternity of death makes sex more urgent, its pleasures more intense. The body is precious because it dies.

Marvell's poem also participates in this reversal of values. It is chastity, not lechery, which is punished after death by worms. In the Dance of Death the dead mimic lovers: in "To his Coy Mistress" it is love which emulates death. To choose love rather than asceticism is to defy eternity and choose the world, to choose to be a world. And yet the imagery of this challenge, the imagery of emulation, abolishes the opposition between love and death set up in the first two sections of the poem and thus, ironically, reinstates asceticism. To make love is to die; to choose the world and the flesh is to repudiate the values which promise eternal life; to choose the pleasures of the body is thus to reject immortality. In its account of time and death the poem reproduces the terms of the medieval contempt of the world. Indeed, in the mid seventeenth century it cannot escape them. At the same time it defies them. Asceticism condemns the world as inadequate, as merely temporal. The poem's lovers, also recognizing the inadequacy of the temporal world, make their own world, and opt for that – and in doing so they opt for death.

III

In the late middle ages the iconography of death was elaborate, complex and pervasive. In the Renaissance death invaded the newly defined privacy of the home in the form of skulls displayed among the furniture or reflections on mortality inscribed on mantelpieces and sundials.[15] Death's-heads commonly decorated personal possessions, jewellery and weapons.[16]

But in the twentieth century death has become unspeakable. Death is concealed from our knowledge as far as possible. Friends and relations often preserve in conjunction with the dying person a conspiracy of silence, of apparent ignorance, of optimism. We debate whether the doctor should tell the patient the truth. The moment of death is a private one: the family no longer assemble at the bedside. Death tends increasingly to take place in the solitude of the hospital. Children are kept away, perhaps not told: death is an adult secret. Sudden death is a blessing: "at least we have the satisfaction of knowing that she knew nothing about it". Mourning has become a discreet and reticent affair compared with the elaborate funerals of earlier periods. It is a consequence of individualism that the death of the individual is no longer the concern of the community. Monuments, unless to public figures, are rare. Sorrow, however, is no less intense for that. On the contrary, it has become an inner, private anguish to which ritual cannot do justice – that within which passes show. Meanwhile, the bereavement of other people is a source of embarrassment, a topic to be avoided. An interest in death is morbid. As Ariès, who lists most of these modern developments, suggests, "this is a way of denying the presence of death in practice, even if one accepts its reality in principle . . . Death has been banished."[17]

At the end of his elegant and challenging book, *Renaissance Self-Fashioning*, Stephen Greenblatt recounts how he was unable to mime the words, "I want to die". He had been asked to do so by a stranger on a plane, whose suicidal son, he understood, had lost the power of speech. The stranger was anxious to try out his own ability to lip-read. Why, Greenblatt wonders, could he not carry out the man's request. Superstition? Fear that his fellow passenger was some kind of homicidal maniac? The desire to be the author of his own sentences?[18] All those things, perhaps, and, I suggest from a post-structuralist point of view, one more: that the self, the subject, constructs itself in the act of speaking, is an effect of its own utterances, and that the supreme fear of the modern self, the subject of liberal humanism, is the fear of death. To say, "I want to die" is simultaneously to produce the self and to will the abolition it dreads.

Liberal humanism makes the subject sovereign, the ultimate location of presence. In liberal humanism the subject is absolute. While Marvell was putting the finishing touches to his poem in the 1670s, Locke had already begun his twenty years' work on *An Essay Concerning Human Understanding*, which theorized the nature of subjectivity in the new order of sovereignty brought about by the Revolution of the 1640s against the absolutism of Charles I. In the *Essay*, published in 1690, Locke makes clear that the only evidence we have of the existence of anything outside ourselves is our experience of it. That we exist, on the other hand, is self-evident, and here Locke amplifies Descartes. My experience confirms that I exist: "I think, I reason, I feel pleasure and pain"; and if I doubt that, my very doubt confirms my existence (IV.ix.3).[19]

Even God cannot be shown to exist independently of the subject. The evidence that God exists is that I exist as a knowing subject and, since nothing can come of nothing, there must eternally have been something intelligent and knowing (IV.x). Locke's humanism is, as the term implies, basically (though not very explicitly) secular. The subject is the guarantee of the existence of God. Good and evil are no more than what is synonymous with our pleasure and pain (II.xx.2). The afterlife is never identified as more than a probability (II.xxi.70), a matter of faith (IV.xviii.7). The subject itself is the only certainty.

In Locke's account the origin of knowledge is experience, and the subject is the place where experience is assembled and interpreted. Experience shows that people die. We know therefore that we die, but we do not know what death is like. We cannot have experience of our own death. Death is fearful because it is in this sense unknown. When Claudio in *Measure for Measure* thinks of death with horror for this reason, "Ay, but to die, and go we know not where" (III.i.119), or when Hamlet dreads "something after death – / The undiscover'd country" (*Hamlet*, III.i.78–9),[20] they approach the modern consciousness of death as the unknown and unknowable.

But if in liberal humanism the evidence for the existence of the world is the existence of the subject, nonetheless the liberal-humanist subject needs the world as other, as that which defines the subject by its difference. The subject is necessarily a knowing subject, differentiated as an entity from the objects of its knowledge. Knowledge (experience) is the guarantee of our existence as subjects, of the consciousness which, according to Locke in the seventeenth century – and to common sense in the twentieth – constitutes personal identity (II.i.11). But our death exceeds consciousness. It is an end to consciousness of which, precisely, we cannot be conscious. That our own death is unknowable thus marks the sovereign subject as finite in more than a merely chronological sense. The fear of death is the recognition of the limits of the subject's imaginary sovereignty.

This absence at the heart of consciousness brings the subject to confront that other absence which is the condition of its being. As an effect of language, the subject is never able to be fully present to itself in its own utterances. From moment to moment, as it speaks, the self which is the guarantee of the world slips, slides and perishes in the very act of affirming its own supremacy. The project of liberal humanism is to reaffirm the sovereign subject by denying the discontinuity of the self.

The nineteenth century specialized in ways of disavowing death, defining it as the gateway to heaven, a sort of large-scale home (what could be more inviting?) beyond the sky, where loved ones would recognize each other and be reunited. But in the more sceptical twentieth century the fear of death is correspondingly more acute. Freud, who so shrewdly observed the emotional contortions of the liberal-humanist subject, draws attention to the contradiction between our recognition that everyone must die and our evasion of the thought of our own death. He also points to the solution we tend to propose: "It is indeed impossible to imagine our own death; and whenever we attempt to do so we can perceive that we are in fact still present as spectators."[21] By this ingenious means the secular subject reasserts its own immortality, preserving its knowing essence as it imagines itself hovering over its own body, watching how the world goes on, missing people – and being missed. Even suicides, who must seem, after all, a counter-example to the modern denial of death, tend apparently to share this impulse. Writers of suicide notes commonly pay considerable attention to the future. They often "appear to be profoundly interested in what is going to happen after their death, as if they were still going to participate in events".[22]

What survives in this imagined future is consciousness, identity. The denial of death thus reaffirms the sovereignty of the subject. Greenblatt, who began, he says, by assuming the autonomy of the subject, and came increasingly to doubt it, ends his narrative and his book as follows:

I have related this brief story of my encounter with the distraught father on the plane because I want to bear witness at the close to my overwhelming need to sustain the illusion that I am the principal maker of my own identity.[23]

But "To his Coy Mistress", acknowledging death, makes no attempt to sustain such an illusion. Marvell's speaker hears time's chariot; his gaze encounters the deserts of vast eternity; his lust is turned to ashes. His song, the poem, the utterance which constructs the speaker as subject, is inaudible in the grave. If it is the fate of the woman's body which most appals and thrills us in the second section of the poem, the force and strangeness of that medieval image should not distract us from this new element in the text, death as the end of consciousness, of desire as well as of the body which is its object.

> The Grave's a fine and private place,
> But none I think do there embrace.   (lines 31–2)

What is the sense of that "I think"? Hesitant, possibly, or perhaps admonitory. But does it not also mark the tentative entry of the Cartesian *cogito* into the terrain of death, a terrain which has hitherto been above all that of the body?

IV

In the middle ages people were surrounded by the iconography of death. But as early as 1658 the Dance of Death had already become a matter of antiquarian interest, reprinted as an appendix to Dugdale's *History of St Paul's Cathedral*. In the twentieth century it is the iconography of love which everywhere proclaims our commitment to life. Advertising, popular music, novels and films make sexuality synonymous with vitality, with psychic and bodily health. In the system of differences brought into being in the seventeenth century, the set of meanings which frame our modern convictions and practices, romantic love and marriage become indissolubly linked with each other and with life.[24] The conjugal family, as the authorized location of the creation of life in a literal sense, centres on the loving couple, whose concord guarantees the growth of their children in moral and physical health. As the alternative to the brutality and impersonality of the market, its other, the family constitutes and circumscribes the legitimate realm of intimate and intense feeling.

From this moment onwards until the nineteenth century, fiction becomes increasingly concerned with the family and family relationships. The obvious identity of love with life, and of both with the family, is reaffirmed in a great many mid-Victorian novels. Lucy Snowe, for instance, heroine of *Villette* and, like so many nineteenth-century protagonists, an orphan (what could be worse?), is haunted by the figure of a spectral nun, emblem of the loveless and thus deadly future she dreads. Caroline Helstone in *Shirley*, another orphan, begins to decline spiritually and physically when she is cut off from the love of Robert Moore. There is nothing organically wrong, but gradually Caroline at eighteen begins to share the "bloodless pallor" and the "corpse-like" appearance of the "old maids" the novel struggles so valiantly to treat with respect. The effects of unrequited love are defined in the imagery of death:

she wasted, grew more joyless and more wan . . . an elegy over the past still rung constantly in her ear; a funereal inward cry haunted and harassed her: the heaviness of a broken spirit, and of pining and palsifying faculties, settled slow on her buoyant youth. Winter seemed conquering her spring: the mind's soils and its treasures were freezing gradually to barren stagnation.[25]

Shirley's friendship, though precious, is not enough to protect her, and Caroline slowly sinks towards death. It is her long-lost mother who saves her life, and the love of Robert which restores her to youth and beauty with "the cordial of heart's ease".[26] Within the family, and within romantic love which is its foundation, is health and vitality: outside it, solitude and death. The figure of Miss Havisham, in *Great Expectations*, skeletal in her faded wedding dress which is also a shroud, conflates the elegiac and the Gothic strands in the Victorian image of the sexless woman. Abandoned on what was to have been her wedding day, Miss Havisham, in a grotesque parody of motherhood, brings up Estella an enemy to love and life.

But the equation of life with love is not confined to women, though they are its foremost victims. The dividing line between public and private, economic and affective, is transgressed by Mr Dombey, who has no identity outside his firm ("the House"), and who brings death into his home in consequence. Incapable of love, and thus deadly to his first wife and to the doomed son who is permitted to be no more than a repetition of his own (public and economic) being, Mr Dombey dismisses little Paul's nurse, the apple-cheeked and fecund Polly Toodle, and consigns him to the care of the loveless Cornelia Blimber, "dry and sandy with working in the graves of deceased languages. None of your live languages for Miss Blimber. They must be dead – stone dead."[27] The dying Paul solicits and secures the love of everyone in that unloving academy, but the totality of their kindness does not stand in for the vital and vitalizing love of father and mother. Without such nourishment he shrinks and fades.

The coerciveness of this series of equations of life with love and love with the family is at once apparent. Emotional fulfilment is to be found within the family and not outside it. Friendship is always secondary. Celibacy is a kind of death. The world of work is legitimately harsh, since the family provides what the market-place fails to supply. And meanwhile, the economic and political relations which exist within the patriarchal family are disavowed, dissolved in the naturalness of domestic concord.

In the twentieth century attention narrows to the sexual relation itself. Connie Chatterley, married to an impotent husband, begins to lose touch with "the substantial and vital world".[28] The terms are familiar: there is nothing organically wrong, but she wastes. The doctor tells her, "You're spending your life without renewing it . . . You're spending your vitality without making any."[29] Sexual experience brings her back to life – or rather to life for the first time. The male sensuality of Mellors causes Connie at last to be "born: a woman".[30] In a society which is rapidly losing touch with the primordial centre of the truly human, Mellors holds on to the real value of the sexual. "For me it's the core of my life: if I have a right relation with a woman."[31] A right relation: the coercion is there again, and more palpably in this overtly proselytizing work. Mellors has already systematically listed all the possible wrong relations – which is to say the wrong kinds of sexual behaviour on the part of women.[32]

Lawrence was familiar with the work of Freud,[33] and would no doubt have endorsed Freud's valuation of "the greatest pleasure attainable by us, that of the sexual act".[34] It was in the 1920s in *Beyond the Pleasure Principle* and *The Ego and the Id* that Freud helped to cement the existing system of differences by theorizing an opposition between two contrary drives, the sexual which presses towards life, and the death drive which issues in hate, destructiveness or sadism. Though Freud concedes that the death drive may be brought into the service óf sexuality,[35] and that love may alternate with hate,[36] the texts struggle to keep sex and death apart, insisting that there is a fundamental opposition between them.[37] A similar opposition informs the work of Freud's most Oedipal of descendants, Gilles Deleuze and Félix Guattari, who propose an antithesis between paranoid/fascist signification, which is deadly, and the liberation of desire in schizo-revolutionary nonsense.[38]

How can we account for this great dualism of love and death in liberal humanism? Conjecturally, by returning to the subject, so absolute and yet so precarious. Identity is an effect of language. Subjects are constituted and take up their places in discourses which define "reality", a set of evident truths, perceived and lived, experienced. But the maintenance of their subject-positions depends on the constant and reiterated confirmation of this reality, a complicity with other subjects to recognize the same objects of knowledge, to share their experience. Our social organization divides work from leisure, the public and the political from the personal. The public world offers confirmation that subjects participate adequately in the consensual knowledges in the form of material rewards, promotion or prestige. It thus reaffirms their identity. In the personal realm, however, only sexual love, the sexual act, self-evidently requires the undivided attention of subjects to each other, depends on a complicity to share the same experience, and promises the reassurance that that implies. Hence the value attached to simultaneous orgasm. Lovers act as mirrors for each other, reflect back in the act an experience of loving each other's imaginary identity. Reciprocal love is the affirmation of the subject, as death is its dissolution.

V

But in the seventeenth century the liberal-humanist dualism of love and death was not yet fixed, and an ironic parallel between them was still in play. The collision between two orders of sovereignty and subjectivity which took place in the period produced strange and shifting alignments between love and death. The swooning death, the quasi-sexual beatitude of the expiring Counter-Reformation saints, is one of these. The element of sadistic pleasure that invades the depiction of violence and torture in the baroque era is another. Marvell's poem is distinct from either. If "To his Coy Mistress" identifies a similarity as well as a distance between love and death, it does not confuse the two.

But the obscurity of the third section of the poem, its difficulty for us now, is, I suggest, an effect of its historical moment. The majority of twentieth-century readings, in quest of coherence, the single, unified meaning which is the impress of the author-subject's consciousness, follow the text's apparent logic (if . . . but . . . therefore . . .), and treat the final section as a celebration of love and life victorious over time and death. Read in this way, the poem elegantly restates an evident truth, confirms the familiar antithesis between love and death, and so reaffirms our experience and thus our identity.

There is, however, a motive for refusing this majority reading, seeking out instead a set of inter-discursive relations that the poem does not name but cannot ignore, a collision between the asceticism it both defies and defers to and the humanism which it cannot yet recognize. Read in this way, the poem indicates that there have been other dispositions of knowledge, that in the mid seventeenth century (liberal-humanist) consciousness began to supplant the (medieval) soul and to invade the realm of the body, bringing about a new alignment of love and death, and a new place for the body and its pleasures.

Our sense of history determines our sense of the present, of its naturalness and inevitability on the one hand, or its relativity on the other. To read texts from the past in their historical difference is to relativize the present, to locate it as a moment in a continuing process of change. It is consequently to release the present – and the future – from the determinism of the natural, and so to place them both rather more firmly in our hands.

Notes

[1] Philippe Ariès, *The Hour of our Death*, tr. Helen Weaver (Harmondsworth: Penguin, 1983), p. 392.

[2] H. M. Margoliouth (ed.), *The Poems and Letters of Andrew Marvell*, revised by Pierre Legouis and E. E. Duncan Jones, vol. 1, *The Poems* (Oxford: Oxford University Press, 1971). All references are to this edition.

[3] Barbara Herrnstein Smith, *Poetic Closure* (Chicago, Ill.: University of Chicago Press, 1968), p. 134.

[4] Barbara Everett, "The Shooting of the Bears: poetry and politics in Andrew Marvell", *Andrew Marvell: essays on the tercentenary of his death*, ed.

120   CATHERINE BELSEY

R. L. Brett (Oxford: University of Hull and Oxford University Press, 1979), pp. 62–103, p. 70.
5 Quoted in Michael Craze, *The Life and Lyrics of Andrew Marvell* (London: Macmillan, 1979), p. 322.
6 James M. Clark, *The Dance of Death in the Middle Ages and the Renaissance* (Glasgow: Jackson, Son and Co., 1950), p. 15.
7 Florence Warren (ed.), *The Dance of Death*, Early English Text Society O.S. 181 (London: Oxford University Press, 1931), Ellesmere MS., lines 194–5.
8 Richard Day, *A Booke of Christian Prayers* (London, 1578), p. 94v.
9 "The Definition of Love", Margoliouth ed., *Poems and Letters*.
10 Edward F. Chaney (ed.), *La Danse Macabre* (Manchester: Manchester University Press, 1945), lines 235–6, 204.
11 Warren (ed.), *The Dance of Death*, Ellesmere MS., lines 173–83.
12 *The Doleful Dance and Song of Death* (London(?), 1625(?)).
13 Warren (ed.), *The Dance of Death*, Ellesmere MS., lines 449–53.
14 Kathleen Cohen, *Metamorphosis of a Death Symbol* (Berkeley: University of California Press, 1973), pp. 29–30 and fig. 10.
15 Ariès, *The Hour of our Death*, pp. 330–1.
16 For examples see William R. Levin, *Images of Love and Death in Late Medieval and Renaissance Art* (Ann Arbor: The University of Michigan Museum of Art, 1976).
17 Ariès, *The Hour of our Death*, p. 580.
18 Stephen Greenblatt, *Renaissance Self-Fashioning* (Chicago and London: University of Chicago Press, 1980), pp. 255–6.
19 John Locke, *An Essay Concerning Human Understanding*, ed. Peter H. Nidditch (Oxford: Oxford University Press, 1975). All references are to this edition.
20 William Shakespeare, *The Complete Works*, ed. Peter Alexander (London and Glasgow: Collins, 1951).
21 Sigmund Freud, "Thoughts for the Times on War and Death", *The Standard Edition of the Complete Works*, vol. 14 (London: Hogarth Press, 1957), pp. 273–302, p. 289.
22 Erwin Stengel, *Suicide and Attempted Suicide* (Harmondsworth: Penguin, 1964), p. 36.
23 Greenblatt, *Renaissance Self-Fashioning*, p. 257.
24 Catherine Belsey, *The Subject of Tragedy* (London: Methuen, 1985) pp. 206–16.
25 Charlotte Brontë, *Shirley*, ed. Andrew and Judith Hook (Harmondsworth: Penguin, 1974), pp. 195, 199.
26 Ibid., p. 557.
27 Charles Dickens, *Dombey and Son*, ed. Alan Horsman (Oxford: Oxford University Press, 1982), p. 120.
28 D. H. Lawrence, *Lady Chatterley's Lover* (Harmondsworth: Penguin, 1960), p. 21.
29 Ibid., p. 81.
30 Ibid., p. 181.
31 Ibid., p. 213.

[32]Ibid., pp. 208–12.

[33] Stephen Heath, *The Sexual Fix* (London: Macmillan, 1982), p. 102.

[34] This is not offered as a declaration of personal preference: it lays claim to the status of a scientific truth. Sigmund Freud, *Beyond the Pleasure Principle*, *The Standard Edition of the Complete Works*, vol. 18 (London: Hogarth Press, 1955), p. 62.

[35] Sigmund Freud, *Pleasure Principle*, p. 54; *The Ego and the Id*, *The Standard Edition of the Complete Works*, vol. 19 (London: Hogarth Press, 1961), p. 41.

[36] Freud, *The Ego and the Id*, pp. 42–4.

[37] So firmly is sex identified with life that Freud sees the fear of death as in reality a development of the fear of castration, *The Ego and the Id*, p. 58.

[38] Gilles Deleuze and Félix Guattari, *Anti-Oedipus: Capitalism and Schizophrenia* (New York: Viking, 1977); Félix Guattari, *Molecular Revolution* (Harmondsworth: Penguin, 1984).

Towards the autonomous subject in poetry: Milton's "On His Blindness"

ANTONY EASTHOPE

It is convenient to begin with a recent essay on "The Continuity of Milton's Sonnets". William McCarthy argues that the twenty-three sonnets (he sets aside the caudate one "On the new forcers") published in 1645, 1673 and 1694 "are a sequence",[1] numbers 1 to 6 representing young love, 8 to 18 maturity and 20 to 23 retirement, with number 7 ("How soon hath Time") and number 19 ("On his Blindess") as turning-points in the series. The argument is convincing, and given that these are Renaissance sonnets it is hard to see how they could not be read as a sequence. Nevertheless McCarthy's argument gives him some anxiety. The sonnets were clearly written and published at different times over forty years; McCarthy cannot feel secure in reading them in sequence unless this is guaranteed by a conscious intention in an individual mind, John Milton, the "real man" behind the "implied author" of the poems. In default of this intention he fears collapse into absolute relativism, reading the sonnets "only as I construe them". As he recognizes, the difficulty is that "we lack access to Milton's consciousness" – apart from the texts – and so he imputes intention to the fact that many (not all) of the sonnets were published together in 1673 and thus "brought by Milton deliberately to our attention". He also admits (in a footnote) that "Milton ordered his sonnets chiefly in the process of writing them".[2]

The unnecessary and impossible search for a transcendental subject – the "real man" "behind" the text – is familiar in literary criticism. As is its necessary consequence: that the reader in the present should be alienated from his or her own productive energies while the text is expropriated as the private property of its supposed metasubject, the Author. Serious literary analysis has recently made advances on the basis that the subject is constituted as an effect of discourse; there is no space, no "John Milton" behind the discourse in which the sonnets take place; subject position is effected across the text and its readings.

The sonnets are texts whose materiality resists, cannot be exhausted in any reading. Further they are historical texts which work to inscribe

122

a subject position determined historically and not just psycho-analytically, a subject-in-history. While deriving from the basic conception, some modes of analysis, as in a recent book on genre, lead to an abstracted and de-historicized version of discourse and subject position: "As Jacques Lacan stressed, 'Repetition demands the new.' Moreover, repetition and difference . . . function as a relation. There is hence not repetition *and* difference, but repetition *in* difference."[3] There is a necessary economy of the subject in which difference is always expressed and contained in repetition. But the forms of this process and structure are historically determinate and historically variable, an expression and containment that is simultaneously ideological. And so it is not "that there is first of all the construction of a subject for social/ideological formations and then the placing of that constructed subject-support in those formations, it is that the two processes are one, in a kind of necessary simultaneity – like the recto and verso of a piece of paper."[4] The specific problem is to provide terms for the subject of discourse in its historical constitution, the historical text and *its* subject.

"Modern poetry is *capitalist* poetry",[5] meaning by "modern" the poetic tradition since the Renaissance. Possibly, then, it will offer an epochal position, the bourgeois conception of the subject as autonomous, self-present, self-originating, hard-edged, defensively phallocratic, "As if a man were author of himself" (*Coriolanus*). But a more specific historical concern poses questions of conjuncture and the need to discriminate within a general poetic development. The distinctions between *discours* and *histoire*, between enunciation and enounced may permit appropriate discriminations to be made between typical and representative texts of Shakespeare, Milton and Dryden.

Enunciation/enounced

We have inherited a grammatical notion that there are three persons: first, second and third. Pointing for example to Arabic grammarians who emphasize the first person ("the one who speaks") as coupled to the second ("the one who is addressed") and contrasted with the third ("the one who is absent"), Benveniste in 1946 argues that "very generally, person is inherent only in the positions 'I' and 'you'. The third person, by virtue of its very structure, is the non-personal form of verbal inflection . . . They contrast as members of a correlation, the correlation of personality: 'I–you' possesses the sign of person; 'he' lacks it."[6] Developing from this (1959) he differentiates two kinds of discourse, *discours* and *histoire*: briefly, *discours* is marked by signs of person while in *histoire* they are absent: "We shall define historical narration as the mode of utterance that excludes 'autobiographical' linguistic form. The historian will never say *je* or *tu* or *maintenant* . . . we shall find only the forms of the 'third person' in a historical narrative strictly followed."[7] In a further development Benveniste goes on to relate "I-you", the mark of *discours*, with enunciation, and Todorov (1972) defines enunciation as "the imprint of the process of uttering on the utterance".[8] As forms of enunciation Todorov lists: personal pronouns (I/you), demonstratives (this/that), relative adverbs and adjectives (here/there), tense of verb, performative verbs ("I swear that"), evaluative and emotive meaning, modifying terms such as "perhaps", "certainly".

At this point in its development the theoretical account risks a technicist error — that is, it risks identifying enunciation with the linguistic *marks* of enunciation. That the equation would be mistaken can be demonstrated in two ways. First on linguistic grounds. Taking up the term "shifters" from Jespersen (1923) and looking back to both Voloshinov and Benveniste on "The Nature of Pronouns" (1956) Roman Jakobson (in 1957) distinguished between "the speech act (*procès de l'énonciation*)" and "the narrated event (*procès de l'énoncé*)" dependent upon it: "four terms are to be distinguished: a narrated event (E^n), a speech event (E^s), a participant of the narrated event (P^n), and a participant of the speech event (P^2), whether addresser or addressee."[9] As there cannot be a signified without a signifier, so there cannot be an enounced without enunciation. It follows that Benveniste's distinction must be reworked: *discours* and *histoire* "are both forms of enunciation, the difference between them lying in the fact that in the discursive form the source of enunciation is present, whereas in the historical it is suppressed."[10] The distinction is not in the enunciation but in the enounced: whether marks of person are present or absent there. Secondly, on grounds of subjectivity. Unless the subject is imagined as metaphysically prior to language,[11] all discourse — including *histoire* — presupposes the subject: "a signifier is that which represents the subject for another signifier".[12] Enunciation precedes enounced; there is always the speaker/listener/reader/writer of the discourse, that is, the subject of enunciation in a determinate position. *Histoire* lacks signs of the subject, *discours* is marked by them — both are forms of the enounced. The difference is that *discours* contains shifters and so a subject of the enounced. Further, even when someone is talking about themselves, the subject of enunciation remains disjunct from the subject of the enounced: "the *I* of the enunciation is not the same as the *I* of the enounced, that is to say, the shifter, which, in the statement, designates him."[13] Since the enounced takes place on the grounds of enunciation, the subject of enunciation can never fully occupy the place of the subject of the enounced. It is as fixity and closure in the enounced that the subject finds a possibility of presence endlessly displaced along the syntagmatic chain in the process of enunciation – a repetition in difference which is the structuring of desire.

These terms relate directly to the analysis of poetry. For the bourgeois tradition – "Modern poetry" – can be defined precisely as a regime of representation aiming to disavow enunciation and its subject in favour of the subject of the enounced.[14] Ideologically predicated on the bourgeois tradition, literary criticism would deny the active productivity of readers in the present. Its central term, the notion of "Imagination", is designed precisely to elide disjunction between subjects of enunciation and enounced. The reader is always the enunciative subject, producing the poem in the continuous present of enunciation, just as from a script actors and technicians produce a play. Milton speaks about his blindness only because I make him. His ghost, however, is not an illusion ("false consciousness") but a material effect of discourse. A full voice, a coherent presence as subject of the enounced is represented through poetic artifice. Its fixity is contrived in various ways, of which four will be emphasized here: the attempt to control sliding of the signifier, to hold signifier onto signified in a sustained syntagmatic order, to contain materiality of language in verse form, to suppress marks of enunciation in the enounced by moving from *discours* to *histoire*.

Shakespeare

Shakespeare's Sonnet 136 was written before 1609. It is not easy to speak and follow, perhaps because it is about female desire and this disturbs the habitual control of male propositional discourse. Its sexual reference is only just kept inexplicit and at a level of innuendo. Modern editors refuse to elucidate it[15] – "will" means sexual desire, "treasure" and "thing" mean vagina ("thing" also later means penis), "prove" means ejaculate:

> If thy soul check thee that I come so near,
> Swear to thy blind soul that I was thy "Will",
> And will thy soul knows is admitted there,
> Thus far for love, my love-suit sweet fulfil.
> "Will", will fulfil the treasure of thy love,
> Ay, fill it full with wills, and my will one,
> In things of great receipt with ease we prove,

Among a number one is reckoned none.
Then in the number let me pass untold,
Though in thy store's account I one must be,
For nothing hold me, so it please thee hold,
That nothing me, a something sweet to thee.
  Make but my name thy love, and love that still,
  And then thou lov'st me for my name is Will.

Sliding of the signifier is most dramatically illustrated here by the seven instances of "will" which variously and simultaneously suggest: wish (both noun and verb), sexual desire, sexual organ, last will and testament, a name (William), part of the future tense. The materiality of the signifier − its active work/play − is thus insisted upon in "fill it full with wills, and my will one", and " 'Will', will fulfil" (a play avoided by say, " 'Will' may fulfil"). There is also instability in "come so near" (= 1. conscience; 2. bed), "treasure", "one", "none", "thing", "nothing" (or "no-thing" in Elizabethan pronunciation), "something"; and sustained ambiguity with "In things of great receipt with ease we prove" (= 1. "It is easy to deal with large numbers of items"; 2. "It is nice to ejaculate in easily available vaginas").

The sliding, the play of will/fill, sounds like the childish pleasure in "treating words as things" analysed by Freud:

I'm Dirty Bill from Vinegar Hill,
Never had a bath and never will.[16]

Strictly this children's rhyme is not nonsense but jest, since language play is already contained in a meaningful sentence, though not one that is "valuable or new or even good".[17] In contrast, to persist with Freud's taxonomy, the play will/fill, is a joke and in fact a tendentious one: will fulfils the treasure of her love, both as Will the man becoming her lover and when sperm fills her vagina.

Overall the floating of the signifier in Sonnet 136 is marginal. Unlike the children's jest it remains a disturbance rather than a disorder of the planes of enunciation and enounced. It is held firmly but not completely onto the signified by closure in the syntagmatic chain. The briefest way to make the point is from a syntactic outline of the sonnet, particularly its conjuctions: "If . . . And . . . Thus . . .", followed by general proposition ("Among a number one is reckoned none" is a mathematical proverb, "one is no number") leading to "Then . . . Though" and a conclusion "Make . . . And then . . . ". It's possible that the very disturbance of the signifier corresponds to the idea of female desire and requires compensation in ideas of number and calculation. Certainly there is syntagmatic closure, the form of a logical argument. The speaker of the enounced (named as Will) is sustained in a general coherence, and the sonnet partakes fully of the tradition by foregrounding enounced over enunciation.

Milton

Milton's sonnet "On his Blindness" (the title added by Newton) is usually dated 1652 or 1655. It refers to a number of passages in the Bible. Whereas the Parable of the Talents (Matthew 25) promises that the servant who hides his one talent (others get five and two) instead of trading with it shall be cast into "outer darkness", the sonnet asserts that the labourer "standing idle in the marketplace" (Matthew 20) is performing adequate service. It is in fact "a flat rejection of the whole point of the parable of the talents":[18]

> When I consider how my light is spent,
> Ere half my days, in this dark world and wide,
> And that one Talent which is death to hide,
> Lodg'd with me useless, though my Soul more bent
> To serve therewith my Maker, and present
> My true account, least he returning chide,
> Doth God exact day labour, light deny'd,
> I fondly ask; But patience to prevent
> That murmur, soon replies, God doth not need
> Either man's work or his own gifts, who best
> Bear his milde yoak, they serve him best, his State
> Is Kingly. Thousands at his bidding speed
> And post o're Land and Ocean without rest:
> They also serve who only stand and waite.

At no point does the signifier insist upon itself, as do will/fill in Shakespeare's sonnet. Rather there is a repeated and controlled oscillation of the signifier over a delimited circle of signifieds. "Light" means sight and inward illumination, "dark" means blindness and fallen human nature, "talent" means a coin and ability, "useless" means not used and not producing interest through usury, "yoak" means wooden cross-piece and the obligation of service, "waite" means attend as a servant and stay in expectation. This consistent movement between concrete and moral abstract as well as the plain diction ("work", "gifts", "bent") rejoins the text to seventeenth-century theological and particularly Puritan discourses. Accumulation of consistent connotation helps to give the language of the sonnet the effect of transparency.

It is now familiar wisdom that in Milton's poetry the reader is to be surprised by syntax: "That the syntax of the octave here seems almost out of control gives the poem a perilous suspense, which the straightforward structure of the sestet then disperses and transcends."[19] But syntactic inversions and delays cause surprise in relation to the extraordinarily high expectation of coherence established. For example, after line 7 ("lest he returning chide") "it seems as if the syntax has collapsed . . . we expect the quotation marks will tell the chiding of 'He', but instead they tell the complaint of 'I'".[20] Any dislocation is temporary, is fully resolved, and only confirms the decisive and unequivocal closure of the syntagmatic chain strung across these fourteen lines and two sentences.

Contrast between the syntax of this text and the Elizabethan sonnet has been remarked elsewhere: "For all its involutions, sonnet xix (When I consider) turns effortlessly on the simplest axis ('I ask: Patience replies') and is at once intelligible: it differs in its fluency from the typical Elizabethan sonnet, which moves forward from point to point, in that it possesses a controlling centre."[21] Whereas Shakespeare's Sonnet 136 develops progressively in a cumulative linearity, Milton's sonnet exhibits only superficial coruscations over a structure rigidly determinate at a deeper level. Through this attempted closure, signifier nailed onto signified in univocal syntax, the sonnet produces the effect of a coherent centre, a fixed subject of the enounced, a voice represented speaking, a presence. Wordsworth's response to Milton's sonnets is significant; he thinks of each as "an orbicular body − a sphere − or dew-drop".[22]

Poetry is written in lines; as discursive form it is specified by "parallelism of the signifier".[23] The economy of poetry is to express enunciative difference by containing it in repetition of the signifier. Verse form in Modern English is determined by line length and rhyme, and it is in rhyme particularly that the materiality of the signifier may open up. The usual contrast between two uses of the sonnet form − respectively Shakespearean and Miltonic − can be understood on this basis. Sonnet 136 is built from three quatrains (each with different rhyme sounds) and a concluding couplet while Milton's sonnet rhymes across an octave (abba abba) and sestet (cde cde), so avoiding the couplet conclusion (only 16, "To Cromwell" so concludes). Milton has less rhyme variation and more phonetic recurrence than Shakespeare, and so one might suppose comes closer to "treating words as things" as in the children's jest rhyme ("Dirty Bill"). The opposite is the case.

Each of Shakespeare's four rhyme divisions (three quatrains and a couplet) coincides with a syntactic unit and semantic development (except perhaps in the already dislocated first two lines of the second quatrain). Milton's monolinear syntactic development rides straight across the rhyme scheme with seven run-on lines and with syntactic junctures in the middle (not the end) of lines 8 and 12 and further terminal junctures in lines 9 and 11 ("replies, God", "best, his"). Milton's practice derives from Italian models, from Tasso and particularly Giovanni della Casa,[24] its aim being – as in *Paradise Lost* – "the sense variously drawn out from one Verse into another". The attempt, then, in Shakespeare's sonnet is to *contain* the enunciative activity of the signifier by holding it onto syntax and meaning; relatively the Milton sonnet would *efface* the signifier through syntagmatic closure and so offers a position of closer identification with the subject of the enounced.

Nevertheless the poem remains a sonnet. Although its usage in 1652 is appropriately idiosyncratic and Milton almost alone cultivated the sonnet in the middle of the seventeenth century, through its verse form the text partakes of the elaborated courtly mode of its Elizabethan precedents. This was recognized by Milton (another Milton?) who mocked Charles I for ascribing "*all vertue* to his Wife, in straines that come almost to Sonnetting".[25]

Dryden

Whatever local commitments it is engaged with during the revolutionary period after 1660 "the plain style wins the day".[26] Transparency becomes an explicit ideal, to be effected as signified is carefully fixed under signifier (in Sprat's formulation of 1667, "so many *things*, almost in equal number of words") in a carefully sustained syntagmatic chain (in Hobbes's recommendation of 1673, an "order of words . . . whereby a man may foresee the length of his period", that is, the sentence).

The sonnet becomes completely marginal and "even including translation only thirteen persons are known to have used the form between 1660 and 1740".[27] Instead there is the reified use of the couplet uniformly across the texts and within. In the couplet the phonetic, syntactic and semantic levels coincide simultaneously in a single closure constantly repeated throughout the poem. It could be argued that Shakespeare's use of the quatrain and indeed the couplet itself anticipates the Augustan couplet (which of course it does) more than the scrupulous avoidance of quatrain and couplet in Milton's sonnet. But the overriding consideration is that Shakespeare's thematic progression is relatively enclosed and acts in correspondence with the rhyme scheme while Milton's transcends rhyme and line length to form its own coherence. In this Milton's sonnet comes very close to the Augustan ideal in which sense is developed ever onwards from one couplet to the next. An apt illustration is the famous opening of *Absalom and Achitophel* (1681):

> In pious times, e're Priest-craft did begin,
> Before *Polygamy* was made a sin;
> When man, on many, multiply'd his kind,
> E're one to one was, cursedly, confin'd:
> When Nature prompted, and no law deny'd
> Promiscuous use of Concubine and Bride;
> Then, *Israel's* Monarch, after Heaven's own heart,
> His vigorous warmth did, variously, impart
> To Wives and Slaves: And, wide as his Command,
> Scatter'd his Maker's Image through the Land.
> *Michal*, of Royal blood, the Crown did wear,
> A Soyl ungratefull to the Tiller's care:
> Not so the rest: for several Mothers bore
> To Godlike David, several sons before.

And so on.

There is hardly need to recall in detail how both sonnets are forms of *discours* and bear the marks of enunciation, with twenty-two instances of "I-thou" in Shakespeare and eight of the first person in Milton; nor to demonstrate fully that the Dryden passage is an example of the dominance in Augustan poetry of *histoire*. Only "cursedly" (line 4) is manifestly a mark of enunciation. To cite Benveniste: "No one speaks here; the events seem to narrate themselves."[28] With marks of enunciation suppressed the text offers itself as fully transparent medium, the enounced disavows its enunciation.

In relation back to Shakespeare and forward to this, Milton's sonnet can be read as a transitional text. While in verse form it rejoins the now residual courtly mode of the sonnet in sonnet sequence, in its syntagmatic closure it intervenes to make possible the Augustan aim of discursive transparency returning the subject to itself as a unity. Transition is also exemplified within the sonnet where there is a shift from the *discours* of the octave to *histoire* in the sestet. As a result the sestet may be reworked with ease into Augustan couplets, however limping:

> God needs nor His own gifts nor yet man's work.
> For those who learn to bear His easy yoke,
> Continue those who serve their Maker best.
> God's state is regal, and at His request,
> Some speed o're land and sea without abate,
> While others serve who only stand and wait.

To insist: *discours/histoire* is a distinction within the enounced. It only operates to provide subject position as part, possibly a minor aspect, of a whole regime of representation, the relation of enunciation and enounced. Instance of this is the easy transposition between the two modes; a passage in one can be rewritten in the other with only minor alteration.[29] Yet within the represented *discours/histoire* need to be discriminated, possibly as demand and desire. Sonnet 136 clearly represents the would-be closed circle of "a request for love".[30] The male "I" supposes the female "thou" as "already possessing the privilege of satisfying needs", even though the circuit is already broken by her "will" which the speaker would rejoin by closing her desire onto his name ("Make but my name thy love"). Only through major alteration could this sonnet be re-written into *histoire*.

Milton's sonnet could easily be transposed ("When he considers how his light is spent", or "considered"). In it desire is represented beginning "to take shape in the margin in which demand becomes separated from need". The first person is repeated eight times in the octave unreciprocated by the second. The sonnet articulates both energetic rebellion against loss (classically blindness is a metaphor for castration) and a controlled assertion that the loss be accepted. Progress across these two is enabled as the speaker's "I" becomes the voice of the Father ("patience . . . soon replies") – "*God* is satisfied" and by identification " 'I' is satisfied".[31] Theologically the poem is unorthodox since there is still "this deep strength of ego"[32] deliberately asserting submission to superego; George Herbert is more orthodox in "The Holdfast":

> to have nought is ours, not to confess
> That we have nought.

Progress from egoistic rebellion to identification with the Father develops from octave to sestet, turning on a paternalist self-recognition in "fondly" (line 8) and the personification of patience which speaks the unquestionable authority of the Father. The turn is also from forms of enunciation to third person discourse, from *discours* to *histoire* (a shift recurrent in *Paradise Lost* and *Samson Agonistes*). In contrast, *histoire* is exemplified in the beginning of *Absalom and Achitophel* by a passage of confident phallocentrism in which His Majesty the Father almost transparently reiterates sons in his own image.

This essay may be best read in conjunction with the theory of poetry developed in *Poetry as Discourse* (London: Methuen, 1983). In its history of English poetry in the seventeenth century the book does not refer to Milton or Dryden and so this essay may serve as a supplement to it.

Notes

[1] W. McCarthy, "The Continuity of Milton's Sonnets", in *Publications of the Modern Language Association of America*, 92 (January 1977), 96–109, p. 96.

2 Ibid., pp. 97, 96, 107, 98, 108 (footnote 7).

3 S. Neale, *Genre* (British Film Institute, London: 1980), p. 50.

4 S. Heath, *"Anata mo"* in *Screen*, 17 (Winter 1976/7), 62.

5 C. Caudwell, *Illusion and Reality* (London: Lawrence and Wishart, 1946), p. 55.

6 E. Benveniste, *Problems in General Linguistics* (Miami: University of Miami Press, 1971), p. 199.

7 Ibid., p. 206.

8 See entry on "Enunciation" in O. Ducrot and T. Todorov, *Encyclopedic Dictionary of the Sciences of Language*, trans. Catherine Porter (Baltimore: Johns Hopkins, 1979).

9 R. Jakobson, "Shifters, Verbal Categories and the Russian Verb", in *Word and Language* (The Hague and Paris: Mouton, 1971), pp. 134, 133.

10 G. Nowell-Smith, "A Note on History/Discourse", in *Edinburgh '76 Magazine* (British Film Institute), p. 27. See also C. MacCabe, "On Discourse", in *Economy and Society*, 8 (August 1979), esp. pp. 280–8.

11 For which Benveniste has been traduced by Greimas (see A. J. Greimas and J. Courtès, *Sémiotique: Dictionnaire Raisonné de la Théorie du Langage* (Paris: Presses Universitaires de France, 1979), entry under "Enonciation") – wrongly as it happens (see Benveniste, cited MacCabe, "On Discourse", p. 285).

12 J. Lacan, *Écrits* (London: Tavistock, 1977), p. 316.

13 J. Lacan, *Four Fundamental Concepts of Psychoanalysis* (London: Hogarth Press, 1977), p. 139 ("énoncé" is translated as "statement" and here retranslated as "enounced").

14 The argument is more fully developed in A. Easthope, *Poetry as Discourse* (London: Methuen ["New Accents"], 1983).

15 W. G. Ingram and T. Redpath (in *Shakespeare's Sonnets* [London: Macmillan, 1964] "feel no obligation to elucidate" and A. L. Rowse (in *Shakespeare's Sonnets*, also London: Macmillan, 1964) finds it hard to discuss the sonnet "with any decency". For a clear account, see *Shakespeare's Sonnets*, ed. S. Booth (New Haven: Yale University Press, 1977).

16 Cited in I. and P. Opie, *The Lore and Language of Schoolchildren* (Oxford: Clarendon, 1967), p. 20.

17 S. Freud, *Jokes* (Harmondsworth: Penguin, 1976), pp. 168, 179.

18 W. R. Parker, *Milton, A Biography* (Oxford, Clarendon Press, 1968), p. 471.

19 T. Stoehr, "Syntax and Poetic Form in Milton's Sonnets", in *English Studies*, 45 (1964), 293.

20 P. Goodman, *The Structure of Literature* (Chicago: University of Chicago Press, 1954), pp. 206, 209–10.

21 E. A. J. Honigman (ed.), *Milton's Sonnets* (London: Macmillan, 1966), p. 41.

22 See Wordsworth's letter to A. Dyce in *Poetical Works*, ed. E. de Selincourt and H. Darbishire, vol. 8 (Oxford: Oxford University Press, 1954), p. 417.

23 *Écrits*, p. 155.

24 See J. S. Smart, *The Sonnets of Milton* (Glasgow: Maclehose, Jackson and Co., 1921) which established the derivation from Della Casa (1503–56); also

F. T. Prince, *The Italian Element in Milton's Verse* (Oxford: Oxford University Press, 1954). Smart shows that the *volta* (meaning by this a break between octave and sestet) is not in any way a rigorous requirement of the Italian sonnet.

25 *Eikonoklastes* in *Works*, ed. F. A. Patterson *et al.* (New York: Columbia University Press, 1931–40), vol. 5, p. 139.

26 Stanley E. Fish, "Epilogue: The Plain Style Question", in *Self-Consuming Arti-facts* (Berkeley: University of California, 1972), p. 379.

27 R. D. Havens, *The Influence of Milton on English Poetry* (Cambridge, Mass.: Harvard University Press, 1922), p. 488.

28 *Problems in General Linguistics*, p. 208.

29 As was demonstrated by M. Barrett and J. Radford in "Modernism in the 1930's", *1936: The Sociology of Literature* (Colchester: University of Essex Press, 1979), vol. 1, pp. 267–9.

30 This and the next two quotations are from *Écrits*, pp. 311, 286, 311 respectively.

31 Goodman, *Structure of Literature*, p. 206.

32 Stoehr, "Syntax and Poetic Form", p. 294.

Pope among the Formalists: textual politics and "The Rape of the Lock"

CHRISTOPHER NORRIS

I

Except in its most obvious physical aspect – the shape of words on the page – it is hard to attach any clear meaning to the idea of poetic "form". This concept may indeed be a species of enabling fiction, having more to do with the interpretative rage for order than with anything objectively "there" in the text. Or it may be the product – in Paul de Man's words – of a close "dialectical interplay" between poem and reading, such that the poem takes on a precarious unity of form in answer to the critic's subtle teasing-out of unifying themes and figures.[1] Criticism would then be caught up in a process of aesthetic mystification whereby its own desire for unity and closure was ceaselessly confirmed in the act of reading. To interpret is always to aim at an encompassing grasp of the text which would charge every detail with relevant meaning and so demonstrate the presence of genuine "organic" form. Yet clearly it is the reading, as much as the poem, whose integrity is at stake in this quest for a validating wholeness of vision. Interpretation must always be able to show that its methods are sufficiently subtle, complex and responsive to bring out the deep-lying sources of coherence vested in the literary text. Any reading that fails in this objective – that leaves certain details unaccounted for, or confesses to finding the text incoherent – is thereby shown up as inadequate.

This assumption runs largely unchallenged from Coleridge to the American New Criticism. It is taken for granted that poetry possesses a richness and complexity of verbal resource that mark it off clearly from "ordinary" language, and that criticism is best, most usefully employed in drawing attention to this difference. Poetry becomes an autonomous mode of discourse, belonging to a separate linguistic domain where commonplace logic no longer holds good and truth is bodied forth through metaphor, paradox and other such privileged rhetorical figures. Interpreters may bring great subtlety to bear in their reading of literary texts. They may even, like Coleridge, carry speculation to the point where it becomes very hard to draw any firm categorical line between poetry, criticism and theory. And there were those among the New Critics, like Allen Tate, who sometimes suspended the orthodox bans to the extent of wondering what criticism might become if freed from its strictly subservient status *vis-à-vis* the literary text.[2] But these were entertained as heretical notions to be set firmly aside when it came to the business of serious practical criticism. T. S. Eliot's pitying reference to "the sad ghost of Coleridge, beckoning from the shades" was sufficient reminder of the ills and delusions to which criticism was prone once it abandoned its proper subordinate role.[3]

For the orthodox New Critics this amounted to a virtual policing operation, a matter of beating the strict ontological bounds that separated poetry from other kinds of language, including the language of criticism. A whole apparatus of doctrinal checks and sanctions was erected to maintain this division of realms. Critics might theorize as much as they pleased, but only on the understanding that their theories belonged to a second-order discourse which reflected on the powers and the limits of criticism itself, rather than seeking to make sense of poetry by imposing an alien logic of explanatory concepts. Thus Cleanth Brooks declared flatly that "the principles of criticism define the area relevant to criticism; they do not constitute a method for carrying it out".[4] Poetry has its own special claim to truth, quite distinct from those of rational explication on the one hand or generalized interpretative theory on the other. To confuse these realms – so the New Critics argued – was to lose sight of whatever gave value to poetry as a language transcending commonplace habits of thought and perception. It is this danger that John Crowe Ransom has in mind when he remarks that any adequate "logic of poetic figure" would effectively constitute "a logic of logical aberrations, applicable to the conventions of poetic language".[5] And this because poetry – unlike criticism or critical theory – need have no truck with the standard requirements of logical consistency or truth. Only by respecting its inwrought structures of rhetorical implication ("paradox", "irony" and other such figures) can criticism hope to preserve poetic truth against the various "heresies" that constantly threaten its autonomous mode of existence.

Chief among these heresies was the idea that poetry could be paraphrased, or made to yield up its meaning in a language of perspicuous plain-prose sense devoid of "poetic" figuration. Thus the New Critics admired William Empson for his extraordinary close-reading skills, but sounded a warning note when it came to Empson's habit of providing all manner of paraphrastic hints and suggestions by way of making the poem more accessible. Empson's readings, as Ransom put it, might just as well apply to "a piece of infinitely qualified prose".[6] For the New Critics it was a high point of principle that poetry existed in a separate dimension of rhetorical complexity which no prose paraphrase – however subtly qualified – could hope to reach. And the same applied to those other rampant "heresies" which sought to interpret poetry in terms of such "extraneous" contexts of knowledge as history, biography or cultural politics. Of course the New Critics never quite lived up to their own high principles here. Reading (say) Brooks on Marvell's "Horatian Ode", one is aware of the way that historical facts and biographical background are smuggled in, so to speak, under cover of mere close attention to "the words on the page".[7] Like Eliot before him, Brooks wants to argue that the special quality of Marvell's poem – its poise, sophistication, perfected balance of attitude – comes of its detachment from the pressures of politics and historical circumstance. The "Ode" thus becomes a test-case for criticism, or more specifically for the kind of criticism that values such qualities of civilized wit and finds little use for mere documentary "background". Yet it is clear that Brooks starts out with a good working knowledge of Marvell's highly ambivalent career during and after the Civil War period. His apparently easy switch of loyalties from Cromwell to the restored monarchy is implicit in everything that Brooks has to say about Marvell's sophisticated handling of civic and martial themes. What Brooks's essay achieves on its own account – and programmatically, as part of the wider New Critical enterprise – is the same aesthetic distancing from history and politics that it finds so strikingly embodied in Marvell's poem.

But this achievement is not without its own specific weight of ideological prejudice. Behind Brooks's reading – nowhere spelled out but informing every last detail – is a potent mythology of English cultural decline which T. S. Eliot raised into a virtual dogma of modern literary opinion. Marvell stands in as the last representative of that civilized tradition whose values were threatened, even as he wrote, by the turmoils of the English Civil War. At about this time, in Eliot's famous phrase, there occurred a "dissociation of sensibility", a lapse from political and cultural grace whose effects we have yet to understand, let alone overcome.[8] The Civil War marked the transition from a stable, divinely sanctioned order of society to one in which religious and political discords would henceforth work their mischief. And along with these social upheavals went a seismic shift in what might be called – though Eliot would scarcely have used such a phrase – the relations of literary production. For Shakespeare, Donne and their contemporaries, "thought" and "emotion" had existed in a happily un-selfconscious harmony, with the intellect existing (as Eliot wrote of Donne) "at the tips of the senses". But then there set in that long sad period of secular decline when poetry could only alternate between extremes of "dissociated" thought and emotion, the Augustans on the one hand (to adopt Eliot's drastically simplified picture) and the Romantics – or their latter-day Georgian descendants – on the other. It is not hard to see how Marvell fits in with this wholesale historical myth. Living through the period of civil strife, and living on (what is more) to become a satirist and a party-political poet in the new age, Marvell yet managed to produce a handful of lyrics and obscurely "topical" poems whose complexity lifts them above mere history or circumstantial record. He thus becomes the touchstone for a critical method which elevates the virtues of "paradox" and "irony" into a measure of poetry's power to transcend the mundane realities of history and politics.

This background narrative, worked up from the myth of Eliot's devising, is deeply inscribed within New Critical practice. More specifically, it goes along with that rhetoric of detachment or aesthetic autonomy which works to keep such interests safely at bay. Eliot's "tradition" is effectively what substitutes for history when the latter is reduced to a potent myth of secular decline and fall. It is a timeless dimension of aesthetic transcendence where the great creative minds of European culture converse without hindrance of mere historical or socio-cultural difference. "Tradition" thus becomes a kind of imaginary museum, a space where the "monuments" of past achievement compose themselves into an ideal order, determined by a sense of deep-laid cultural continuity and not by mere accidents of historical time and place. All these factors converge in the reading of Marvell proposed by Eliot and refined upon by Brooks. Leaving out the politics – or treating it as incidental background, fit matter only for the poet's play of non-committal attitude – the "Ode" can then serve as a perfect example of poetry transcending such unworthy concerns.

II

Post-structuralism takes issue with the "old" New Critics on each of these closely connected points of principle. It rejects the idea that poetry is a special kind of language, radically different from those other discourses (of history, criticism, literary theory) which must therefore learn to respect its sovereign autonomy. De Man's essay on the New Criticism shows how this doctrine self-deconstructs as soon as one

focusses attention on its characteristic language and strategies of argument. The discrepancy between precept and practice becomes most
apparent when the New Critics draw upon metaphors and images of
natural process to support the idea of "organic" form. In de Man's
words:

Instead of revealing a continuity affiliated with the coherence of the natural
world, [this] takes us into a discontinuous world of reflective irony and ambiguity. Almost in spite of itself, it pushes the interpretative process so far that
the analogy between the organic world and the language of poetry finally ex-
plodes. This unitarian criticism finally becomes a criticism of ambiguity, an
ironic reflection on the absence of the unity it had postulated.[9]

The upshot of de Man's essay is to show that the New Critics were
unable to maintain any strict demarcation between the language of
poetry and those other kinds of language that belong (so they thought)
to a separate discursive realm. And this leads on to a further implication: that criticism itself is often drawn into complex and duplicitous
strategies of reading which deserve the same close attention that interpreters normally pay to "literary" texts. It is precisely by *failing* to
discover any firm ontological ground for their distinction between
poetry and criticism that these interpreters point beyond their own
express doctrines to a deconstructive reading of poetry and criticism
alike. According to de Man, it is often in their moments of singular
"blindness" − blindness, that is, to the rhetorical complexity of their
own texts − that critics may provide the maximum "insight" for
readers alert to such symptoms.

    And this is to suggest that we should read criticism in a way quite
distinct from received ideas of its proper utility and purpose. It is not
(as the New Critics would have it) a discourse standing apart from the
literary text, supplying certain insights and even, on occasion, certain
guidelines of "method" but in no sense aspiring to occupy the same
rhetorical domain. For post-structuralists, on the contrary, poetry and
criticism exist in a close (if often strained and contradictory) relationship, such that no dogmatic conviction on the critic's side can hold
them forcibly apart. And this because texts of *all* kinds − poetry,
criticism, philosophy, historical narrative − can be shown to exploit
the same rhetorical techniques and to place similar problems in the way
of any straightforward (veridical or referential) reading. It is no longer
a case, as it was for the New Critics, of resisting the claims of a
positivist literary scholarship bent upon reducing the text to so many
background facts or evidential sources. Such claims rested on the
presupposition that *other* forms of discourse gave access to a truth
beyond the equivocal, self-occupied character of "literary" language.

Thus the old quarrel between "scholars" and "critics" was not so much a genuine difference of principle as a matter of seeking opposite solutions to the same root dilemma. For all that they resisted its intrusive claims, the New Critics effectively yielded to scholarship the right to adjudicate in questions of straightforward textual self-evidence. Their only defence in face of such attack was to tighten up the sanctions surrounding that imaginary entity, the "literary" text.

Post-structuralism goes various ways around to subvert this rigid demarcation of textual bounds. In de Man it takes the form of a deconstructive reading that presses the logic of New Critical theory to the point where it has to confront its own aberrant rhetorical drift. Elsewhere the point is made by taking texts from supposedly different discursive realms and reading them alongside each other to draw out their co-implicated rhetorics and strategies of argument. Some of the best recent criticism of Wordsworth has more or less explicitly read him in the light of concepts and analogies drawn from Hegel's *Phenomenology of Mind*.[10] The point of such readings is not to claim "philosophical" authority for what would otherwise be just another piece of workaday literary criticism. Philosophy is not conceived as an ultimate truth-telling discourse whose superior logical grasp enables it to illuminate the poem's more perplexed or obscurely metaphorical passages. Rather it is a question of allowing both texts to enter into a process of mutual interrogative exchange where commonplace distinctions between "poetry" and "philosophy" become increasingly hard to maintain. For the "old" New Critics there was just one concept from Hegel – that of the "concrete universal" – that served to underwrite their claims for the absolute autonomy of poetic form.[11] Removed from the context of Hegelian dialectic – of everything pertaining to history and change – it figured as a purely metaphysical support for the idea of poetry as a self-contained language indifferent to everything outside its own domain. What T. S. Eliot derived from Hegel (*via* his philosophic mentor F. H. Bradley) was the same kind of de-historicized idealist doctrine which enabled him to formulate "tradition" as a timeless communing of minds, and poetry as a matter of unconsciously discovering some "objective" verbal form for one's otherwise inchoate emotions.[12] As with Bradley, so with Eliot, this led to a species of transcendental solipsism. "Tradition" becomes a kind of echo-chamber for the mind disenchanted with history and withdrawn into its own private vision of a purely synchronic cultural order.

It is a very different Hegel who figures so importantly in current post-structuralist criticism. In place of the "concrete universal" – that ideal pretext for lifting poetry clean out of contact with history, philosophy and other kinds of discourse – Hegel now provides the means to articulate these languages together and open up an intertextual dialogue between them. One result of this process is that criticism can now be read with an eye to those rhetorical strategies and blind-spots which give it a symptomatic interest on its own account. In the remainder of this essay I shall be looking at one fairly typical modern compilation – a *Casebook* on Pope's "The Rape of the Lock", edited by John Dixon Hunt[13] – and attempting to draw out some of these problematic issues. The *Casebook* I have chosen for two main reasons. First, it is a kind of implicit New Critical manifesto, reprinting several essays (by Brooks among others) which are clearly meant as exemplary readings of their kind. Furthermore they are presented as in some sense resolving those "problems" with the poem encountered by earlier, less sophisticated critics. So the *Casebook* has a narrative line of its own, a tale of confusions and partial insights eventually redeemed by a criticism capable of rising above such limited views. Secondly, anthologies like this are often prescribed as "background" reading for students, whose use of them – as a handy source of ideas but certainly not as *texts* for close reading – falls in exactly with New Critical precept. So my argument here is intended to have pedagogical as well as "purely" theoretical implications. What those students had much better do, instead of mining the *Casebook* for authoritative "insights", is read the critics with a mind alert to their interpretative strategies and moments of symptomatic blindness.

There is likewise more than one reason for selecting "The Rape of the Lock" as a suitable case for this kind of intertextual reading. It is a "problem" poem not only in the sense that it has generated volumes of commentary, but also in the way that it has set these critics at odds with each other and even – at times – with their own principled commitments. As with Marvell, there is a marked tendency to insulate the poem from its social and political context, thus making it the more amenable to modern techniques of close-reading. And this goes along with the desire to turn back the clock of history and treat Pope (again like Marvell) as a poet in whom there survived – intermittently at least – something of the old "metaphysical" virtues. Leavis's essay "The Line of Wit" is a classic example of this strategy at work.[14] It sets out to identify those elements in Pope's verse that relate him to Donne and the early seventeenth century, qualities that almost disappeared from later English poetry – so the argument runs – partly through Milton's malign influence and partly through the pressures of socio-political change engendered by the Civil War. That Milton was preeminently the poet of Civil War politics – an out-and-out partisan and not, like

Marvell, an artful balancer of options – gives this story an added plausibility. In Pope's case, as even the New Critics can hardly deny, poetry and politics are so far intertwined as to make it very hard to read him without some knowledge of the relevant "background". Nevertheless there are certain techniques – most of them represented in this *Casebook* – for minimizing the historical damage and restoring Pope to something very like the "metaphysical" state of innocence and grace.

What comes across most strikingly in Brooks's reading is his effort to contain the poem's *sexual* politics by treating it – in standard New Critical style – as an allegory of aesthetic transcendence. More precisely, it is Pope's special virtue to supply such a perfectly assured ironic gloss to his narrative war-of-the-sexes that the episode becomes a fine demonstration of New Critical theory in practice. Thus, according to Brooks, the whole purpose of Pope's supernatural machinery (the "iridescent little myth of the sylphs") is to symbolize the working of those social conventions that "govern the conduct of maidens". The poem represents a good-humoured and tolerant attempt to "do justice", as Brooks puts it, to "the intricacies of the feminine mind" (p. 141). Like the modern critic, Pope is well provided with sophisticated means of taking pleasure in the episode without permitting more serious thoughts to intrude. "For in spite of Pope's amusement at the irrationality of that mind, Pope acknowledges its beauty and its powers." Powers to seduce, to beguile and entertain, but always within the strict limits laid down by a male sense of realism, balance and proportion. For there are – as both Pope and Brooks do well to remind us – certain elementary natural facts behind the shadow-play of Pope's delightful "machinery" and Belinda's equally delightful courtship rituals. The poet and the critic are neither of them *seriously* deceived by the elaborate conventions which Belinda – to her cost – takes for real. Pope "has absolutely no illusions about what the game is". Like Brooks, he is in possession of a balanced outlook which knows precisely where to draw the line between convention and reality, civilized pretence and natural fact. That he can hold these opposites so perfectly in balance is a tribute not only to Pope's artistry but also to his male-commonsense firmness of judgment. He is certainly "not to be shocked", Brooks writes, "by any naturalistic interpretation of the elaborate and courtly conventions under which Belinda fulfils her natural function of finding a mate" (p. 144).

Beyond the surface detail of Brooks's reading is a scene of recognition where the critic discovers exactly those admirable qualities in the poem that characterize his own interpretative stance. Of course one

could hardly expect otherwise, given that the critic was drawn or impelled to interpret the poem in the first place. But there is more going
on when it comes to Brooks's reflections on Belinda and the nature of
female sexuality. His reading produces a series of implicit equations
that associate poetry (or poetic convention) with "the intricacies of the
feminine mind", and criticism – or Brooks's kind of formalist criticism
– with the masculine power to comprehend and sensibly judge those
intricacies. If "Pope's interpretation of Belinda's divinity does not need
to flinch from bawdy implications", it is because both Pope and his
like-minded critic have the fine breadth of judgment to take these opposed attitudes on board with perfect equanimity. Women (like poems)
have a special licence to indulge their "intricate" subtleties of feeling
far beyond the limits properly observed by the discourse of male
reason. Thus Belinda can display all the giddy symptoms of
"feminine" temperament – from coquetry to an absurdly exaggerated
horror at her own (merely symbolic) "rape" – and yet remain an object
of male delectation. For it is a mark of Pope's maturity of judgment
(and no less a virtue in Brooks's reading) that these female vagaries are
not condemned but transformed into fit material for a wise and witty
poem. Thus Pope "definitely expects Belinda to be chaste; but, as a
good humanist, he evidently regards virginity as essentially a negative
virtue, and its possession, a temporary state" (p. 147). Belinda's
histrionics are a passing show, the product of an overwrought virginal
mind whose hypocrisies her male admirers (poet and critic) can afford
to treat with humorous indulgence. "She'll soon get over it" is the
worldly-wise moral that Brooks finds implicit in Pope's supreme
equanimity of tone.

    All this chivalry turns out to have sharp limits when it comes to the
more disturbing implications of Belinda's "rape". Brooks follows Pope
in his will not to flinch from a manly recognition of the literalized
meaning that persistently lurks within the metaphor. Thus he quotes
Belinda's "anguished" exclamation:

> Oh hadst thou, cruel! been content to seize
> Hairs less in sight, or any hairs but these!

and remarks that it "carries on, unconsciously, the sexual suggestion"
present throughout the poem (p. 146). But in this case the message is
clear enough: that Belinda is more concerned with superficial appearances than with any real threat to her maidenly virtue. In Brooks's
words, "something of the bathos carries over to the sexual parallel: it
is hinted, perhaps, that for the belle the real rape might lose some of
its terrors if it could be concealed". So there is, it seems, another and

less attractive side to the terms on which criticism tolerates Belinda's character. *Either* the rape is just an elaborate game, in which case her reactions are absurdly overwrought (and perhaps, Brooks suggests, an extension of Belinda's seductive powers by other, more devious means). *Or*, if there is a hint of some real as opposed to merely metaphorical rape, then Belinda's concern for social appearances does begin to look like vanity or worse. Thus the upshot of all Pope's fine generosity – his attempt, as Brooks describes it, to "do justice to the intricacies of the feminine mind" – is to place Belinda in a classic double-bind or no-win situation.

Brooks sees nothing of this, convinced as he is that "Pope's tact is perfect", a matter of delicately making allowance for the whims and caprices of female temperament. What he chiefly admires is the poet's ability to fend off premature judgements by maintaining an attitude of finely poised ironic reflection. "The detachment, the amused patronage, the note of aloof and impartial judgement – all demand that the incident be viewed with a large measure of aesthetic distance" (p. 152). But even here Brooks's language betrays the slide into a tone of condescending male amusement at Belinda's expense. And behind this rhetorical shift lies the familiar New Critical evaluative stance which rates poems according to their level of "detached" ironic self-containment. The very notion of poetic "form" is equated by Brooks with this power to keep a multitude of feelings and responses in play while refusing to judge between them. "It is, finally, the delicate balance and reconciliation of a host of partial interpretations and attitudes" (p. 152). Yet it is hard to square such statements with the cruder forms of irony and the patronizing tone that enter Brooks's language when he lines up with Pope on the side of male "realism". Then most often it is a matter of insinuating home truths which the "feminine mind", for all its intricate turns, cannot properly grasp. And this superior knowledge on the male's part is not without its moments of unguarded brutality. "Pope knows that the rape has in it more of compliment than of insult, though he naturally hardly expects Belinda to interpret it thus. He does not question her indignation, but he does suggest that it is, perhaps, a more complex response than Belinda realizes" (p. 152). "Naturally" Belinda can hardly appreciate the ultimate achievement of civilized wit that discovers such rich possibilities for irony in treating the rape as more "compliment" than "insult". That pleasure is reserved for those unflinching spirits whose largeness of view equips them to write – or fully appreciate – such poetry as this.

In the course of Brooks's reading one can make out another covert drift of analogical thinking, this time one that associates the finely

wrought balance of poetic "form" with the elusive, precarious nature
of female "virtue". Brooks makes a point of denying that "form" has
anything to do with mechanical conventions or rigid ideas of how
poetry ought to be structured. Rather it is a question of tonal balance,
of that infinitely subtle and qualified irony through which Pope
achieves his best effects. The New Critics were collectively ill at ease
when it came to defining precisely what they *meant* by "form" in
poetry. The various rhetorical tropes that they raised into touchstones
of poetic value ("paradox", "irony", etc.) were all too easily taken for
dogma and reified as structures objectively "there" in the poem. So the
New Critics often had to insist, like Brooks, that these tropes were
devices of no special value in themselves, but only in so far as they
served to communicate a complex and rewarding variety of sense. The
effect of such qualifications was to set up a kind of infinite regress, with
"form" defined only in tentative, provisional terms and always subject
to further complicating hints of ambivalence or irony. In some of
Brooks's essays – like the piece on Donne's "Canonization" in *The
Well-Wrought Urn*[15] – the poem has a tight enough rhetorical structure for its "form" to be presented as more or less synonymous with
its play of tone and attitude. Thus Brooks can turn the poem into a
perfect New Critical allegory of reading, with the urn as symbol of
poetry's power to contain and memorialize the extremes of human experience. But elsewhere – as when writing about Marvell or Pope –
it is more difficult for Brooks to effect this transition from the level of
meaning and attitude to the level of totalizing "form". His response,
as we have seen, is to invoke a series of detached or "placing" ironies
on the poet's part, such as to forestall any premature reduction to a
crudely moralizing import. The effect of this manoeuvring is to set
them both up – poet and critic – as arbiters of a rich and complex
experience beyond the mere conventions of literary style. And it is
woman (Belinda) who figures in Brooks's reading as a creature so far
taken in by those conventions as to exemplify the same liabilities and
limits as the notion of poetic "form". What this notion must include,
according to Brooks, is "much more than the precise regard for a set
of rules and conventions mechanically applied" (p. 152). As Pope sees
beyond the female self-regard that attaches such importance to appearances, so Brooks envisages a larger, inclusive realm of poetic meaning that puts the mere mechanics of "form" firmly in its place. "Belinda's is plainly a charming, artificial world; but Pope is not afraid to let
in a glimpse of the real world which lies all about it" (p. 152). Unlike
the well-wrought urn of Donne's devising, Belinda is a frail vessel
whose womanly flaws the critic obligingly rotates to view.

Other commentators on "The Rape of the Lock" are far less subtle than Brooks in announcing this commonplace prejudice. Aubrey Williams hunts out all manner of sources for the emblem of woman as "the weaker vessel", from the New Testament to Shakespeare, Herrick, Gay, Keats and Freud.[16] And he sets up a similar suggestive parallel between Belinda's weakness and the complex fascination which she – like the poem – exerts upon the male reader. Thus: "although Pope's view of her is laced with irony, Belinda's beauteous virginity is somehow rendered more precious, and our regard for it somehow more tender, by recognition of how easily it can be marred or shattered" (p. 227). When Williams takes issue with Brooks, it is on account of Brooks's failure to heed these omens of catastrophe and his consequent tendency to make the poem turn on matters of "taste" rather than moral questions. What they signify to Williams is a deeper-running current of serious suggestion: that Belinda does indeed suffer some kind of "fall", that her perfection is rudely shattered, and that (in Williams's deft phrasing) "she does lose her 'chastity', in so far as chastity can be understood, however teasingly, as a condition of the spirit" (p. 228). There are several kinds of "teasing" suggested here, all from a male point of view. There is Belinda's artful use of her own virgin sexuality, deployed (however "unconsciously") as a means to heighten her seductive charms. There is the teasing implicit in the male critic's down-to-earth reminder that chastity "as a spiritual condition" is really beside the point, though good for some neatly turned displays of poetic conceit. But along with these suggestions goes a hint of how the *poem* – itself a frail vessel of seductive contriving – puts itself constantly at risk (like Belinda) from the wrong kind of male attention. There seems, Williams writes, "as much danger in taking the poem too lightly as there is in taking it too seriously: the poem seems able to tease us into thought as well as out of it" (p. 228). The two kinds of teasing, sexual and aesthetic, both have to do with form, convention and the risks attendant on mistaking artifice for real-life behaviour.

Williams's glancing allusion to Keats suggests how issues of aesthetic form here become closely intertwined with sexual and erotic implications. If the poem teases criticism into and out of thought, then it shares this power with Belinda's artful yet dangerous use of her feminine charms. The aesthetic ideal implicit in formalist criticism – that of the poem as a pure, self-enclosed product of verbal artifice – exacts the same tribute of mixed feelings as Belinda's dissimulating conduct. Thus Williams's language oscillates between a "tender regard" for her "beauteous virginity" and talk of the "narcissistic self-love" that drives her to make such a show of it. In the same way, Williams reproaches Brooks for yielding too readily to the poem's aesthetic blandishments – to matters of form, taste, convention – and thus ignoring its moral import. If Brooks had only attended more closely to the implications of Belinda's "fall" (along with the associated metaphors of woman as the "weaker vessel") he would surely have resisted this temptation. The beguiling influence of aesthetic form is as powerful yet also as fragile as anything mustered by Belinda's arts. In the last analysis Williams, like Brooks, wants an end to this teasing play and an honest acknowledgment (on the poet's, if not on Belinda's part) that the sexual situation is for real. Thus: "Pope further intensifies the issues (and the element of free choice) by his hints, delicate though they be, that Belinda actually acquiesces, however faintly, in the 'rape' " (p. 228). Thus poet and critic are agreed in demanding that the girl leave off her artificial pretences and face up – at whatever "unconscious" level – to some plain home truths about the female mind.

III

There are two main topics or centres of attention in this running debate among the modern commentators. One is the question of Belinda's "character", shading off easily (as we have seen) into generalized pronouncements about female nature. The other has to do with interpretative method and the balance of priorities between such matters as form, attitude and tone. That these topics are linked in devious ways – that the "problem" of Belinda is oddly tied up with the "problem" of aesthetic form – I have suggested through the reading of Brooks and Williams. A familiar pattern begins to emerge as the critics take issue over various details of Pope's elusive text. On the one hand they conceive themselves as speaking up for truth against the falsehoods or the partial insights of other, less sophisticated readings. Thus the *Casebook* has several essays of a broadly New Critical persuasion that compete in their attempts to do full justice to Pope's satiric range and subtlety of tone. On the other hand these critics adopt a certain stance in regard to Belinda (or "woman" in general), the effect of whose presence in the poem is both to disconcert and to redouble their truth-seeking efforts. Woman takes on those aesthetic attributes – of ambivalence, paradox, dissimulating irony – which the New Critics expressly prized yet obscurely mistrusted in poetry. So Belinda becomes, in effect, a surrogate victim of the tensions and strains which these critics are unable to resolve in their own methodology. Her "world" is represented as a self-enclosed domain of mere "good form" and polite convention.

Meanwhile the interpreters can confidently join voice with Pope in discovering the limits of the female world and gently but firmly reminding Belinda of the sexual realities outside.

One is reminded of those passages in Derrida's *Spurs* where he shows how the image of woman has figured obsessively as lure and provocation in the discourse of male reason. Woman provokes by her "unmasterable" distance, her standing-off from the masculine protocols of wisdom, dignity and truth. With Nietzsche especially, this issues in a kind of mixed fascination and loathing, a fix upon woman as the virtual embodiment of everything that philosophy − "serious" philosophy − needs to abjure. Thus Nietzsche in his overtly misogynist vein excoriates woman for her fickleness, her concern with appearances and scandalous disregard for truth. Yet Nietzsche is himself in the process of challenging (or deconstructing) those very claims-to-truth that have ruled the discourse of philosophic reason from Socrates to Hegel and beyond. And so there develops, in Nietzsche's writing, a perverse association of themes by which "woman" comes to stand − however obliquely − for those liberating energies that might yet break with the weight of received ideas.

Woman . . . is twice model, at once lauded and condemned. Since she is a model for truth she is able to display the gift of her seductive power, which rules over dogmatism, and disorients and routs those credulous men, the philosophers. And because she does not believe in the truth (still, she does find that uninteresting truth in her interest) woman remains a model, only this time a good model. But because she is a good model, she is in fact a bad model. She plays at dissimulation, at ornamentation, deceit, artifice, at an artist's philosophy. Hers is an affirmative power. And if she continues to be condemned, it is only from the man's point of view where she repudiates that affirmative power and, in her specular reflection of that foolish dogmatism that she has provoked, belies her belief in truth.[17]

Other names for this "dissimulating non-truth of truth" are (as Derrida suggests) "style" and "writing", since philosophy has traditionally repressed the knowledge of its own rhetorical character in pursuit of an idealized self-presence of truth immune to such trivial distractions. So "woman" becomes, by this strangest of involuntary reversals, the emblem of everything that beckons beyond the delusive regime of metaphysical truth.

The drastic ambivalence of Nietzsche's writing on the "woman question" is reproduced − albeit more tactfully − in critical discussion of Pope's Belinda. Here also there is a strain of manly disapproval which occasionally rises to shuddering contempt at the artifice of female life. Dr Johnson strikes this tone in a passage from his "Life" of Pope which the *Casebook* includes among its "Extracts From Earlier Critics". "The whole detail of a female life is here brought before us, invested with so much art of decoration that, . . . we feel all the appetite of curiosity for that from which we have a thousand times turned fastidiously away" (p. 69). It is the word "fastidious" that heightens the sense of outraged masculine values, suggesting as it does that Johnson's reaction has about it something of the exaggerated "female" sensitivity to matters of form and appearance. As with Nietzsche, the topic is one that gets under the critic's elaborate defences and then proceeds to work a subtle confusion of established gender-role ideas. Thus Johnson goes on – in yet more absurdly hyperbolical style – to justify his own animadversion by remarking the effect of female behaviour on the conduct of society at large. "The freaks, and humours, and spleen, and vanity of women, as they embroil families in discord, and fill houses with disquiet, do more to obstruct the happiness of life in a year than the ambition of the clergy in many centuries" (p. 69). Of course one wouldn't find any modern critic prepared to let prejudice ride in such an overtly moralizing style. Yet the upshot of all their sophisticated reading techniques is still to devise new and more elaborate ways of putting Belinda down.

In fact those "earlier critics" were often more aware of the politics – sexual and dynastic – bound up with the problems of interpreting Pope's allegorical design. Thus Hazlitt cites a passage from Shakespeare, remarking on its elemental grandeur, and then observes how "there is none of this rough work in Pope . . . His Muse was on a peace establishment, and grew somewhat effeminate by long ease and indulgence" (p. 92). Hazlitt is writing from the standpoint of a later, more pressured situation when events in France and the backlash in Britain had forcibly involved poetry with politics and put an end to the idea of poets living undisturbed "on a peace establishment". There is a certain contempt in Hazlitt's description, carried (as usual) by the habit of thought which associates poetic artifice with all things womanish or "effeminate". But there is also a clear understanding that Pope's peculiar kind of formal perfection has political and ideological overtones beyond this immediate impression. "The balance between the concealed irony and the assumed gravity is as nicely trimmed as the balance of power in Europe" (pp. 93–4). If there is something effete about Pope's way of writing, it is nonetheless a style whose formal attributes and implicit values can always be enlisted on the side of conservative reaction. To celebrate Pope – as the modern critics do – for his qualities of "balance" and perfect ironic detachment is to fall in with that mystified image of a bygone civilized order which Hazlitt was quick to perceive in the conservative ideologues of his day.

One can see this process very plainly at work in Martin Price's essay "The Problem of Scale: the game of art". Price goes through most of the usual moves to establish the poem as a well-nigh miraculous achievement of verbal art and Belinda as the vessel whose graces and flaws enable the poet to bring this miracle about. The sylphs and gnomes of Pope's supernatural "machinery" are, says Price, "in their diminutive operation, like those small but constant self-regarding gestures we may associate with a lady conscious of her charms" (p. 238). And yet these very frailties of female nature are so worked upon by Pope's transformative art that they become an emblem of everything that raises humanity above mere animal instinct. Like many of the commentators, Price invokes the time-honoured trope by which poetry is seen as an agent of redemption, a means of lending ideal permanence to the passing show of mortal beauty. Thus: "the elevated lock is, in a sense, the poem, shining upon beaux and sparks, but upon all others who will see it, too". So the lock stands in synecdochically, not only for Belinda (who is thereby redeemed from all the ills that female flesh is heir to), but also for the poem, by whose magical powers this whole transformation is successfully carried through. But if woman is thus saved from her natural state, it is only on condition that she play the proper role as defined by prevalent male ideas of "feminine" artifice and charm. She then becomes the acme of perfection for a backward-looking vision of order which locates the social virtues in a bygone age and discovers mere chaos and anarchy in everything since.

So it is hardly surprising when Price caps his argument by quoting Edmund Burke on the sad decline from older standards of moral and aesthetic taste: "It is gone, that sensibility of principle, that chastity of honour, which felt a stain like a wound, which inspired courage while it mitigated ferocity, which ennobled whatever it touched, and under which vice lost half its evil, by losing all its grossness" (quoted by Price, *Casebook*, p. 242). This passage lends itself ideally to the purposes of a criticism bent upon refining away all the traces of history and sexual politics inscribed within Pope's text. Any crudely literal understanding of the "rape" is discountenanced by Burke's harking back to a time when "grossness" was rendered unthinkable – sublimated out of view – by a more refined state of moral sensibility. In Hazlitt this notion of a lost golden age went along with a sense – a keenly historical sense – of the politics implied by any such form of retrospective idealization. Burke's example was evidence enough that the transposition of aesthetic values into the sphere of history and politics was a move now coopted by the forces of reaction, whatever its earlier, more radical claims. There is something of the same differentiating irony when Byron speaks of "the ineffable distance in point of sense, harmony, effect . . . between the little Queen Anne's man, and us of the Lower Empire" (p. 101). What Hazlitt and Byron implicitly resist is the kind of ahistorical mythologizing impulse that annuls such distance in the name of some ideal aesthetic or social order. But when Price quotes the passage from Burke, it is assumed to carry a timeless authority and weight of self-evidence beyond all mere fluctuations of political climate. Like the poem itself, Burke's words are translated to a realm of precarious yet somehow enduring truth where they hold out against the ravages of secular decline. In the Cave of Spleen episode we are offered, according to Price, "one of the strongest pictures of disorder in the age . . . a sense of the strength of the forces that social decorum controls and of the savage distortion of feeling that it prevents" (p. 240). Thus the tonings of Burke's counter-revolutionary rhetoric are carried over perfectly intact into Price's reading of Pope.

There is one modern essay in the *Casebook* that does raise questions about the politics of interpretation and the New Critical tendency to render such questions invisible by placing poetry beyond reach of historical discourse and critique. The author is Murray Krieger, himself a noted defender of the "old" New Criticism, but also a theorist aware of its failings from the viewpoint of other, more politically sensitive modes of reading. Krieger's title − "The 'Frail China Jar' and the Rude Hand of Chaos" − suggests that his essay will follow the by now familiar pattern, constructing a mythology of aesthetic form against the "chaos" of modern (political) reality. And indeed, up to a point, this is the line his argument adopts. Thus it happens − as so often in New Critical debate − that Krieger takes issue with a fellow-interpreter (Cleanth Brooks once again), suggesting that there is more to be said, or more subtle and adequate ways of saying it. Even Brooks, according to Krieger, has "not quite pursued his approach to this poem to a unified conclusion". He has rested content with "merely complicating the dimensions of the poem . . . and so leaving it, exposed but not regrouped, in all its multiplicity" (p. 203). It is thus left for Krieger to press Brooks's scattered insights to their proper (formalist) conclusion and thereby demonstrate both the unifying power of Pope's imagination and the full splendours of a method that can adequately celebrate that power.

In Krieger's closing statement − after an intertextual reading with

The Dunciad and parts of the *Essay on Man* − this method achieves its own apotheosis. The passage is worth quoting at length since it brings out very clearly the aims and ontological commitments of New Critical method.

Powerless against chaos − that disintegrating force of historical reality whose "uncreating word" extinguished "Art after Art" − the frail universe could win immortality with the very evanescent quality that doomed it: for "quick, poetic eyes" it glows, gem-like, a sphere beyond the reach of the "universal Darkness" that buried all.   (p. 219)

On the face of it, this stands as the perfect summation of all those rhetorical strategies and ploys that the New Critics raised to such a high point of principle. Allusions to *The Dunciad* are skilfully interwoven with an argument that sets off the timeless values of art against the "chaos", the "disintegrating force" of historical process. And this attitude is confirmed elsewhere in Krieger's essay when he states simply that "the permanence of art must be preferred to the dynamic causality of history".

As usual, it is Belinda − and Belinda's virginity − that serves as a focus for this contrast between natural and artificial orders of being. Krieger is more precise, more rhetorically exacting than most interpreters when he isolates the two chief tropes − metonymy and zeugma − through which the transformation is achieved. Metonymy (taking the lock to stand for Belinda's body) is what enables the allegory to work its effect while keeping its distance from any crudely literal sense. Zeugma, the yoking of two distinct idioms to a single verb ("Or stain her honour, or her new brocade") is the single most effective of Pope's rhetorical tricks, in so far as it creates an ironic clash between seemingly disparate orders of value. Thus Krieger can argue that the poem finally brings about a "miraculous conversion", such that "the 'frail china jar' becomes more precious than virginity − in effect comes to be not merely a symbol for virginity, but even an artificial substitute for it in this world of artifice" (p. 212). In so far as it deploys a more "technical" idiom to refine upon this commonplace trope, Krieger's essay rejoins the New Critical tradition whose values and priorities it scarcely disturbs.

And yet, on a closer reading, there are signs in Krieger's text that the different analytical terms go along with a tendency to problematize those truths about poetic language that the New Critics took as a matter of working faith. For one thing, Krieger holds out against the somewhat homespun New Critical rhetoric which assimilates *metonymy* to *metaphor*, and thus ignores any problems in the way of its own transcendentally unifying vision. Krieger's essay was published in 1961, long before the advent of deconstruction or of Paul de Man's powerful demystifying texts on the rhetoric of metaphor and symbol. Nevertheless there are moments when Krieger very strikingly anticipates de Man's astringent critique of the truth-claim vested in these privileged figures of thought. The more orthodox New Critics were apt to build a vision of universal harmony and truth on the basis of details (like Belinda's lock) which they took – in a vaguely encompassing sense – as metaphors of the human condition. Krieger is himself intermittently willing to go along with such claims. But elsewhere he insists (like de Man) that it is wrong to be taken in by this rhetorical ploy; that metonymy and metaphor need to be distinguished; and that most "metaphors" come down in the end to aggregates of metonymic detail. Thus with Pope it is a question of resisting inflated metaphorical accounts by viewing the poem as "a mockery of the self-conscious seriousness displayed by trivial characters over a trivial occurrence". And in that case we will see them "indulging the logical fallacy of metonymy: they have mistaken the lock of hair, actually incapable of being violated, for the lady's body – vulnerable, but unassaulted by the baron" (p. 203). There is more to this passage than a simple insistence on getting one's terminology right and not confusing two distinct figures of speech. What Krieger is effectively deconstructing – against the main drift of his essay – is the strong vested interest in totalizing tropes (like metaphor and symbol) which underwrites the claims of New Critical method.

The comparison with de Man will seem less far-fetched if one takes account of a symptomatic footnote to Krieger's essay. The note conceeds that he has been using the key-term "zeugma" in two distinct senses, only one of them answering to its proper usage as defined by rhetorical theory. A genuine case of zeugma is one where the double meaning hangs on a single verb, thus involving a *grammatical* as well as a rhetorical dimension to the well-wrought pun. This condition is satisfied by classic examples of the kind ("Here thou, great Anna! whom three realms obey, / Dost sometimes counsel take – and sometimes tea.") Of Krieger's instances, only one (he thinks) conforms to the strict pattern: "Or stain her honour, or her new brocade". The others are cases where the rhetorical effect is much the same although the grammar doesn't properly conform to type. These figures Krieger describes as "mere antitheses of four distinct parts, with each object controlled by its own verb" (p. 219). Thus in the lines "Whether the nymph shall break Diana's law, / Or some frail China jar receive a flaw" there is no instance of zeugma, strictly defined, but there *is* the strong sense that disparate scales of value are being neatly played off through a shrewd turn of style. This enables Krieger to claim that, "in a rhetorical if not in a grammatical sense", these tropes all exploit the same kind of verbal resource. Only in rare cases do we find what Krieger calls "the short-circuited perfection of the grammatical device". The others are "effective, but less complete, and thus less brilliant examples yielding the same rhetorical effect".

In several late essays de Man drew attention to the link between rhetorical and ideological forms of mystification. In particular he pointed to the ways in which philosophers and literary critics had effectively collapsed the vital distinction between logic, grammar and rhetoric.[18] This threefold division – basis of the classical *trivium* – was pushed out of sight (so de Man argues) by the rise of an aesthetic ideology which privileged metaphor and symbol as the highest, most expressive forms of language. What this attitude entailed, on the negative side, was a marked disregard for metonymy, allegory and other such merely "mechanical" tropes. These figures held out against the Symbolist drive to sink ontological differences and treat language as a visionary discourse of pure, unmediated truth. They insisted on the arbitrary nature of the sign, the irreducible gap between signifier and signified, and the fact that meaning was constructed in language by a process that constantly deferred or undermined the hypostatic union dreamt of in Symbolist aesthetics. Thus the "valorization of Symbol" always occurs at the expense of allegory and coincides historically with "the growth of an aesthetics that refuses to distinguish between experience and the representation of this experience".[19] What metonymy and allegory have in common is their power to deconstruct this mystification of language by ceaselessly revealing the rhetorical sleights of hand upon which its claims are ultimately based. In "the world of the Symbol", de Man writes, "it would be possible for the image to coincide with the substance", since sign and reality are "part and whole of the same set of categories". With allegory, on the other hand, meaning can only consist "in the *repetition* of a previous sign with which it can never coincide, since it is of the essence of this previous sign to be pure anteriority".[20] And metonymy exerts a similar force of deconstructive leverage since it focusses attention on the artifice involved – the element of random or piecemeal selectivity – in any act of figural substitution. Where metaphor implies a totalizing grasp, a perfect reciprocity between "vehicle" and "tenor", metonymy puts up an active resistance to this strong rhetorical drift.

Hence de Man's repeated demonstration of the ways in which underprivileged tropes (like metonymy and allegory) work to undo the high romantic claims of symbol and metaphor. Hence also his suggestion that criticism returns to that division of discourse (logic, grammar, rhetoric) laid down by the classical *trivium*. For it is precisely in the tension *between* these disciplines or levels of analysis that de Man locates the most important area for deconstructive critique. It is here, he argues, that mystified rhetorical strategies get a hold upon language by systematically eliding the conflicts of sense which would otherwise threaten their self-assured grasp. This comes out most clearly in the problems that develop as one reads a text with an eye to those repetitive (or 'quasi-automatic') patterns of meaning that resist a purely metaphorical account. By calling attention to this resistance – showing, as de Man very often does, how metaphor typically self-deconstructs into chains of metonymic detail – theory can effectively hold out against the powers of linguistic mystification. And from this it follows, according to de Man, that "more than any other mode of enquiry . . . the linguistics of literariness is a powerful and indispensable tool in the unmasking of ideological aberrations, as well as a determining factor in accounting for their occurrence".[21] On the one hand literary language gives endless opportunities to those who would erect a wholesale system of mystified values on the basis of a favoured few rhetorical tropes. Such is the New Critical way of elevating figures like "paradox" and "irony" to the status of touchstones for the absolute measurement of poetic worth. But there is also – as de Man would argue – an opposite, demystifying use for the "linguistics of literariness", one that can recognize those strategies for what they are precisely by virtue of its own close involvement with textual and rhetorical critique. Thus de Man writes contemptuously of critics who attack deconstruction on the grounds of its supposed "apolitical" character. "Those who reproach literary theory for being oblivious to social and historical (that is to say ideological) reality are merely stating their fear at having their own ideological mystifications exposed by the tool they are trying to discredit. They are, in short, very poor readers of Marx's *German Ideology*."[22] If deconstruction makes a virtue of attending closely to the rhetoric of literary (and critical) texts, this is *not* – as some Marxist critics would have it – a last-ditch retreat from the pressures of political commitment. For it is often at this level of textual analysis that thought can best unmask those effects of ideological blindness and duplicity to which language is always prey.

IV

This brief excursion into de Man's later essays may help to define the exact point at which Krieger parts company with the orthodox New Critical reading of "The Rape of the Lock". His insistence on distinguishing metonymy from metaphor is a move beyond the mystified ontology of poetic language that treats all the kinds and varieties of trope as aspiring to a single, metaphorical condition. It is true that Krieger takes only a cautious and limited step in this direction. Thus his footnote no sooner explains the distinction than it seems to withdraw, for all practical purposes, onto safer New Critical ground. ("My point is, however, that in a rhetorical if not a grammatical sense, there is a similar yoking of two disparate worlds in all these instances.") And his reading is indeed, to a very large extent, organized around those selfsame rhetorical strategies that operate in Brooks and other such adepts of formalist method. In this sense Krieger's essay differs from itself as much as it differs from orthodox New Critical practice. But this difference is by no means confined to a somewhat more exacting deployment of rhetorical terms. Ultimately it leads to a questioning of all those aesthetic assumptions which the New Critics raised into a safeguard against the pressures of historical awareness.

Not that Krieger deconstructs the formalist position with anything like de Man's tenacity or will to expose its blind-spots of argument. He remains a New Critic by rooted persuasion, arguing that poetry has the power to express lasting truths through a language that transcends the limiting conditions of plain prose statement. More recently Krieger has defended such claims against the threat of a deconstructionist theory that would seem to annul every kind of ontological privilege and reduce poetry to an undifferentiating rhetoric of tropes. In his book *Poetic Presence and Illusion* (1979) Krieger suggests that Renaissance poets like Sidney and Spenser effectively prefigured all these modern debates.[23] On the one hand they were trained up in a long tradition of rhetorical theory which laid great stress on the elaborate conventions and the artificial character of poetic language. On the other, they devised a whole range of redemptive tropes by which to thematize the permanence of verbal art-forms, their power to resist the encroachments of time and the vicissitudes of cultural change. Hence those metaphors in the courtly-love tradition that represent the poem as conferring on the beloved an immortality beyond reach of her natural charms and graces. Such tropes are an emblem – so Krieger would argue – of poetry's power to hold out against the various disintegrating forces that afflict other kinds of language. And among those forces must be counted the drift toward a generalized intertextuality whose effect is to undermine belief in the "presence" (or capacity for autonomous self-preservation) traditionally ascribed to poetry.

These themes are all present in Krieger's reading of "The Rape of the Lock". They amount – as I have said – to a highly refined and sophisticated set of variations on the standard New Critical technique that treats the poem as a self-sustaining allegory of aesthetic transcendence. Thus Pope can finally afford to acknowledge the hard truths of Belinda's mortal condition, but "only because he is granting a resurrection to that metonymic lock which has been appropriately hailed by the 'beau monde' that it symbolizes" (p. 218). The rhetorical drift here – from "metonymy" to "symbol" – shows very clearly what de Man has in mind when he writes of the prematurely "totalizing" drive that motivates all rhetorics based upon symbol and metaphor. In this case it allows Krieger's essay to rise to an impressive peroration where the poem is inscribed "midst the stars" (with Belinda's name), and "the illusory universe . . . like the 'Beau monde' constructed as a work of art . . . testifies to the persistence, the indomitable humanity of its creator's classic vision" (pp. 218–19). It would be hard to find a more consummate example of formalist poetics in the service of a transcendental aesthetic creed.

But one can set against this the various indications that Krieger had already found problems with the "old" New Criticism, not least with its tendency to lift poems into a realm of timeless contemplative truth immune to the assaults of time. One such indication is the fact that his essay brings in *The Dunciad*, not merely as a source of local contrasts and comparisons, but by way of a genuinely *intertextual* reading that threatens the whole aesthetic ideology built upon "The Rape of the Lock". In the end Krieger sees a victory for art against the "uncreating word" of anarchic reality, the "disintegrating force" that history applies to the products of human imagination. But it is a victory achieved through such a complex and tortuous process of argument that Krieger appears to be constantly setting up obstacles to his own wished-for interpretative vision. Of all texts (or intertexts), *The Dunciad* goes furthest to undermine that sense of metaphysical grace that Krieger glimpses, precariously figured, in "The Rape of the Lock". And the point is made again, from a different angle, when he takes Epistle I of the "Essay on Man" as an instance of Pope's rather shallow and simplistic benevolist creed, his belief that all was for the best if one could only make out the hidden purpose of things. Krieger regards this as a piece of slightly desperate nostalgia, a backdated myth quite out of touch with the realities of Pope's time and place. It offers "a kind of *ersatz* and decapitated replica of the unified, catholic, psychologically and aesthetically soothing thirteenth-century universe" (p. 212). Krieger is firm enough in rejecting this myth and the species of naive wish-fulfilment that goes along with it. Yet there are, as we have seen, still signs in Krieger's essay of that other powerful myth of historical decline and aesthetic transcendence which Eliot and the New Critics after him took as an article of faith. And this puts considerable strain on his argument when it comes to distinguishing the good from the bad (or the merely escapist) uses of myth. Once again, the interpreter is on trial along with the poem, his reading subject to the same kinds of complicating doubt and tension. For it is only through the highest refinements of formalist method that "The Rape of the Lock" can be made to appear an object of such transcendent aesthetic worth that it stands apart from the naively idealizing strain of Pope's lesser productions. Otherwise the poem *and* Krieger's reading must seem to fall into the same habit of substituting myth for the complex realities of human experience.

Krieger's intentions are plain enough. He wants to point up the peculiar excellence of "The Rape of the Lock" by contrasting it firstly with Pope's pious platitudes in the *Essay On Man*, and then with the vision of universal chaos vouchsafed in *The Dunciad*. This allows him to take the most completely "artificial" of Pope's creations and argue that in truth it represents a supremely balanced response to those fallacious opposite extremes. His rejecting the archaic mythology of the *Essay On Man* is a credibilizing gesture which insists that Krieger's essay − like the better poem − is strong enough to withstand a good deal of demythologizing treatment. "Once Pope feels secure that he has established Belinda's world as one we can cherish . . . he dares introduce materials from other and realer worlds more openly as if to prove the power of his delicate creation" (p. 209). The same can be said of Krieger's essay, balanced on a knife-edge of critical tact between the claims of an ideal aesthetic order and those of a tough-minded demythologizing stance. Hence the uneasy coexistence within that essay of orthodox New Critical tropes with tentative moves into a larger domain of aesthetic and historical speculation. The signs of this incipient passage "beyond formalism" are there to be read in Krieger's attentiveness to intertextual meaning, his insistence (up to a point) on the metaphor/metonymy distinction, and his refusal to countenance wholesale Spenglerian mythologies of Western cultural decline.

This commentary will seem rather off-the-point if one accepts what Krieger has to say in his opening paragraph. Here he maintains that New Criticism is not − as popular prejudice would have it − a species of "ivory-tower" formalism that ignores history on principle. His essay is intended partly as a practical demonstration that the close-reading of literary texts "can illuminate even so un-New-Critical an area as the history of ideas" (p. 201). But at this point Krieger feels obliged to enter a series of methodological caveats. It may be, he writes, that this exercise will turn into "a kind of mythology of idealized generalizations", a myth which allows certain "ideological commonplaces" to bear more weight than the "careful historian" would permit. To this extent, as Krieger seems willing to acknowledge, the interests of history are still subdued to those of a harmonized aesthetic understanding. But if this results in his essay "doing violence" to those other kinds of commonplace that govern the historian's enterprise, then Krieger remains unrepentant. For "surely", he argues, "this is one of the chief functions of poetry, this violation of the commonplace" (p. 201). His language here can hardly fail to call up echoes of that other "violation" whose literal or figurative sense the poem and its critics so skilfully hold in balance. Oddly enough, in this particular passage, it is the myth-making artifice of poetry that inflicts such "violence" on historical understanding, and not – as one might suppose – the other way round. But there are similar ironies and double-edged comparisons everywhere in Krieger's essay. Thus: "the rape of the lock is more to be avoided in honor's world than are the more sordid, but less openly proclaimed, assaults in classical legend and in London back-alleys" (p. 204). Once again Pope's achievement is precariously balanced between opposite extremes: brute fact and fiction, sordid reality and myths of Arcadian innocence. What Krieger visibly strives to maintain is an attitude transcending these hateful antinomies. But equally visible in the rhetoric of his essay are the twists and argumentative detours that result from a formalist aesthetic pushed up against its limits of self-valorizing method.

One result of what he calls "this somewhat reckless allegorical excursion" is that Krieger brings poetry more closely into contact with philosophy and the history of ideas. The contact is fleeting and offered in the spirit of a merely suggestive analogy. Nevertheless it prefigures, in a tentative way, that erosion of the old ontological bounds that ensued upon the break with New Critical precept and practice. In this passage Krieger is reflecting on the extreme fragility and artificial nature of that civilized world whose ideal embodiment is the rhyming couplet of Pope.

As the Humes and the Kants convincingly reveal in shattering the false, dogmatic security of this world, the price of the construct is a metaphysical flimsiness – a naiveté, the reverse side of its symmetrical delicacy – that made it easy prey to the rigours of critical philosophy and the ravages of social-economic revolution.   (p. 213)

Here again there is an element of mythical projection, a running-

together of "critical philosophy" (conceived in no very precise terms)
with the process of cultural attrition through social change. Certainly it
is a passage that bears all the marks of that gloomy prognosis which was
T. S. Eliot's legacy to modern criticism. But in Krieger's version there is
a countervailing stress on the "flimsiness", the lack of historical foundations for any mythology that sets up a golden age of past achievement
against which to measure the symptoms of latter-day decline. Kant is
drawn in, not merely as a typecast "rationalist" destroyer of communal
wisdom, but also – more pointedly – as one who called such myths to
account by exposing their dependence on the ideal constructions of
human intellectual and imaginative vision. Thus the passage – like so
much in Krieger's essay – seems to allegorize its own predicament,
caught between a powerful literary myth of origins and a will to
deconstruct that myth by moving outside its privileged aesthetic ground.

Krieger is among the subtlest and most resourceful of those theorists
who have continued to work within the broad confines of New Critical
method. Others – like Geoffrey Hartman – have seized upon the
hermeneutic freedoms offered by alternative sources in (mainly Continental) theory.[24] In Hartman's case the move beyond formalism has
led to his dispensing with all those customary terms of distinction that
mark off "literature" from "criticism" on the one hand, and criticism
from philosophy (or "theory") on the other. His writing thus breaks
altogether with that principled division of realms which the New
Critics sought to maintain. Yet in reading their texts – as I have tried
to show here – one is constantly aware of those other discourses
crowding in upon the narrow preserves of aesthetic autonomy and
truth. What Krieger writes of the "Essay on Man" could just as well
apply to his own beleaguered position as a rearguard defender of New
Critical values. In Pope's reassertion of a bygone "cosmic solidarity"
one detects, according to Krieger, "the insecurity that was aware of its
vulnerability and of the surrounding hordes of modernism already closing in" (p. 213). Such criticism verges on a conscious recognition of
its own deep involvement with the vision of order so precariously
achieved by Pope. At this point it becomes quite impossible to draw
a line between commentary "on" the poem and commentary as a kind
of reflexive critique that both displays and interrogates its own founding assumptions.

Of course Pope guessed what the critics would soon be at, and determined to play them off the field by supplying an absurd pseudonymous
gloss. "A Key to the *Lock*" by Esdras Barnivelt appeared soon after the
poem and affected to warn the innocent reader against being taken in
by its subtle contrivances. "This unhappy division of our Nation into

Parties" is the cause, Pope suggests, of all the covert political meanings that are presently passed off upon an unsuspecting public by poets of deeply mischievous intent. Hence the need for an answering subtlety of method on the interpreter's part.

In all things which are intricate, as Allegories in their own Nature are, . . . it is not to be expected that we should find the Clue at first sight; but when once we have laid hold on that, we shall trace this our Author through all the Labyrinths, Doublings and Turnings of this intricate Composition.   (p. 35)

And indeed the poem has not lacked for ingenious commentators ready to pursue those labyrinthine doublings and tropes. But Pope's prediction is wide of the mark – in the long term at least – when he attributes this seeking-out of occult meanings to the spirit of rampant party-political prejudice. Far from reading politics *into* the poem, criticism has developed the most elaborate techniques for keeping such questions either safely out of sight or firmly subordinate to its own aesthetic concerns. "Unhappy divisions" of any kind – sexual or political – give way to the desire for a harmonizing myth that transcends all forms of disruptive or complicating difference. It is in the moments when this project encounters resistance that the critics are beguiled into allegories of reading more intricate than anything dreamed of by Pope's pseudonymous scribe.

Notes

[1] See Paul de Man, "Form and Intent in the American New Criticism", in *Blindness and Insight: essays in the rhetoric of contemporary criticism* (London: Methuen, 1983), pp. 20–50.
[2] See especially Allen Tate, *The Forlorn Demon* (Chicago: University of Chicago Press, 1953).
[3] T. S. Eliot, *The Use of Poetry and the Use of Criticism* (London: Faber, 1933), p. 63.
[4] Cleanth Brooks, "My Credo" (contribution to "The Formalist Critics: a symposium"), *Kenyon Review*, vol. 18 (1951), 72–81; p. 78.
[5] John Crowe Ransom, in *Critical Responses to Kenneth Burke*, ed. William Ruekert (Minneapolis: University of Minnesota Press, 1969), p. 156.
[6] John Crowe Ransom, "Mr Empson's Muddles", *The Southern Review*, vol. 4 (1938/9), pp. 322–39; p. 330.
[7] See Cleanth Brooks, *The Well-Wrought Urn* (New York: Harcourt, Brace and World, 1947).
[8] T. S. Eliot, "The Metaphysical Poets", in *Selected Essays* (London: Faber, 1964), pp. 288–99.
[9] de Man, *Blindness and Insight*, p. 28.
[10] See the two essays on Wordsworth reprinted in Paul de Man, *The Rhetoric of Romanticism* (New York: Columbia University Press, 1984). Also

Geoffrey Hartman, *Wordsworth's Poetry, 1787–1814* (New Haven: Yale University Press, 1964) and David Simpson, *Wordsworth and the Figurings of the Real* (London: Macmillan, 1982).

11 See especially W. K. Wimsatt, *The Verbal Icon* (Lexington: University of Kentucky Press, 1954).

12 See T. S. Eliot, *Knowledge and Experience in the Philosophy of F. H. Bradley* (London: Faber, 1964).

13 John Dixon Hunt (ed.), *"The Rape of the Lock": a casebook* (London: Macmillan, 1968).

14 See F. R. Leavis, "The Line of Wit", in *Revaluation* (Harmondsworth: Penguin, 1967), pp. 10–41.

15 Cleanth Brooks, *The Well-Wrought Urn*, pp. 10–20.

16 Aubrey Williams, "The 'Fall' of China", in Hunt (ed.), *A Casebook*, p. 220–36. All further references to essays in the *Casebook* given by page number in the text.

17 Jacques Derrida, *Spurs: Nietzsche's styles*, trans. Barbara Harlow (Chicago: University of Chicago Press, 1979), pp. 67–9.

18 See especially Paul de Man, "The Resistance To Theory", *Yale French Studies*, 63 (1982), pp. 3–20. Also, for a more summary statement, "The Return To Philology", *Times Literary Supplement*, No. 4158 (10 December 1982), 1355–6. *The Resistance to Theory* – a posthumous volume of essays on this and related topics – has been announced for publication by the University of Minnesota Press.

19 de Man, "The Rhetoric of Temporality", in *Blindness and Insight*, pp. 187–228; p. 188. See also Daniel O'Hara's discussion of de Man on Yeats, pp. 360–4 of this volume.

20 Ibid., p. 207.

21 de Man, *The Resistance to Theory*, p. 11.

22 Ibid., p. 11.

23 Murray Krieger, *Poetic Presence and Illusion* (Baltimore and London: Johns Hopkins University Press, 1979). See also Krieger's essay in the present volume, where he develops a related line of argument.

24 See for instance Geoffrey Hartman, *Beyond Formalism* (New Haven: Yale University Press, 1979); *"The Fate of Reading" and Other Essays* (Chicago: University of Chicago Press, 1975); *Criticism in the Wilderness: the study of literature today* (New Haven: Yale University Press, 1980); and *Saving the Text: literature/Derrida/philosophy* (Baltimore and London: Johns Hopkins University Press, 1981).

Gray's "Elegy": inscribing the twilight

STEPHEN BYGRAVE

I

One tendency of the professionalization of certain French writing as American "deconstruction" in the 1970s was to deny the "history" which more traditional scholarship assumed to interinanimate its texts. The denial was tactical, and that history was meant to return as a problem. History may indeed be, as Fredric Jameson suggests, the return of our repressed: interpretation *is*, as de Man and others insist, a rewriting of rewriting, but Jameson insists that *what* it rewrites is a historical subtext rather than (as traditional scholarship would have it) context. History remains as a "ground" or "absent cause", the necessary fiction which fictions rewrite, *re*present.[1] However, since that professionalization was carried out rather in Departments of Comparative Literature or of English than in History or Philosophy some unease may remain at reading a history out of rather than into the text.

At the end of his essay "Literary History and Literary Modernity", Paul de Man writes that "history" cannot be the object of knowledge, since the data of historical understanding "are not empirical facts but written texts, even if these texts masquerade in the guise of wars or revolution".[2] Thus de Man's *Allegories of Reading* "started out as a historical study and ended up as a theory of reading" within which he can mock any talk of a *hors texte* which is historical as not merely presumptive but as the return of a recurrent delusion:

With the internal law and order of literature well policed we can now confidently devote ourselves to the foreign affairs, the external politics of literature. Not only do we feel able to do so, but we owe it to ourselves to take this step: our moral conscience would not allow us to do otherwise.[3]

Our kingdom for a *hors texte*. De Man has shrewdly anticipated objections to his own practice. With de Man (as with a critic like Michael Riffaterre) the logic cannot be faulted once the premises have been accepted. But is the insistence that history may produce readings rather than the reverse attributable only to the promptings of "our moral conscience"? And why does de Man write "*external* politics"? What sort of "*internal* politics" is he claiming for his own practice? In an essay called "The Dead-end of Formalist Criticism" he posits a "historical poetics" which – although it does not yet exist, Marxism being tied to an idealist teleology – remains a consummation devoutly to be wished: "Such a poetics promises nothing except the fact that poetic thought will keep on becoming, will continue to ground itself in a space beyond its failure" (*BI*, p. 242). It is no coincidence that this reads like a quotation from Schlegel's *Athenäum Fragments* or Shelley's *Defence of Poetry*. De Man's characteristic procedure is first to pressurize the explicit claims made by a text, then to show how they must collapse under such pressure. Second, he introduces an alternative set of terms of his own, only to show how these too must finally collapse, and what remains is either a question or a paradox. These alternatives are not unlike the endings of Keats's "Ode to a Nightingale" and "Ode on a Grecian Urn" respectively, a (rhetorical) question or a (paradoxical) complementary. De Man's refusal of determinate meaning is then Romantic but principled: it swerves away from the dead end of a pragmatist reader-response theory.

A second tendency has been for the play of language, of interpretation, only to heap the shrine of the set text with incense kindled from the graduate school's flame. Now your "deconstructive" reading of the canonical text can be set alongside (some would say, is parasitical upon) the New Critical, archetypal, or whatever: professionalization was also domestication. Calling that against which you define yourself "Western metaphysics" may only be like calling it "Philistinism" or "technologico-Benthamite civilization". Particularly at Yale the extraordinary productivity of the 1970s was a productivity of attention to texts which, although devalued by the New Critics, were hardly outside the canon. The readings of Bloom and Hartman especially were belated readings of the words on the page, and their attention was expended on those texts which risked the most on the self-subsistence (the atemporality) of their figures: that is to say, Romantic poetry. Although a literary history has been the least important of its proclaimed goals the project of Harold Bloom has invited us to read literary history as the history of the Romantic poem. If as readers we are all post-Romantic then all poets, at least from Milton on, are Romantic.

Thomas Gray's "Elegy Written in a Country Churchyard" has been canonical almost since its first publication in 1751. It is now no longer read – professionally at least – as the expression of timeless and unchanging human feeling which Dr Johnson found in it. At the end of his *Life of Gray* Johnson says that he prefers Gray's life to any of his works but then goes on to exempt this one:

In the character of his Elegy I rejoice to concur with the common reader; for by the common sense of readers uncorrupted with literary prejudices, after all the refinements of subtlety and the dogmatism of learning, must be finally decided all claim to poetical honours. The *Church-yard* abounds with images which find a mirror in every mind, and with sentiments to which every bosom returns an echo.[4]

Nowadays, rather than being read like the epitaph it claims to become, the "Elegy" is read as a poem which dramatizes the Augustan ideal under stress, incapable of being extended to accommodate certain forms of personal rather than common or social experience. It is read then as a poem whose time has not quite come. The word deconstruction, if not always its practice, suggests a clearing of the ground, a working through the text. Gray's poem works rather by a textual suspension which harks back, as much eighteenth-century prose does, to a mythical era in which society was simpler and could be more easily grasped. Thus the literary history of pastoral is not extraneous to the political: William Empson has described pastoral as a "process of putting the complex into the simple".[5] The "Elegy" evokes a twilight which it cannot then move beyond: this text itself (Gray's self) must finally be displaced onto another (the epitaph) which has, it can be claimed, *already* gone through that twilight. That claim is, I think, Gray's own in the (rewritten) ending of the poem: in what Landor called "the tin-kettle of an epitaph tied to its tail".[6]

Displacement may be too strong a word for a poem so concerned with the integration of individual into common experience, and so often read as having achieved it. I shall try to show however that the "private" syntax of the "Elegy" itself problematizes the reading its "public" diction appears to seek. We might compare Collins's "Ode to Evening" which does not reach a main verb until its fifteenth line (and his "Ode on the Poetical Character" never seems to arrive at its main verb at all). As John Barrell shows, this creates a tension with the placidity of the diction. In the "Ode to Evening" he finds syntactic warrant in the suspension of the main verb and the multiple dependent clauses preceding it for a series of Empsonian paraphrases which might defuse such tension: to so defuse it however would be to rewrite it. We are left with readings which are alternative but cannot be simultaneous, readings of the poem as either "allegorical" or "descriptive" – terms offered by the title of the volume in which the "Ode" first appeared. The allegorical figure of personification is an abstraction from disparate, individual experience where the poem's descriptive particulars, which would be below common notice, are brought into contiguity. In Gray's "Elegy", also set at twilight, there is a similar tension, here ending with a personification, the prosopopoeia, as I shall suggest, of the epitaph. In an epitaph the individual is most generalized, most abstracted, in death. The qualities which Johnson finds in the "Elegy" are those which, as we shall see, Wordsworth finds in epitaphs. The epitaph joins name, verse and time in publicly legible form. Thus Barrell suggests that the extension of forms in the mid eighteenth century from the hegemony of the heroic couplet to, amongst other forms, odes and elegies, "could be argued as attempts to recover the range that has been lost to poetry, and even to propose versions of an ideal, less complex society for the poet to operate in, where private experience was not separable from public, or not suppressed in favour of an abstract idea of the typical, the representative, the common".[7]

With the "Elegy" as with Collins's "Ode" beginning at the beginning is difficult because it takes so long to begin.

> The curfew tolls the knell of parting day,
> The lowing herd winds slowly o'er the lea,
> The ploughman homeward plods his weary way,
> And leaves the world to darkness and to me.[8]

This is an iteration of particulars which, together with its insistence on the gradual departure of light and of human and animal company from the scene, suggest that what is to follow will be a personal meditation. Yet the rhyme-word "me" at the end of the stanza is the only occurrence of the first-person pronoun in the poem. This corresponds, I suggest, to that syntactic suspension noticed in Collins's "Ode". (In Gray's "Ode on a Distant Prospect of Eton College" – a poem which, as even its title suggests, depends on a withdrawn, superior position for the perceiver – the first-person is withheld until the fifteenth line, which is its only mention.)

Such a characteristic could be compared with Gray's earlier poems, many of which are concerned with a kind of lapsarian exclusion, or with his biography. For example, Lonsdale tells us in his edition that it has "never been doubted" that where Gray refers, in a letter to Walpole written from Stoke Poges in 1750, to "having put an end to a thing, whose beginning you have seen long ago", he refers to the "Elegy" which he encloses. The letter is worth quoting in full:

Dear Sir,
As I live in a place, where even the ordinary tattle of the town arrives not till it is stale, and which produces no events of its own, you will not desire any excuse from me for writing so seldom, especially as of all people living you are the least a friend to letters spun out of one's own brains, with all the toil and constraint that accompanies sentimental productions. I have been here at Stoke a few days (where I shall continue good part of the summer); and having put

an end to a thing, whose beginning you have seen long ago, I immediately send it you. You will, I hope, look upon it in the light of a *thing with an end to it*; a merit that most of my writings have wanted, and are like to want, but which this epistle I am determined shall not want, when it tells you that I am ever

Yours,

T. GRAY

Not that I have done yet; but who could avoid the temptation of finishing so roundly and so cleverly in the manner of good queen Anne's days? Now I have talked of writings; I have seen a book, which is by this time in the press, against Middleton (though without naming him), by Asheton. As far as I can judge from a very hasty reading, there are things in it new and ingenious, but rather too prolix, and the style here and there savouring too strongly of sermon. I imagine it will do him credit. So much for other people, now to *self* again. You are desired to tell me your opinion, if you can take the pains, of these lines. I am once more

Ever Yours.[9]

The poem could be read as though it were this letter: it claims to have ended but its ending is a false ending; it strives for the elegantly assured solidity of the high-Augustan mode ("the manner of good queen Anne's days") but finally forgets those it has claimed to recover from being forgotten ("So much for other people, now to *self* again"). The danger of such a (parodic) reading would be in replacing a historical with an antiquarian approach: in domesticating Gray's gesture toward a "space" beyond the poem as a gesture explicable only hermetically. Such a reading of the "Elegy" then might merely re-present Gray's representation of his own confusion.

Clearly there is a superficial politics of the poem. The tragedy of lost opportunities is presented in terms of very different valuations of Hampden and Milton compared with that of Cromwell (lines 57–60). The Eton College MS. of the poem has the names Cato, Tully and Caesar for Hampden, Milton and Cromwell. This too is indicative of the tension between the generalizing, moralizing tone and the historical particular. But beneath the surface there are also tremors – in, for example, the preceding stanza (lines 53–6):

> Full many a gem of purest ray serene
> The dark, unfathomed caves of ocean bear;
> Full many a flower is born to blush unseen
> And waste its sweetness on the desert air.

Now clearly this is an important figure for Gray, because he uses it again in his much later "Ode for Music":

> Thy liberal heart, thy judging eye,
> The flower unheeded shall descry,

And bid it round heaven's altars shed
The fragrance of its blushing head:
Shall raise from earth the latent gem
To glitter on the diadem.

Yet a classic piece of literary criticism itself brings into the light the implications of the figure. This is from William Empson's *Some Versions of Pastoral*:

What this means, as the context makes clear, is that eighteenth century England had no scholarship system or *carrière ouverte aux talents*. This is stated as pathetic, but the reader is put into a mood in which he would not try to alter it . . . By comparing the social arrangement to Nature he makes it seem inevitable, which it was not, and gives it a dignity which was undeserved. Furthermore a gem does not mind being in a cave and a flower prefers not to be picked; we feel that the man is like the flower, as short-lived, natural, and valuable, and this tricks us into feeling that he is better off without opportunities. The sexual suggestion of *blush* brings in the Christian idea that virginity is good in itself, and so that any renunciation is good; this may trick us into feeling it is lucky for the poor man that society keeps him unspotted from the world. The tone of melancholy claims that the poet understands the considerations opposed to aristocracy, though he judges against them; the truism of the reflections in the churchyard, the universality and impersonality this gives to the style, claim as if by comparison that we ought to accept the injustice of society as we do the inevitability of death.   (p. 4)

Although it offers itself, tentatively, as only an example of how such analysis might look, this seems to me a fine example of a Marxist analysis, wrenching the text from the context it tries to make for itself and forcing it to confront (some version of) history.

Without such a reading of the "bourgeois" pastoral much later work would have been impossible. Let me quote from a book which has helped as much as any to provide us with a context for reading eighteenth-century poems which is reconstructed from eighteenth-century assumptions (without sharing them as, say, Paul Fussell seems to). It is such a procedure at least which John Barrell claims for his book *English Literature in History, 1730–1780: an equal, wide survey*:

Instead of attempting to write a summary of one or more aspects of the history of the period as it can be reconstructed from the late twentieth century, and then attempting to compare that construction with what we can learn from the literature, I have tried to ask how some writers of the period themselves attempted to construct an understanding of contemporary social changes. What was it that most struck *them* about what was happening in their society, and in what ways did they try to comprehend what was happening as an historical process? What sorts of knowledge did that effort require of them, and from what perspective, and in what language, could social change be described?[10]

This is not a plea for the innocence of historical scholarship but the pre-emptive defence of an oppositional procedure. Barrell constructs but does not name a critic who only reproduces the eighteenth century's sense of its own history as teleology. His claim is to replace teleology with archaeology. As the rest of his book demonstrates, "perspective" here is a metaphor not for the privilege assumed by the twentieth-century critic or historian but for that ideological vantage-point assumed by, among others, Thomson, Dyer, several eighteenth-century grammarians, and Smollett. The stance of withdrawn "superiority" rationalizes a political as well as a metaphysical subject–object distance. Writers on society want at once to be involved in the picture as useful producers and to be possessed of a panoramic view of it: yet it is impossible to be convinced at once of right action and of "an equal, wide survey". Barrell reads Thomson's "Seasons" and Dyer's *The Fleece* as symbolic legitimations of a perspective which although not unchallenged nor unfalsifiable was one upon which the social order depended. As Barrell goes on to say, "the writing of such poets [as Collins or Gray] seems reduced to questioning the possibilities of writing 'true' poetry at all in a 'progressive' age: it does not so much challenge the confident vision of Georgic, as resent it". And that resentment issues in what might look like nostalgia. Gray's "Elegy" can take its place among "discourses to which the freedom of disaffection is accorded on the understanding that they are private".[11]

In the "Elegy" however this privacy is externalized to the extent that Johnson could see it as the apotheosis of "common sense". Although the impulses in the poem are toward making a durable text it seems also to foreground the exigencies of interpretation: there is not just the problem of the epitaph but that of the scroll of Knowledge never being unrolled for the rustic dead (lines 49–52) and their being forbidden to "read their history in a nation's eyes" (line 64) as the English revolutionaries could. Forgetfulness is "dumb" (line 85). This might lead us to interpret the reference to poetry and poets within the poem differently. In line 41 there is a "storied" urn – that which remains, but remains to no avail. The epitaph memorializes a living Melancholy very like that of the pensive poet at the beginning. *These* allegories of reading suggest some anxiety about Gray's ability to determine how his text will be read. The truly durable text is not the one which we are given finally in the epitaph: even the written epitaph seems devalued in favour of "the voice of Nature" out of the tomb (line 91). So, rather than take the poem's pre-history to be that of Gray's "development" we might examine, in the manner suggested by Barrell, the way it constructs its own history. (Of course literary history will be a constituent part of that construction too: the re-writing of "Lycidas" and other pastorals by a poet who invokes "mute inglorious Miltons".) That construction in turn ends with the writing of an epitaph, an inscription.

Edward Said describes a comparable moment in Swift's "Verses on the Death of Dr Swift", a poem in which Swift wittily anticipates the reception of his own death in the mouths of his acquaintances. By doing so, Swift "constructed the continuity he wished to perpetuate . . . Swift's death is transformed from a variety of gossipy stories into an event."[12] But it is an event only within the disparate accents of gossip – and "nowhere else" (p. 69). Such an "event", however, though contained within "the transcendent judgement of history" (p. 68), gives its own terms to history: "It becomes Swift's problem . . . to show language as the arena in which fictions battle each other until only the most worthy remain. What remains of Swift can only be described, a long time later, by an impartial, anonymous voice that . . . understands Swift as a man who was *too much* for his own time" (p. 69). What finally remains is not the dispersal of meanings among the trivial words and pastimes of the idle urban bourgeoisie but the "objective chronology" of historic time, two movements which are gathered together triumphantly by the movement of the poem. The poem is a synthesis which transcends such chat, and can control it, because "this conversation belongs neither to the public nor to the private world but to an entirely independent verbal order that obliterates every worthwhile distinction" (p. 69). The poem – this "powerful verbal structure" – literally makes history and the subject – Swift – supplements the particular time of his existence. Said is addressing the problem which was addressed, from the other side of the institutional fence, by Hayden White in his *Metahistory* (1973): the problem of the relationship of text (textuality) and history. For Said, Swift *solves* this problem, and it is never clear whether the "impartial, anonymous voice" is his conclusion as to the success of this inscription or his paraphrase of Swift's desire for that inscription. The problem of the disparate "voices" offered us by this poem – as by the "Elegy" and, behind both, Milton's "Lycidas" – is precisely the difficulty of that final, univocal inscription. Can we be happier with the notion of "history" as a speaking subject than we were with the notion of "authors"? (The latter at least had finite dates.)

Barrell, Empson and Said each pursue a metaphor of eighteenth-century poetry: Barrell takes that of the perspective, the gaze; Empson Gray's (local) flower and gem figure; and Said a moment of self-inscription very similar to that in the "Elegy". Their technique is to stand inside these metaphors and see where they get taken. It depends on their taking the poem at its word. The text is interrogated for what it *does* (which includes what it claims to do), rather than held as the triumphantly reconciling effect of vagrant causes in previous texts or in its author's biography. It entails a figuring *through* rather than a figuring *out* of the figures of a text. The poem should speak for itself, as a tombstone must: letting it speak will let it reveal its figural hand. De Man, with his strangely elephantine whimsy, calls this activity disfigurement.

II

The best reading of Gray's "Elegy" that I know of is by George T. Wright, who subtly traces the dialectic of motion and sound with the absence of these qualities through the figures of the poem. He takes his cue from its fifth line, "And all the air a solemn stillness holds", rightly suggesting that "stillness" in the poem signifies absence of sound as well as absence of movement and that, further, there is an objectification or reification of that stillness: so that the verb "to hold" signifies both to grasp and to remain.[13] I would add an emphasis on the setting of the poem at twilight, a hovering between states, a stilled moment in a process of transition. Evening is when withdrawing can seem communal rather than anti-social. Barrell's reading of Collins concludes that "evening becomes more than a time of day: it comes to represent that position, conscientiously sought for by a number of eighteenth-century poets, from which, withdrawn from the world, we can experience as concord whatever, within the world, we experienced as discord".[14] Wright also recognizes that the ending of the poem is not (or not only) a conventional gesture tagged on to some naturalizing, mythologizing reflections which patronize the rural poor. The close of the poem is not a renunciation of ambition and the committal of Gray's soul to God. Instead, it functions analogously to the epitaph of Swift's "Verses": "Gray does not, in fact, choose a simple 'unlettered' epitaph for himself but one that is cast in sophisticated heroic quatrains and has far too many lines for a 'frail memorial' . . . The central subject of the *Elegy* is not the contrast between the poor and the great, but the nature and meaning of epitaphs."[15]

Gray concludes the first version (1742) with a self-apostrophe, "thou who mindful of the unhonour'd Dead / Dost in these Notes their artless Tale relate", which leads to a final Christian–Stoic reconciliation:

> No more with Reason & thyself at Strife
> Give anxious Cares & endless Wishes room
> But thro' the cool sequester'd Vale of Life
> Pursue the silent Tenour of thy Doom.[16]

This conclusion, as his editor comments,

ultimately failed to satisfy Gray, partly because it was too explicitly personal for publication, but also no doubt because its very symmetry and order represented an over-simplification of his own predicament, of the way he saw his own life and wished it to be seen by society. A simple identification with the innocent but uneducated villagers was mere self-deception.[17]

In the final version, the pervading melancholy of Gray's concern with the prospect of his own annihilation is projected on to the rural society.

There remains a tension between the luck of the "cool sequester'd Vale" and the acknowledged repression of "chill Penury" in village life; but a new tension is created within the decorous *sententiae* of the end-stopped quatrains: a tension between the soliloquy and the fact that its only audience can be the dead villagers, its ostensible subject (Gray calls the poem "an elegy", another change from the earlier, Eton College manuscript, which has "Stanza's"). Gray ascribes to the villagers a quiet heroism, "far from the madding crowd", but the ambivalent praise for retirement is due also to a bitter lack of faith in the possible reception of the poet's work by the literary culture of the madding crowd. The art of the panegyrist is contrasted with the retirement of the villagers who were

> Forbade to wade through slaughter to a throne,
> And shut the gate of mercy on mankind;
>
> The struggling pangs of conscious truth to hide,
> To quench the blushes of ingenuous shame,
> Or heap the shrine of Luxury and Pride
> With incense kindled at the Muse's Flame.[18]

Yet retirement implies a prior engagement: which entails that the tension is felt by the poet alone. The poet who is "overheard" in the first twelve lines is an observer of rather than participant in nature and the villagers' lifestyle – which is presented in lines 17–28 as a pastoral reconciliation with nature. The analogy of spatial with psychological distance is one to which de Man and Barrell have both drawn attention.[19] Here of course the gap is primarily social. Gray is an outsider within the rural society as well. Indeed, as the "hoary-headed swain" evokes the poet-figure at the end of the poem, the nearest he comes to filling a role within the rural society is as the village idiot:

> Muttering his wayward fancies he would rove;
> Now drooping, woeful-wan, like one forlorn,
> Or craz'd with care, or cross'd in hopeless love.

This "rustic" poet too is an outsider, rapt in himself like Gray in the churchyard, yet distanced from him. We are unable to identify this poet-figure because of the way in which he is addressed prior to the inquiry as to his "fate": "For thee, who mindful of the unhonoured dead / Dost in these lines their artless tale relate." "For thee", we are told, but "thee" in this final version is less clearly Gray himself than the earlier "thou" who is finally enjoined to accept obscurity. Is this a self-apostrophe, or is it addressed to the stonecarver who, although "unletter'd", has incised the epitaph? "These lines" could be either the lapidary epitaph or this poem written by Thomas Gray. If Gray is addressing himself there is a grammatical displacement. The only occurrence of the first-person pronouns is in the fourth line, "And leaves the world to darkness, and to me". While "and to me" is made to seem syntactically superadded, almost an afterthought, it is of course foregrounded by its stanzaic position and, therefore, by rhyme.

In then going on to detail the "homely joys and destiny obscure" of the villagers, Gray implicitly sets theirs beside his own, paradoxically suggesting the promise of poetic immortality by its denial. The question whether he too may be a "mute inglorious Milton" is never asked. It is the headstones not the "Elegy" whose "uncouth rhymes . . . the place of fame and elegy supply". If, then, "these lines" are not the lines Gray writes, ostensibly to elegize the villagers, but those written by a rustic poet, now himself in the oblivion of death, it must be the "fate" of the dead stonecarver not of Gray which is related by the "hoary-headed swain". As a result, the identity of the "youth" for whom "th' unletter'd muse" has composed the epitaph is ambiguous. Gray does not emerge from this rural babble as Swift does from the urban – but do we expect or desire that he should?

Lest it be thought that I am playfully finding difficulties in a poem which, as Johnson says, finds an echo in every bosom, I shall here cite John Walker, from a rhetorical textbook which was reprinted nine times up to 1823. Walker assumes a sharp division between the voices of the "melancholy" Gray and the "indifferent" swain, in advising against accenting this second voice when reading the poem aloud:

Nothing can be conceived more truly ridiculous, in reading this passage, than quitting the melancholy tone of the relator, and assuming the indifferent and rustic accent of the old swain; and yet no error so likely to be mistaken for a beauty by a reader of no taste; while a good reader, without entirely dropping the plaintive tone, will abate it a little, and give it a slight tincture only of the indifference and rusticity of the person introduced.[20]

Walker is referring to lines 93–100, the point at which Gray himself ostensibly "quits" narration of his poem, displacing his own voice first onto "some hoary-headed swain" and then onto the epitaph. The salient point here is that Walker's advice is contained within his chapter on prosopopoeia – defined as "the investing of qualities or things inanimate with the character of persons"[21] – so Walker implicitly accepts that the villagers have as little animation as the gravestones, that the "person introduced" merely ventriloquizes for the poet who has withdrawn.

Assuredly, what Walker explicitly recognizes is a homogeneity of tone which is more important than the voice of any individual "character" in the poem. (This is also the consensus reached by essays which the editor of a casebook on the "Elegy" has grouped under the rubric of " 'The Stonecutter' Controversy".)[22] The problem I have just elaborated is not one that can be "solved", for the textual evidence of this tension is incontrovertible. Gray however is implicated in his own irony, as I hope I have shown. There is room for more speculation as to the reasons for the withdrawal I have mapped in the "Elegy".

This withdrawal is strategic, displacing the responsibility for the achievement of signification on to a series of voices other than the "me" of the fourth line, a progressive distancing which is indeed achieved by something like prosopopoeia. The "Elegy" then is a paradigm of the form to be taken by the Romantic "conversation poem". It moves from that single first-person singular into a kind of repressed dialectic of self and society, finally withdrawing from an assertion of the reintegration of the self at a higher level. Alienated from the public language Gray tries almost literally to carve himself a niche in "the short and simple annals of the poor". However, reading it as a Romantic poem we find that it doesn't behave as the Romantic poem should. Wright finds analogues in T. S. Eliot, Byron, Scott and Wordsworth, concluding that the poem disappoints (though it does not collapse into incoherence) because Gray didn't have the resources of the Wordsworthian symbol at his disposal, was too myopic "to see the divine as powerfully involved in the mortal" (p. 389). It is particularly surprising then that he doesn't mention Wordsworth's three "Essays on Epitaphs".

De Man's reading of these texts concludes a meditation upon "autobiographical discourse as a discourse of self-restoration".[23] The trope of autobiography, he says, *is* prosopopoeia, of which he gives the etymology as *prosopon poien*, to confer a mask or face. The fiction of coming face to face with an ideal self is, as de Man shows, one that is active in Wordsworth's "spots of time". After the "Elegy" Coleridge's "conversation poems" rely on the fictional attribution of a tongue to the dead, the voiceless or inanimate – and the turn in "Frost at Midnight" for example ("But thou . . . ") is comparable to that in the

"Elegy" accomplished by "For thee". Wordsworth chides Gray and Milton for the *fiction* of prosopopoeia, and de Man deftly shows metaphor returning from this denunciation, making the unknown known (or knowable) by becoming accessible to the senses. The Romantic poem, for de Man, is a text in which history is no more than a function continually effaced (and *de*faced, *dis*figured) by language. His closing paradox, "Death is a displaced name for a linguistic predicament", invites the *faux naif* retort from Wordsworth's churchyard "Where are all the *bad* people buried?"[24] – a passage de Man does not quote. Wordsworth's insistent faith in something always beyond rhetoric seems to counterpoise de Man's conclusion of some rhetoric always beyond things. The necessity to "put an end to a thing", as Gray's letter has it, may always look like a lapidary simplification. Gray's epitaph, like Swift's, does indeed make history (history, as we know, is made by dead people) but it is not the name inscribed on the stone. The displaced name of de Man's formulation is not death but "Romanticism". In Gray's "Elegy", I suggest, we read not a displaced name but a displacement of naming. Whether we read this as a retreat or a refusal we are within that historical twilight which the poem inscribes.

Notes

[1] See *The Political Unconscious: narrative as a socially symbolic act* (Ithaca, NY: Cornell University Press, 1981), especially pp. 81–2.

[2] *Blindness and Insight: essays in the rhetoric of contemporary criticism*, second edition, revised and enlarged (London: Methuen, 1983), p. 165. Hereafter abbreviated *BI* and cited in the text.

[3] *Allegories of Reading: figural language in Rousseau, Nietzsche, Rilke and Proust* (New Haven and London: Yale University Press, 1979), p. x, p. 3.

[4] Samuel Johnson, *Lives of the Poets*, edited by G. Birkbeck Hill, 3 volumes (Oxford, 1905), vol. 3, pp. 441–2.

[5] William Empson, *Some Versions of Pastoral* (London: Chatto and Windus, 1935), p. 22. Hereafter cited in the text.

[6] Cited by Donald Davie, *The Late Augustans: longer poems of the later eighteenth century* (London: Heinemann, 1958), p. 114.

[7] John Barrell, "Collins' 'Ode to Evening' ", in *Teaching the Text*, ed. Suzanne Kappeler and Norman Bryson (London: Routledge and Kegan Paul, 1983), pp. 1–17, p. 12.

[8] *The Poems of Gray, Collins and Goldsmith*, edited by Roger Lonsdale (London: Longman Annotated English Poets, 1969). The text of the "Elegy" is quoted from this edition, pp. 117–40.

[9] *The Correspondence of Thomas Gray*, ed. Paget Toynbee and Leonard Whibley, 3 volumes (Oxford: Oxford University Press, 1971), vol. 1, 326–7.

[10] *English Literature in History, 1730–1780: an equal, wide survey* (London: Hutchinson, 1983), p. 13.

[11] Barrell, Ibid., pp. 108–9.

[12] Edward Said, "Swift's Tory Anarchy", in *The World, the Text and the Critic* (Cambridge, Mass.: Harvard University Press, 1983), pp. 54–71, pp. 66–7. Further references are given in the text.

[13] George T. Wright, "Stillness and the Argument of Gray's *Elegy*", *Modern Philology*, 74 (May 1977), 381–9, p. 381.

[14] *Teaching the Text*, p. 15.

[15] Wright, "Stillness and the Argument of Gray's *Elegy*", p. 382.

[16] *Poems of Gray, Collins and Goldsmith*, pp. 130–1, note to line 72.

[17] Ibid., p. 115.

[18] It is at this point that the new ending is added.

[19] See de Man,"The Rhetoric of Temporality", *BI*, pp. 187–228.

[20] John Walker, *A Rhetorical Grammar (1785)*, reprinted, English Linguistics Facsimile Reprints, 266 (Menston, Yorks.: Scolar Press, 1971), p. 202.

[21] Ibid., p. 198.

[22] See *Twentieth Century Interpretations of Gray's Elegy: a collection of critical essays*, edited by Herbert W. Starr (Englewood Cliffs, NJ: Prentice-Hall, 1968), pp. 41–81. Lonsdale rejects the problem of the "swain" in a terse footnote to his edition (*Poems of Gray, Collins and Goldsmith*, p. 135, line 93n.), yet in a 1973 lecture to the British Academy he recognizes exactly this instability, though chiefly in the earlier version – see Roger Lonsdale, "The Poetry of Thomas Gray; versions of the self", *Proceedings of the British Academy*, 59 (1973), 105–23, 107–8.

[23] de Man, "Autobiography as De-Facement", in *The Rhetoric of Romanticism* (New York: Columbia University Press, 1984), pp. 67–81, p. 74, hereafter cited in the text. For a fine reading of Wordsworth based on his "Essays on Epitaphs" see Frances Ferguson, *Wordsworth: language as counter-spirit* (New Haven: Yale University Press, 1977).

[24] *Wordsworth's Literary Criticism*, ed. W. J. B. Owen, Routledge Critics Series (London: Routledge and Kegan Paul, 1974), p. 134. Wordsworth is quoting from Lamb's *Rosamund Gray* (1798): he says nevertheless that "no Epitaph ought to be written upon a bad Man, except for a warning" (p. 151).

From topos to trope, from sensibility to Romanticism: Collins's "Ode to Fear"

HAROLD BLOOM

Doubtless there are many perspectives that could reveal to us the essential continuities between four apparently disjunctive entities: the topics of classical rhetoric, the ideas of Associationist psychology, the tropes of High Romantic poetry, the mechanisms of defense named by Sigmund Freud and eventually codified by his daughter Anna. But I have only my own perspective to offer, and I seek here to develop certain notions that have obsessed me in a series of works, culminating in an essay called "Poetic Crossing", to be found as a coda to my book on Stevens (Ithaca and London: Cornell University Press, 1976). Much that I have to say will be rather technical, but at least it will not be dry. I propose to take William Collins's "Ode to Fear" and to read it rhetorically and psychologically, so as to contrast within it the representations of two related but distinct poetic modes, Sensibility (as Northrop Frye suggested we call it) and Romanticism.

The "Ode to Fear", a remarkable poem by any standards, is perhaps too Spenserian in its diction, and too Miltonic in its procedures, to sustain its own implicit prayer for originality, its own yearnings for strength. Collins was a very learned young poet of real genius, and he seems to have intuited how few years of sanity and control would be available to him. His "Ode to Fear" is a daemonic exercise, a desperate gamble with his poetic limits that rightly reminds us how attractive he was to Coleridge and to Hart Crane, poets who shared his temperament and his ambitions. The modern critical theorist who best illuminates daemonic or Sublime poetry is Angus Fletcher, both in his remarkable early book, *Allegory* (1964), and in his more recent essays on threshold rhetoric and personification. But before I expound Fletcher's liminal visions, I need to say something about the puzzling gap between the poets, in their advanced conceptions of rhetoric and psychology, and the critics of later eighteenth and early nineteenth-century Britain..

We are currently in a literary situation where much critical theory and *praxis* is more on the frontier than most of our best poetry tends to be, a situation infrequent though hardly unique in the history of culture. The criticism and formal psychology of the Age of Sensibility and of Romantic times lagged considerably behind the experiments of Collins and of Shelley. When I began to write criticism, in the middle fifties, it seemed to me that Wallace Stevens was well out in front of available criticism, though not of the speculations of Freud. We are catching up to Stevens, and perhaps we begin to see precisely what Freud was *not* doing, anyway. Collins implicitly had a Miltonic theory of imagination, as presumably the commentaries on Aristotle that he wished to write would have shown. But what marks both British psychology and literary theory from the mid 1740s down to (and beyond) the time of Coleridge is its conservatism. Hazlitt is a formidable exception, and his theories helped to free Keats from some of the inadequacies of British intellectual tradition, but the main story is elsewhere, with Wordsworth and Coleridge, where the puzzles of the relation between thought and art are still just beyond the analytical range of our critical scholarship.

Dr Johnson, who wrote of Collins with personal warmth but lack of critical discernment (rather like Allen Tate on Hart Crane), was of course the strong critic contemporary with Collins's experiments in the ode. With his neoclassic bias, Johnson was critically just not what Collins needed, though humanly the compassionate and sensible Johnson did Collins much good. Poetically, I would say, Collins needed a vital critic to tell him that the trope for time, particularly *literary* time, could be only irony or else metalepsis (also called transumption) and Collins was deliberately one of the least ironic of all gifted poets. He needed a critic rather like Angus Fletcher, who is discussing Coleridge in the passages I am about to quote, but who might as well be describing Collins:

Coleridge, whose heart is so full, if sometimes only of its own emptiness, its desire to be filled, seems fully aware that the betweenness of time-as-moment, pure thresholdness, barren liminality, at least in what Einstein would call a "space-like" way, must be a nothingness. Between the temple and labyrinth there must be a crossing which, viewed from the perspective of time, does not stand, stay, hold or persist. Yet the poet craves persistence and duration . . .

A new or renewed Renaissance mode of personification would seem to be the main yield of the poetry of threshold . . .

. . . Formally, we can say that personification is the figurative emergent of the liminal scene . . . Personifications come alive the moment there is psychological breakthrough, with an accompanying liberation of utterance, which in its radical form is a first deep breath.

A Sublime or Longinian critic this acute would have strengthened Collins where he needed it most, in his own sense of poetic election. The "Ode to Fear" could have been called "Ode to Poetic Election", and

its opening invocation makes us wonder just what the personification
Fear can mean:

> Thou, to whom the world unknown
> With all its shadowy shapes is shown;
> Who see'st appalled the unreal scene,
> While Fancy lifts the veil between:
> Ah Fear! Ah frantic Fear!
> I see, I see thee near.

Why name one's own daemon or genius as Fear? Indeed as "frantic
Fear"? Is this a free choice among available personifications, a kind of
Aristotelian "fear" to be dispelled by an aesthetic catharsis, or is it an
over-determined fear, belonging more to Freud's cosmos than Aristotle's? Perhaps these questions reduce to: is there not a sexual,
perhaps a sado-masochistic element, in what Collins calls Fear? The
"mad Nymph", Fear, is nothing less than Collins's Muse, rather in
the sense that Lacan called Freud's earliest patients, those gifted and
charming hysterical young women of Jewish Vienna, Freud's Muses.

The most illuminating reading of the "Ode to Fear" that I know is
by Paul Sherwin in his superb book, *Precious Bane: Collins and the
Miltonic legacy* (Austin, 1977). Sherwin rightly emphasizes Collins's
teasing technique; we never do see anything of the presumably attractive mad Nymph beyond her "hurried step" and "haggard eye". I
agree with Sherwin that there is an affinity here between Collins and
Burke. Collins too favors sympathy over imitation, the effect of things
on the mind over a clear idea of the things themselves. Milton's
"judicious obscurity", as Burke admiringly called it, is followed by
Collins, who also rejects mere mimesis. Sherwin approvingly quotes
Mrs Barbauld, that Mrs Alfred Uruguay of her age, as remarking that
Collins's Fear is at once the inspirer of passion and its victim. And so,
in Sherwin's reading, is Collins:

If, on the one hand, his sympathy is drawn out by Fear's all-too-human
vulnerability, it is perplexed by her apparent divinity; and whereas the former
aspect of the personification establishes the possibility of intimacy, it is the
latter aspect, enticing the speaker with the dangerous allure of numinous experience and heightening his sense of self, that provokes him to seek out this
precarious communion.

I don't wish to be accused of assimilating William Collins to Ernest
Dowson, but I am going to urge a reading rather less ontological and
more sexual even than Sherwin's. How, after all, experientially speaking, does one go about renewing the link between rhetorical personification and daemonic possession? There is religion of course,

presumably more in its esoteric than in its normative aspects. There is intoxication, by drink and by drug, and there is, yet more poetically, the always beckoning abyss of sexuality as taken to its outer limits, where pleasure and pain cease to be antithetical entities. I am not going to give us a William Collins as heroic precursor of the Grand Marquis, or a critical vision of the "Ode to Fear" as a grace note preceding *The Hundred and Twenty Days of Sodom and Gomorrah*. But the pleasures of the "Ode to Fear" are uneasily allied to its torments, and there is an element of sexual bondage in those torments. That even this element should be, ultimately, a trope for influence-anxieties is hardly a revelation, since I know no ampler field for the study of belatedness than is constituted by the sadomasochistic elements in our psyches.

Is it too much to say that Collins, throughout his Ode, attempts to work himself up into a frenzy of fearful apprehension, in the hope that such frenzy will grant him the powers of the tragic poet, of Aeschylus, Sophocles, above all of Shakespeare? Yes, that is to say too much, because we then underestimate what Freud would have called Collins's overvaluation of the object, when his Fear is that object. Fear indeed is Collins's wounded narcissism, and so becomes the entire basis for the aggressivity of his poetic drive. But that requires us to name more clearly the Nymph or daemon, since Aristotle's tragic fear hardly seems an apt name for the Sublime hysteria that Collins confronts and desires.

Shall we not call her the Muse of repression, and so of the Counter-Sublime? Perhaps, in Freudian terms, we could call her the Counter-Transference, the analyst's totemic and repressed apprehension that he is in psychic danger of being, as it were, murdered and devoured by his devoted patient. Fear, as Fletcher and Sherwin tell us, is Collins's *own* daemon, his indwelling Urania. Our twentieth-century Collins was Hart Crane, and I turn to Crane for his versions of Collins's Nymph. In a late, unfinished lyric, "The Phantom Bark", Crane rather strangely alludes to Collins, and evidently not to any actual poem Collins wrote:

> So dream thy sails, O phantom bark
> That I thy drownèd man may speak again
> Perhaps as once Will Collins spoke the lark,
> And leave me half adream upon the main.

The reference is purely visionary, as though Collins came back from the dead, say, in Shelley's "To a Skylark". In some truer sense Collins speaks to his Nymph Fear again when Crane addresses his nymph Helen in *For the Marriage of Faustus and Helen*. Crane too cries out:

"Let us unbind our throats of fear and pity", while he goes on to give us his version of "*Vengeance,* in the lurid Air, / Lifts her red Arm, expos'd and bare" as "the ominous lifted arm / That lowers down the arc of Helen's brow / To saturate with blessing and dismay". Crane's later versions of this antithetical Muse include the Paterian Venus of *Voyages* VI, who "rose / Conceding dialogue with eyes / That smile unsearchable repose – ", and the woman of "The Broken Tower", a Collinsian poem where the Muse's "sweet mortality stirs latent power" in her poet. A late fragment by Collins actually prophesies Crane's death lyric: "Whatever dark aerial power, / Commission'd, haunts the gloomy tower." Like Collins, Crane invokes the Evening Star as the gentlest form of his Daemon, though Crane's invocation necessarily is more desperate: "O cruelly to inoculate the brinking dawn / With antennae toward worlds that glow and sink – "

What Crane helps us see is that Collins's Fear is a Muse not so much called on to help the poet remember, as one invoked to help the poet forget. A Muse who forgets, or who needs to forget, is *en route* to Moneta in "The Fall of Hyperion", but Collins is rather more Coleridge's precursor than he is Keats's. Except for Scripture and Milton, and perhaps Shakespeare, what passage in poetry haunted Coleridge more productively than this:

> Through glades and glooms the mingled measure stole,
> Or o'er some haunted steam with fond delay,
>   Round an holy calm diffusing,
>   Love of peace and lonely musing,
> In hollow murmurs died away.

From "The Passions" to "Kubla Khan" is a movement from one threshold to another, and liminal poets have a particularly intense way of recognizing their family romance and its nuances. Fletcher, the theoretician of thresholds, reminds us that etymologically the *daemon* is the spirit of division, a reminder that I remember using as a starting-point in working out the revisionary ratio of *daemonization* or the Counter-Sublime. The Sublime trope for such dividing tends to be breaking, a making by breaking, or catastrophe creation. I return to the "Ode to Fear" to trace just such a breaking.

How specific ought we to be in finding an identity for Collins's "world unknown" and "unreal scene"? The late Thomas Weiskel brilliantly argued for something like Freud's Primal Scene Fantasy, but here as elsewhere I would prefer some version of what I have theorized as the Scene of Instruction. Not that the two fantasies are wholly exclusive, since what passes between the Poetic Father and the Muse has its sexual overtones in the evening ear of the belated ephebe. Yet

Collins's scene can be called more Yeatsian than Freudian, more at home in the world of *Per Amica Silentia Lunae* than in that of *Totem and Taboo*. This may be simply because Collins's "sources" are mostly Spenserian (Masque of Cupid, Temple of Venus), but I suspect a more crucial reason also; Fear is indeed Collins's own Daemon, but he has not yet possessed her or been possessed by her. The scene she partly inhabits by seeing is populated by the fathers, by Spenser, Shakespeare and Milton, but not by Collins himself. As the Ode begins, Fear sees the visionary world, but all that Collins sees is Fear. We are in the ancient topos of Contraries and Contradictories but not yet in the trope of Romantic Irony. And there I touch at last upon my first theoretical speculation in this essay: Sublime Personification seems to me an uneasy transitional phase or crossing between Associationist topos and Romantic trope. Collins's Fear is a commonplace burgeoning but not yet burgeoned into an irony, or as Freud called it, a reaction-formation. Fear *sees* and is frantic; Collins sees *her*, and becomes rather less persuasively frantic:

> Ah Fear! Ah frantic Fear!
> I see, I see thee near.
> I know thy hurried step, thy haggard eye!
> Like thee I start, like thee disordered fly.

That repetition of "I see, I see" is already quite Coleridgean, so that we almost expect Collins to burst forth with "And still I gaze – and with how blank an eye!" What restrains Collins is an awareness still just short of irony, certainly short of Spenserian irony, regardless of all the Spenserian diction. The contraries of seeing and not-seeing the visionary scene yield to the topoi of definition and division in the remainder of the strophe, as Collins enumerates the monsters appearing in Fear's train. Division is properly daemonic here, with one giant form, a Spenserian Danger, thousands of phantoms: "Who prompt to deeds accursed the mind", as well as an indefinite number of fiends who: "O'er nature's wounds and wrecks preside". All these lead up to a highly sadistic Vengeance, who requires considerable scrutiny. But even Danger has his peculiarities:

> Danger, whose limbs of giant mould
> What mortal eye can fixed behold?
> Who stalks his round, an hideous form,
> Howling amidst the midnight storm,
> Or throws him on the ridgy steep
> Of some loose hanging rock to sleep;

The sources here – in Spenser and Pope – are not developed with any particular zest or inventiveness on Collins's part. But we should note the obsessive emphasis again upon the eye of the beholder, the horrified fixation that is one of the stigmata of repression. Spenser's Daunger, that hideous Giant, was associated with hatred, murder and treason, which may have been daily intimations for Spenser to dread, whether in Ireland or at court, but cannot have had much reality for Collins in the years when he still was sane. His Danger "stalks his round" amid more commonplace sublimities, storm and impending rock fall. These represent surely the psyche's potential for violence, whether aggressivity is to be turned against others or against the self:

> And with him thousand phantoms joined,
> Who prompt to deeds accursed the mind;
> And those, the fiends who, near allied,
> O'er nature's wounds and wrecks preside;

These wounds and wrecks of nature include internalized disorders, which is what prompts the vision of a ferociously personified feminine superego, as it were, an image of sadomasochistic Vengeance:

> Whilst Vengeance in the lurid air
> Lifts her red arm, exposed and bare,
> On whom that ravening brood of fate,
> Who lap the blood of sorrow, wait;

Again the sources (Milton, Dryden, Pope) are of little consequence except for Collins's own noted reference to the hounds of vengeance in Sophocles's *Electra*. The curious doubling, almost redundant, of Vengeance's lifted arm as both "exposed and bare" enforces how lurid Collins's scopic drive dares to become. There is a troubling ambiguity in the image, as Weiskel noted. Vengeance is a kind of phallic woman, appropriate to a masochistic fantasy, and in some curious way Collins blends her into an Artemis figure, waited upon by destined hounds. There is thus a hint of an Actaeon identity for poor Collins himself, a hint taken up in the couplet closing the strophe:

> Who, Fear, this ghastly train can see,
> And look not madly wild like thee?

Like his daemonic Muse, Collins really does expect to be hunted down and torn apart by the Furies, for his tone lacks any playful element. That he more than half desires his fate is clear enough also. What is beautifully not clear is just who is seeing what in this rather confused scene of sadomasochistic instruction. Fear sees it all, yet Collins is by no means as yet fully one with his own Fear. She sees and yet does not wish to see; Collins sees only in and by visionary fits, yet he does want to see, whatever the cost. Lacan's grim jest about the scopic drive comes to mind: that which we are fixated upon, obsessively stare upon, is precisely what cannot be seen. Only the creativity of Fear can impel Collins beyond this daemonic threshold.

Of course, like Weiskel or to some extent also Sherwin, or Paul Fry in his fine reading of this Ode, I am giving a kind of Freudian reading (broadly speaking) and Collins's own overt psychology was Associationist. But the line between Associationism and Freud is a blurred one, for a number of reasons. One is merely genetic, despite all Freudian denials. Freud's theory of language essentially came from John Stuart Mill (whom Freud had translated) and so was essentially a late version of Associationism. But far more crucially, both the Associationist categories and the Freudian mechanisms or fantasies of defense rely implicitly upon rhetorical models, these being the topoi or commonplaces for Associationism and the prime tropes or figures for Freud. Romanticism is of course the connecting link here between topos and trope, association and defense, or to phrase this more saliently, Collins's "Ode to Fear", though a monument of and to Sensibility, is itself a version of that connecting link, a poem verging on High Romanticism and kept back from it mostly by two barriers. Call one of these decorum or diction, and the other Collins's own anxieties, human and creative, and you may be calling a single entity by two misleadingly different names.

I am aware that I am telling what is hardly a new story, scholarly or critical, but this twice-told tale always does need to be told again. The story's troublesome phantom is what we go on calling personification, an old term I have no desire to protest provided we keep remembering that primarily it means not humanization but masking, or as Fletcher has taught us, masking at the threshold, at the crossing between labyrinth and temple, or as I want to say, between limitation and a representation that is a restitution. Such masking, in Associationist terms, is a movement through categorical places. In Romantic or Freudian terms, it is a movement between tropological or defensive configurations, marked always by ambivalence and duplicity.

The masterpiece of emotive ambivalence, in Freud or in the poets, is called variously the Oedipal conflict, taboo, and transference, and this is where Collins chooses to center his Epode:

> In earliest Greece to thee with partial choice
>   The grief-full Muse addressed her infant tongue;
> The maids and matrons on her awful voice,
>   Silent and pale, in wild amazement hung.

> Yet he, the bard who first invoked thy name,
>   Disdained in Marathon its power to feel:
> For not alone he nursed the poet's flame,
>   But reached from Virtue's hand the patriot's steel.
>
> But who is he whom later garlands grace,
>   Who left awhile o'er Hybla's dews to rove,
> With trembling eyes thy dreary steps to trace,
>   Where thou and Furies shared the baleful grove?
>
> Wrapped in thy cloudy veil the incestuous queen
>   Sighed the sad call her son and husband heard,
> When once alone it broke the silent scene,
>   And he, the wretch of Thebes, no more appeared.

Sophocles of course is hardly Collins's poetic father, but the Oedipal scene is very much Collins's own, and the echo of *Comus* in the condition of the maids and matrons has considerable force. Freud has taught us to look for meaningful mistakes, and the learned Collins errs remarkably here. The "sad call" in *Oedipus Colonus* is not sighed once by Jocasta, but frequently by the god, who is summoning Oedipus to join him. I take it that Collins himself is being summoned, not by Apollo, but by the Oedipal Muse, for whom another name, we now can see, is Fear:

> O Fear, I know thee by my throbbing heart,
>   Thy withering power inspired each mournful line,
> Though gentle Pity claim her mingled part,
>   Yet all the thunders of the scene are thine!

Pity here is as little Aristotelian as Fear has been. Collins now recognizes Fear as being not only daemon and Muse but as mother, a recognition scene that is the Sublime crisis-point of the Ode. In Associationist terms, the Epode has moved from the categories of Contiguity to those of Comparison, from matters of cause and effect to those lying, beyond causation, in the heights and depths of the daemonic Sublime. Collins's heart recognizes what his occluded sight could not, and so he learns, as Stevens phrased it, that the mother's face is the purpose of the poem. But a mother who is more fear than pity, whose power is withering, and who inspires a thunderous Scene of Instruction, is a most extraordinary version of the mother, and suggests an Orphic as well as an Oedipal fate for poor Collins.

But this is of course Collins's own direct suggestion, and the puzzle of the "Ode to Fear" grows ever greater. The Pindaric, from its origins through Collins on to Shelley, courts disaster, as suits the most overtly agonistic of all lyric forms. Paul Fry charmingly suggests that all the "monsters" Collins invokes "appear to be nothing other than Pindaric odes". I would modify Fry by observing that Collins is a strong enough poet to know that anything he wishes to get into his Pindaric ode must be treated as if it already was a Pindaric ode. A motherly Muse so fearful, indeed so hysterical as to require the analogue of Jocasta, belongs to the same principle of strength and its costs. Collins is frightening himself to some purpose, and I swerve for a brief interval from Collins into Freud not to seek a reductive version of that purpose but rather to show that every strong anxiety is in some sense an *achieved* anxiety, so that Collins mimes a profound constant in the civil wars of the psyche.

Freud, in his later (post-1926) revision of his theory of anxiety, wrote a kind of commentary upon the Sublime ode, not least upon the "Ode to Fear". In Freud's earlier theory, neurotic anxiety and realistic anxiety were rigidly distinguished from one another, since neurotic anxiety was dammed-up libido, caused by unsuccessful repression, while realistic anxiety was caused by real danger. But after 1926, Freud gave up the notion that libido could be transformed into anxiety. Anxiety, Freud came to insist, is prior to repression, and indeed was the motive for repression. The causal distinction between neurotic anxiety and real fear was thus abandoned for good. The doctrine of the priority of anxiety depends upon a mapping of the psyche in which the ego itself is viewed as being in large part unconscious, so that we must say we are lived by the id. Oppressed from the other side by the superego, or the ego's own abandoned earlier affections, the poor ego is exposed to the death drive, the final form of sadomasochistic ambivalence aggressively turned in against the self. Real fear and neurotic anxiety alike become interchangeable with the fear of castration, which is to say, the fear of death. But the hapless ego's surrender of its aggressivity, whether against the self or others, does not appease the superego, which progressively grows more murderous toward the ego.

Associationist psychology had no such vision of man, but Collins's "Ode to Fear" does, probably against Collins's own desires and intentions. Weiskel shrewdly observed that Collins had discovered "a fantasy code appropriate to the special crisis of discourse in his day". Freud admitted that the poets had been there before him, and it is uncanny that Collins was more *there* than poets far stronger. We think of Blake in this dark area, but Blake was enough of an heroic vitalist to disengage from his own Spectre of Urthona. Collins, like Cowper, is all but one with that Spectre, with the temporal anxiety that cannot be distinguished from the poetic ambitions of the Sensibility poets.

If we glance back at the Strophe of the "Ode to Fear" we can see that its hidden subject is the tormented question: "Am I a poet?" Collins indeed is the Muse's true son, but can the Muse be Fear and nothing more? In the Epode the question is altered, since there the true poet, Aeschylus, is revealed as being fearless. The question therefore becomes: "Can I love, or get beyond poetic self-love?", and the answer seems to be highly equivocal, since Oedipal love is narcissistic beyond measure. In the Antistrophe, much the strongest of the poem's three divisions, Collins makes a fierce endeavor to introject poetic immortality, but the Miltonic shadow intervenes, with startling results. The question becomes not what it should be, more life or a wasting death, but the truth and decorum of the romance mode. Collins is, I think, creatively confused throughout the Antistrophe but the confusion, as in so much of Tennyson, becomes an aesthetic gain:

> Thou who such weary lengths hast passed,
> Where wilt thou rest, mad nymph, at last?
> Say, wilt thou shroud in haunted cell,
> Where gloomy Rape and Murder dwell?
> Or in some hollowed seat,
> 'Gainst which the big waves beat,
> Here drowning seamen's cries in tempests brought!

The sentiment here, though not the mode, suggests Thomas Lovell Beddoes and George Darley, a good three generations later. The "mad nymph" desperately requires rest, but the Miltonic verb "shroud" for "shelter" suggests that no rest is possible for this personification of the poetic. A rested Fear would cease to fear, and so the poem would have to close prematurely. But the transmogrification of personification into phantasmagoria moves Fear from visual to auditory hallucination, which increases psychic disorder, both in the Muse and in her poet. What seem to me the poem's most effective lines mark Collins's crisis of identification, as he seeks to internalize Miltonic power while continuing his avoidance of naming that source of paternal strength:

> Dark power, with shuddering meek submitted thought
> Be mine to read the visions old,
> Which thy awakening bards have told:
> And, lest thou meet my blasted view,
> Hold each strange tale devoutly true.

The Archangel Michael, instructing Adam just before the expulsion from Eden, says it is time to wake up Eve, who has been calmed with gentle dreams: "and all her spirits compos'd / To meek submission". Collins here takes up that feminine and passive stance imposed upon Eve by angelic power, and so I think that his union with his Muse Fear now has become a very radical interpenetration. In this progressive internalization, the topos of Resemblance engenders characteristic metaphor, in which nature and consciousness bewilderingly perspectivize one another. Weiskel, acutely aware of this progress from Sensibility to Romanticism, caught it up in an eloquent formulation:

The "reader's" mind is deeply divided between the powerful and dark appeal the fantasies are making and his conscious renunciation of the desires they excite. An attitude of meek submission holds off his recognition of these desires, but it also prevents his Longinian appropriation of the precursor's power as his own. The power remains dark, instinct with danger; the liberating power of a symbolic identification with the bards is just what is missing.

Sherwin emphasizes "the radical bivalence of the daemon" here, saying of Collins that:

He has so thoroughly absorbed the rage of his dark angel that the daemon, no longer threatening the poet with engulfment, is viewed as a guide leading beyond itself to the special prerogatives of the prophetic seer.

Both these critics of Collins's Sublime help us to see that Collins is on the verge of strength, yet hesitant to cross over into it, though Sherwin's tone is more positive than Weiskel's. I would add that Collins's baffled version of the Longinian or reader's Sublime is very difficult indeed to interpret. Unlike the idealized Eve's, Collins's meek submission is a "shuddering" one, and that modifier "shuddering" is his ironic response to Milton as an "awakening" bard, that is, a bard who imposes upon the reader a very intense affective burden. So empathic is this response, however ironic, that Collins's eyes are threatened with being blasted, darkened by shock, unless he assents to the Miltonic fable, however strange. If the precise tale here be the expulsion from Eden, then one sees why Collins's subsequent passage returns to the Milton of "L'Allegro" and "Il Penseroso", and of "Comus", and perhaps to the Shakespeare of *A Midsummer Night's Dream*:

> Ne'er be I found, by thee o'erawed,
> In that thrice-hallowed eve abroad,
> When ghosts, as cottage-maids believe,
> Their pebbled beds permitted leave,
> And goblins haunt, from fire or fen
> Or mine or flood, the walks of men!

That an urbane tone has entered cannot be questioned, but what has departed is the voice of William Collins. We hear the octosyllabic Milton, and not his venturesome and daring ephebe. Had Collins dared further, he would have found the Miltonic rhetoric of transumption or metalepsis for a triumphant closure, but instead he ends quite elegantly but weakly, in an interplay of the topoi of Antecedents and Consequences:

> O thou whose spirit most possessed
> The sacred seat of Shakespeare's breast!
> By all that from thy prophet broke,
> In thy divine emotions spoke,
> Hither again thy fury deal,
> Teach me but once like him to feel:
> His cypress wreath my meed decree,
> And I, O Fear, will dwell with thee!

Collins was capable of strong closure, as the "Ode on the Poetical Character" demonstrates. What defeated him here? Paradoxically, I would assert that the relative failure is in the generation of sufficient anxiety. What fails in Collins is his own capacity for an infinite Fear. Not that courage becomes the issue, but trauma. Apathy dreadly beckons, and Collins prays for the power *to feel*. Yet I do not think he means affect. His knowing failure is in cognition, and I want to look closely at Dr Johnson's moving dispraise of his learned and gifted young friend in order to see if we can recover a clue to Collins's self-sabotage:

He had employed his mind chiefly upon works of fiction, and subjects of fancy; and, by indulging some peculiar habits of thought, was eminently delighted with those flights of imagination which pass the bounds of nature . . .

This was however the character rather of his inclination than his genius, the grandeur of wildness, and the novelty of extravagance, were always desired by him, but were not always attained . . . His poems are the productions of a mind not deficient in fire . . . but somewhat obstructed in its progress by deviation in quest of mistaken beauties.

To pass natural bounds, to wander beyond limits, *extra vagans*, that surely was Collins's poetic will, his intended revenge against time's: "It was." Johnson is shrewd, as always, in saying that Collins not only desired too much, but beyond the range of his genius. The fault was not ambition, but rather that Collins had to ask his inventive powers to give him what neither contemporary criticism nor contemporary psychology afforded. Milton stands on the verge of the European Enlightenment, but when it begins to reach him it breaks over him, confirming only his recalcitrant furies. Collins puzzles us because he is spiritually close enough to Milton to acquire more of the Miltonic power than actually came to him. Geoffrey Hartman's sad summary is just, noble and restrained, and joins Johnson as the classical verdict upon Collins:

Collins rarely breaks through to the new poetry . . .

Collins does teach us, however, that the generic subject of the sublime ode (as distinct from that of individual poems) is the poetical character: its fate in an Age of Reason. The odes are generally addressed to invited powers and, like the gothic novel, raise the ghosts they shudder at. Their histrionic, sometimes hysterical, character stems from the fact that they are indeed theatrical machines, evoking a power of vision that they fear to use. Collins, like a sorcerer's apprentice, is close to being overpowered by the spirit he summons.

My friend's simile of the sorcerer's apprentice is particularly effective if associated with the version of Dukas in Disney's *Fantasia*. The vision of William Collins as Mickey Mouse overcome by a host of mops is more than any poet's reputation could sustain. Poor Collins indeed! I would prefer another vision of Collins's limitations, one that emphasizes the odd splendor, or splendid oddness, of his liminal achievements. Daemonic poetry is a strange mode, whether in Collins, Coleridge, Shelley, Beddoes or Hart Crane. When Collins gets it exactly right, then he has the uncanniness of an original, as this cento intends to illustrate:

> And she, from out the veiling Cloud,
> Breath'd her magic Notes aloud:
> And Thou, Thou rich-hair'd Youth of Morn,
> And all thy subject Life was born!

> To the blown *Baltic* then, they say
> The wild Waves found another way,
> Where *Orcas* howls, his wolfish Mountains rounding;
> Till all the banded West at once 'gan rise,
> A wide wild Storm ev'n Nature's self confounding,
> With'ring her Giant Sons with strange uncouth Surprise.

> Now Air is hush'd, save where the weak-ey'd Bat,
> With short shrill Shriek flits by on leathern Wing,
> Or where the Beetle winds
> His small but sullen Horn,
> As oft he rises 'midst the twilight Path,
> Against the Pilgrim born in heedless Hum:

> What though far off, from some dark dell espied
> His glimm'ring mazes cheer th'excursive sight,
> Yet turn, ye wand'rers, turn your steps aside,
> Nor trust the guidance of that faithless light;
> For watchful, lurking 'mid th'unrustling reed,
> At those mirk hours the wily monster lies,
> And listens oft to hear the passing steed,
> And frequent round him rolls his sullen eyes,
> If chance his savage wrath may some weak wretch surprise.

These are among the breakthroughs from Sensibility into Romanticism, though never into the Wordsworthian mode. What Collins
could not learn was what Wordsworth had to invent, a transumptive
or time-reversing kind of trope as original as Milton's own, yet plainly
not Miltonic. Collins's stance was neither ironic nor transumptive, and
so temporality remained for Collins a choking anxiety. If Collins was
no mere sorcerer's apprentice, it must be admitted he was also no
sorcerer, as the baffled closure of the "Ode to Fear" renders too obvious. I circle back to the question prevalent in all criticism of Collins:
what made him poor? Why was his psychic poverty, his imaginative
need, so scandalously great? To have crossed into the Romantic
Sublime only a year or two after the death of Pope was hardly the act
of a weak poet, yet Collins will never lose the aura that Johnson gave
him and that Hartman has confirmed.

I go back to Collins's true spiritual companion among the critics,
Fletcher, though Fletcher alas has published only a few remarks about
Collins. In his early masterpiece, *Allegory*, Fletcher has a fine observation on the function of the Sublime: "Graver poems like the sublime
odes of Collins and Gray, and later of Shelley, have the direct and
serious function of destroying the slavery of pleasure."

I interpret Fletcher as meaning that Collins, Gray, Shelley in their
uncanny Pindarics are bent on persuading the reader to forsake easier
in exchange for more difficult pleasures. Paul Fry, acutely but perhaps
too severely, says of the School of Collins and Gray: "An ode that
remembers the pastness of others and not the otherness of the past can
have nothing to say of fallen experience as a distinct phase." I think
that Collins met Fry's challenge by refusing to admit that fallen experience *was* a distinct phase. As Coleridge's precursor, Collins
pioneered in representing what Thomas McFarland calls the
"modalities of fragmentation" or "forms of ruin" in Romantic poetry.
As McFarland is showing us, there *are* modalities, these *are* achieved
forms, with aesthetic arguments and structured intensities all their
own.

Repetition, as Paul Fry has noted in this context, is very much the
issue when we bring Collins to an aesthetic judgment: "Repetition is
what unlearns the genealogical knowledge of the ode, which creates a
world and a god with every stroke of the pen, only in the same movement to absent these creations from the poet's field of vision."

Fry knowingly follows Paul de Man's theory of lyric here, but I
would suggest Kierkegaard's "repetition" rather than de Man's as
being closer to Collins's Sublime project. Kierkegaard's "repetition"
literally means in Danish "a taking again", and is described by Mark

Taylor as "the willed taking-again of a transcendental possibility". Collins wills to take again the transcendental possibility of poetry as he knows it in Spenser, Shakespeare and Milton. Or rather, he wills to will such a taking-again, so as to affirm again the possibility of poetic strength. But a will two degrees from the possibility is a troubled will, too troubled to attempt what McFarland, following Plato, calls "the Place Beyond the Heavens", the "true being, transcendence, and the symbolic indication of wholeness" that make up the synecdoches of visionary poetry. Collins's synecdoches are wounded aggressivities, turned in against themselves, sado-masochistic vicissitudes of the thwarted poetic drive against time's "It was". Collins cannot say: "I am" in his poems. Instead of the synecdoches of wholeness, Wordsworthian or Keatsian, he can offer only the Associationist categories of Definition and Division.

Yet the "Ode to Fear" remains a unique poem, as do three or four other major performances by Collins, and its deep mutual contamination of drive and defense is far closer to the psychic cartography of Freud than to Locke. Collins survives not so much as a voice, but as the image of a voice, perhaps even as the topos of image-of-voice itself. What Collins knows in that daemonic place is the "continuous present" that Northrop Frye said was representative of the mode of Sensibility and of its exercise of repetition. Gray and Cowper and Smart perhaps were more at home in that "continuous present" than Collins was, and what we know of his life shows us how little Collins ever felt at home anywhere. Only the place of the daemon could have been home for Collins, and to that occult place I turn for my conclusion.

Collins, as all his critics rightly say, is a poet always engaged at invocation, in calling, until he seems quite giddy with the strain. Recall that our word "god" goes back to a root meaning "called" or "invoked", and that the word "giddy", possessed by god, has the same root. Yeats, in his beautiful daemonic reverie, *Per Amica Silentia Lunae*, gives us the formula for Collins's sense of place, for the exact topos of Sensibility: "The Daimon, by using his mediatorial shades, brings man again and again to the place of choice, heightening temptation that the choice may be as final as possible, imposing his own lucidity upon events, leading his victim to whatever among works not impossible is the most difficult."

Collins's odes enact that drama over and again. That there should have been a religious element in his final mania is not surprising, for he is nothing but a religious poet, as Shelley and Hart Crane are Orphic religionists also. But to be an Orphic prophet in the mode of

Sensibility was plainly not possible, and again it was not surprising that Collins, and his odes, alike were slain upon the stems of Generation, to adapt a Blakean conceptual image. Yeats, so much stronger a poet than Collins ever could be, must have the final words here. The tragedy of Sensibility is that it could suffer but not write this liminal passage of High Romantic self-revelation, which again I quote from *Per Amica Silentia Lunae*:

When I have closed a book too stirred to go on reading, and in those brief intense visions of sleep, I have something about me that, though it makes me love, is more like innocence. I am in the place where the Daimon is, but I do not think he is with me until I begin to make a new personality, selecting among these images, seeking always to satisfy a hunger grown out of conceit with daily diet; and yet, as I write the words "I select", I am full of uncertainty, not knowing when I am the finger, when the clay.

Sex and history in *The Prelude* (1805): Books IX to XIII

GAYATRI CHAKRAVORTY SPIVAK

Whatever the "truth" of Wordsworth's long life (1770–1850), Books IX through XIII of the 1805 version of his autobiographical poem *The Prelude* present the French Revolution as the major crisis of the poet's poetic formation. As one critic has put it, "his allegiance to revolutionary enthusiasm was so strong that, when, as he saw it, the revolutionary government resorted to nationalistic war (and after he had set up residence with his sister, as they had so long desired), Wordsworth was thrown into a catastrophic depression that has led many modern critics to treat the Revolution (or having a child by and 'deserting' Annette Vallon, one is never quite sure) as the trauma of his life."[1] As this analysis reminds us, the "revolution" in Wordsworth's life also involved two women. As in the critic's sentence, so also in *The Prelude*, the story of Annette is in parenthesis, the desertion in quotation marks. "His sister" – and indeed Wordsworth does not name her – is also in parenthesis.

The consecutive parts of *The Prelude* were not consecutively composed. The account in the text is not chronological. I have taken the textual or narrative consecutivity imposed by an authorial decision as given. Such a decision is, after all, itself part of the effort to cope with crisis.

As I read these books of *The Prelude*, I submit the following theses:
(1) Wordsworth not only needed to exorcise his illegitimate paternity but also to reestablish himself sexually in order to declare his imagination restored.
(2) He coped with the experience of the French Revolution by transforming it into an iconic text that he could write and read.
(3) He suggested that poetry was a better cure for the oppression of mankind than political economy or revolution and that his own life had the preordained purpose of teaching mankind this lesson.

My critique calls for a much more thorough reading of the history and politics of the French Revolution and the English reaction than I am able to provide here.

I sometimes use the Derridian words "trace" and "trace-structure" in the following way. In our effort to define things, we look for origins. Every origin that we seem to locate refers us back to something anterior and contains the possibility of something posterior. There is, in other words, a trace of something else in seemingly self-contained origins. This, for the purposes of my argument, "is" the trace-structure.

The trace, since it breaks up every first cause or origin, cannot be a transcendental principle. It would thus be difficult to distinguish clearly between the trace as a principle and cases of the trace, such as writing or a stream. The trace-structure does not simply undermine origins; it also disrupts the unified and self-contained description of things. By isolating three theses in Wordsworth's work, I am inconsistent with the notion of the trace-structure. No discourse is possible, however, without the unity of *something* being taken for granted. It is not possible to attend to the trace *fully*. One's own self-contained critical position as attendant of the trace also refers back and forward. It is possible to read such references as one's "history" and "politics". Since the trace cannot be fully attended to, one possible alternative is to pay attention to the texts of history and politics as the trace-structuring of positions, knowing that those two texts are themselves interminable.

Wordsworth's exorcism of illegitimate paternity; sexual self-establishment to restore imagination

It is commonly acknowledged that the story of Vaudracour and Julia, as told in Book IX of *The Prelude* (1805), is a disguised version of the affair between Wordsworth and Annette Vallon. The real story is much more banal: Annette did not have a chance to begin with. She was romantic and undemanding. Plans for marriage were tacitly dropped over the years. No money was forthcoming even after Wordsworth received his modest legacy. Annette got deeply involved in the Royalist resistance and died poor at seventy-five. The story is told in detail in Emile Legouis's *William Wordsworth and Annette Vallon*.[2] "It is only fair to add that Wordsworth made some provision for his daughter from the time of her marriage in February, 1816. This took the form of an annuity for £30, which continued until 1835 when the annuity was commuted for a final settlement of £400."[3] In "Vaudracour and Julia" the woman is in a convent, the child dead in infancy, and the man insane.

It is not my concern in this section to decide whether Wordsworth can be excused or if Annette was worth his attentions. It is rather to remark that, in these books of *The Prelude*, one may find textual signs of a rejection of paternity, of a reinstatement of the subject as son (rather than father) within Oedipal law, and then, through the imagination, a claim to androgyny.

The acknowledgment of paternity is a patriarchal social acknowledgment of the trace, of membership in what Yeats called "those dying generations". Through this acknowledgment, the man admits that his end is not in himself. This very man has earlier accepted sonship and admitted that his *origin* is not in himself either. This makes it possible for the man to declare a history. Wordsworth the autobiographer seems more interested at this point in transcending or coping with rather than declaring history – in producing a poem rather than a child. He deconstructs the opposition and cooperation between fathers and sons. The possibility of his being a father is handled in the Vaudracour and Julia episode. The rememoration – the symbolic reworking of the structures – of his being a son is constructed in the famous "spots of time" passages. Then, since mothers are not carriers of names, by means of nature as mother, Wordsworth projects the possibility of being son *and* lover, father *and* mother of poems, male *and* female at once.

I will try to show this projection through the reading of a few passages. But first I should insist that I am not interested in a personal psychoanalysis of William Wordsworth, even if I were capable of undertaking such a task. The thematics of psychoanalysis as a regional science should be considered as part of the ideology of male universalism, and my point here would be that Wordsworth is working with and out of that very ideology. If indeed one wished to make a rigorous structural psychoanalytic study, one would have to take into account "the death of Wordsworth's mother when Wordsworth was eight". One would have to plot not only "the repressions, fixations, denials, and distortions that attend such traumatic events in a child's life and the hysteria and unconscious obsessions that affect the life of the grown man, and more than likely his poetic practice"[4] but also the search for "the lost object" and the recourse to fetishism in the text as signature of the subject.

The story of Vaudracour and Julia begins as a moment of dissonance in the story of the French Revolution, marking a deliberate postponement or substitution:

> *I shall not, as my purpose was, take note*
> Of other matters which detain'd us oft
> In thought or conversation, *public* acts,
> And *public* persons, and the emotions wrought
> Within our minds by the ever-varying wind
> Of *Record* or *Report* which day by day

> Swept over us; but I will here *instead*
> Draw from obscurity a tragic Tale
> *Not in its spirtit singular indeed*
> But haply worth memorial.   (IX, 541–50; italics mine)

Not only does the story not have its proper place or singularity, but its narrative beginning is given as two random and not sufficiently differentiated choices out of plural possibilities: "Oh / Happy time of youthful Lovers! thus / My story may begin, Oh! balmy time . . ." (IX, 554–5). In the final version of *The Prelude* (1850), its revisions dating probably from 1828, the beginning is even less emphatic: "(thus / The story might begin)" is said in parenthesis, and the story itself is suppressed and relegated to the status of nothing but a trace of a record that exists elsewhere: "So might – and with that prelude did begin / The record" (IX, 557–8 [1850]). If in the serious public business of *The Prelude* such a non-serious theme as love and desertion were to be introduced, the 1850 text asks, "Fellow voyager! / Woulds't thou not chide?" (IX, 563–4).

The end of Book IX in both versions gives us an unredeemed Vaudracour, who, situated in an indefinite temporality, remains active as an unchanging pre-text at the same time as the prospective and retrospective temporality of Books X to XIII puts together a story with an end. The mad Vaudracour is "always there":

> Thus liv'd the Youth
> Cut off from all intelligence with Man,
> And shunning even the light of common day;
> Nor could the voice of Freedom, which through France
> Soon afterwards resounded, public hope,
> Or personal memory of his own deep wrongs,
> Rouse him: but in those solitary shades
> His days he wasted, an imbecile mind.   (IX, 926–33)

In this autobiography of origins and ends, Vaudracour simply lives on, wasting his days; the open-ended temporality does not bring his life to a close. In this story of the judgment of France, he remains unmoved by the voice of Freedom. In this account of the growth of a poet's mind, his mind remains imbecile. This is the counterplot of the origin of The Prelude, the author's alias. The author stands in contrast to, yet in complicity with, the testamentary figures of the endings of the later books, who are in fact sublated versions of Vaudracour.

At the end of Book X an acceptable *alter ego* is found. He is quite unlike the Vaudracour who marks the story of guilt. This is of course Coleridge, the Friend to whom *The Prelude* is addressed. Rather than remain suspended in an indefinite temporality, this sublated *alter ego* looks toward a future shaped by the author:

> Thou wilt stand
> Not as an Exile but a Visitant
> On Etna's top.   (X, 1032–4)

Unlike the fictive Vaudracour in his uncomfortable suspension, Coleridge, now in degraded Sicily, *is* the parallel of Wordsworth, then in unruly France. Wordsworth had not been able to find a clue to the text of the September Massacres in Paris:

> upon these
> And other sights looking as doth a man
> Upon a volume whose contents he knows
> Are memorable, but from him lock'd up,
> Being written in a tongue he cannot read,
> So that he questions the mute leaves with pain
> And half upbraids their silence.   (X, 48–54)

That failure seems recuperated in all the textual examples – Empedocles, Archimedes, Theocritus, Comates – brought to bear upon contemporary Sicily, precisely to transform it to a pleasant sojourn for Coleridge. Imagination, a faculty of course denied to Vaudracour's imbecile mind, is even further empowered:

> by pastoral Arethuse
> Or, if that fountain be in truth no more,
> Then near some other Spring, *which by the name*
> *Thou gratulatest, willingly deceived,*
> Shalt linger as a gladsome Votary,
> And not a Captive   (X, 1034–98; italics mine)

As I will show later, the end of Book XI welcomes Coleridge as a companion in an Oedipal scene, and the end of Book XII cites Coleridge as guarantor that in Wordsworth's early poetry glimpses of a future world superior to the revolutionary alternative are to be found. The end of Book XIII, the end of *The Prelude* as a whole, is a fully negating sublation of Vaudracour. If *his* life was a waste of days, by trick of grammar indefinitely prolonged, the poet's double is here assured:

> yet a few short years of useful life,
> And all will be complete, thy race be run,
> Thy monument of glory will be raised.   (XIII, 428–30)

If Vaudracour had remained unchanged by revolution as an imbecilic mind, here the poet expresses a hope, for himself and his friend, that they may

> Instruct . . . how the mind of man becomes
> A thousand times more beautiful than

> . . . this Frame of things
> (Which, 'mid all the revolution in the hopes
> And fears of men, doth still remain unchanged)
>
> (XII, 446–50)

Julia is obliterated rather quickly from the story. By recounting these successive testamentary endings and comparing them to Vaudracour's fate, which ends Book IX, I have tried to suggest that Vaudracour, the unacknowledged self as father, helps, through his disavowal and sublation, to secure the record of the progress and growth of the poet's mind. Let us now consider Wordsworth's use of Oedipal signals.

There is something like the use of a father figure by a son – as contrasted to acknowledging oneself as father – early in the next book (X, 467–515). Wordsworth recounts that he had felt great joy at the news of Robespierre's death. Is there a sense of guilt associated with ecstatic joy at *anyone's* death? We are free to imagine so, for, after recounting this excess of joy, Wordsworth suddenly recalls the faith in his own professional future felt by a father figure, his old teacher at Hawkshead. (As is often the case in *The Prelude*, there is no causal connection between the two episodes; however, a relationship is strongly suggested.) The memory had come to him by way of a thought of the teacher's epitaph, dealing with judgments on Merits and Frailties, written by Thomas Gray, a senior and meritorious member of the profession of poetry. This invocation of the tables of the law of the Fathers finds a much fuller expression in later passages.

In a passage toward the beginning of Book XI, there is once again a scene of disciplinary judgment. Of the trivium of Poetry, History, Logic, the last has, at this point in Wordsworth's life, seemingly got the upper hand. As for the other two – "their sentence was, I thought, pronounc'd" (XI, 94). The realization of this inauspicious triumph of logic over poetry is given in a latent image of self-division and castration:

> Thus strangely did I war against myself
> . . . Did like a Monk who hath forsworn the world
> Zealously labour to cut off my heart
> From all the sources of her former strength.   (XI, 74, 76–8)

Memories of the "spots of time" bring enablement out of this predicament. The details are explicit and iconic.[5] The poet has not yet reached man's estate: "When scarcely (I was then not six years old) / My hand could hold a bridle" (XI, 280–1). As he stumbles lost and alone, he accidentally discovers the anonymous *natural* inscription, *socially* preserved, of an undisclosed proper name, which is all that remains of the phallic instrument of the law:

The Gibbet-mast was moulder'd down, the bones
And iron case were gone; but on the turf,
Hard by, soon after that fell deed was wrought
Some unknown hand had carved the Murderer's name.
The monumental writing was engraven
In times long past, and still, from year to year,
By superstition of the neighbourhood
The grass is clear'd away; *and to this hour*
The letters are all fresh and visible.

(XI, 291–9; italics mine)

At the time he left the spot forthwith. Now the memory of the lugubrious discovery of the monument of the law provides:

A virtue by which pleasure is enhanced
That penetrates, enables us to mount
When high, more high, and lifts us up when fallen.

(XI, 266–8)

Many passages in these later books bring the French Revolution under control by declaring it to be a *felix culpa*, a necessary means toward Wordsworth's growth as a poet: this is such a suggestion. Nothing but the chain of events set off by the Revolution could have caused acts of rememoration that would abreactively fulfill memories of Oedipal events that childhood could not grasp.

As in the case of the memory of the teacher's grave, a metonymic though not logical or metaphoric connection between the second spot of time and the actual father is suggested through contiguity. Here Wordsworth and his brothers perch on a parting of the ways that reminds us of the setting of Oedipus's crime: "One of two roads from Delphi, / another comes from Daulia".[6] Ten days after they arrive at their father's house, the latter dies. There is no logical connection between the two events, and yet the spiritual gift of this spot of time is, precisely, that "the event / With all the sorrow which it brought appear'd / A chastisement" (XI, 368–70).

One might produce a textual chain here: joy at Robespierre's *judgment* (averted by a father figure); the self-castrating despair at Poetry's *judgment* at the hand of Logic (averted by a historical reminder of the *judgment* of the Law); final acceptance of one's own gratuitous, metonymic (simply by virtue of temporal proximity) guilt. Now, according to the canonical Oedipal explanation, "Wordsworth" is a man as son. And just as the murderer's name cut in the grass can be seen *to this day*, so also the rememorated accession to manhood retains a continuous power: "in this later time . . . unknown to me" (XI, 386, 388). It is not to be forgotten that the false father Vaudracour, not established within the Oedipal law of legitimate fathers, also inhabits this temporality by fiat of grammar.

Near the end of Book XI, Coleridge, the benign *alter ego* – akin to the brothers at the recalled "original" event – is once again called forth as witness to the Oedipal accession. Earlier, Wordsworth had written:

> . . . I shook the habit off
> Entirely and for ever, and again
> In Nature's presence stood, *as I stand now,*
> A sensitive, and a creative soul.
>
> (XI, 254–7; italics mine)

Although the "habit" has a complicated conceptual antecedent dispersed in the argument of the thirty-odd previous lines, the force of the metaphor strongly suggests a sexual confrontation, a physical nakedness. One hundred and fifty lines later, Wordsworth welcomes Coleridge into the brotherhood in language that, purging the image of all sexuality, still reminds us of the earlier passage:

> Behold me then
> Once more in Nature's presence, thus restored
> *Or otherwise,* and strengthened once again
> (*With memory left of what had been escaped*)
> To habits of devoutest sympathy.
>
> (XI, 393–7; italics mine)

History and paternity are here fully disclosed as mere traces, a left-over memory in parenthesis (line 396), or one among alternate methods of restoration (line 394–5). All that is certain is that a man, stripped and newly clothed, stands in front of Nature.

It is interesting to note that Wordsworth's sister provides a passage into the rememoration of these Oedipal events, and finally into the accession to androgyny. Unlike the male mediators who punish, or demonstrate and justify the law – the teacher, the murderer, the father, Coleridge – Dorothy Wordsworth restores her brother's imagination as a living agent. And, indeed, William, interlarding his compliments with the patronage typical of his time, and perhaps of ours, does call her "wholly free" (XI, 203).[7] It is curious, then, that the predication of *her* relationship with Nature, strongly reminiscent of "Tintern Abbey", should be entirely in the conditional:

> Her the birds
> And every flower she met with, could they but
> Have known her, would have lov'd. Methought such charm
> Of sweetness did her presence breathe around

> That all the trees, and all the silent hills
> And every thing she look'd on, should have had
> An intimation how she bore herself
> Towards them and to all creatures.   (XI, 214–21)

The only indicative description in this passage is introduced by a controlling "methought".

Although Wordsworth's delight in his sister makes him more like God than like her – "God delights / In such a being" (XI, 221–2) – she provides a possibility of transference for him. The next verse paragraph begins – "Even like this Maid" (XI, 224). Julia as object of desire had disappeared into a convent, leaving the child in Vaudracour's hands. Vaudracour as the substitute of the poet as father can only perform his service for the text as an awkward image caught in an indefinitely prolonged imbecility. Dorothy as sister is arranged as a figure that would allow the poet the possibility of a replaying of the Oedipal scene, the scene of sonship after the rejection of premature fatherhood. If the historical, though not transcendental, authority of the Oedipal explanation, especially for male protagonists, is given credence, then, by invoking a time when he was like her, William is invoking the pre-Oedipal stage when girl and boy are alike, leading to the passage through Oedipalization itself, when the object of the son's desire is legally, though paradoxically, defined as his mother.[8] Nature sustains this paradox: for Nature is that which is not Culture, a place or stage where kinships are not yet articulated. "One cannot confound incest as it would be in this intensive nonpersonal régime that would institute it, with incest as represented in extension in the state that prohibits it, and that defines it as a transgression against persons. . . . Incest as it is prohibited (the form of discernible persons) is employed to repress incest as it is desired (the substance of the intense earth)."[9]

Wordsworth would here clear a space beyond prohibitions for himself. Dorothy carries the kinship inscription "sister" and provides the passage to Nature as object choice; Wordsworth, not acknowledging paternity, has not granted Annette access to a kinship inscription (she was either Madame or the Widow Williams). The text of Book XI proceeds to inscribe Nature as mother and lover. The predicament out of which, in the narrative, Dorothy rescues him, can also be read as a transgression against both such inscriptions of Nature:

> I push'd without remorse
> My speculations forward; yes, set foot
> On Nature's holiest places.   (X, 877–9)

The last link in this chain is the poet's accession to an androgynous

self-inscription which would include mother and lover. Through the
supplementary presence of Nature, such an inscription seems to embrace places historically "outside" and existentially "inside" the poet.
We locate a passage between the account of the discovery of the name
of the murderer and the account of the death of the father:

> Oh! mystery of Man, *from what a depth*
> *Proceed* thy honours! I am lost, but see
> In simple childhood something of the base
> On which thy greatness stands, but this I feel,
> That from thyself it is that thou must give,
> Else never canst receive. The days gone by
> Come back upon me from the dawn almost
> Of life: *the hiding-places of my power*
> *Seem open; I approach*, and *then they close*;
> I see by glimpses now; when age comes on,
> May scarcely see at all, and I would give,
> While yet we may, as far as words can give,
> A substance and a life to what I feel:
> I would enshrine the spirit of the past
> For future restoration.   (XI, 329–43; italics mine)

We notice here the indeterminacy of inside and outside: "from thyself"
probably means "from myself", but if addressed to "mystery of man",
that meaning is, strictly speaking, rendered problematic; there are the
"I feel"s that are both subjective and the subject matter of poetry; and,
of course, the pervasive uncertainty as to whether memory is ever inside or outside. We also notice the double inscription: womb or depths
that produce the subject and vagina where the subject's power finds a
hiding place. Consummation is as yet impossible. The hiding places of
power seem open but, upon approach, close. It is a situation of seduction, not without promise. It is a palimpsest of sex, biographic
memorialization, and psychohistoriography.

Dorothy is in fact invoked as chaperon when Nature is his hand-
maiden (XIII, 236–46). And when, in the same penultimate passage of
the entire *Prelude*, she is apostrophized, William claims for the full-
grown poet an androgynous plenitude which would include within the
self an indeterminate role of mother as well as lover:

> And he whose soul hath risen
> Up to the height of feeling intellect
> Shall want no humbler tenderness, his heart
> Be tender as a nursing Mother's Heart;
> Of female softness shall his life be full,
> Of little loves and delicate desires,
> Mild interests and gentlest sympathies   (XIII, 204–10)

The intimation of androgynous plenitude finds its narrative opening in the last book of *The Prelude* through the thematics of self-separation and autoeroticism, harbingers of the trace. The theme is set up as at least twofold, and grammatically plural. One item is Imagination, itself "another name" for three other qualities of mind, and the other is "that intellectual love" (XIII, 186), with no grammatical fulfillment of the "that" other than another double construction, twenty lines above, where indeed Imagination is declared to be *another* name for something else. Of Imagination and intellectual love it is said that "they are each in each, and cannot stand / Dividually" (XIII, 187–8). It is a picture of indeterminate coexistence with a strong aura of identity ("each in each", not "each in the other"; "dividually", not "individually"). In this declaration of theme, as he sees the progress of the representative poet's life in his own, Wordsworth seems curiously self-separated. "This faculty", he writes, and we have already seen how pluralized it is, "hath been the moving soul / Of our long labour." Yet so intrinsic a cause as a moving soul is also described as an extrinsic object of pursuit, the trace as stream:

> We have traced the stream
> From darkness, and the very place of birth
> In its blind cavern, whence is faintly heard
> The sound of waters.   (XIII, 172–5)

The place of birth, or womb, carries a trace of sound, testifying to some previous origin. The explicit description of the origin as place of birth clarifies the autoerotic masculinity of "then given it greeting, as it rose once more / With strength" (XIII, 179–80). For a time the poet had "lost sight of it bewilder'd and engulph'd" (XIII, 178). The openness of the two adjective/adverbs keeps the distinction between the poet as subject (inside) and Imagination as object (outside) indeterminate. The autoerotic image of the subject greeting the strongly erect phallus that is his moving soul slides quickly into a logical contradiction. No *rising* stream can "reflect anything in its 'solemn breast'", let alone "the works of man and face of human life" (XIII, 180–1). It is after this pluralized and autoerotic story of Imagination as trace that Wordsworth assures "Man" that this "prime and vital principle is thine / In the recesses of thy nature" and follows through to the openly androgynous claims of lines 204–10, cited above.

The itinerary of Wordsworth's securing of the Imagination is worth recapitulating. Suppression of Julia, unemphatic retention of Vaudracour as sustained and negative condition of possibility of disavowal, his sublation into Coleridge, rememorating through the mediation of the figure of Dorothy his own Oedipal accession to the Law, Imagination as the androgyny of Nature and Man – Woman shut out. I cannot but see in it the sexual-political program of the Great Tradition. If, in disclosing such a programmatic itinerary, I have left aside the irreducible heterogeneity of Wordsworth's text, it is also in the interest of a certain politics. It is in the interest of suggesting that, when a man (here Wordsworth) addresses another man (Coleridge) in a sustained conversation on a seemingly universal topic, we must *learn* to read the microstructural burden of the woman's part.

Transforming revolution into iconic text

To help introduce this section, let us reconsider those lines from Book X:

> upon these
> And other sights looking as doth a man
> Upon a volume whose contents he knows
> Are memorable, but from him lock'd up,
> Being written in a tongue he cannot read,
> So that he questions the mute leaves with pain
> And half upbraids their silence.   (X, 48–54)

The contents of the book of revolution must be transformed into a personal memory. The autobiographer assures us that, at twenty-two, he knew them to be "memorable". He uses strong language to describe the task of learning to read them. It would be to transgress an interdiction, for the book is "lock'd up" from him.

In Book IX help in reading the text of the landscape and, then, of the landscape of revolution, comes from Tasso, Spenser, and the Milton of *Paradise Lost*. As his despair thickens, Wordsworth begins to *identify* with Milton's personal position, as described, say, in *Samson Agonistes*. The sleepless city articulates its guilt through Macbeth. His own guilt by transference (including perhaps the unacknowledged guilt of paternity) makes him echo Macbeth's nightmares. He admires and sympathizes with the Girondists because they identified with the ancient Greeks and Romans.

A little over halfway through Book X, Wordsworth does a double take which seems to purge the experience of the Revolution of most of what one would commonly call its substance. In line 658, he "reverts from describing the conduct of the English government in 1793–4, to recount his own relation to public events from the time of his arrival in France (Nov. 1791) till his return to England. He is therefore traversing again the ground covered by Books IX and X, 1–227" (de Selincourt, p. 583).

This gesture of distancing seems to mark an important advance in the chain I am now describing. Instead of leaning on the great masters of art and poetry for *models* by means of which to organize the discontinuous and alien landscape and events, in the latter half of Book X Wordsworth begins to compose *icons* out of English and natural material. The vision of the sacrifice on Sarum Plain can be seen as the last link in this chain. (The great icon of the ascent of Mount Snowdon in Book XIII triumphantly takes us back to a time *before* Wordsworth's experience in France.) Since we have looked at the occluded chain of the thematics of paternity, sonship, and androgyny, this overt and indeed often ostensive effort should not occupy us long. This section will involve little more than fleshing out, through a reading of a few passages, of what I have summarized in the last two paragraphs. It remains merely to add that this is of course rather different from a consideration of Wordsworth's own declared political allegiance at the time of the composition of these Books.[10]

The sensible or visible is not simply the given of immediate experience. It carries the trace of history. One must learn to read it. Wordsworth records this impulse in a reasonable way when he judges his initial response to French events as follows:

> I was unprepared
> With needful knowledge, had abruptly pass'd
> Into a theatre, of which the stage
> Was busy with an action far advanced.
> Like others I had read, and eagerly
> Sometimes, the master Pamphlets of the day;
> Nor wanted such half-insight as grew wild
> Upon that meagre soil, help'd out by talk
> And public News; but having never chanced
> To see a regular Chronicle which might shew,
> (If any such indeed existed then)
> Whence the main Organs of the public Power
> Had sprung, their transmigrations when and how
> Accomplish'd, giving thus unto events
> A form and body . . .   (IX, 91–106)

As far as the record in *The Prelude* is concerned, Wordsworth never did go in search of an ordinary, formalizing as well as substantializing chronicle of the power structure of the French Revolution. Instead he sought alternate literary-historical cases within which he could insert the historical and geographical landscape. If I quote Marx in his middle twenties here, it is only because we should then witness two textualist solutions to similar problems, going in opposed directions. Ludwig Feuerbach also seems not to know how to read a social text, and Marx proposes the following:

the sensuous world around [us] is not a thing given direct from all eternity, remaining ever the same, but the product of industry and of the state of society; and, indeed, in the sense that it is an historical product, the result of the activity of a whole succession of generations, each standing on the shoulders of the preceding one, developing its industry and its intercourse, and modifying its social system according to the changed needs. Even the objects of the simplest "sensuous certainty" are only given [us] through social development, industry and commercial intercourse. [Because he lacks this approach] Feuerbach sees [in Manchester] only factories and machines, where a hundred years ago only spinning-wheels and weaving-looms were to be seen, or in the Campagna of Rome he finds only pasture lands and swamps, where in the time of Augustus he would have found nothing but the vineyards and villas of Roman capitalists.[11]

Confronted with a little-known historical text, Wordsworth's solution is to disavow historical or genealogical production and attempt to gain control through a private allusive positing of resemblance for which he himself remains the authority and source; at least so he writes almost a decade later. Most of these "resemblances", being fully implicit, are accessible, of course, only to a reader who is sufficiently versed in English literary culture. For example, Wordsworth makes his task of describing the French experience "resemble" the opening of *Paradise Lost*, Book IX, where Milton turns from the delineation of sinless Paradise to describe

> foul distrust, and breach
> Disloyal on the part of Man, revolt,
> And disobedience; on the part of Heav'n
> Now alienated, distance and distaste,
> Anger and just rebuke, and judgment giv'n.
>
> (de Selincourt, p. 566)

It must be pointed out that the "sin" is not just France's against Paradise, which Wordsworth will judge. It could more "literally" be Wordsworth's own carnal knowledge, which this text must subliminally obliterate.

Michel Beaupuy makes an attempt to fill Wordsworth in on the sources of the present trouble, and on the hope for the future. As Wordsworth commemorates these conversations, which for him came closest to a "regular Chronicle" of the times, he gives them apologetic sanction, for Coleridge's benefit, in the name of Dion, Plato, Eudemus, and Timonides, who waged a "philosophic war / Led by philosophers" (lines 421–2). Indeed, Wordsworth's sympathies were with Girondists because they "were idealists whose speeches were full of references to ancient Greece and Rome" (de Selincourt, p. 576). Here too it is interesting to compare notes with Marx:

Luther put on the mask of the apostle Paul; the Revolution of 1789–1814 draped itself alternately as the Roman republic and the Roman empire; and the revolution of 1848 knew no better than to parody at some points 1789 and at others the revolutionary traditions of 1793–5. In the same way, the beginner who has learned a new language always retranslates it into his mother tongue: he can only be said to have appropriated the spirit of the new language and so be able to express himself in it freely when he can manipulate it without reference to the old, and when he forgets his original language while using the new one.[12]

A new and unknown language has been thrust upon William Wordsworth. Even as its elements are being explained to him, he engages in a bizarre "retranslation" into the old. What he describes much more carefully than the substance of the conversation is when "from earnest dialogues I slipp'd in thought / And let remembrance steal to other times" (IX, 444–5). In these interstitial moments, the preferred chronicle is sidestepped through the invocation of "straying" hermit and "devious" travelers (IX, 446, 448). Next the poet reports covering over the then present discourse with remembered stories of fugitive maidens or of "Satyrs . . . / Rejoicing o'er a Female" (IX, 460–1). Geography, instead of being textualized as "the result of the activity of a whole succession of generations, each standing on the shoulders of the preceding one", is "retranslated" into great literary accounts of the violation or flight of women. The sight of a convent "not by reverential touch of time / Dismantled, but by violence abrupt" (IX, 469–70) takes its place upon this list and prepares us for Julia's tale. The verse paragraph that intervenes between the two does give us something like an insight into Beaupuy's discourse. Let us consider the strategy of that paragraph briefly.

First, an invocation of an unrememorated castle (third on the list after Romorentin and Blois) – "name now slipp'd / From my remembrance" (IX, 483–4) – inhabited by a nameless mistress of Francis I. This visual object, as Wordsworth remembers, gives Imagination occasion to enflame two kinds of emotions: one was, of course, "virtuous wrath and noble scorn" though less so than in the case of "the peaceful House / Religious" (IX, 496, 492–3); the other was a

> mitigat[ion of] the force
> Of civic prejudice, the bigotry,
> So call it, of a youthful Patriot's mind

and, Wordsworth goes on, "on these spots with many gleams I look'd / Of chivalrous delight!" (IX, 500–1). Beaupuy in the written text is able to produce a summary of his argument only by metaphorizing the object of the French Revolution as "a hunger-bitten Girl" . . . " 'Tis against *that* / Which we are fighting' " (IX, 510, 517–18). Here is the summary:

> All institutes for ever blotted out
> That legalised exclusion, empty pomp
> Abolish'd, sensual state and cruel power
> Whether by the edict of the one or few,
> And finally, as sum and crown of all,
> Should see the people having a strong hand
> In making their own Laws, whence better days
> To all mankind.   (IX, 525–32)

This admirable summary is followed by a proleptic rhetorical question that reminds us that due process was suspended under the Reign of Terror. As a deviation from the theme, the story of Vaudracour and Julia is broached. One is reminded that Beaupuy, the only good angel on the Revolutionary side, is himself a deviation, "of other mold", and that his own retranslation of the events into art and sexual courtesy (in an unwitting display of class and sex prejudice) serves, as it were, to excuse his Revolutionary sentiments:

> He thro' the events
> Of that great change wander'd in perfect faith,
> As through a Book, an old Romance or Tale
> Of Fairy, or some dream of actions . . .
> . . . Man he lov'd
> As Man; and to the mean and the obscure . . .
> Transferr'd a courtesy which had no air
> Of condescension, but did rather seem
> A passion and a gallantry, like that
> Which he, a Soldier, *in his idler day*
> Had pay'd to Woman [!]
> (IX, 303–6, 311–12, 313–17; italics mine)

It is the passage through the long Book X that allows the poet of *The Prelude* to represent himself as generative subject. The literary-historical allusions and retranslations of Book IX change to icons of the poet's own making. In an intermediate move, Wordsworth tells the tale of lost control by *interiorizing* literary analogues. We have seen how, in the final passages about the androgynous Imagination, the distinction between inside and outside is allowed to waver. As Wordsworth tries to transform revolution into iconic text, again the binary opposition between the inside of literary memory and the outside of the external scene is no longer sufficient. The distinction begins to waver in a use of Shakespeare that has puzzled many readers.

Book X, lines 70–7, is worth considering in all its versions.

"The horse is taught his manage, and the wind
Of heaven wheels round and treads in his own steps,
Year follows year, the tide returns again,
Day follows day, all things have second birth;
The earthquake is not satisfied at once."
And in such a way I wrought upon myself,
Until I seem'd to hear a voice that cried,
To the whole City, "Sleep no more."

Most of it is within quotation marks, the poet "wrighting" upon himself. About two years after the completion of the 1805 *Prelude*, the quotation marks were lifted, and thus the sense of a unique sleepless night was removed. As the passage stands in 1805, the exigency seems to be more to invoke Shakespeare than to achieve coherence. The lines begin with a peculiarly inapt quotation from the lighthearted opening of *As You Like It*, where Orlando complains that his brother's horses are treated better than he. Wordsworth wrests the line from its context and fits it into a number of sentences, all either quotations or self-quotations (thus confounding the inside of the self with the outside), which seem to echo two different kinds of sentiments: that wild things are tamed and that things repeat themselves. The sentences do not seem to provide much solace against the massacres, guaranteeing at once their taming and their return, though perhaps the idea of a wild thing obeying the law of its own return is itself a sort of taming.

In the allusion to *Macbeth* that follows, however, the result of becoming so agitated seems to be an acknowledgment of the guilt of the murder of a father/king. The voice in Shakespeare had seemingly cried, "Sleep no more!" to all the house because Macbeth had murdered Duncan. Although in Wordsworth's eyes it is Paris who is guilty of killing the king, the Shakespearean reference where the guilty Macbeth is himself the speaker implicates Wordsworth in the killing of his own paternity through the rejection of his firstborn. A peculiar line in the collection of sayings stands out: "All things have second birth." When in an extension of the *Macbeth* passage nearly two hundred lines later, he confides to Coleridge that although the infant republic was doing well, all the injustices involved in its inception gave him sleepless nights, an overprotesting parenthesis stands out in the same unsettling way:

Most melancholy at that time, O Friend!
Were my day-thoughts, my dreams were miserable;
Through months, through years, long after the last beat
Of these atrocities (*I speak bare truth,*
As if to thee alone in private talk)
I scarcely had one night of quiet sleep

> Such ghastly visions had I of despair
> And tyranny, and implements of death,
> And long orations which in dreams I pleaded
> Before unjust Tribunals, with a voice
> Labouring, a brain confounded, and a sense
> Of *treachery and desertion* in the place
> The holiest that I knew of, my own soul.
>
> (X, 369–81; italics mine)

The image of the victorious republic is that of a Herculean female infant (Annette bore a daughter, Caroline) who had throttled the snakes about her cradle. I am suggesting, of course, that even as Wordsworth seeks to control the heterogeneity of the Revolution through literary-historical and then iconic textuality, the occlusion of the personal guilt of the unacknowledged paternity is still at work.

Shakespearean echoes are scattered through the pages of *The Prelude*. Most of the time, however, Milton helps Wordsworth get a grip on the Revolution. I have already mentioned that Book Nine opens with a Miltonic echo. Wordsworth describes the beginning of the Reign of Terror in words recalling the Miltonic lines, "So spake the fiend, and with necessitie, / The Tyrant's plea, excus'd his devilish deeds" (*Paradise Lost*, IV, 394–5; de Selincourt, p. 579).

Lines 117–202 of Book X are limpid in their conscious sanctity. These are the lines that end in recounting that Wordsworth left France merely because he was short of funds and that this was by far the best thing that could have happened because this way his future contributions as a poet were spared. Here Wordsworth speaks of himself as comparable to an angel and of his courageous hopes for France, not in the voice of Shakespeare's guilty Macbeth, but as Milton's saintly Samson, undone by a woman:

> But patience is more oft the exercise
> Of saints, the trial of their fortitude,
> Making them each his own Deliverer
> And Victor over all
> That tyrannie or fortune can inflict.
>
> (*Samson Agonistes*, 1287–91; de Selincourt, p. 577)

Indeed, it is the language of *Paradise Lost* that helps give that joy at Robespierre's death the authority of just condemnation: "That this foul Tribe of Moloch was o'erthrown, / And their chief Regent levell'd with the dust" (X, 469–70).

We have so far considered some examples of allusive textualization and also of the interiorization of literary allusion. Let us now turn to the composition of icons.

The point is often made that it was not so much the experience of the French Revolution, but the fact of England's warring with France, that finally brought Wordsworth to despair. Wordsworth's initial reaction to the Revolution matched a good English model: "There was a general disposition among the middle and upper classes to welcome the first events of the Revolution – even traditionalists argued that France was coming belatedly into line with British notions of the 'mixed constitution'."[13] In addition, Wordsworth claims three personal reasons for sympathy: "born in a poor district", he had never, in his childhood, seen

> The face of one, who, whether Boy or Man,
> Was vested with attention or respect
> Through claim of wealth or blood   (IX, 223–5)

At Cambridge he had seen that "wealth and titles were in less esteem / Than talents and successful industry" (IX, 234–5). (A superficial but understandable analysis.) And all along, "fellowship with venerable books . . . and mountain liberty" prepared him to

> hail
> As best the government of equal rights
> And individual worth.   (IX, 246–8)

Support for idealistic revolutionary principles based on such intuitive-patriotic grounds would be ill prepared for England's French policy. Fortunately for Wordsworth's long-term sanity, the martial conduct of the French, the "radicalization of The Revolution", and the fear of French invasion provided him with a reason to withdraw into the ideology-reproductive "passive" politics that is apolitical and individualistic, as it allowed Pitt to become "the diplomatic architect of European counter-revolution".[14] If the reverence due to a poet is laid aside for a moment and Wordsworth is seen as a human being with a superb poetical gift as defined by a certain tradition, then his ideological victimization can be appreciated:

The invasion scare resulted in a torrent of broadsheets and ballads . . . which form a fitting background for Wordsworth's smug and sonorous patriotic sonnets:

> It is not to be thought of that the Flood
> Of British freedom, which, to the open sea
> Of the world's praise, from dark antiquity
> Hath flowed, "with pomp of waters, unwithstood," . . .

"Not to be thought of"; and yet, at this very time, freedom of the press, of public meeting, of trade union organisation, of political organisation and of election, were either severely limited or in abeyance. What, then, did the common Englishman's "birth-right" consist in? "Security of property!" answered Mary Wollstonecraft: "Behold . . . the definition of English liberty."[15]

It might be remembered that the elation of first composition at the inception of *The Prelude* is not unmixed with the security of a legacy and a place of one's own.

This "revolutionary" nationalism articulates itself in one of the first full-fledged icons that will situate politics and history for Wordsworth, his select readership, and students of the Romantic period. The components of the icon are scattered through lines 254 to 290 of Book X: a tree, a steeple, a congregation, plucked flowers. The overt argument begins by setting up a strong binary opposition of nature and anti-nature. Wordsworth uses the honorable but confused appellation of patriotism as a "natural" sentiment, based on the assumption of a "natural" tie between man and the soil (as if indeed he were a tree), rather than an "ideological" connection needed to support a political and economic conjuncture bearing its own history.[16] Thus the initial feeling against England's French policy is already dubbed "unnatural strife / In my own heart" as the icon is set up. And since the so-called conceptual justification for the icon is based on what may as well be called the "metaphoric" axiomatics of a man as a tree, or an organism "literally" rooted in the soil, the metaphor which is the first component of the icon has more than a sanction by analogy:

> I, who with the breeze
> Had play'd, a green leaf on the blessed tree
> Of my beloved country; nor had wish'd
> For happier fortune than to wither there,
> Now from my pleasant station was cut off,
> And toss'd about in whirlwinds.

A limited and controlling play is changed by the war into an untimely death which, in an induced motion, imitates life. Just as the subjectivistic element of the anti-Vietnam War movement was not for communist principles but a cleaner America, so also Wordsworth's icon casts a vote here not for revolutionary principles but an England worthy of her name.

The tree is a natural image. The next bit of the icon secures the social and legal dimension. Although the situation is a church, the iconic elements are steeple, congregation, Father worship. Wordsworth's practice is different when he wants to invoke transcendental principles. Here the preparation slides us into a situation where Wordsworth feels alienated because, unlike the "simple worshippers" (sharing in "mountain liberty") who gave him his taste for revolution, he cannot say,

"God for my country, right or wrong." The power of the icon, with the status of conceptual-literal-metaphoric lines made indeterminate, wrests our support for Wordsworth's predicament without questioning its strategic structure; indeed indeterminacy is part of both the rhetorical and the thematic burden of the passage, as the opening lines show:

> It was a grief,
> *Grief call it not, 'twas anything but that*
> *A conflict of sensations without name,*
> Of which he only who may love the sight
> Of a Village Steeple as I do can judge
> When in the Congregation, bending all
> To their great Father, prayers were offer'd up,
> Or praises for our Country's Victories,
> And 'mid the simple worshippers, perchance,
> I only, like an uninvited Guest
> Whom no one own'd, sate silent, shall I add,
> Fed on the day of vengeance yet to come?
>
> (X, 264–75; italics mine)

It is not by chance that the responsibility for such a mishap is thrown on an unspecified "they":

> Oh much have they to account for, who could tear
> By violence at one decisive rent
> From the best Youth in England, their dear pride,
> Their joy, in England.   (X, 276–9)

We are no longer sure whether the warmongers of England or revolution itself is to blame. The condemned gesture is still the act of cutting or rending. But the icon ends with an ambiguous image. At first it is alleged that, at the time, the French Revolution was considered a higher advent than nationalism – just as Christ was greater than John the Baptist. Then this very thought is "judged" in the following lines:

> A time in which Experience would have pluck'd
> Flowers out of any hedge to make thereof
> A Chaplet, in contempt of his grey locks.   (X, 289–91)

This is indeed a contemptuous picture of a revolution that goes against any established institution. The image of age pretending to youthful self-adornment is unmistakable in tone. The force of the whirlwind has been reduced to weaving a chaplet, cutting off a leaf to plucking flowers. The coherence of a historical or revolutionary argument is on its way to being successfully rejected as mere folly.

I now turn to what in my reading is the place where the chain stops and the mind triumphs over the French Revolution: Book XII, lines 298–353, the reverie on Sarum Plain. The lines are addressed to that certain Coleridge who, as "Friend", is witness, interlocutor, and *alter ego* of *The Prelude*. They are an apology for a hubristic professional concept of self: poets like prophets can see something unseen before. This is not a unique and self-generative gift, for poets are connected in "a mighty scheme of truth" – a "poetic history" that is presumably other and better than "history as such", which by implication here, and by demonstration elsewhere in *The Prelude*, has failed in the task of prediction and prophecy. The gift is also a "dower" from an undisclosed origin, but the Friend is encouraged to establish something like a relationship between that gift or "influx" and *a* work of Wordsworth's (not necessarily *The Prelude?*), whose origin is caught in a negative which necessarily carries the trace of that which it negates. The thing negated (logically "prior") would, in this case, seem paradoxically to imply a chronological posteriority: "the depth of untaught things". This vertiginous deployment of indeterminacy of traces culminates in the hope that this work will deconstruct the opposition between Nature and Art – "might become / A power like one of Nature's". Yet to be like *one* of Nature's powers, bringing in the entire part–whole/identity problem, makes even that possible deconstruction indeterminate. Such a collocation of indeterminacy, where nothing can be fixed, is the antecedent of the deceptively simple and unified word "mood" to which Wordsworth was "raised" and which is, presumably, both the origin and the subject matter of what I am calling an iconic recuperation of the events of 1791–3. (The date of the "actual" walk is July–August, 1793.)

It is by now no longer surprising that the immediate setting of the reverie is also marked by tracings and alternations. The ranging walks took place either *without* a track or *along* the dreary line of roads. The trace-structure here is not the obstreperous heterogeneous material or opening of political history; a vaster time scale seems to make the experience safe for poetry: "through those vestiges of ancient times I ranged". The disingenuous line "I had a reverie and saw the past" carries this overwhelming and conditioning frame.

In his vision of Sarum Plain, the poet sees multitudes *and* "a single Briton". This Briton is a *subject*-representative or *alter ego* of great subtlety. He is also the *object* of Wordsworth's attentive reverie. There is the same sort of self-deconstructive ego splitting as in the autoerotic passage on the Imagination as object of attention that I discussed earlier. He is not necessarily singular though "single", as the following words make clear: "Saw . . . here and there, / A single Briton . . ." The relationship between him and the prophetic voice is one of metonymic contiguity, not of agency or production. The voice itself, though "of spears" and thus war-making, is "heard" like that prophetic "voice of the turtle", announcing peace and safety from God's wrath: a revolution controlled and soothed into the proper stuff of poetry. The consciousness that produced the voice is itself undermined and dispersed into a compound image and common nouns that hold encrypted the proper name of the leader of Wordsworth's calling, Shakespeare:

> The voice of spears was heard, the rattling spear
> Shaken by arms of mightly bone, in strength
> Long moulder'd of barbaric majesty.   (XII, 324–6)

I have already remarked upon Wordsworth's use of a metonymic or sequential, rather than a metaphoric or consequential, rhetoric. Here that habit seems specifically to blur the relationship between selves and voices. Imagination, or Poetry, is presented as an august trace, other and greater than what can be uttered by a mere individual. Since the poet carefully orchestrates this presentation, the intolerable trace-structure of history as catastrophe can now be tamed.

The relationship between Shakespeare's encrypted name and the poet's successful invocation of a darkness that took or seemed to take (the rhetoric of alternation yet again) all objects from his sight to produce a highly precarious "center" where the icon is finally visible is thus predictably metonymic: "It is the sacrificial Altar." At last the carnage of the French Revolution is reconstructed into a mere image of a generalized "history" on the occasion of a highly deconstructive and self-deconstructed Imagination. Wordsworth can now "read" the September Massacres:

> It is the sacrificial Altar, fed
> With living men, how deep the groans, the voice
> Of those in the gigantic wicker thrills
> Throughout the region far and near, pervades
> The monumental hillocks.   (XII, 331–5)

"History" has at last come alive and animated the native landscape. And indeed the next few images are of a collective possibility of reading; no longer a reverie but actual geometric shapes which figure over a precultural soil – the very image of the originary institution of a trace, what Heidegger would call "the worlding of a world".[17] The precultural space of writing is as carefully placed within a *mise-en-abîme* as the origin of Wordsworth's unspecified work a few lines earlier: "untill'd ground" matching "untaught things". This particular inscription is not a reminder of Oedipal law but a charming and pleasant access to science. The principle of figuration is multiple:

"imitative form", "covert expression", "imaging forth" of the constellations. This principle, the relationship between representation and represented, is finally itself figured forth as that connection among poets (the Druids and Wordsworth) with which the argument began:

> I saw the bearded Teachers, with white wands
> Uplifted, pointing to the starry sky
> Alternately, and Plain below.   (XII, 349–51)

The icon is sealed at the beginning of the next verse paragraph: "This for the past" (XII, 356).

The intolerable trace-structure of history is thus brought under control by the authorial positing of the elaborate trace-structure of the Imagination and the brotherhood of poets. The control is emphasized all through the next verse paragraph, the closing lines of Book XII. Coleridge is called forth to testify that at this time Wordsworth began to produce good poetry. But even Coleridge is superseded, for "the mind is to herself / Witness and judge". Out of the self-evidence of such supreme self-possession, and by way of an elaborate iconic self-deconstruction, Wordsworth competes successfully with the Revolution and records the articulation of a new world; the double privilege matches the accession to androgyny:

> I seem'd about this period to have sight
> Of a new world, a world, too, that was fit
> To be transmitted and made visible
> To other eyes, as having for its base
> That whence our dignity originates   (XII, 370–4)

and so on. Reading Romantic poetry will bring about what the French Revolution could not accomplish. What we need to learn from is " 'An unpublished Poem on the Growth and *Revolutions* of an Individual Mind' ", as Coleridge's description of *The Prelude* has it "as late as February 1804" (de Selincourt, p. xxvi; italics mine).

Yet a postscript must be added. These books of *The Prelude* have curious moments when what is suppressed projects into the scene. Vaudracour and the murderer's name operate unceasingly as textual time passes. And elsewhere the poet apologizes most unemphatically for having neglected details of time and place, and for not having given his sister her rightful place in his poem. If these two items are seen as hardly displaced representatives of the matter of France and the matter of woman, the poet is here excusing the very constitutive burden of these Books:

> Since I withdrew unwillingly from France,
> The Story hath demanded less regard

> To time and place; and where I lived, and how
> Hath been no longer scrupulously mark'd.
> Three years, until a permanent abode
> Receiv'd me with that Sister of my heart
> Who ought by rights the dearest to have been
> Conspicuous through this biographic Verse,
> Star seldom utterly conceal'd from view,
> I led an undomestic Wanderer's life   (XIII, 334-43)

(The sister, incidentally, disappears completely from the 1850 version.) I comment on a comparable narrative intrusion at the end of this next section.

Poetry as cure for oppression: a life preordained to teach this lesson

Wordsworth offers his own poetry as a cure for human oppression and suffering because it teaches one where to look for human value.

In lines 69–158 of Book XII, the ostensible grounds of such a suggestion are researched and presented. The narrative has just passed through the Oedipal encounters. Now Wordsworth is ready to undertake his own critique of political economy. His conclusion is that the true wealth of nations is in

> The dignity of individual Man,
> Of Man, no composition of the thought,
> Abstraction, shadow, image, but the man
> Of whom we read [a curious distinction!], the man whom we behold
> With our own eyes.   (XII, 84-8)

Man as a category is of course always an abstraction, whether we see him, read of him, or make him a part of "public welfare", which last, according to Wordsworth in this passage, is "plans without thought, or bottom'd on false thought / And false philosophy" (XII, 74-5). Without pursuing that point, however, let us insist that although, following his rhetorical bent, Wordsworth does not equate the true wealth of nations with individual male dignity, but leaves them suggestively contiguous on a list, there can be no doubt that he here recounts the history of someone who *seriously* and with experience, knowledge, and wisdom confronts the problems of social justice and political economy. He refers to "the Books / Of modern Statists" (XII, 77-8), most specifically, of course, to Adam Smith's *The Wealth of Nations*, first published in 1776.[18] (In the 1850 version of *The Prelude*, the phrase – "The Wealth of Nations" – is put within quotation marks, as the title of a book.)

Quite appropriately, though always by implication, Wordsworth finds the increasing of the *wealth* of nations, as understood by classical economists, to be a hollow goal. Adam Smith was a proponent of the labor-command theory of value: "The value of any commodity, therefore, to the person who possesses it, and who means not to use or consume it himself, but to exchange it for other commodities, is equal to the quantity of labour which it enables him to purchase or command. Labour, therefore, is the real measure of the exchangeable value of all commodities."[19] His method of increasing the wealth of a nation is therefore greater division of labor, greater specialization, deregulation of trade, economic interaction between town and country, the establishment of colonies – all based on a view of human nature reflected in the following famous passage:

Man has almost constant occasion for the help of his brethren, and it is in vain for him to expect it from their benevolence only. He will be more likely to prevail if he can interest their self-love in his favour, and shew them that it is for their own advantage to do for him what he requires of them. . . . It is not from the benevolence of the butcher, the brewer, or the baker, that we expect our dinner, but from their regard to their own interest. We address ourselves, not to their humanity but to their self-love, and never talk to them of our own necessities but of their advantages.[20]

Wordsworth predictably does not concern himself with the practical possibilities of *laissez-faire* capitalism. He implicitly questions its presuppositions regarding human nature – which he considers an aberration. He does not, however, suggest that the production of commodities requires and produces this aberrant version of human nature. He posits, rather, a subjective theory of human value, where the work of salvation would consist of disclosing that man's essential wealth lay inside him.

He therefore asks: Why is the essential individual who is the standard of measurement of this subjective theory of value (yet, curiously enough, not an abstraction) so rarely to be found? Wordsworth poses a rhetorical question: "Our animal wants and the necessities / Which they impose, are these the obstacles?" (XII, 94–5). If this question were answered in the affirmative, then the entire occluded chain of the non-acknowledgment of paternity might, even in so seemingly self-assured a passage, be making itself felt; in other words, Wordsworth would then be in the most uncharacteristic position of "taking himself as an example", making of his animal nature the inevitable reason for the failure of perfectibility. If in the negative, then Wordsworth's case against political justice, against Godwin, Adam Smith, and the French Revolution is won. As in all rhetorical questions, the questioner obliquely declares for one alternative: "If not, then others vanish into thin

air" (XII, 96). And the asymmetry of the rhetorical question constitutes *The Prelude*'s politics as well as the condition of its possibility.

The position, then, is that social relations of production cannot touch
the inner resources of man. The corollary: revolutionary politics, seeking to change those social relations, are therefore superfluous; poetry,
disclosing man's inner resources, is the only way. Although Wordsworth cannot ask how there will come to pass a set of social relations
in which everyone will have the opportunity and education to value
poetry for its use, he does ask a preliminary question that seems appropriate if the poet is to disclose the wealth of man:

> how much of real worth
> And genuine knowledge, and true power of mind
> Did at this day exist in those who liv'd
> By *bodily labour, labour far exceeding*
> *Their due proportion*, under all the weight
> Of that injustice which upon ourselves
> *By composition of society*
> Ourselves entail   (XII, 98–105; italics mine)

If this question is asked rigorously, we arrive at the problem of
human alienation in the interest of the production of surplus-value:

The fact that half a day's labour is necessary to keep the worker alive during
twenty-four hours does not in any way prevent him from working a whole day.
Therefore the value of labour-power and the value which that labour-power
valorizes [*verwertet*] in the labour-process, are two entirely different magni-
tudes; and this difference was what the capitalist had in mind when he was pur-
chasing the labour-power.[21]

Whether he has stumbled upon the crucial question of social injustice or not, Wordsworth's ideological preparation and predilection
lead him to a less than useful answer. The ground rules of the academic
subdivision of labor would make most of us at this point piously
exclaim, "One does not judge poets in this way! This is only Wordsworth's personal story, and since this is poetry, it is not even that –
the 'I' of *The Prelude* is to be designated 'the speaker', not 'Wordsworth'." Suffice it to say that I am deliberately calling Wordsworth's
bluff, seeing if indeed poetry can get away with a narrative of political
investigation when it never in fact "irreducibly intends" anything but
its own "constitution".

Although

> an intermixture of distinct regards
> And truths of individual sympathy often might be glean'd
> From that great city,   (XII, 119–21)

Wordsworth, "to frame such estimate [of human worth]",

> . . . chiefly look'd (what need to look beyond?)
> Among the natural abodes of men,
> Fields with their rural works.   (XII, 105–8)

"What need", indeed! Wordsworth is tracing out a recognizable ideological circuit here, deciding that the peculiarities of one's own locale give the *universal* norm. (In fact, even in terms of *rural* England, the situation in Cumberland and Westmorland was not representative.)[22] "Feuerbach's 'conception' of the sensuous world [in the *Principles of a Philosophy of the Future*] is confined on the one hand to mere contemplation of it, and on the other to mere feeling; he posits 'Man' instead of 'real historical man'. *Man is really 'the German'*."[23]

There is something to admire in Wordsworth's impulse. Not only does he ask the question of disproportionate labor, he also emphasizes that the excluded margins of the human norm are where the norm can be properly encountered; his own thematics are of depth and surface:

> There [I] saw into the depth of human souls,
> Souls that appear to have no depth at all
> To vulgar eyes.   (XII, 166–8)

This is all the more laudable because of the deplorable consequences of the vagrancy laws, some of them of Tudor origin, that began to be sharply felt as a result of the rise of industrial capitalism. It is noteworthy, however, that at the crucial moment of decision in *The Prelude* Wordsworth does not speak of the dispossessed "small proprietors" of the Lake Country, of whose plight he had considerable knowledge, nor of "an ancient rural society falling into decay".[24]

The ideological benevolent perspective Wordsworth had on these vagrants would not allow him to argue here for a fairer distribution of labor or wealth, but would confine him to the declaration that virtue and intellectual strength are not necessarily the property of the so-called educated classes – and hedge even that declaration by an "if" and a personal preference:[25]

> If man's estate, by doom of Nature yoked
> With toil, is therefore yoked with ignorance,
> If virtue be indeed so hard to rear,
> And intellectual strength so rare a boon
> I prized such walks still more   (XII, 174–8)

It is of course worth noticing that the conditions for prizing the walk are askew. In terms of the overt argument of this part of *The Prelude*, we are not sure whether Wordsworth thinks the first "if" is correct;

this uncertainty makes the "therefore" rhetorically undecidable, since the declared charge of the argument suggests that the last two "ifs" are false suppositions. But I prefer to ask simpler questions: Why is the doom of Nature not equally exigent upon everyone, and why should a man who does not want to reduce Man (*sic*) to a homogenizing abstraction be unable to entertain the question of heterogeneity?

If, indeed, one continues the analogy, it looks like this: Wordsworth will work on the human wealth represented by the solitaries and produce poetry which will teach others to be as wealthy as the originals. It should be repeated that such an analogy ignores such questions as "Who reads poetry?" "Who makes laws?" "Who makes money?" as well as "What is the relationship between the interest on Wordsworth's capital and the production of this theory?" The greatness of Marx was to have realized that, within capitalism, that interest is part of a surplus the production of which is the sole prerogative of wage labor and that production is based on exploitation. "Productive labor" and "free labor" in this context are not positive concepts; they are the bitter names of human degradation and alienation: "the 'productive' worker cares as much about the lousy rubbish he has to make as does the capitalist himself who employs him, and who also couldn't give a damn for the junk."[26] Within the historical situation of the late eighteenth century, to offer only poetry as the means of changing this definition of "productive" is class-bound and narrow. Since it denies the reality of exploitation, it need conceive of no struggle. An example of this attitude can still be found in the official philosophy of current Departments of English: "The goal of ethical criticism is transvaluation, the ability to look at contemporary social values with the detachment of one who is able to compare them in some degree with the infinite vision of possibilities presented by culture."[27]

Wordsworth's choice of the rural solitary as theme, then, is an ideologically symptomatic move in answer to a critical question about political economy. It is neither to lack sympathy for Wordsworth's predicament nor to underestimate "the verbal grandeur" of the poetry to be able to recognize the program.

We have so far considered Wordsworth's suggestion that poetry is a better cure for human oppression or suffering than revolution. His second suggestion is that his own life is preordained to teach this lesson. In making my previous arguments, I have amply presented the elements of this well-known suggestion. So much so, that I will not reformulate it here. Suffice it to mention that this particular chain of thought in *The Prelude* is rounded off most appropriately, in a verse paragraph of exquisite beauty, where Wordsworth expresses an unconvincing uncertainty about that very telos of his life; even as he finds, in the "private" memory of the "public" poetic records of his "private" exchange with Coleridge, a sufficient dialogic justification for *The Prelude*:

> To thee, in memory of that happiness
> It will be known, by thee at least, my Friend,
> Felt, that the history of a Poet's mind
> Is labour not unworthy of regard:
> To thee the work shall justify itself. (XIII, 406–10)

Yet, just as there is a moment when France and Dorothy jut into the text as apology when all seemed to have been appeased, so also is there a moment when, in this final book, something apparently suppressed juts into the scene. Life is seen to have a telos or at least a place that is distinct from the poet's self. And such a life is seen as capable of launching an unanswerable or at least unanswered reproach. There is even a hint that *The Prelude* might be but an excuse. If the passage I quote above narrates a poetic career, this passage narrates the career of *The Prelude* not just as text but as discourse:

> O Friend! the termination of my course
> Is nearer now, much nearer; yet even then
> In that distraction and intense desire
> I said unto the life which I had lived,
> Where art thou? Hear I not a voice from thee
> Which 'tis reproach to hear? Anon I rose
> As if on wings, and saw beneath me stretch'd
> Vast prospect of the world which I had been
> And was; and hence this Song, which like a lark
> I have protracted . . . (XIII, 372–81)

No answer to Wordsworth's question of the first six lines is articulated in the next four; only a strategy is described. If one pulled at a passage like this, the text could be made to perform a self-deconstruction, the adequacy of *The Prelude* as autobiography called into question. But then the politics of the puller would insert itself into the proceeding. I have stopped short of the impossibly duped position that such a person with pull is politics-free, oscillating freely in "the difficult double bind" of an aporia, like the Cumaean sybil in a perpetual motion machine.

In these pages I have read a poetic text attempting to cope with a revolution and paternity. I have not asked the critic to be hostile to poetry or to doubt the poet's good faith; although I have asked her to examine the unquestioning reverence or – on the part of the poets themselves – the credulous vanity that seems to be our disciplinary requirement. As a feminist reader of men on women, I thought it useful to point out that, in the texts of the Great Tradition, the most remotely occluded and transparently mediating figure is woman.

Notes

[1] Wallace W. Douglas, *Wordsworth: The Construction of a Personality* (Kent: Kent State University Press, 1968), pp. 3–4.

[2] Legouis's approach is so sexist and politically reactionary that the reader feels that it was Annette's good fortune to have been used by Wordsworth, Wordsworth's good sense to have treated her with exemplary pious indifference and no financial assistance, and his magnanimity to have given his daughter money in her adult life, to have allowed this daughter, by default, to use his name, and to have probably addressed her as "dear Girl" in "It is a beauteous evening", when, on the eve of his marriage to sweet Mary Hutchinson, Dorothy and William were walking with ten-year-old Caroline, *without* Annette, because the latter, "although inexhaustibly voluble when she pours out her heart, . . . seems to be devoid of intellectual curiosity" (Emile Legouis, *William Wordsworth and Annette Vallon* [London: J. M. Dent, 1922], pp. 68, 33). Critical consensus has taken Wordsworth's increasingly brutal evaluation of the Annette affair at face value: "In retrospect [his passion for Annette] seemed to him to have been transient rather than permanent in its effects upon him, and perhaps to have arrested rather than developed the natural growth of his poetic mind. . . . Consequently, however vital a part of his biography as a man, it seemed less vital in the history of his mind" (*The Prelude, or Growth of A Poet's Mind*, ed. Ernest de Selincourt [Oxford: Clarendon Press, 1926], p. 573; this is the edition of *The Prelude* that I have used. References to book and line numbers in the 1805 version are included in my text.) Female critics have not necessarily questioned this evaluation: "What sort of girl was Annette Vallon that she could arouse such a storm of passion in William Wordsworth?" (Mary Moorman, *William Wordsworth: A Biography* [Oxford: Clarendon Press, 1957], p. 178.) More surprisingly, "it would not be possible to read *The Prelude* without wondering why on earth Vaudracour and Julia suddenly crop up in it, or why Wordsworth does not make any more direct mention of Annette Vallon. Nevertheless, although one cannot help wondering about these things, they are not really what the poem is about" (Margaret Drabble, *Wordsworth* [London: Evans Brothers, 1966], p. 79). Herbert Read did in fact put a great deal of emphasis on Annette's role in the production of Wordsworth's poetry (*Wordsworth*, The Clark Lectures, 1929–30 [London: Jonathan Cape, 1930]). His thoroughly sentimental view of the relationship between men and women – "the torn and anguished heart [Wordsworth] brought back to England at the end of this year 1792" – and his discounting of politics – "he was transferring to this symbol France the effect of his cooling affection for Annette" – make it difficult for me to endorse his reading entirely (pp. 102, 134).

[3] Read, *Wordsworth*, pp. 205–6. "It is impossible to date *Vaudracour and*

Julia accurately; we know of no earlier version than that in MS.'A' of *The Prelude*, but it is possible that the episode was written some time before 1804" (F. M. Todd, "Wordsworth, Helen Maria Williams, and France", *Modern Language Review*, 43 [1948], 462).

4 Richard J. Onorato, *The Character of the Poet: Wordsworth in The Prelude* (Princeton: Princeton University Press, 1971), p. 409.

5 I refer the reader to my essay, partially on a passage from *The Prelude*, "Allégorie et histoire de la poésie: hypothèse de travail" (*Poétique*, 8 [1971]), for a working definition of the "iconic" style. An "icon" is created in "passages where the [putative] imitation of real time is momentarily effaced for the sake of a descriptive atemporality [*achronie*]" (p. 430). Such passages in Romantic and post-Romantic allegory characteristically include moments of a "temporal menace . . . resulting in a final dislocation" (p. 434). This earlier essay does not relate Wordsworth's "iconic" practice to a political program. Geoffrey Hartman's definition of the concept of a "spot of time", also unrelated to a political argument, is provocative: "The concept is . . . very rich, fusing not only time and place but also stasis and continuity" (*Wordsworth's Poetry, 1787–1814* [New Haven: Yale University Press, 1964], p. 212).

6 *Sophocles I*, ed. David Grene (Chicago: University of Chicago Press, 1954), p. 42.

7 For the sort of practical but unacknowledged use that Wordsworth made of Dorothy, see Drabble, *Wordsworth*, pp.111 and *passim*. The most profoundly sympathetic account of the relationship between William and Dorothy is to be found in F. W. Bateson, *Wordsworth: A Re-interpretation*, 2nd ed. (London: Longmans, Green, 1954).

8 "Femininity", in *The Standard Edition of the Complete Psychological Works of Sigmund Freud*, trans. James Strachey (London: Hogarth Press, 1964), vol. 22.

9 Gilles Deleuze and Félix Guattari, *Anti-Oedipus: capitalism and schizophrenia*, trans. Mark Seem *et al.* (New York: Viking Press, 1977), p. 161.

10 A sense of the field may be gleaned from A. V. Dicey, *The Statesmanship of Wordsworth: An Essay* (Oxford: Clarendon Press, 1917); Crane Brinton, *The Political Ideas of the English Romanticists* (New York: Russell and Russell, 1926); Kenneth MacLean, *Agrarian Age: a background for Wordsworth* (New Haven: Yale University Press, 1950); E. P. Thompson, "Disenchantment or Default? A Lay Sermon", in *Power and Consciousness*, ed. Conor Cruise O'Brien and William Dean Vanech (London: University of London Press, 1969); George Watson, "The Revolutionary Youth of Wordsworth and Coleridge", John Beer, "The 'Revolutionary Youth' of Wordsworth and Coleridge: another view", David Ellis, "Wordsworth's Revolutionary Youth: how we read *The Prelude*", in *Critical Quarterly*, 18, 19, nos. 3, 2, 4 (1976, 1977; I am grateful to Sandra Shattuck for drawing my attention to this exchange); and Kurt Heinzelman, *The Economics of the Imagination* (Amherst: University of Massachusetts Press, 1980).

11 Karl Marx and Friedrich Engels, *The German Ideology*, in *Collected Works*, ed. Jack Cohen *et al.* (New York: International Publishers, 1976), vol. 5, pp. 39–40. I do not say Marx and Engels here because the passage is from Part

I of *The German Ideology*. "It gives every appearance of being the work for which the 'Theses on Feuerbach' served as an outline; hence we may infer that it was written by Marx" (*The Marx-Engels Reader*, ed. Robert C. Tucker [New York: Norton, 1972], p. 110).

12 Karl Marx, "The Eighteenth Brumaire of Louis Bonaparte", in *Surveys from Exile*, ed. David Fernbach (New York: Vintage Books, 1974), pp. 146–7.

13 E. P. Thompson, *The Making of the English Working Class* (New York: Vintage Books, 1966), p. 105.

14 Ibid., p. 107.

15 Ibid., p. 79; only first ellipsis mine.

16 A contrast is to be encountered in Rousseau. "A man is not planted, in one place like a tree, to stay there the rest of his life" (*Emile*, trans. Barbara Foxley [London: Modern Library, 1911], p. 20). Although Derrida (*Of Grammatology*, trans. Gayatri Chakravorty Spivak [Baltimore: Johns Hopkins University Press, 1976], pp. 222–3) shows us how even "this criticism of the empirical Europe" can be used in the service of ethnocentric anthropology, it is certainly a less insulated world view than Wordsworth's. It is in this spirit that, at the end of *Emile*, the hero is encouraged to travel in order to choose that system of government under which he would find greatest fulfillment. He does of course come back to woman and mother country.

17 See "The Origin of the Work of Art", in *Poetry, Language, Thought*, trans. Albert Hofstadter (New York: Harper and Row, 1971), pp. 44 ff.

18 "From the context, Wordsworth clearly means 'statist' not only in the sense of 'a politician, statesman' (*OED* 1, which cites as example a Wordsworthian usage from 1799) but also in the sense of a political economist (which might include *OED* 2, 'one who *deals* with statistics', the earliest usage of which is given as 1803)" (Heinzelman, *Economics of the Imagination*, p. 305, n. 18).

19 Adam Smith, *An Inquiry into the Nature and Causes of the Wealth of Nations*, ed. Edwin Cannan (New York: Modern Library, 1937), p. 30.

20 Ibid., p. 14.

21 Karl Marx, *Capital*, trans. Ben Fowkes (New York: Vintage Books, 1977), vol. 1, p. 300.

22 "Wordsworth as a social poet would seem to have preferred to be faithful to the experience of his own northern counties rather than to the greater experience of England, which he certainly knew about" (MacLean, *Agrarian Age*, p. 95).

23 Marx, *German Ideology*, p. 39; italics mine.

24 MacLean, *Agrarian Age*, p. 89.

25 "Feeling as imagination he reserved for himself and the child, our 'best philosopher'; feeling as affection he conferred, with just a slight air of condescension and shame, upon the peasant world" (MacLean, *Agrarian Age*, p. 96). "He obviously no longer believed [in Michel Beaupuy's philosophy], and he perhaps had convinced himself that there was a difference between English and French beggary, but this does not justify him in rationalizing beggary, no matter how eloquently, as a fundamental good"

(Edward E. Bostetter, *The Romantic Ventriloquists: Wordsworth, Coleridge, Keats, Shelley, Bryon* [Seattle: University of Washington Press, 1963], p. 56).

26 Karl Marx, *Grundrisse: Foundations of the critique of political economy*, trans. Martin Nicolaus (New York: Vintage Books, 1973), p. 273.

27 Northrop Frye, *Anatomy of Criticism: four essays* (Princeton: Princeton University Press, 1957), p. 348.

Bounding lines: *The Prelude* and critical revision

JONATHAN ARAC

This essay addresses the process of rewriting *The Prelude*, begun by Wordsworth in 1798, protracted through his lifetime, and continuing posthumously in the work of critics and editors, culminating in the remarkable efforts of the Cornell Edition to create, at last, the "original text" (Parrish, p. vii).[1]

I

Even a century now after Walter Pater suggested it, Wordsworth remains exemplary for the "initiation" he offers into "reading between the lines" (p. 40). But what should we make of our interlinear relationship? We might try to hold the lines ever more closely together through adding our presence to them, engage in a glossing that knits parts into a comprehensive totality.[2] Such a reading of *The Prelude* would find example in the expansion from two parts in 1798–9 to five and then thirteen books in 1805.[3] In spinning out more and more material to stand between parts that were originally compacted together, Wordsworth suggests an interlinear glossing comparable to Coleridge's marginal revision of "The Rime of the Ancient Mariner".[4] Such inscription of part into whole would return to Romantic principles, the literary symbol and the philosophical dialectic. It would find in *The Prelude* what Coleridge sought in *The Recluse*, "a redemptive process in operation", an "idea" that "reconciled all the anomalies and promised future glory and restoration" (*Table Talk* [21 July 1832], vol. 6, p. 404).

Instead, however, we might recognize that Wordsworth never wrote *The Recluse* and was dissatisfied by *The Prelude*. He had looked forward to the day of its completion "as a most happy one", but he found it "not a happy day":

I was dejected on many accounts; when I looked back upon the performance it seemed to have a dead weight about it, the reality so far short of the expectation. . . . [T]he doubt whether I should ever live to write the Recluse and the

227

sense which I had of this Poem being so far below what I seem'd capable of
executing, depressed me much.   (*Letters*, 594 [3 June 1805])

For its force to be felt, this must be set beside the closing lines:

> [T]he mind of man becomes
> A thousand times more beautiful than the earth
> On which he dwells, above this frame of things . . .
>
> In beauty exalted, as it is itself
> In substance and of fabric more divine.   (1805, XIII, 446–52)

To contrast this elation to the dejection of the letter is to pose starkly
the problems of disjunction between the empirical self and the poetic
self.

An alternative position "between the lines" might try thinking
through the relations of these two selves in *The Prelude*. Such a reading
might open the spaces between parts of the poem, perhaps by noting
that *The Prelude* is less a fixed text than a poem in process for some
forty years (1798–1839). The differences that emerge between an
"original" line (whether in the text of 1799 or 1805) and its ultimate
successor (1850 text) might point toward problems within any state of
the text, lines that run in different directions to form a "palimpsest"
(Smith, p. 156). Varieties of such "reading asunder", of *The Prelude* as
of all Wordsworth's poetry, characterized A. C. Bradley and Matthew
Arnold no less than Pater. Each of these great Victorian critics strove
to discriminate the essential Wordsworth, the true virtue that remained
when "the electric thread untwined" (Pater, p. 41) lay before us. They
renewed motifs from Longinus on the sublime in their concern with
the great moment, their reliance upon touchstones, and their concern
for finding and sharing the greatness of the poet's mind.

In *The Prelude, or Growth of a Poet's Mind*,[5] these earlier readers
sought the mind. New Criticism, however, owed more to Aristotle than
to Longinus, attended more to poems than to poets, downplayed the
violence of separation to emphasize the harmony of integration, the
totality that results from organic "growth". In *The Mirror and the
Lamp*, M. H. Abrams greatly clarified the differences between these
two positions (p. 22), but his own practice in *Natural Supernaturalism*
sided with Aristotle. He flexibly cast aside strict New-Critical distinctions of intrinsic versus extrinsic ("Rationality and Imagination", p.
461), but only in order to understand *The Prelude* as an even grander
"heterocosm". In the middle of *The Prelude*, Abrams found a world he
shared, and invited us to share, with the poet, whose scene articulates
"a truth about . . . the ineluctable contraries that make up our human

existence" (*Natural Supernaturalism*, p. 107). But this world changes. Finally by Book XIV Wordsworth has "progressed" in his fiction to a "higher realization" (p. 112), now "collects and resolves the contrary qualities" (p. 111), and, transforming his "life into a landscape", from the "high perspective" of "metaphoric flight" can "discern that all its parts are centered in love" (p. 114). Such discernment has cognitive value not as a view of the world but only as a reading of *The Prelude* as a world apart, a "heterocosm" (*Mirror and Lamp*, p. 272). Even that value, however, is severely limited if we recall that shortly before the passage Abrams emphasized (XIV, 381–9), Wordsworth had, with equal authority, claimed that love is inseparably linked to imagination, the "feeding source" of the poem (XIV, 189–94). Thus he pre-emptively displaces the centrality of love. Wordsworth himself wanted a reading of *The Prelude* that bound together all the parts, eclipsing imagination with love, but he could not in fact achieve it, and it is not clear that we should.

We do ourselves little good as readers if we allow our pleasure in a new relation to *The Prelude*, our recent conviction of its crucial greatness, to mask the problems posed between its lines. Attention to these problems will be more productive than hyperbolic acclaim for success. *Natural Supernaturalism* most distinguishedly repre-sents the danger I am posing.[6] The massive learning, the cogent shaping of rich materials, the compositional finesse of the work all lend authority to its arguments that in *The Prelude* Wordsworth achieves a "circular shape" (p. 79) "centered in love", a romantic version of Christian and neoplatonic commonplaces that figure the progress of the soul as a journey leading through a circuitous path to home (chs. 3–5, esp. pp. 278–92). I recognize the wish of Words-worth's that this reading fulfills, but I find in *The Prelude* discrepancies from such a pattern, crevices that interrupt the smooth path around. If "circular shape" suggests a satisfying, compensatory return, circles may also figure a lack or an excess. Thus Emerson wrote, "Our life is an apprenticeship to the truth, that around every circle another can be drawn; that there is no end in nature, but every end is a beginning; that there is always another dawn risen on mid-noon, and under every deep a lower deep opens" (p. 403). Emerson opens up the circle in two respects: it may be a limit rather than a ful-fillment; it is liable to internal rupture. He jams together two contradic-tory moments from *Paradise Lost*, Raphael's appearance in Eden (V, 310–11) and Satan's sense of having "no place", for "in the lowest deep a lower deep / Still threat'ning to devour me opens wide" (IV, 76–7). This astonishing juxtaposition suggests the double pull that spoils Wordsworth's circle — the expansion of its end into "something ever more" and the recession of its origin.

The boat-stealing episode provides focus for these issues:

> It was an act of stealth
> And troubled pleasure, nor without the voice
> Of mountain-echoes did my boat move on;
> Leaving behind her still, on either side,
> Small circles glittering idly in the moon, (365)
> Until they melted all into one track
> Of sparkling light. But now, like one who rows,
> Proud of his skill, to reach a chosen point
> With an unswerving line, I fixed my view
> Upon the summit of a craggy ridge, (370)
> The horizon's utmost boundary; for above
> Was nothing but the stars and the grey sky.
> She was an elfin pinnace; lustily
> I dipped my oars into the silent lake,
> And, as I rose upon the stroke, my boat (375)
> Went heaving through the water like a swan;
> When, from behind that craggy steep till then
> The horizon's bound, a huge peak, black and huge,
> As if with voluntary power instinct
> Upreared its head. I struck and struck again. (380)
> And growing still in stature the grim shape
> Towered up between me and the stars, and still,
> For so it seemed, with purpose of its own
> And measured motion like a living thing,
> Strode after me. With trembling oars I turned, (385)
> And through the silent water stole my way
> Back to the covert of the willow tree;
> There in her mooring-place I left my bark, —
> And through the meadows homeward went, in grave
> And serious mood; but after I had seen (390)
> That spectacle, for many days, my brain
> Worked with a dim and undetermined sense
> Of unknown modes of being; o'er my thoughts
> There hung a darkness, call it solitude
> Or blank desertion.   (1850, I, 361–95)

This sequence represents several crucial elements of *The Prelude*. As in rowing one strives to "reach a chosen point" by looking backward, so *The Prelude* by retrospective inquiry aims to project the poet forward into *The Recluse*, for which *The Prelude* was "preparatory" (Preface to *The Excursion* in *Prose Works*, vol. 3, p. 5). *The Prelude* tries to integrate "spots of time" into the consecutive history of a life project, just as each of the single "small circles" made by the fall of the oar, each new trace of energy, finally "melted all into one track". Wordsworth is trying to open circles to achieve an "unswerving line". But this typical spotting and knotting, doubling back to single out moments that can be joined each to each to define a direction for the present, is interrupted. The outer circle, which was to contain the projected line, fails to hold. The "huge peak" breaks open "the horizon's utmost boundary", supplanting the "summit" which was to serve as point of reference for the line. The terror of disruptive recession at the origin precludes the goal. The return "back to the covert" marks a frustration, a triumph of anxiety to make a closure against both the yawning backward abysm and the unspecified and unreachable goal. If end and origin fall away, the starting-point at least remains.

In *The Prelude*, by 1850 if not in 1805, Wordsworth's return to his own imaginative starting-point comforts the double failure to achieve *The Recluse* and to find the origin. Whatever his wishes, Wordsworth could no more write *The Recluse* than he could keep ascending after he had reached the highest point of his journey in the Alps. That Alpine experience of crossing limits repeats the characteristic movement of *The Prelude*: a compromise is suddenly resolved into its conflicting components: the solid ground opens downward into the "mind's abyss"; outward into "something evermore about to be"; and upward into the rising of imaginative "Power" (VI, 591–608).

In revising the boat-stealing sequence between 1805 and 1850, Wordsworth made a number of changes that suggest his own "reading asunder". He tried to clarify ambivalence by reducing blurring and blending, reinforcing the sense by textually distancing from each other elements that once fell together. Through adding "to reach a chosen point / With an unswerving line" (368–9), Wordsworth highlighted the fact of interruption by introducing the goal and emphasizing the direction of will toward it. Furthermore, Wordsworth reinforced with a superlative the apparent firmness of the origin: "The horizon's utmost boundary" (371) replaces "the bound of the horizon" (1805, 399). Similarly, "above" (371) replaces "behind" (1805, 399), because to mention a "behind" already weakens a "bound" by extending it. Such a pairing of "bound" and "behind" in 1805 proleptically figures the later usurpation of "bound" by "behind" (377–8). Instead of reserving the thrust of the peak for a sudden point of emergence as in 1850, the prolepsis spreads over the whole scene the rising power of imagination. Likewise in establishing the surroundings, Wordsworth deleted the lines "A rocky steep uprose / Above the cavern of the willow-tree" (1805, 394–5). He thereby preserved for its punctual presence the sudden verticality of the "grim shape" (381).

Yet however carefully he read between his lines and wrote out the differences produced, Wordsworth never wholly untangled the elements of the scene. If the "steep uprose" (1805, 394) is deleted, in its place stands "one who rows" (367). The nonsense of homophony (rose-rows) reasserts the imaginative disruption. Wordsworth no doubt heard this problem in writing that the peak "towered" (382), replacing "rose" (1805, 410), but this attempt at discrimination only blurs the point anew in losing the precise identity between how "I rose" (375) and how the cliff did, and in displacing from a privileged spot one of Wordsworth's characteristic words of imaginative activity. Finally, the crucial word "bound" (378) resounds disturbingly; it already contains within itself the discrepant elements of the episode. The word suggests not only limitation and geographical fixity (its literal function in the passage), not only integration ("my days . . . bound each to each") and obligation, but also directed mobility. To summarize: while the rower is outward bound, a shape bounds up beyond the bounds of the horizon, and he feels bound to return.

II

This episode suggests both the failure of Wordsworth's career to reach its goal and its correlative fascination with origins. The revision sharply illuminates this line, suggesting Wordsworth's own awareness of it. The message sounds throughout the rest of *The Prelude* and of Wordsworth's other writings: let the interruption be the end; overlook nothing that comes athwart your path. Such dislocations from the expected circuit are the true reward. The Boy of Winander episode, bound up in MS. JJ with the boat-stealing (see Parrish, pp. 84–9), amplifies upon this pattern. Calling out to the owls, the boy awaits a response from them. Sometimes they respond with "concourse wild / Of jocund din", but at other times:

> When a lengthened pause
> Of silence came and baffled his best skill, (380)
> Then sometimes, in that silence while he hung
> Listening, a gentle shock of mild surprise
> Has carried far into his heart the voice
> Of mountain torrents; or the visible scene
> Would enter unawares into his mind, (385)
> With all its solemn imagery, its rocks,
> Its woods, and that uncertain heaven, received
> Into the bosom of the steady lake.   (1850, V, 379–88)

The suspended middle state, in which the boy "hung" while the goal of owl-sound was held off, allows for the "gentle shock of mild

surprise", the taking in of voice and scene that replaces the anticipated hoots. In 1805 the first lines of this passage read, "When it
chanced / That pauses of deep silence mocked his skill" (404–5). In
replacing "mocked", "baffled" opens the experience to a more positive
tone through suggesting the *self*-vexation that often accompanies
imagination for Wordsworth. The major effect of the revision is to
lengthen the pause by the addition of an adjective ("lengthened"), by
singularizing it, and by placing it at the line's end. This transformation
of the pause and the antithetical balancing in revision of the beginnings
of lines 379 ("Of jocund din") and 380 ("Of silence") combine sufficiently to "deepen" the silence without further need for the adjective.
Just as in revising the boat-stealing Wordsworth drew special attention
to the frustration of the goal, the truncation of the proposed journey, so
here too the weight falls increasingly on the length of the intermediate
state. In revision, the poet holding vigil over the boy's grave stands
"mute", like the boy, "a long half hour" (396), replacing "a full half-
hour" (1805, 421). The boy's time is thus explicitly paralleled to the
poet's ("lengthened" – "long"), and the time is emptied ("full" yields to
"long"). It is a time of receptivity, of potential only.

I read in these revisions Wordsworth's increasingly active grappling
with the change that had come over *The Prelude* between its first completion and its final revision. We ourselves hardly have the concepts to
disentangle so complex a knot of intention, text, and history. One easy
gauge, however, is to recognize in *The Prelude* of 1805 "the poem to
Coleridge", as it was regularly called in the Wordsworth household
(*Prelude*, 529, 530, 535).[7] The addresses to Coleridge in the poem
were at first no literary fiction; even when written in his absence they
solicited his return, and Coleridge's "To William Wordsworth"
responded in kind to *The Prelude* when it finally reached its destination.
By the final revision, Coleridge was dead. What had at first been addresses to the reader turn to apostrophe.[8] The whole question of
Wordsworth's relations to his hearers and readers requires much more
study. Bateson illuminates the significance of Wordsworth's addressing
his intimates rather than the public (187–97), but confusion often
arises. So Abrams cites a passage from *The Prelude* of 1805 to show
"the deliberately . . . affirmative stance" the Romantics adopted when
"they undertook to speak with an authoritative public voice" ("Rationality and Imagination", 462–3), but only a New Critical refusal of
history can grant "public voice" to a work that its author never
published and never spoke save to a few intimates. Abrams deprecates
the "ingenious exegetic" (*Natural Supernaturalism*, p. 446) of those
who find self-division in Wordsworth's "stance", or alienation in the

privacy of his "public voice", but he does not acknowledge the processes that produce his own reading or the historical transformations
that redefine the status of Wordsworth's text. In this instance, after
Coleridge's death the decorum shifts from epistolary (address) to lyrical
(apostrophe), intimate to monumental; the poem gains at once a dimension of fiction.

The relation *The Prelude* bears to *The Recluse* resembles its relation
to Coleridge, whose pet project was *The Recluse*. Just as *The Prelude*
was intended to reach Coleridge, so it was "subsidiary" to *The Recluse*
(*Prose Works*, vol. 3, p. 5). But in the final revisions the means become
the end, no longer a stage to pass through in life but a posthumous life,
the "poem on his own life" (*The Prelude*, 535–6) to be given to the
world when he is dead. In both of the relations – to Coleridge and to
The Recluse – *The Prelude* moves from transitivity to intransitivity; it
becomes that aesthetically self-focussed message that Jakobson defined
as fundamentally poetic ("Linguistics and Poetics", 356). The poem
runs the danger of yielding to a nostalgic wish to annihilate half
a lifetime and of becoming purely recollective – not of the earlier
self remembered in 1805 but of the younger poetic self *writing* in
1805.

Yet to recall what Coleridge awaited, required in *The Recluse* makes
even the dangers of *The Prelude* a good alternative. Wordsworth was
to "assume the station of a man in mental repose . . . whose principles
were made up . . . prepared to deliver upon authority a system of
philosophy" (*Table Talk*, vol. 6, p. 403). Even Wordsworth was never
so perfect a "*Spectator ab extra*" as to arrogate this "position". Wordsworth never achieved such grounding and was therefore unwilling to
"assume" it. He recognized that his life as a poet depended upon
disturbance, "shock" and "surprise", however gentle and mild. If he
could speak "upon authority", it was derived not from the stability of
truth but from the lability of moments in which the world slipped away
as a shape rose from behind the bound, or in which one felt "the sentiment of being spread / O'er all" (1805, II, 420–1).

There is a humane liberation in letting go – even with indecision,
anxiety, and guilt – such a project as *The Recluse*, in deferring the end,
keeping suspended in receptivity like the Boy of Winander. There is
reward too in replacing the end, letting the interruption stand for the
achievement, the wandering for goal: "something evermore about to
be" (VI, 608), "The budding rose above the rose full blown" (XI, 121).
The revisions to *The Prelude* demonstrate the continuing liveliness of
response in Wordsworth, his continuing power to find between the
lines of the earlier text places where imagination would come to him.

Even in first composing the childhood scenes of *The Prelude*, Wordsworth relied not on "naked recollection of the past" but instead im-
aginatively produced memories through "after-meditation" (III,
614–16). So in revising, he did not merely recollect a younger self
writing, he repeated that writing and made it different.

The situation of the spectator *ab intra*, the man poised between an
origin that bounds up always just beyond grasp and an evermore excessive goal, recalls Wordsworth's definition of the writer of epitaphs.
The writer of epitaphs occupies a "midway point" between the contrasting views of humankind as spirit and humankind as embodied
("Essays upon Epitaphs", in *Prose Works*, vol. 2, p. 53). Although
deduced from the "consciousness of . . . immortality" (p. 50), the
desires epitaphs serve begin from the fact of human finitude, in
attempting "to preserve the memory of the dead, as a tribute due to
his individual worth, for a satisfaction to the sorrowing hearts of the
survivors, and for the common benefit of the living" (p. 53). As a further figure of the writer's attempt to negotiate extremes, Wordsworth
offered the circle. He declared that views which "seem opposite to each
other" (humankind as spirit, humankind as body) have "a finer connection than that of contrast. – It is a connection formed through the subtle progress by which . . . qualities pass insensibly into their contraries,
and things revolve upon each other." The analogy is then developed
to a "voyage . . . sailing upon the orb of this planet" (p. 53). But such
a fidelity to the surface of earth immediately suggests the circle as a
figure of human limitation, rather than of triumphant completion as
in Abrams. Compare the answer Wordsworth suggested to a child
wondering about the origin and tendency of a stream: "The spirit of
the answer must have been, though the word might be sea or ocean,
accompanied perhaps with an image gathered from a map, or from the
real object in nature – these might have been the *letter*, but the *spirit*
of the answer must have been . . . a receptacle without bounds or
dimensions; – nothing less than infinity" (p. 51). Only through a
spiritual gloss can we make our parts whole. Since we cannot achieve
the boundlessness of pure origin or ultimate end, we rest in between
closed into a circle by the failure of our line to extend itself infinitely,
"our little life rounded".

Such observations elucidate *The Prelude* better than does Abrams's
ingenious exegetic thrust toward infinity. Not only do they echo
the boat-stealing, where the circle defines limitation in the face of
the unbounded surroundings, but they clarify a puzzle from the
ending. Throughout *The Prelude*, origins, as in the boat-stealing, have
receded. For each initiatory attempt of the "blest . . . infant Babe" an

answering "already" is there before him (II, 232–51), and not just phenomenologically, Wordsworth would have it, but logically as well: "in the words of Reason deeply weighed", each thought "hath no beginning" (228–32). The "native rock" that had been "goal / Or centre" of childhood activity is "gone", and "in its place / A smart Assembly-room usurped the ground." The disconnection from origins figured here is so intense that Wordsworth felt "Two consciousnesses, conscious of myself / And of some other Being" (II, 32–3). The revision once again makes the point. In 1805 the stone was "split, and gone to build / A smart Assembly-room" (38–9), a process that however violent still preserves a continuity between a native single wholeness and the "assembly-room" where differences meet and crowd together in shifting combinations.

Just as the origin recedes, the hope to "reach a chosen point" is repeatedly frustrated. "The story of my life" fails to remain a "theme / Single and of determined bounds" for which the "road lies plain before me " (I, 639–41). This problem stems less from the "broken windings" (II, 274) than from a growing fear of the path's end. Such windings become not obstacles but devices serving a wish never to end, a fear of the unbounded goal that turns one back:

> Even as a river, – partly (it might seem)
> Yielding to old remembrances, and swayed
> In part by fear to shape a way direct,
> That would engulph him soon in the ravenous sea –
> Turns, and will measure back his course, far back,
> Seeking the very regions which he crossed
> In his first outset; so have we, my Friend!
> Turned and returned with intricate delay.   (1850, IX, 1–8)

We recognize the Freudian circuitous path, the "intricate delay" that knots our life together, delaying death. In 1805 this moment was followed by its opposite, "An impulse to precipitate my verse" (IX, 9–10), the wish for total expenditure that hastens the end and undoes the bindings of economy. Wordsworth reconsidered the dangers of urging on too rapidly the end of the story of one's own life. The root sense of "precipitate" is "headlong, head over heels" (perhaps too "verse" echoes French "verser", "to pour out, overturn") and Wordsworth revised this dangerous plummet with an image of overview, the retrospect of "a traveller, who has gained the brow / Of some aerial Down" (IX, 9–10). The dangers of the end fuel a wish for transcendence, a safe height (an "aerial Down" names the danger of descent while sublimating it upwards). Paths attract Wordsworth not by reaching a goal, but to the extent that a "disappearing line" is like "an invitation into space / Boundless" (XIII, 146–51). Just as in the "Essays upon Epitaphs" "origin and tendency are . . . inseparably correlative" (p. 51), so in *The Prelude* too the infinite distancing of one answers to that of the other.

But if the poem is to reach any conclusion, some halt must be called to this double regress, and in the last book Wordsworth arbitrarily did so. He could only make the poem end by declaring that the origin had been found. Declaring imagination the "moving soul" of the work, Wordsworth wrote in 1805:

> We have traced the stream
> From darkness, and the very place of birth
> In its blind cavern, whence is faintly heard
> The sound of waters.   (1805, XIII, 172–5)

But this attempt at grounding an end did not work. The poem was not finished; it did not prepare for *The Recluse*, and Wordsworth continued for the rest of his poetic life to wander within it: "Along the mazes of this song I go. / . . . Thus do I urge a never-ending way / Year after year" ("Fragments . . . akin to *The Prelude*", in *Poetical Works*, vol. 5, p. 347). While still in revision retaining the terminal gesture, Wordsworth significantly attenuated the "very place of birth":

> We have traced the stream
> From the blind cavern whence is faintly heard
> Its natal murmur   (XIV, 194–6)

The effect is like that described by Lamb many years earlier: "Here the mind knowingly passes a fiction upon herself . . . and, in the same breath detecting the fallacy, will not part with the wish" (I, 265, 30 January 1801). Specific place yields to murmur, eye to ear, letter to spirit, as in the "Essays upon Epitaphs".

Similar compromises determine the major intellectual issue of *The Prelude*. A pure naturalism would be as untenable as engulfment in the "ravenous sea", and a pure assertion of imagination as impossible as dwelling in the "blind cavern". So the mind is proclaimed "lord and master" (XII, 222) and countered with the claim, "From Nature doth emotion come" (XIII, 1), and the formula of "ennobling interchange" (XIII, 375) attempts to harmonize them. Such a resolution of radically discordant elements, however, decomposes constantly; the resultant is resolved back into its component forces. The circle figures a wish to deny the opposition of extremes, and in the "Essays upon Epitaphs" the master trope of *Natural Supernaturalism*, "life as a journey", stands as a consolatory commonplace (p. 54). If *The Prelude* fulfills the ambition it expresses, it is not because it has reached its goal, but rather because interrupting accident had intervened, because the means had become the end, as for the Boy, as in the boat-stealing.

In the "Essays upon Epitaphs" Wordsworth considered the relation of means and ends – life and death – and found in immortality the figure necessary to relate the two. Otherwise, "such a hollowness would pervade the whole system of things, such a want of correspondence and consistency, a disproportion so astounding between means and ends, that there could be no repose, no joy" (p. 52). The trope of immortality ("death *is* eternal life") establishes the desired relation between means and ends, truncation and infinitude, just as the imagination does in *The Prelude*. Or in *The Prelude* is it love that centers the system, or nature, or the interaction among various of these elements? *The Prelude* offers "several frames of things", and their relations vary. They may be "mutually indebted" or instead "half lost / Each in the other's blaze" (VIII, 481–4). The process may transform from a totalizing "swallowing up of lesser things in great" to a disruptive "Change of them into their contraries" (XI, 179–80). Wordsworth's terms cut the kind of figures around each other that such crucial notions of neoplatonic art theory as "idea" and "nature" did. They hold what Erwin Panofsky anticipated Jacques Derrida by calling "a peculiar relation of mutual supplementation" (*eigentümlich wechselseitige Suppletivverhältnis*), in which the terms do not oppose each other but "correspond" to each other, "completing or even replacing each other" (*ergänzend oder sogar stellvertretend*) (p. 35).

III

I have tried to suggest ways of reading the circle, the journey, *The Prelude* itself, that differ from those of *Natural Supernaturalism* not only to further an understanding of Wordsworth that I find more humane, although less grand, but also because the current criticism of Wordsworth engages fundamentals of critical practice and principle. This is even clearer now in the middle 1980s than in 1978 when I first wrote this essay. The issue I shall arrive at is the critique of "spatial form", the starting-point for Derrida's reach from philosophy toward literature in "Force and Signification" and for W. V. Spanos in defining the postmodernism of *boundary 2*, where this essay first appeared.

Our current context for understanding *The Prelude* is still defined by the appearance over twenty years ago of works by Herbert Lindenberger, M. H. Abrams ("English Romanticism", the first major step toward *Natural Supernaturalism*), and Geoffrey H. Hartman. Despite notable British essays by Leavis, Knight, and Empson,

American New Criticism had not much attended to *The Prelude*, and these works of the early 1960s look beyond New Criticism in important respects. They have so throughly reoriented Wordsworth criticism as to overshadow the books of David Perkins and David Ferry, which hinted at a valuable turning toward *The Prelude* within the American academy as redefined by New Criticism.

Our new way with Wordsworth came under the sign of comparative literature, engaging emphases at once more theoretical, more international, and more historical than those associated with New Criticism. Our wish for a "new literary history" and our current concern with methods of "critical inquiry" are both prefigured in this eruption within the criticism of Wordsworth. As is so often the case with critical revision, this innovation came through looking back, from engagement with the nineteenth-century German tradition of Romance philology. Hartman dedicated his book to the memory of Erich Auerbach; Abrams's essay drew on Auerbach for its climactic argument; and Lindenberger related *The Prelude* to *topoi* studied by E. R. Curtius. All three located Wordsworth in the history of European rhetoric (as did the early work of Paul de Man, although its influence was not felt until later). Hartman began by isolating the Romantic figure of "surmise", derived from the classical "*fallor . . . an*" construction. Lindenberger devoted his first chapter to "*The Prelude* and the Older Rhetoric" and went on to define Wordsworth's new "rhetoric of interaction". Abrams connected the sublime to the matter-of-fact in Wordsworth through the Christian rhetoric of *sermo humilis*, derived from the low style in which the Bible sets forth the greatest matters.

These new emphases altered the tradition of criticism of Wordsworth. Through their relations to these new studies, several older essays came into new prominence: those by A. C. Bradley, Matthew Arnold, and Walter Pater, all English critics who worked in their differing ways at joining the new thought and writing of Germany to native concerns. Arnold and Bradley have been accepted as the two poles of Wordsworthian criticism (Abrams, "Introduction", pp. 2–4), and one may see Abrams and Hartman as their heirs.[9] Bradley's darkly philosophical, brooding poet, hostile to "sense" and verging on apocalypse (pp. 130–4), has an affinity to Hartman's Wordsworth that is well known because Hartman himself noted it. Rejecting Wordsworth's "philosophy", Arnold in contrast looked back to Wordsworth for a consoling joy that forecast Abrams's argument. In considering the necessity for poetry to engage with "*life*" and not rest in mere formalism, Arnold drew a figure from Epictetus. Perfection of form bears the same relation to life that "inns bear to home": "As if a man, journeying home, and finding a nice inn on the road . . . were to stay forever." Against this negative prototype of the "halted traveler" (Hartman), Arnold inveighed, "Man, thou hast forgotten thine object; thy journey was not *to* this, but *through* this." In contrast, "a poet like Wordsworth", Arnold concluded, "prosecutes his journey home" by choosing to sing "Of truth, of grandeur, beauty, love, and hope. . . . Of joy in widest commonalty spread" (pp. 144–7). Arnold prefigured Abrams's master figure of the journey homeward and his central focus on the "Prospectus" to *The Recluse*. Arnold did not, however, claim that Wordsworth actually reached home, only that he was *en route*, and I take this as a critical judgment, not merely as Arnold's writing before the publication of "Home at Grasmere", on which Abrams relied to supplement *The Prelude*.

Pater has had less impact because he did not fix an image of Wordsworth. Likewise the multiple approaches of Lindenberger's book have prevented it from consolidating a clear position in the critical tradition. But iconoclasm may help evade the impasse of strongly etched but opposite images. Can we set such images into an active relation with each other that is not merely synthetic? Just as Lindenberger followed one strand at a time of *The Prelude* and did not strive for a coherent picture, so Pater emphasized that "sometimes" Wordsworth felt a pure, imaginative solipsism, in which "the actual world would, as it were, dissolve and detach itself, flake by flake". "At other times", however, he felt a pantheistic "spirit of life in outward things, a single, all-pervading mind in them, of which . . . even the poet's imaginative energ[ies] are but moments" (pp. 54–5). Pater presented the variety and mobility of writing in *The Prelude* without, like Abrams, demanding a harmonious resolution to a triumphant plot, and without, like Hartman, insisting upon a fierce, debilitatingly self-conflicting struggle. At best, such a strategy of reading encourages a fresh sensitivity to more of the poem than would a strategy prepared to find only a single story. Such sensitivity, I have been arguing, is required if we are to respect and analyze the poem's historical complexity, rather than freezing it into an idealized emblem.

Yet how can we read the work as a whole without fixing an image? This is a version of the problem of "totality" and "representation" that has provoked such controversy in the last decade across the humanities and social sciences. Within literary study this problem vexes the reading of nineteenth-century novels as well as poetry. For realistic fiction works by eroding conventional forms, which are set up only to be undermined. If one "stands at a distance" from such a work, it seems the very image of what it is attacking. Apart from local texture, *Don*

Quixote looks like a heroic romance, *Madame Bovary* like a love story.
The issue becomes even more difficult when the technique of realism
is less ironic than these and more allegorical, depending like Thackeray
or George Eliot on the sequence of larger units, so that any portion of
such a plural work may show only one emphasis. Nonetheless, attention to rhetoric (in its largest sense of how words work different effects
from those of grammar or logic) offers some resistance to fascination
by the image.[10]

Pater implied one rhetorical reading of *The Prelude* in analyzing the
problems of means and ends (which have already engaged us in thinking through the relations between *The Prelude* and *The Recluse* and then
in following Wordsworth's meditations on epitaphs). Pater suggested
that the way we relate means to ends is the "type or figure under which
we represent our lives to ourselves". He offered three instances: that
which subordinates means to end, "a figure, reducing all things to
machinery"; that which justifies the end by means – "whatever may
become of the fruit, make sure of the flowers and the leaves"; that in
which "means and end are identified" (pp. 60–2). These figures correspond to metonymy, synecdoche, and metaphor. They offer rhetorical
models for the major intellectual elements of *The Prelude*: the
metonymic "reducing" of associational psychology ("an unrelenting
agency / Did bind my feelings even as in a chain" [III, 168–9]); the
synecdochic organicism of pantheistic totality (that "grows / Like harmony in music" and "reconciles / Discordant elements" [I, 340–3]);
the metaphoric leap of pure imagination that achieves identity without
mediation ("the light of sense / Goes out, but with a flash" [VI,
600–1]).[11]

These rhetorical models support Lindenberger's reading of *The
Prelude* in terms of three separate organizing principles: a memoir of
facts in order (a metonymic reading Lindenberger ascribed to the nineteenth century); the principle of which "Wordsworth himself was most
aware . . . the threefold pattern of early vision, loss, and restoration",
modeled on the "traditional cycle of paradise, fall, and redemption"
(Abrams's synecdochic, Hegelian reading); and a third principle that
"stands at odds with the other two, for . . . it recognizes no beginning,
middle, or end" (pp. 190–1). This third principle, metaphoric in its
eclipse of mediation, Lindenberger calls "repetition", drawing from
Kierkegaard's critique of Hegel (pp. 196–7). A fourth principle might
be adduced (tropologically, a type of irony) on the model of Derrida's
"differance". It would find an unbridgeable gap between means and
end. The end, or origin, would not exist, but our consciousness of
its absence would nonetheless define our life as medial. I have tried

reading *The Prelude* along this line, to challenge the dominance of the second.

Even if rhetorical analysis helps prevent fixation on an image, the German philological tradition that made rhetoric available to us for the study of Wordsworth has problems of its own. Although to Americans they are both German Romanticists, Auerbach and Curtius each felt strong distress at the work of the other. Auerbach's reviews criticized Curtius's *European Literature and the Latin Middle Ages* for its fundamentally unhistorical method, for neglecting Christian innovations and choosing a topical, synoptic emphasis on classical continuity. This criticism bears directly on the opposing positions of the two men toward literary modernism. Auerbach was strongly disturbed by modernism, despite his acute comments on it in *Mimesis* and his recognition that his own method bore the marks of modernity. Curtius, however, wrote early defenses and interpretations of Joyce, Eliot, and others. As early as 1929 he adumbrated Joseph Frank's analysis of "spatial form": "In order really to understand *Ulysses* one would have to have the entire work present in one's mind at every sentence" (p. 353). Curtius cast his own *European Literature* into this modernist form, describing it in terms of "aerial photography" (p. ix) and "spiral ascent" (p. 381).[12] Auerbach's *Mimesis* remained resolutely chronological, yet committed as well to articulate disturbances and breakthroughs. Although Auerbach's crucial conception of "figuralism" shows a resemblance to spatial form (according to Frank, p. 237), Christian figuralism is only a phase in the overall history Auerbach pursues. Abrams's *Natural Supernaturalism* put some of Auerbach's topics to use, but it followed Curtius's organization, deliberately echoing the "spiral form" ("Rationality and Imagination", 450) it found in Romantic writing. Thus through the German heritage from Hegel,[13] Abrams arrived at the formalist cancellation of time, along with the New Critics, despite their other differences.

Yet a more resolute focus on rhetoric, on language in action, might evade the totalizing, binary opposition of spatial versus temporal. Rhetorical studies, such as Miller's "Fiction of Realism" (123–6) have undermined a similar dichotomy, Roman Jakobson's polarizing of metaphor and metonymy, by recalling the necessary interplay between the two in any articulated work (since to rest wholly at one pole is to suffer an aphasia). Is it possible wholly to segregate space and time, any more than Wordsworth's 1850 revision of the boat-stealing wholly segregated the elements and eliminated blending? In contrasting Homer to the Bible, the first chapter of *Mimesis* set in motion the terminology of space and time. The "complete externalization" (p. 2) and "foregrounding" in the *Odyssey* create a static icon in which all time is present, while in the Bible matters of history, formation, and development determine what is presented and how (pp. 14–15). Auerbach argued (as later of *Ulysses*) that the *Odyssey* may be analyzed structurally (pp. 11, 487), but that only in the Bible is the temporality of interpretation necessary (p. 12). Yet within Auerbach's text, the critical metaphors follow an opposite line as well. Connections in the Bible are "vertical", in Homer horizontal (p. 14). The parts of Homer's world link contiguously, metonymically, as the text moves along the syntagmatic axis that marks the flow of language in time; in the Bible, however, the leap of metaphor relates a human event to its paradigm in divine providence. "History" (pp. 15ff.), as in the Bible, is understood from a perspective that lifts up every moment into eternal significance, while the Homeric icon, complete at every moment, from moment to moment metamorphoses. That is, the radical opposition of Homer to the Bible, with which Auerbach acknowledged discomfort ("Epilegomena", 2), proves unstable; the curse of fixity, the privilege of change, move across the bounding line.

In the palimpsest of our cultural history, the languages of space and time are both inscribed. A purifying revision, or retranscription, that tried to straighten out the tangles of these lines, to free us from our need to read between them, would no doubt like Wordsworth achieve some fresh moments and new emphases. Should it strive to do better? The "peculiar relation of mutual supplementation", by which minor terms become major and opposites complete, or replace one another, saved Wordsworth from the complacency of *The Recluse*; his position was never wholly "made up" or composed but always liable to displacement. This is the interest of his situation. Should we strive for the disinterestedness of stepping out from between the lines, into the position of the ideal recluse, released by omitting "all cross currents, all friction . . . everything unresolved, truncated, and uncertain" (*Mimesis*, p. 16)? This would be, in Auerbach's terms, to will ourselves from "history" into "legend". I have tried to argue against Abrams's legend of Wordsworth and replace it with the "friction" of history, to unfix the firmness of his image. Such a project could undertake much more than I have here. For example, it is remarkable, but I believe uncommented, that Wordsworth's three major periods of revisionary labor on *The Prelude* correspond to the major historical crises of post-Napoleonic England in his lifetime: 1816–19, the movement up to Peterloo on which E. P. Thompson has written so powerfully; 1831–2, the period of Reform agitation; and 1838–9, the time of Chartism and the "Condition-of-England Question". So too, one could further historicize the critical revision in our understanding of *The Prelude*, to begin with by relating its revival to the speculative hopes of the 1960s.

For now, this beginning has attempted to indicate both that ways of reading associated with "deconstruction" have a history (including figures so different as Pater and Panofsky) and that such ways of reading may help to address matters of history (in this case, the textual status of *The Prelude*) more flexibly and precisely than our established practices of literary history (such as Abrams's), which prove closer to New Critical ahistoricism than has usually been acknowledged.[14]

Notes

[1] References in parentheses are to the list of works cited, below.

[2] On the gloss and the relation of part to whole, see Lipking (pp. 612, 622).

[3] On the early stages of *The Prelude*, see MacGillivray, Parrish, and Jonathan Wordsworth.

[4] Cf. Arac, "Repetition and Exclusion", (pp. 268–9).

[5] de Selincourt reproduces the 1850 title-page with this subtitle (p. 1), which the Norton editors make it almost impossible to discover, in their vendetta against Victorian "alterations and intrusions" (p. xii).

[6] In contrast to Miller's important critique (in "Tradition and Difference") of Abrams's premises, I focus on theoretical issues that emerge from Abrams's actual reading of *The Prelude*.

[7] It is not clear from the evidence in the Norton *Prelude* (pp. 531–3), however, that Wordsworth "always" (p. ix) thought of it in these terms.

[8] On the structural distinction between address and apostrophe, see Culler; on the historical relation between the two, see Auerbach, "Dante's Addresses".

[9] I discuss Hartman more fully in "Afterword" (pp. 190–7).

[10] See my "Rhetoric and Realism".

[11] My tropology here is indebted to White.

[12] These motifs from the Foreword and Epilogue recur throughout. On Curtius's Joycean "perspectivism" see Evans (p. 142).

[13] Curtius and Auerbach specifically align their enterprises with Hegel, *European Literature* (p. 4); and "Epilegomena" (p. 15).

[14] My thanks to Paul Bové, who edited the special issue of *boundary 2* where this first appeared, and to Dan O'Hara, who put us in contact.

Works cited

Abrams, M. H. "English Romanticism: the spirit of the age." In *Romanticism Reconsidered*. Ed. Northrop Frye. New York: Columbia University Press, 1963.

"Introduction: two roads to Wordsworth." In *Wordsworth: a collection of critical essays*. Englewood Cliffs, N. J.: Prentice-Hall, 1972.

The Mirror and the Lamp: Romantic theory and the critical tradition (1953). New York: Norton, 1958.

Natural Supernaturalism: tradition and revolution in Romantic literature. New York: Norton, 1971.

"Rationality and Imagination in Cultural History", *Critical Inquiry*, 2 (1976).

Arac, Jonathan. "Afterword." In *The Yale Critics: Deconstruction in America.* Minneapolis: University of Minnesota Press, 1983.

"Repetition and Exclusion: Coleridge and New Criticism Reconsidered." In *The Question of Textuality: strategies of reading in contemporary American criticism.* Ed. William V. Spanos *et al.* Bloomington: Indiana University Press, 1982.

"Rhetoric and Realism in Nineteeth-Century Fiction: Hyperbole in *The Mill on the Floss*", ELH, 46 (1979).

Arnold, Matthew. "Wordsworth" (1879). In *Essays in Criticism: second series* (1888). London and New York: Macmillan, 1896.

Auerbach, Erich. "Dante's Addresses to the Reader" (1954). In *Gesammelte Aufsätze zur romanischen Philologie.* Berne and Munich: Francke, 1967.

"Epilegomena zu *Mimesis*", *Romanische Forschungen*, 65 (1953).

Mimesis: the representation of reality in Western literature (1946). Trans. Willard Trask (1953). New York: Doubleday, 1957.

[Reviews of Curtius, *Europäische Literatur und Lateinisches Mittelalter*], *Romanische Forschungen*, 62 (1950) and *Modern Language Notes*, 65 (1950).

Bateson, F. W. *Wordsworth: a re-interpretation.* 2nd ed. London: Longmans, 1956.

Bradley, A. C. "Wordsworth." In *Oxford Lectures on Poetry* (1909). Bloomington: Indiana University Press, 1961.

Coleridge, Samuel Taylor. *Complete Works.* Ed. W. G. T. Shedd. New York: Harper, 1853.

Culler, Jonathan. "Apostrophe", *Diacritics*, 7.4 (1977).

Curtius, Ernst Robert. *European Literature and the Latin Middle Ages* (1948). Trans. Willard R. Trask (1953). New York and Evanston: Harper, 1963.

"James Joyce and His Ulysses" (1929). In *Essays on European Literature.* Trans. Michael Kowal. Princeton: Princeton University Press, 1973.

Derrida, Jacques. "Differance" (1968). In *Speech and Phenomena.* Trans. David B. Allison. Evanston, Ill.: Northwestern University Press, 1973.

"Force and Signification" (1963). Trans. Alan Bass. In *Writing and Difference.* Chicago: University of Chicago Press, 1978.

Of Grammatology (1967). Trans. Gayatri Chakravorty Spivak. Baltimore: Johns Hopkins University Press, 1976.

de Selincourt, Ernest (ed.). *The Prelude, or Growth of a Poet's Mind.* By William Wordsworth. 2nd ed. Rev. Helen Darbishire. Oxford: Clarendon, 1959.

Emerson, Ralph Waldo. "Circles" (1841). In *Essays and Lectures.* New York: Literary Classics of the United States, 1983.

Empson, William. "'Sense' in *The Prelude*." In *The Structure of Complex Words* (1951). Ann Arbor: University of Michigan Press, 1967.

Evans, Arthur R., Jr. "Ernst Robert Curtius." In *On Four Modern Humanists.* Princeton: Princeton University Press, 1970.

Ferry, David. *The Limits of Mortality.* Middletown, Conn.: Wesleyan University Press, 1959.

Frank, Joseph. "Spatial Form: an answer to critics", *Critical Inquiry*, 4 (1977).

Hartman, Geoffrey H. *Wordsworth's Poetry 1787–1814*. New Haven: Yale University Press, 1964.

Jakobson, Roman. "Linguistics and Poetics." In *Style in Language*. Ed. Thomas A. Sebeok. Cambridge, Mass.: MIT Press, 1960.

"The Metaphoric and Metonymic Poles." In *Fundamentals of Language*. The Hague: Mouton, 1956.

Knight, G. Wilson. "The Wordsworthian Profundity." In *The Starlit Dome* (1941). London: Oxford University Press, 1971.

Lamb, Charles. *The Letters of Charles and Mary Anne Lamb*. Ed. Edwin W. Marrs, Jr. Ithaca and London: Cornell University Press, 1975.

Leavis, F. R. "Wordsworth." In *Revaluation* (1936). Harmondsworth: Penguin, 1972.

Lindenberger, Herbert. *On Wordsworth's "Prelude"*. Princeton: Princeton University Press, 1963.

Lipking, Lawrence. "The Marginal Gloss", *Critical Inquiry*, 3 (1977).

MacGillivray, J. R. "The Three Forms of *The Prelude*, 1798–1805." In *Essays in English Literature from the Renaissance to the Victorian Age*. Ed. Millar MacLure and F. W. Watt. Toronto: University of Toronto Press, 1964.

Miller, J. Hillis. "The Fiction of Realism." In *Dickens Centennial Essays*. Ed. Ada Nisbet and Blake Nevius. Berkeley: University of California Press, 1971.

"Tradition and Difference", *Diacritics*, 2 (1972).

Panofsky, Erwin. *Idea*. Leipzig and Berlin: Teubner, 1924.

Parrish, Stephen (ed.). *The Prelude, 1798–1799*. By William Wordsworth. Ithaca: Cornell University Press, 1977.

Pater, Walter. "Wordsworth." In *Appreciations* (1889). London and New York: Macmillan, 1897.

Perkins, David. *The Quest for Permanence*. Cambridge, Mass.: Harvard University Press, 1959.

Smith, James. "Wordsworth: a preliminary survey" (1938). In *A Selection from "Scrutiny"*, vol. 2. Ed. F. R. Leavis. Cambridge: Cambridge University Press, 1969.

Spanos, William V. "Modern Literary Criticism and the Spatialization of Time: an existential critique", *Journal of Aesthetics and Art Criticism*, 29 (1970).

"The Detective and the Boundary: some notes on the postmodern literary imagination", *boundary 2*, 1 (1972).

Thompson, E. P. *The Making of the English Working Class*. New York: Random House, 1963.

White, Hayden V. *Metahistory*. Baltimore: Johns Hopkins University Press, 1973.

Wordsworth, Jonathan. "The Five-Book *Prelude* of Early Spring 1804", *Journal of English and Germanic Philology*, 76 (1977).

Wordsworth, William. *The Letters of William and Dorothy Wordsworth: The Early Years, 1787–1805*. Ed. Ernest de Selincourt. 2nd ed. Rev. Chester Shaver. Oxford: Clarendon Press, 1967.

The Poetical Works of William Wordsworth. Ed. Ernest de Selincourt and Helen Darbishire. Oxford: Clarendon Press, 1949.

The Prose Works of William Wordsworth. Ed. W. J. B. Owen and Jane Worthington Smyser. Oxford: Clarendon Press, 1974.

The Prelude, 1799, 1805, 1850. Ed. Jonathan Wordsworth, M. H. Abrams and Stephen Gill. New York and London: Norton, 1979.

Coleridge and the deluded reader: "The Rime of the Ancient Mariner"

FRANCES FERGUSON

The criticism of "The Rime of the Ancient Mariner" reflects a craving for causes. Opium, or Coleridge's guilt-obsessed personality, or (as Robert Penn Warren would have it) his convergent beliefs in the "One Life within us all" and in the Imagination caused the poem to come into being in its own peculiar form. A "teaching text" like *The Norton Anthology of English Literature* sets out to explicate the lines:

> The Wedding-Guest stood still,
> And listens like a three years' child:
> The Mariner hath his will   (lines 14–16)

– and sets up a nice causal connection by asserting that "the Mariner has gained control of the will of the Wedding guest by hypnosis – or, as it was called in Coleridge's time – by 'mesmerism' " (*Norton Anthology*, vol. 2, p. 292. All direct quotations from the "Rime" follow the text of *The Complete Poetical Works of Samuel Taylor Coleridge*, ed. Ernest Hartley Coleridge, Oxford: Oxford University Press, 1968). There may be some form of hypnosis – or mesmerism – in the rather monotonous rhythms of the lines, but the annotation converts hypnosis into a misguidedly "scientific" explanation of why the Wedding Guest couldn't or didn't bother to get away.

This construction of causes – for the poem as a whole or for individual passages – is particularly striking because it appears as a series of belated rejoinders to the many complaints that greeted the poem's first public appearance. The "Rime" was quite widely censured for extravagance, unconnectedness, and improbability. Even Wordsworth in his Note to the "Rime" in the 1800 edition of *Lyrical Ballads* registered various objections that amounted to the assertion that the poem was deficient in connections and causes:

The Poem of my Friend has indeed great defects; first, that the principal person has no distinct character, either in his profession of Mariner, or as a human being who having been long under the controul of supernatural impressions might be supposed himself to partake of something supernatural: secondly, that

248

he does not act, but is continually acted upon: thirdly, that the events having no necessary connection do not produce each other; and lastly, that the imagery is somewhat too laboriously accumulated.

(*Lyrical Ballads*, ed. R. L. Brett and A. R. Jones, New York: Barnes and Noble, 1963, pp. 270–1).

Wordsworth's account of the poem's "defects" in a note that is a manifesto for its being reprinted may well be of a piece with the simultaneously published Preface to *Lyrical Ballads*, in which he sought to avoid the appearance of *"reasoning* [the reader] into an approbation of these particular Poems" (Brett and Jones, *Lyrical Ballads*, pp. 236–7). Everywhere in his account of defects Wordsworth cites formal features (albeit in the extended sense) – character, plot, motive, and imagery; and it is hard to believe that Wordsworth was doing anything more than repeating – and thereby acknowledging – the categories of poetic appreciation that he and Coleridge were explicitly attacking in *Lyrical Ballads*. But if the author of "The Thorn", "We are Seven", and *The Prelude* seems improbable in the role of someone wedded to clearly delineated character, plot, motive, and imagery, Coleridge's own remarks about the poem are even more difficult to assimilate to the critical search for causes and consequences. For example, Coleridge's famous account of Mrs Barbauld's opinion of the "Rime" figures in almost every article on the poem, but to diverse ends:

MRS. BARBAULD once told me that she admired the Ancient Mariner very much, but that there were two faults in it, – it was improbable, and had no moral. As for the probability, I owned that that might admit some question; but as to the want of a moral, I told her that in my own judgment the poem had too much; and that the only or chief fault, if I might say so, was the obtrusion of the moral sentiment so openly on the reader as a principle or cause of action in a work of such pure imagination. It ought to have had no more moral than the Arabian Nights' tale of the merchant's sitting down to eat dates by the side of a well, and throwing the shells aside, and lo! a geni starts up, and says he *must* kill the aforesaid merchant, *because* one of the date-shells had, it seems, put out the eye of the geni's son.

(*Specimen of the Table Talk of the late Samuel Taylor Coleridge*, ed. H. N. Coleridge, 2nd edn., revised, Oxford: OUP, 1836, p. 111)

On the one hand, critics have harnessed this passage to an attempt to eschew interpretation; the poem as a "work of . . . pure imagination" has no discursively translatable meaning. (This is the "What-do-you-think-when-you-think-nothing?" school of criticism.) On the other hand, perhaps the most influential modern critic of the poem, Warren, confesses that he is "inclined to sympathize with the lady's desire that poetry have some significant relation to the world, some meaning"

(*Selected Essays*, p. 199). Thus, his reading of the passage from *Table Talk* about Mrs Barbauld is this: "If the passage affirms anything, it affirms that Coleridge intended the poem to have a 'moral sentiment', but felt that he had been a trifle unsubtle in fulfilling his intention" (p. 200).

The no-moral position seems patently unconvincing because it becomes an excuse for hanging in one's confusions; but even though Warren's essay remains the most provocative interpretation, it also seems progressively to overspecify the "moral sentiment". What Warren calls the sacramental vision, the theme of the "One Life" that is expressed in the poem's conclusion ("He prayeth best. . .") and what he calls the imagination (the symbols of the poem) are both models of unity and fusion. And since unity and coherence are poetry for Warren, this poem must be both unified and unifying by definition; images must be symbols, and the symbols must speak of the Mariner's – and the reader's – "expressive integration" (p. 262) with the universe and "with other men, with society" (p. 255). Warren's interpretation suggests not merely that the sin of pride is involved in the "Rime" but also that the poem in some sense involves teaching one – all of us – to avoid that sin. But while I agree with Warren that morals are at issue in the poem, Coleridgean morality seems to me consistently more problematic than he suggests. For the difficulty of the poem is that the possibility of learning from the Mariner's experience depends upon sorting that experience into a more linear and complete pattern than the poem ever agrees to do. For the poem seems almost as thorough a work of backwardness – or *hysteron proteron* – as we have.

One aspect of this backwardness led a contemporary reviewer (Charles Burney) to fulminate in 1799 against *Lyrical Ballads* in general and against the "Rime" in particular:

Though we have been extremely entertained with the fancy, the facility, and (in general) the sentiments, of these pieces, we cannot regard them as poetry, of a class to be cultivated at the expence of a higher species of versification, unknown in our language at the time when our elder writers, whom this author condescends to imitate, wrote their ballads. Would it not be degrading poetry, as well as the English language, to go back to the barbarous and uncouth numbers of Chaucer? . . . Should we be gainers by the retrogradation? . . . None but savages have submitted to eat acorns after corn was found.

> (*Coleridge: the critical heritage*, ed. J. R. deJ. Jackson, London:
> Routledge and Kegan Paul, 1979, p. 55)

But the archaistic diction is only one aspect of the poem's "retrogradation". For Coleridge not only reverses linguistic and poetic *progress* in the "Rime", he so thoroughly compounds the past with the present tense that the action or progress of the poem hovers in a temporal limbo:

> The Wedding-Guest he beat his breast,
> Yet he cannot choose but hear;
> And thus spake on that ancient man,
> The bright-eyed Mariner.   (lines 37–40)

And even such a basic question as that of the Mariner's motive for killing the bird is given a tardy (and insufficient) answer. The event of the killing is recounted in the first section of the poem; and the suggestion that the Mariner may have been trying to confute his shipmates' superstitious connections between the Albatross and the weather emerges only in the second section. The possibility that the Mariner may have hoped – scientifically – to disprove their superstition is the closest thing to an hypothesis we are offered, and it appears only when we desire a motive so strongly that we must mistrust our own efforts to reestablish a cause-and-effect sequence.

But how does any reader and critic sort out the action that presumably points the moral of the poem? Or, in other words, how does one sort out the moral value of the agents of the poem? The Mariner concludes his story to the Wedding Guest with the following "good" words:

> He prayeth well, who loveth well
> Both man and bird and beast.

> He prayeth best, who loveth best
> All things both great and small;
> For the dear God who loveth us,
> He made and loveth all.   (lines 612–17)

But the Mariner has a decidedly malignant effect on the persons who save his body after his spiritual redemption on the ship: the Pilot collapses in a fit, and the Pilot's boy goes mad. Likewise, the Albatross seems good, then bad, then good, because the death of the Albatross causes first fog and mist (bad), then clearing (good), and finally the failure of the breeze (bad). Our difficulty is that all the evidences of moral value are mutually contradictory.

There is, however, one element of the poem that leads us. In 1815–16 Coleridge added the Gloss along the left margin as he was readying his work for the 1817 edition of *Sibylline Leaves*. And the critical "advances" that have been made in the last century and a half pay tribute to Coleridge's sagacity in having supplied this helpful commentary. John Livingston Lowes notes the literary elegance of the Gloss's prose.

B. R. McElderry, Jr., sees the Gloss as an "artistic restatement and ornament of what is obvious in the text", and as a chance for Coleridge to relive the pleasure of writing his "one completed masterpiece". And Robert Penn Warren peppers his long essay on the "Rime" with statements like this: "The Gloss here tells us all we need to know, defining the Mariner's relation to the moon" (*Selected Essays*, p. 243). The almost universal opinion seems to be that Coleridge wrote the Gloss (either as Coleridge or in the role of a fictitious editor) because he was attempting to clarify and unify the poem after entertaining the legion of hostile comments upon its confusions and inconsequence.

But the Gloss provides a strange kind of clarity and unity. Consider some examples. As the Wedding Guest speaks for the first time about anything except the wedding he wishes he could attend, this is what the text offers:

> "God save thee, ancient Mariner!
> From the fiends, that plague thee thus! –
> Why look'st thou so?" – With my cross-bow
> I shot the ALBATROSS.   (lines 79–82)

And the Gloss comments – "The ancient Mariner inhospitably killeth the pious bird of good omen." "Inhospitably", "pious", and "good omen" bespeak conclusions that do not echo the main text because the main text never reaches such value judgments.

The Argument that Coleridge deleted from the poem after 1800 recounted that "the Ancient Mariner cruelly and in contempt of the laws of hospitality killed a Sea-bird", but the Gloss here seems even stronger than the Argument had been. However forceful the ancient laws of hospitality, the notion of a man's hospitality toward a bird contains a rather anomalous and itself prideful assumption – that the bird is a visitor in the Mariner's domain. If the Mariner commits a sin of pride in killing the Albatross and thereby asserting his power over it, even the Mariner's refusal to kill the bird would in this context involve the pride-laden assurance that man's domain measures the universe. But the even more striking feature of the Gloss is the attribution of unambiguous moral qualities to the bird – "the pious bird of good omen". And while the text of the poem proper registers only the sailors' vacillations on the moral standing of the bird, the Gloss is conspicuously conclusive on that point. The main text offers the sailors' contradictory opinions:

> And I had done a hellish thing,
> And it would work 'em woe:
> For all averred, I had killed the bird

> That made the breeze to blow.
> Ah wretch! said they, the bird to slay,
> That made the breeze to blow!
>
> Nor dim nor red, like God's own head,
> The glorious Sun uprist:
> Then all averred, I had killed the bird
> That brought the fog and mist.
> 'Twas right, said they, such birds to slay,
> That brought the fog and mist.   (lines 91–102)

And the Gloss seems merely to scorn the sailors' confusions: first "His shipmates cry out against the ancient Mariner, for killing the bird of good luck"; then, "But when the fog cleared off, they justify the same, and thus make themselves accomplices in the crime."

When the ship is stalled, and everyone aboard is desperately searching the horizon in hope of rescue, the text recounts things this way:

> A weary time! a weary time!
> How glazed each weary eye,
> When looking westward, I beheld
> A something in the sky.
>
> At first it seemed a little speck,
> And then it seemed a mist;
> It moved and moved, and took at last
> A certain shape, I wist.   (lines 145–52)

And the Gloss makes this remark: "The Ancient Mariner beholdeth a sign in the element afar off." Nothing is ever really "afar off" for the Gloss. What for the main text is merely "a something" and "a certain shape" is already categorized for the Gloss as a sign, a symbol. The Gloss, in assuming that things must be significant and interpretable, finds significance and interpretability, but only by reading ahead of – or beyond – the main text.

Now the only portion of the Gloss that has been cited as an editorializing incursion upon the main text is the scholarly comment that supports the dreams which some of the sailors have about an avenging spirit: "A Spirit had followed them; one of the invisible inhabitants of this planet, neither departed souls nor angels; concerning whom the learned Jew, Josephus, and the Platonic Constantinopolitan, Michael Psellus, may be consulted. They are very numerous, and there is no climate or element without one or more." But both the entire Gloss and the bulk of critical opinion of the poem may well be editorializing, in that they mold contradictory evidences into a cause-and-effect pattern that the main text never quite offers: the Albatross was a good bird, the Mariner killed it, the Mariner was punished for his crime, the Mariner learned to acknowledge the beauty of all natural creatures and was saved to proselytize for this eminently noble moral position.

But let us return to the remarks on the poem in the *Specimens of the Table Talk of the late Samuel Taylor Coleridge*. In Coleridge's account of the first tale from the *Arabian Nights* the geni "says he *must* kill the aforesaid merchant, *because* one of the date-shells had, it seems, put out the eye of the geni's son" (emphasis Coleridge's). If the poem should have had no more moral than this, we may ask, what kind of moral is it? The merchant, presumably, would not have thrown his date-shells into the well if he had dreamed that he would do harm to the geni's son; and by the same logic, the Mariner would, presumably, not have killed the Albatross if he had recognized its goodness and significance. As is common in Coleridge's work generally, intention and effect are absolutely discontinuous, and the moral is that morality appears to involve certainty only if you can already know the full outcome of every action before you commit it.

Coleridge's recounting his conversation with Mrs Barbauld about the poem seems to me particularly striking in the context of this moral problem. A rather sizable collection of reviewers had complained about the poem's improbability and lack of moral, but Mrs Barbauld became his most significant interlocutor on the poem's moral import. A brief excursus on Anna Laetitia Barbauld may suggest why she in particular would be an appropriate real or fictitious disputant of record. Mrs Barbauld was firmly committed to the education of children, and she demonstrated her commitment by authoring *Lessons for Children* (1780) and *Hymns in Prose for Children* (1781). *Lessons for Children* was divided into four parts – *Lessons* . . . (1) For Children from Two to Three Years Old; (2) and (3) For Children of Three Years old; and (4) For Children from Three to Four Years old, so that the readings moved from simple to more complex in a gradual scale. As Mrs Barbauld stated in her Preface to *Hymns in Prose*, this was her purpose:

to impress devotional feelings as early as possible on the infant mind . . . to impress them by connecting religion with a variety of sensible objects; with all that he sees, all that he hears, all that affects his young mind with wonder of delight; and thus by deep, strong, and permanent associations to lay the best foundation for practical devotion in future life.

Reading was thus not merely a neutral exercise; reading and religion were to be taught simultaneously. Now in this respect Mrs Barbauld's project was not exactly unheard of. Such a linkage was explicit in the practice of using the Bible as the textbook for reading; and from the sixteenth century, when people began to be concerned about the heretical interpretations of the Bible that neophyte readers produced, the primer had been seen as a temporary substitute for the Bible or as a preparation for the Bible itself. Additionally the primer was supposed to supply relevance; it would not merely link reading with religion, it would also prepare the child to recognize the moral dilemmas of his everyday life.

Thus, the child learning to read in the late eighteenth and early nineteenth centuries was given (by Mrs Barbauld, Mrs Trimmer, Thomas Day, Maria Edgeworth, and others) texts that endowed nature with particular significance for the child, and as a religious child, he was to behave with particular moral probity toward nature. In fact, the most frequently recurrent theme in primer literature of the time was the sinfulness of cruelty to animals – particularly birds. Mrs Barbauld's *Lessons for Children of Three Years Old*, Part I, in fact, concludes with two short stories, the first of which enforces the moral of kindness to birds:

A naughty boy will not feed a starving and freezing robin; in fact he even pulls the poor bird's tail! It dies. Shortly after that, the boy's parents leave him because he is cruel, and he is forced to beg for food. He goes into a forest, sits down and cries, and is never heard of again; it is believed that bears ate him.

(Sylvia W. Patterson, *Rousseau's* Emile *and Early Children's Literature*, New York: Scarecrow Press, 1971, p. 44)

No wonder Wordsworth recounts in Book I of *The Prelude* (lines 333–50) that his childish act of stealing eggs from a bird's nest produced a major crisis of guilt.

Now I obviously don't mean to suggest either that Coleridge wrote "The Rime of the Ancient Mariner" or that Wordsworth wrote that passage from *The Prelude* as a direct attack on Mrs Barbauld or primers generally. But I do want to suggest that the moral causality that most critics discern in the "Rime" sounds less appropriate to Coleridge's poem than to the conclusion of Mrs Barbauld's "Epitaph on a Goldfinch":

> Reader,
> if suffering innocence can hope for retribution,
>   deny not to the gentle shade
>   of this unfortunate captive
>   the natural though uncertain hope
>   of animating some happier form,
>   of trying his new-fledged pinions
>   in some humble Elysium,
>   beyond the reach of Man,
>   the tyrant
>   of this lower universe.   (*Works*, vol. 2, p. 323)

The primary difference between Mrs Barbauld's literary morals and Coleridge's seems to lie in her emphasis upon acts and his agonizing explorations of the difficulties of recognizing the full implications of an action before it is committed, put in the context of the full range of human history (particularly the context of the Bible), and interpreted. Mrs Barbauld's story of the little boy who was cruel to the starving and freezing robin is, one might assert, no less improbable than the "Rime", no less committed to what we might see as excessive punishment for the crime perpetrated. But while the critics of the "Rime" almost invariably mock Mrs Barbauld as an obtuse and simplistic moralist, they also subscribe to the moral line of the Gloss, which leads them to a Barbauldian moral.

We must return to a rather simple-minded question: How bad was the Mariner to kill the bird? The act was certainly one of "motiveless malignity", for the Albatross had done nothing to him. But the crucial point is that he "didn't know any better"; it's merely the kind of explanation that enlightened parents of our own century employ to exonerate a child who has just destroyed the drapes in order to "play dress-up" or who has pulled the cat's tail. And while Mrs Barbauld could be said to regard the learning of reading and morals as *technical* skills, Coleridge recognizes reading as moral because one's *techné* can never suffice. One acts, Coleridge would say, on the basis of one's reading or interpretation, but if reading and interpretation are the genesis of moral action, they may be infinitely divorced from moral outcome – may, in fact, reverse one's interpretation of the moral value of the act. Reading as a *techné* and morals as techniques of behavior thus become suspect for Coleridge because they imply that experience – and one's interpretation of it – are both stable and repetitive – that one can learn what one needs to know.

In this context, Coleridge's Gloss to the "Rime" recalls not merely the archetypal glosses – those in the margins of early printed editions of the Bible; it also raises the question of the ways in which such glosses and the primer tradition made the Bible more accessible and comprehensible while also domesticating that main text. For if glosses and primers came to be felt necessary because readers "couldn't understand" the Bible properly, Coleridge's addition of his Gloss to the "Rime" seems to have answered the critics who called his poem incomprehensible, largely by a domestication. Think back to the main text of the poem. The Wedding Guest, in the first stanza, asks, "Now wherefore stopp'st thou me?" Nowhere in the poem is the Wedding Guest's question answered, not even at the end, although we know then:

He went like one that hath been stunned,
And is of sense forlorn:
A sadder and a wiser man,
He rose the morrow morn.   (lines 622–5)

The Mariner's stopping the Wedding Guest is probably the most arbitrary event in a poem filled with arbitrary events, and any explanation that asserts that he was chosen because his callowness needed correction seems far-fetched. The main interest of the Wedding Guest is that he has something to do; he has the intention of going to a wedding. In Part I of the poem he alternately pays attention to the Mariner and to the sounds of the wedding; but then, at the end of the poem he turns "from the bridegroom's door". Most importantly, neither his personality nor his intentions matter; he becomes what he reads (or hears). But if this account seems a fabulous escalation of the power of the word, think of the fate of the other sailors on the Mariner's ship. Nothing happens to them when they denounce the Mariner's act of murder, but then they reverse themselves when the fog clears and the fair breeze continues. The Gloss informs us that they thus become accomplices in the Mariner's crime. But in Part III of the poem, the Mariner is awarded to Life-in-Death while all the rest of the crew become the property of Death. We never know whether this eventuality is a delayed punishment for their first opinion or a more immediate punishment for their second. Since the Mariner did the killing when they only expressed opinions about it, their fate seems cruel indeed. But the implication seems to be that every interpretation involves a moral commitment with consequences that are inevitably more far-reaching and unpredictable than one could have imagined. And neither the sailors' paucity of information (which necessarily produces a limited perspective) nor their intentions (to praise the good and denounce the bad) are any exoneration for them (because most human interpretations are similarly limited, well-intentioned, and unexonerated).

Some of the major revisions of the poem, at least in retrospect, seem designed to make not the moral but the process of arriving at morals the major issue. In 1798 the poem was published under the title, "The Rime of the Ancient Mariner", and its Argument preceding the text provided rather neutral information, primarily geographical – "How a Ship having passed the Line was driven by storms to the Cold Country towards the South Pole; . . . and of the strange things that befell . . ." But in keeping with Coleridge's rather persistent practice of giving with one hand while taking away with the other, the 1800 version was titled "The Ancient Mariner. A Poet's Reverie", as if to emphasize the unreality of the piece, while the Argument was far more morally directive – "how the Ancient Mariner cruelly and in contempt of the laws of hospitality killed a Sea-bird and how he was followed by many and strange Judgements". And a similar doubleness or confusion arises with the introduction of the Gloss in 1817. For while the Gloss sorts out a moral line for the poem, it is accompanied by an epigraph that Coleridge excerpted from Thomas Burnet:

I believe easily that there are more invisible than visible beings in the universe. But of them all, who will tell us the race? and the ranks and relationships and differences and functions of each one? What do they do? What places do they inhabit? The human mind has always circled about the knowledge of these things but has never reached it. Still, it is undeniably desirable to contemplate in the mind, as it were in a picture, the image of a greater and better world: lest the mind, accustomed to the small details of daily life, becomes contracted and sink entirely into trivial thoughts. But meanwhile we must be watchful of truth and must keep within suitable limits, in order that we may distinguish the certain from the uncertain, day from night.

(Translation of Burnet in Coleridge, *Selected Poetry and Prose*,
ed. Elisabeth Schneider, New York: Holt, Rinehart and Winston,
1972, pp. 634–5)

Although a number of critics have taken the epigraph as an ironic foil to the progress of the poem, its waverings between belief and self-cautionary gestures are closer to the pattern of the main text than has been acknowledged. For here an assertion of belief dissolves into a discourse on the lack of information, while an assertion of the necessity of belief even from limited information dwindles into the necessity of accepting limitation. But the most interesting feature of the epigraph is not primarily what it says but what it refuses to say. For the main text of the "Rime" is written in imitation of medieval ballads; and while the persona of the Gloss is that of a seventeenth-century editor who lays claim to sorting out the medieval tale, the author of the epigraph, his contemporary, merely provides us with a record of his lack of certainty. Thus, for a "Rime", a mini-epic of progress that moves largely by retrogradation, we have a Gloss of progress and an epigraph that sees the progress of knowledge only in terms of circling – or, perhaps, hanging on the line. Even Coleridge's revisions not only maintain but also intensify the contradictory interpretations that the main text keeps throwing up to us.

As Coleridge would (and did) say, "I would be understood." Although I have criticized (and perhaps even derided) the Gloss and Gloss-bound criticism, I do not mean to suggest simply that the position of the Gloss is wrong and that uncertainty (or no position) is right. That would be to plunge the poem back into the criticism that maintains that the poem doesn't mean anything because it is a "poem . . . of pure imagination". Coleridge vented his spleen against common schemes of the progress of knowledge – the "general conceit that states and governments might be and ought to be constructed as machines, every movement of which might be foreseen and taken into previous calculation" (*Lay Sermons*, ed. R. J. White, London: Routledge and Kegan Paul, 1972, p. 34) and against education infected by "the vile sophistications and mutilations of ignorant mountebanks" (*The Friend*, Essay XIV, ed. B. E. Rooke, London: Routledge and Kegan Paul, 1969, p. 102). But he was equally virulent on the subject of indolence (especially his own) as an attempt to avoid commitment. Commitment – or belief – is inevitable for Coleridge, but it does not issue in certainty or guides to future action.

So what is "The Rime of the Ancient Mariner" then? Some have maintained that it is an attempt to befuddle the reader with a welter of strange evidence and contradictory interpretations, that it is an elaborate *tour de force* of mystification. This account of the poem casts Coleridge in the role of Milton's Satan, who continually changes shape to lure men to their doom. But it might be said that perhaps no other writer in English worries more concertedly than Coleridge about deluding his readers. One almost hears him saying, "My intentions are good, how can I be misunderstood?" And this discomfort at the possibility of being misunderstood perhaps accounts for the peculiar procedure of stratifying his lay sermons for preselected audiences (*The Statesman's Manual* was "addressed to the higher classes of society"; *A Lay Sermon* was to "the higher and middle classes"; and a projected third lay sermon was to have been directed to "the lower and labouring classes of society"). Even his critique (in *Biographia Literaria*, ed. J. Shawcross, 2 vols., Oxford: Oxford University Press, 1954, ch. XVII) of the theories of poetic diction that Wordsworth expounded in the two Prefaces to *Lyrical Ballads* (and in the Appendix of 1802) involves primarily an argument against the confusions that might arise from importing a "natural" language that would appear strikingly "unnatural" to the audience for poetry. Wordsworth did not really mean what he said about imitating the language of the lower and rustic classes of society, Coleridge insists, because a rustic's language, "purified from all provincialism and grossness, and so far reconstructed as to be made consistent with the rules of grammar" is really a version of the philosophic and ideal language to which all poets and all readers of poetry are accustomed. Coleridge, as he says repeatedly, would be understood.

Why is it, then, that Coleridge is so monumentally difficult to understand? Not only poems like the "Rime", "Kubla Khan", and "Christabel", but also Coleridge's various prose works continually frustrate many readers who struggle to understand what, exactly, he is saying. And this is a particular problem because Coleridge is continually presented to us as important primarily because of his distinctions – between virtue and vice, symbol and allegory, imagination and fancy. Barbauld-like critics of the "Rime" separate good from evil, and I. A. Richards separates the good (the imagination) from the not-so-good (the fancy). What is it that they know that we don't know?

It may be useful here to turn to the *Biographia Literaria* because it provides the most explicit account of Coleridge's experience and views of reading (and of the ways in which reading involves one's entire set of beliefs about the world). Chapter XII is named "A Chapter of requests and premonitions concerning the perusal or omission of the chapter that follows". And Coleridge begins it with the following remarks on his reading:

> [In reading philosophical works, I have made the following resolve] "*until you understand a writer's ignorance, presume yourself ignorant of his understanding*". This *golden rule* of mine does, I own, resemble those of Pythagoras in its obscurity rather than its depth . . . [But the reader] will find its meaning fully explained by the following instances. I have now before me a treatise of a religious fanatic, full of dreams and supernatural *experiences*. I see clearly the writer's grounds, and their hollowness. I have a complete insight into the causes, which through the medium of his body has [*sic*] acted on his mind; and by application of received and ascertained laws I can satisfactorily explain to my own reason all the strange incidents, which the writer records of himself. And this I can do without suspecting him of any intentional falsehood . . . I UNDERSTAND HIS IGNORANCE.
>
> On the other hand, I have been re-perusing with the best energies of my mind the Timaeus of PLATO. Whatever I comprehend, impresses me with a reverential sense of the author's genius; but there is a considerable portion of the work, to which I can attach no consistent meaning . . . I have no insight into the possibility of a man so eminently wise using words with such half-meanings to himself, as must perforce pass into no-meaning to his readers . . . Therefore, utterly baffled in all my attempts to understand the ignorance of Plato, I CONCLUDE MYSELF IGNORANT OF HIS UNDERSTANDING.
>
> (vol. 1, pp. 160–1)

Although Coleridge later speaks of the "organic unity" of this chapter, that "golden rule" of his turns the problem of reading from the text (or the writer) to the reader. For Coleridge's "tolerance" for the ignorant writer – in refusing to suspect him of "any intentional falsehood" – exculpates that writer by turning the reader's own prejudices into a self-reinforcing standard of judgment. No knowledge or virtue or imagination on the part of the author, from this perspective, is susceptible of revealing itself to a reader who does not already believe that such qualities inhere in the work. And the curiosity of the piece is that explanation is fullest (even including physiological causation) when Coleridge describes himself reading a book that he had dismissed before he ever began to read. "Understanding ignorance" and being "ignorant of an author's understanding" are merely techniques through which a reader adjusts his demands to accord with his beliefs.

Such beliefs or prejudices are inevitable, unless, as Coleridge says, we discover "the art of destroying the memory *a parte post*, without injury to its future operations, and without detriment to the judgement" (ibid., p. 162). Now Coleridge described his project in *Lyrical Ballads* as that of writing on "supernatural" subjects "so as to transfer from our inward nature a human interest and a semblance of truth sufficient to . . . [produce] that willing suspension of disbelief for the moment, which constitutes poetic faith" (*Biographia Literaria*, vol. 2, p. 6). But, after all that we have been saying Coleridge said, how is such a "suspension of disbelief" possible? Disbelief is merely a subset of belief, a kind of belief that a thing is not (to paraphrase Gulliver). And the most famous chapter of the *Biographia Literaria*, chapter XIII, "On the imagination, or esemplastic power", reveals this process as well as anything in Coleridge's work. Let us start from the end – the distinction between imagination and fancy – to which Coleridge has, he says, been building through the entire book. The secondary imagination idealizes and unifies in its processes of *vital* understanding. The fancy is merely a mechanical and associationist operation that can only rearrange fixities and definites. At some moments Coleridge uses these terms as classificatory (see *Shakespearean Criticism*, ed. T. M. Raysor, 2 vols., London: Dent [Everyman], 1961, vol. 1, pp. 211–18); and for I. A. Richards they seem to be universally applicable categories. Richards, for instance, quotes four lines of *Annus Mirabilis* and remarks, "To attempt to read this in the mode of Imagination would be to experiment in mania. . ." And then he generalizes that in "prose fiction, the detective novel is a type of Fancy, but any presentation of an integral view of life will take the structure of Imagination" (*Coleridge on Imagination*, pp. 94–5).

But various other elements of Coleridge's chapter would seem to cast doubt on projects like Richards's *Coleridge on Imagination* (London: Routledge and Kegan Paul, 1950) and *Practical Criticism* (London: Routledge and Kegan Paul, 1929) and their assumption that one man's "imagination" is the same as another's. For the letter that Coleridge inserts immediately before the famous distinction is (fictitiously) a letter from a friend "whose practical judgment [Coleridge] had ample reason to estimate and revere" (*Biographia Literaria*, vol. 1, pp. 198–9). And although the friend admits that he may not fully understand Coleridge's chapter on imagination, he continually suggests that Coleridge is guilty of breach of promise – for instance, he cites the *Biographia Literaria's* subtitle, "Biographical Sketches of My Literary Life and Opinions", to argue that it does not lead the reader to anticipate Coleridge's arcane speculations in the *Biographia Literaria*. But the rather major difficulty here is that Coleridge's chapter must do battle with the accumulated expectations of the friend's lifetime: "Your opinions and method of argument were not only so new to me, but so directly the reverse of all I had ever been accustomed to consider as truth . . ." (ibid., p. 199). Once again, we are left with a question about the nature of the text (in this case, a deleted or unwritten text): is the "deficiency" in the text or in the reader?

It seems that a reader can only read the texts that say what he already knows. Thus, the editor of the Gloss reads a text that he knows, while the no-moral critics read a text that they know. And the difficulty is that for Coleridge what you know and what you read are part of a moral dilemma, because one can only act on the basis of what one knows (i.e. believes) and vice is merely the result of incomplete information. Coleridge says in *The Friend* (Essay XIV, p. 104) that "virtue would not be virtue, could it be *given* by one fellow-creature to another" (italics his). In other words, a man must be virtuous to understand the understanding of anyone else's knowledge – and thus to be virtuous.

And if this situation seems to present us with an impasse, it may perhaps explain why Coleridge so desperately wanted to write a summa or *Omniana*, a book of universal knowledge. He continually quotes from an incredibly diverse collection of texts, makes one statement only to confound it with the next, and he even plagiarizes. Many readers feel imposed upon by what they take to be Coleridge's efforts to delude them with airy nothings and falsehoods; and Norman Fruman is merely the latest in the line of critics who "expose" the "scandal" of Coleridge's plagiarisms. But both the plagiarism and the voracious reading perhaps point to related ends: if you are what you read, plagiarism (in a more or less obvious form) becomes inevitable; and if insufficient knowledge or reading is the cause of moral inadequacy, then nothing less than all knowledge – everything – will suffice. Coleridge, like Leibnitz, would "explain and collect the fragments of truth scattered through systems apparently the most incongruous" (*Biographia Literaria*, vol. 1, p. 169). But like so many of Coleridge's projects, the summa was never completed, because incomplete information (as Coleridge recognized) was not the problem.

The problem, rather, was that he could sort information from knowledge, delusion from truth, with no more certainty than anyone else who has lived long enough to have a memory and, thus, prejudice. He said, in the *Aids to Reflection* (London, 1825), that "original sin is not hereditary sin; it is original with the sinner and is of his will" (p. 227). And for Coleridge this original sin was interpretation from a limited perspective that had disproportionate consequences, for the peril was that any apparent extension or reversal might, always, be merely a disguised entrenchment of that particular limitation or prejudice. The Ancient Mariner's redemption or conversion, we are told, occurs when he blesses the sea-snakes. But if it seems like a conversion for a man who killed a rather appealing bird to see beauty in snakes, there is also room for a different interpretation. The bird is spoken of in Part V of the poem as something of a Christ figure, and we all know about the spiritual connotations of snakes. The Mariner's conversion, then, may be a redemption, or, merely a deluded capitulation to the devil. For Coleridge, as for the Ancient Mariner, the problem is that one cannot know better even about whether or not one is knowing better.

Evening star and evening land

GEOFFREY HARTMAN

> to say of the evening star,
> The most ancient light in the most
> ancient sky
> That it is wholly an inner light, that
> it shines
> From the sleepy bosom of the real,
> re-creates,
> Searches a possible for its
> possibleness.   Wallace Stevens
>
> The perished patterns murmur   Emily Dickinson

For most readers the charm of Akenside's "Ode to the Evening Star",
a minor piece of the 1740s,[1] resides in its first stanza, perhaps even in
its first two lines:

> To-night retir'd, the queen of heaven
>   With young Endymion stays:
> And now to Hesper it is given
> Awhile to rule the vacant sky,
> Till she shall to her lamp supply
> A stream of brighter rays.

The rising of the moon is delayed, in Akenside's version of the myth,
because she is dallying with a human lover, the shepherd Endymion;
there is something like a divine, erotic slowing of time, familiar from
myths associated with Jove or the prevention of dawn; the theme of
"staying" (line 2) leads, moreover, into that of "supply" (line 5), so
that it is tempting to connect the moon's dalliance with her brightened
lamp, her refurbished rising. Yet the myth does not flow into the form
of an epyllion or little romance: it glimmers above the action like a distant star of constellated image. The poem remains a curious variant on
addresses to the Evening Star. Hesper's brief reign suits perhaps the
idea of the brief hymn whose prototype the eighteenth century found
in a small poem attributed to Bion.[2]

Bion's influence can only be understood through some ideal of classic decorum, of silver mediocrity. His poem approximates the length of an epigram or what was considered as its modern form, the sonnet – and it is a juvenile sonnet Coleridge will hymn to *his* Evening Star in 1790.[3] But in Akenside a tension is felt between the compact form and its narrative elaboration. If his opening stanza is more condensed and suggestive than anything in Bion, the remainder of this poem of 78 lines (compared to Bion's eight) is devious and prolix. Akenside seems to have a problem with "development" or "manner of proceeding", not uncommon in eighteenth-century lyrics, and especially nature poems.

In the Romantic poets the nature lyric is as much about consciousness as about nature. Moreover, it is often about the *development* of consciousness; and this dynamic factor helps poets in the otherwise paradoxical task to plot, or narrate, nature. Akenside's problem may hinge, similarly, on finding a developmental pattern. Not for nature so much as for poetry: how can poetry, at this time in its life, be developed? Does it have a future or only a past? The course of the poem is so stylized that one thinks of the sorrows of the poet rather than of Olympia's mourning lover – the tears are tears of the muses, cultured pearls. The poet's concern seems to be with literary rather than personal continuity, or how the first bears on the second. Hesper is invoked as a link in a symbolic chain leading from loss to acceptance, and strongly suggesting the centrality of poetic sublimation.

New lamps for old

In its simple form, patterned on Bion, the Hymn to the Evening Star makes Hesper a surrogate moon, a night-light guiding lover to beloved. But Akenside has "herald Hesper" (Keats) light the way to loss rather than to the beloved, for the star leads him to a second symbolic agent, the nightingale, which wakes memories of loss under the very moon that is the traditional sign of consummated love or restored presence. Ben Jonson's famous lyric from *Cynthia's Revels* (1601) with the refrain "Hesperus entreats thy light / Goddess excellently bright" and Milton's "Now came still Ev'ning on" (*Paradise Lost*, VI, 598–609) follow the straight pattern and so illumine the deviousness of the later ode. Hesperus, in Milton, is to the absence of light as the nightingale is to that of sound: both are "wakeful" powers that bridge a dark moment and prepare hierarchically for the emergence of the moon as "Apparent Queen". Compared to the purity of Jonson's, Milton's, and Bion's sequence, Akenside's lyric is the night-ramble of a gloomy egotist.

The formal problem is made more intriguing by the fact that the first three stanzas of the hymn, though prelusive, are a detachable unit. Close in theme and length to Bion's lyric, they constitute a small hailing that sets the scene (first stanza), invokes the star (second stanza), and rounds the invocation with a vow (third stanza). Their internal structure is equally cohesive. What the moon is to Endymion, Hesper is to be for the poet: both condescend, the one for love-brightness, the other for the poet's sake. This descendentalism exists, however, within a vivid sense of hierarchy. The latinate diction, in fact, and the elaborate, even contrived syntax of lines 9 to 12:

> Oh listen to my suppliant song,
> If haply now the vocal sphere
> Can suffer thy delighted ear
> To stoop to mortal sounds

sensitize the reader to the whole question of subordination.

The poem's formal development is closely linked to the tension that surrounds the concept of subordination. If the first three stanzas are contortedly archaic in their evocation of sidereal hierarchy and the last three a moralizing frame aiming at a similar kind of overview, the middle or narrative portion of the ode depicts a reversal of influence. Philomel gradually becomes a star-symbol replacing Hesper, as he the moon. Though we begin in heaven, and stars stoop to conquer, as we approach ritually the magic center or "green space" of the nightingale (a centering movement we meet often in this type of poem), power flows from earth to heaven. In stanza 7 the nightingale's song "holds" the moon above the lovers in a repetition of the "staying" which began the ode, and in stanza 10 breezes that attend the path of the nightingale's song repeat the star's attendance on Hesper (lines 6–7):

> Hark, how through many a melting note
> She now prolongs her lays:
> How sweetly down the void they float!
> The breeze their magic path attends:
> The stars shine out: the forest bends:
> The wakeful heifers gaze.

This transfer of power, or reversal of earthly and starry agents, was foreshadowed by syntactical and phonemic stresses in the opening stanzas.[4]

"Far other vows must I prefer . . ." With these words, and still paying formal tribute to Hesper, Akenside deviates from Bion. He converts the Evening Star poem into something psychic and strange, haunted by loss, memory, sublimation, and the influence of poetic song. He leads us to a symmetrical and cunning space:

> See the green space: on either hand
> Inlarg'd it spreads around:
> See, in the midst she takes her stand . . .

both empty and full, natural yet ghostly. That narrow, clearly framed, yet open space is not unlike poetry, especially when based on the classical sense of centering. The very predominance of a prototype, the very fixation on theme or symbol, becomes the poet's way to a wilder symbolic action and an enlarged vision of continuity.

A phenomenological thematics

The Evening Star poem is a fickle and minor genre. But its brief span of life, mainly as an eighteenth-century idyllion, belies the interest of a theme which poets occasionally renew and which is constantly merging with the larger question of continuity – personal or historical. The dual name of the star, Hesper (Vesper) and Phosphor (Venus), evening and morning star, and its "genial" (Venus-y or procreative) aspect make it symbolic of a continuity that persists within apparent loss. The epigram attributed to Plato and rendered by Shelley as:

> Thou wert the morning star among the living
> Ere thy fair light had fled; –
> Now, having died, thou art as Hesperus, giving
> New splendour to the dead[5]

is the very emblem of triumphant sublimation, of identity maintained in the realms of death.

In its broadest literary aspect, the starry theme becomes expressive of the problematics of *poesy*. Is there a true literary-historical continuity, a great chain of great poets, or how much vision (sublime style) can be saved? By 1750 the starry theme was in doubt; and while Blake in his deep and virtuoso way talks once more of poets "appearing" to him in the "poetical heavens", their succession is generally felt to be uncertain. Gray's "Stanzas to Mr Bentley" (1752) expresses the sense of his age that poetry is in eclipse.

> But not to one in this benighted age
> Is that diviner inspiration given,
> That burns in Shakespear's or in Milton's page,
> The pomp and prodigality of heav'n.

This "not to one" may well echo Collins's "Ode on the Poetical Character", which assumes that each age has "one only one" significant poet and that his own age has not even him:

Heav'n, and Fancy, kindred Pow'rs,
Have now o'erturned th' inspiring Bow'rs,
Or curtain'd close such Scene from ev'ry future View.

Despite this cultural pessimism, hope does not die. Blake realized
that the poets' loss of confidence was related to a wrong understanding
of poetry's high seriousness. The divine makers of the previous era had
raised poetry to the skies. Their strength had shown that Poetry and
Divinity were "kindred pow'rs". But this did not mean poetry could
compete with religion on religion's ground – as Milton had "in-
imitably" done. To burden it with divinity, to raise it to a sky pre-
empted by the frozen forms of national religion, was to sink it under
a weight Dr Johnson's obstinate bass unwearily reiterated: "The good
and evil of Eternity are too ponderous for the wings of wit. The mind
sinks under them in passive helplessness, content with calm belief and
humble admiration." The sidereal universe of religion, as he also said,
could not be magnified.

In these circumstances, to bring an angel down could be more important than to raise a mortal to the skies. I will call this harrowing of the
skies the descendental theme. So Milton enters Blake's left foot, and
was already shown by Collins (in a complex image that goes up and
down simultaneously) in the Eden of his own invention, and raising an
"Evening Ear" from its ethereal dews toward a sphery music.[6]

Yet *poesy* is by no means a direct subject of Evening Star poems. The
larger historical pathos is simply part of their aura. We begin, rather,
with "the nightes dread",[7] a power failure or dangerous interval, a
moment when the light goes out. The evening star rises in that space,
on that loss; and however strongly it rises there is often the fear of new
withdrawal ("Soon, full soon, dost thou withdraw"[8]) and the
dangerous sense that "sacred dew" or starry "influence" no longer
prevails. To the descendental theme we can add, therefore, that of the
dangerous, *interlunar* moment.

It is remarkable that in Blake's poem on the evening star the moon
does not actually rise; but were it to rise it would just be a second star
rather than a transcending presence. "Genius dies with its Possessor,
and does not rise again until Another is born." There is a difference
between Blake and Milton on this: Blake thinks of each great poet as
a new and equal star.

Indeed, though Hesperus is traditionally the moon's precursor, it can
be subversive of that "laboring" planet. As the most brilliant of the
early stars it becomes for the expectant mind a singular mark. It seems
absolute in its "steadfast" (if often brief) presence, and begins to stand
for itself rather than for something to come. It expresses a power of

feeling that is both solipsistic and unchanging, or so transcendently hopeful as not to be fulfilled by a temporal − chronologically easy − next stage. Its "intense lamp" does not die into another light: it narrows into itself, or sets unmodified in a kind of *liebestod*.[9]

With this we reach a difficult and subtle motif. As the moon of its own twilight zone, Hesperus tends to personify the threshold and evoke an enchanted spot of time in which a richly ominous signifier is all there is. The star-signifier appears as a sign accompanied by signs, or leading to other symbols rather than to a sign-transcending reality. Since man cannot live by signs alone, the evening star poem rouses our reality-hunger and perplexes the very idea of *development*.

In this it is like love itself, or desire. The star cannot be more than a sign, given the intensity of the desire invoking it. The poem feeds the sign, even fattens it: it wants it to be, if not more than a sign, then more of a sign. Yet the most successful poetry is still, so Shelley knew, "as darkness to a dying flame". The symbol remains a threshold; and the idea of development, of a waxing and waning that is also a ripening, a movement beyond mutability, remains moot. Darkness re-enters the progression of interlunar moment, evening star, moonrise, at any point.

Why then, one might ask, do we need a starry paradigm at all? Could not any pseudo-progression serve? The reason why there is a star-symbolism is clarified by Los's struggle with his Spectre:

Los reads the Stars of Albion! the Spectre reads the Voids
Between the Stars; among the Arches of Albion's Tomb sublime.

Plate 91 of "Jerusalem" shows Los decreating the sublime structures of traditional visionary poetry, which have been, in Blake's interpretation, a "Tomb sublime", that is, built upon, or in fearful reaction to, "the Voids". Los smites the Spectre, or his ingrained habits of perceiving, until

all his pyramids were grains
Of sand & his pillars: dust on the flys wing: & his starry
Heavens; a moth of gold & silver mocking his anxious grasp.

What is foreseen here, though not attained − for Los remains "anxious", trembling before his new-found mortality as previously before phantoms − is a sublimity not based on sublimation. The stars, therefore, remain, but become as mortal (or immortal) as men. They are "consumed" like erotic desire and reborn out of its satisfaction:

The stars consumd like a lamp blown out & in their stead behold
The Expanding Eyes of Man behold the depths of wondrous worlds

One Earth one sea beneath nor Erring Globes wander but Stars
Of fire rise up nightly from the Ocean & one Sun
Each morning like a New born Man issues with songs & Joy.[10]

The most interesting Romantic lyrics do not begin in the sky. They begin, nevertheless, with an interlunar moment created by the descendental "smiting" so powerfully stylized in Blake. There is a downward displacement of the stars which gives the impression of (1) sidereal darkness and (2) new powers (stars) emerging from below. Poetry itself, at this point in history, is generically associated with this downward displacement of the sky's energies. Our phenomenological thematics, in other words, become poetical.

Let me give two examples of the starry theme no longer in its thematic form, or not purely so. We are, for instance, only subliminally aware on reading

Tyger Tyger, burning bright,
In the forests of the night

that usually stars burn this way and that this "descendental" constellation, Tyger, presides over the moment after Hesper has set, when "the lion glares thro' the dun forest". And while there might seem to be no relation whatsoever between Blake's lyric and Wordsworth's "Daffodils", the poet who wanders "lonely as a cloud / That floats on high o'er vales and hills", could collide with a star. And that is, more or less, what happens: a moment of withdrawal, of Wordsworthian inwardness, is suddenly filled with the shock of *earthly* stars:

When all at once I saw a crowd
A host of golden daffodils . . .

The "golden" hint of these lines is elaborated by "Continuous as the stars that shine / And twinkle on the Milky Way", and the "flash" of the final stanza.[11]

The interlunar moment merges in Wordsworth with the themes of retirement, reflectiveness, and self-renewal. His flowery shock is the descendental obverse of the emotion of the sublime. In other poems, of course, up and down are more dizzyingly related − not only in the great passages from *The Prelude* (Mont Blanc, the Simplon Pass, Snowdon) but also in such evening poems as "Composed by the Side of Lake Grasmere" where the lake that yields a "vivid repetition of the stars" leads him into a curious surmise:

Is it [the lake] a mirror, or the nether Sphere
Opening to view the abyss in which she feeds
Her own calm fires?

But it is not only the content of the surmise which interests here. If we try to go beyond thematics to poetics, the surmise becomes significant as a surmise, as part of a larger act of the poetic mind.

Wordsworth: (1) Star and surmise

The surmise comes from a sonnet composed when "clouds, lingering yet, extend in solid bars / Through the grey west". This lingering, a moment of suspense or interregnum, points to the interlunar rising of Hesperus. The brightest stars are already visible, intensified by the "mirror" of the lake. "And lo! these waters, steeled / By breezeless air to smoothest polish, yield / A vivid repetition of the stars." The word "steeled", which continues the metaphor "solid bars", echoes in the mind as "stilled" – "Tranquillity is here" (line 14). Deeply internal, it repeats the wishful progress of the whole poem from martial to pastoral.

Yet no thematic continuity in Wordsworth is as remarkable as the poet's mind "in the act of finding / What will suffice". Stillness, for that mind, is never loss: life should appear within loss, presence within absence. The evening sight is analogous, therefore, to the poet's morning vision of London from Westminster Bridge. The "lo" (line 2) and "list" (line 11) converge as gestures that skirt a desired epiphany. Yet, even as the mind searches for the sufficient, the twilight nature of the moment is fully respected. The very formality of the sonnet prevents the moment from merging into a next stage – it does not "die" into light. Time is almost suspended, like the clouds of the opening lines. The poem becomes a little sphere, restless within (since neither cloudland nor the battle-scarred earth suffices) but turning on its own axis, and furnished with its twilight, and tutelary, voice.

The image of clouds as bars already betrays the poet's desire for something firmer than cloud, for a *grounding* of eye or imagination. His descendental movement from sky to earth and even into earth is a movement toward both stillness (peace) and that ground. The more human field he reaches is, however, the Napoleonic battlefield, "earth's groaning field". The imagination moves away again, trying the nether sphere just as it had previously stepped among the stars. But the image of "calm fires" is counter-volcanic, and shows how precarious each speculation ("fancy") is: the middle-ground sought by Wordsworth, the twilight moment he respects, is always about to fade into starlight or fire.[12] To call earth's fires "calm" (sated) only emphasizes in its very boldness the restless journeying of his imagination toward a fold. So that the surmise ("Is it a mirror, or the nether Sphere . . .") is a restraint on the epiphanic movement, a "lingering" comparable to that of the clouds. The Wordsworthian imagination remains unpastured: it hungers for calm and finds no shepherd. Except Pan, at the very end, in the form of a piped-in, reedy voice, the opposite of panic.

Wordsworth: (2) Star and symbol

Before showing the deepest use, or displacement, of the evening star theme in Wordsworth, it is best to double back and consider poems where the theme is more explicitly present. Hesperus appears in two earlier poems, "Fair Star of Evening, Splendor of the West", written at Calais in August, 1802, and "It is No Spirit Which from Heaven Hath Flown", composed in 1803. Both exhibit that tension between *zoning* (the star seen as inhabiting its own zone separated by nature's or poetry's magic from various continua) and *zooming* (a sympathetic or ecstatic movement of identification) that we found in very subtle form in the Grasmere sonnet. The idea, for instance, of "the sky / He hath it to himself − 'tis all his own"[13] so corresponds to Wordsworth's own homing instinct that his appropriation of an image he has helped to create threatens to destroy the separateness essential to it. The poem zooms in on the star as his (and England's) encompassing symbol.

Both poems begin in the feeling of distance or exile. The earlier verses are written from Calais, with the poet looking westward toward his country during the fragile Peace of Amiens. The idea of an interregnum enters − however discreetly − if the political situation is kept in mind.[14] The star is "hanging" on the horizon's brink above the dusky spot which is England; and Wordsworth, though he sees the star and his country as twofold − one being the crown or bosom-jewel of the other − merges them finally into "one hope, one lot, / One life, one glory".

The star seems to be a symbol yet participates so nearly in the imaginative essence of "real" England that symbol and reality converge. Wordsworth knows that his imagination needs a "star" but he also knows it must be a "native star". It should encompass his own, human destiny from birth to setting. There is, on the one hand, a finely graded if descendental transformation of Hesperus from "Star of Evening" to "Star of my Country", and, on the other, an identifying movement which collapses distances and degrades the star into an emblem ("my Country's emblem . . . with laughter on her banners").

Wordsworth's later poem expresses a deeper or more general sense of exile. The distance is not that from Calais to Dover but an undefinable one from "my natural race"[15] to "some ground not [presently] mine". The star has transcended its zone by dominating the sky in broad daylight. It is so simply, so startlingly "there" that it at once incites and repels descendental or metamorphic myths (lines 1–4). Wordsworth's need for a center or zoom, felt in the previous poem, culminates now in an almost hypnotic moment of enchanted stasis.

There is a further difference between the poems as acts of mind. The lyric of 1803 is more akin to experiences familiar to us from the great *Prelude* passages. Something startles sight by anticipating itself. Though the star is hoped for – indeed, one of hope's emblems – it defeats the perceptual or mythic apparatus prepared for its coming. It is there so naturally that it appears to be already *in its place* (compare line 13), that is, absolute, beyond temporal change. It has become a "fixed star" to imagination.

The poet, it is true, still talks of it as a sign or "admonition" (line 5). But then the octave of this lengthened sonnet is clearly a sparring for time – for rebounding from a sublime or unexpected impression. The real "admonition" is to himself; and Wordsworth adverts to his own mind in the poem's second half, which no longer seeks to render the immediacy of an external image. It turns instead (note the tense change, from present to past) to what "wrought" within him. With "O most ambitious star" we reach, in fact, the symmetrical center (9–1–9) of the poem, its exact turning-point. This cry, star-oriented yet reflexive, turns us not from image to meaning – nowhere, and certainly not in Wordsworth, is imaging free of the interpretative consciousness – but from an objectifying mode that subsumes the subjective context, back to subjectivity. While Wordsworth's star-staring (lines 1–8) elides the sense of time, now there is an "inquest" – an inward questing – into which time returns as time-for-reflection.

The final verses, presented as a "thought" – an illusion sustained consciously and *in* time – are actually an audacious return to first impressions, and quietly merge the idea of ground and heaven. Their subject is transcendence, but this is depicted as a *stepping*, and compared to the ghostly apparition of the soul in a place (that is, heaven) not its own. Yet Wordsworth preserves, this time, a sense of distance: the soul is not of the place but appropriates it "strong her strength above".

Wordsworth: (3) Death of a star

Sieh, Sie erstand und schlief   Rilke

A signal transformation of the evening star theme is found in the Lucy poems. "Fair as a star when only one / Is shining in the sky" is not, of course, a stingy compliment, but an allusion to Hesper which carries with it the suggestion of brief if intense emergence. Throughout the poems which

have Lucy for subject the thought of her death blends curiously with
that of her presence: she is a twilight or threshold figure that gleams
upon the sight, then disappears. There is, almost simultaneously,
emergence and discontinuity. As in Rilke's "Starker Stern", and in the
later *Sonnets to Orpheus*, an image of setting overtakes that of dawning
life:

> tausendfachen Aufgang überholend
> Mit dem reinen Untergang.

Though the erotic connotations are much stronger in Rilke, where
Hesper is clearly Venus, in Wordsworth too the lover appears together
with love's star. The guiding planet of "Strange fits" is the "evening
moon" rather than the evening star, yet it is already "sinking", and
there occurs a ritual stepping and zoning similar to what guided Akenside's lover to a ghostly center. At the end of the lyric, in a reverse play
of a familiar theme, both moon and Lucy enter on an "interlunar"
phase, and it is only then that "thought" rises. The poem's curious use
of both centering and descendental movements links it clearly enough
to the idylls of Hesperus.

But Wordsworth's poem is as much about symbol as about star: in
a sense, the symbol stars. We have, this time, an act of the mind finding
what exceeds. The lover goes out of himself into star or moon: it is a
mild case of ecstasy in which the distance between lover and Lucy –
that precarious or psychic distance Hesper traditionally lights – is
overcome by a deep, "symbolic" association of her with the moon.
Lucy, to use a Renaissance term, is eternized, but unconsciously so.
The evening moon not only leads to her but she becomes the moon,
love's absorbing center. The narrative progressions of the poem make
us feel the slope of things toward her until she is seen as their infinite
threshold – and sets. When the moon drops it is as if a fixed had
become a falling star; the distance between lover and Lucy is restored;
the symbol proves fallible.

This purgation of the star-symbol is perfected in "A Slumber Did
My Spirit Seal". Here is neither Lucy by name nor the visible image
of a star. But she who is described in the first stanza, who rises on the
poet's "slumber", is immortal as a star. Poet becomes Astrophil. She,
however, who is described in the second stanza is ground not sky, yet
"heaven" and "ground" subtly meet because she has merged with the
rolling planet. The descendental theme is so subtly realized that the
passage from stanza to stanza, which coincides with that from state to
state, is a "stepping" not accompanied by open shock or disillusion.
Because the rise and fall of the star-symbol occurs at a level "too deep

for tears", there is no such formal cry-ing as: "If Lucy should be dead!" or "The difference to me!"

The absence of rhetorical glitter does not mean, of course, absence of structure. It means that Wordsworth has purified *exclamation* even further than in "Strange fits" and "She Dwelt": he has killed the exclamation mark, in fact. Instead of a reversal (↓) followed by point (.) to make (!) we have a star turned asterisk:

> How went the Agile Kernel out
> Contusion of the Husk
> Nor Rip, nor wrinkle indicate
> But just an Asterisk.[16]

Stanza 1 implies the star ("The whole of Immortality / Secreted in a star"), stanza 2 star as asterisk, or sign of an absence. Lucy's essence and that of language coincide. If she is part of a galaxy, it is Gutenberg's. Yet absence here has its own presence, so that asterisk balances star. At last a poem without artificial center, a poem which does not overcondense consciousness into symbol and symbol into star.

An excursus on the Romantic image

A voice, a mystery.   Wordsworth

Wordsworth's revolt against the star-symbol has various reasons: its trivialization in eighteenth-century poetry, a religiously inspired prudence, etc. To conventionalize it we can think of his distrust of personification, which it extends, or of English poetry's recurrent bouts of conscience *vis-à-vis* pagan myth. Yet we read Wordsworth unconscious much of the time of his place in the history of ideas or the polemical history of style. These histories, recovered, allow us to be articulate about his intentions but they describe his novelty rather than his originality. They remain external to his strong poetic presence.

Curiously strong, considering how little "glitter", or conventional texture, his poetry has. Many have suspected, therefore, that his imagery comes from a different loom. They have sought to discover the formula of its secret weave. It is equally inadequate, however – though far more interesting – to describe the diffusion of theme or image in Wordsworth, or the change from parallelistic to chiastic patterns in his metaphors. The only adequate rhetorical analysis is one that views his poems in terms of "mind in act", with the very temptation of symbolizing – that is, overcondensing, or turning contiguity (metonymy) into identity (metaphor) – as its subject.

This kind of rhetorical analysis does not deal with rhetoric but with rhetoricity, or word-consciousness. Speech, written or voiced, is only a special field within semiotics, defined as the study of signs in the context of signification generally. A poem may have a direct theme, subject, or reference, but it also contains, modifying these, an indication concerning the power and poverty of symbols. The older kind of rhetorical analysis (with its interest in stylistics or psycho-practical acts) was bound to emphasize the persuasive, quasi-visual figure, or such subliminal voicings as pseudo-morphemes. It can usefully point out, for example, a pun in line 11 of "It Is No Spirit" (the star "startles") or the pattern of reversal and transference in "A Slumber" (the speaker's slumber seems to have become the girl's as he wakes).

In poetry, however, we respond less to images or figures as such than through them to the *image of a voice*. The newer rhetorical analysis is caught up in this highly complex notion. It does not automatically privilege voice over "dead speech" though it can do so, as when F. R. Leavis attacks Milton. We know, however, that the nostalgia for an "inviolable voice" is based quite consciously on the fact that such a voice is a fiction. It is always associated with prior loss or violation, as the Philomel myth perfectly expresses.[17] Philomel sings in the interlunar moment, when there is silence – and silence is pleased. Through the "wakeful descant" of poetry we become conscious of the immensity of the detour leading from absence to presence, or from symbol to symbol rather than to "the real thing".

What is Wordsworth's image of a voice? It might be said that he seeks to avoid both "writing up" – the artifices of declamation, of raising speech to oratory; and "writing down" – the appearance that verse is mere reflection, the mimesis of a prior event, or speech-event. "Voicing" is clearly part of the subject of the Lucy poems, and thus an older type of rhetorical reading will not suffice. As we have shown, exclamation is more at issue than declamation. Voice becomes intratextual, in the sense of merging with the text rather than seeking to transcend textuality by "opening" into an underlying or originative emotion.

As one moves, therefore, from "Strange Fits" to "A Slumber", not only does quoted speech disappear but something happens to the intentionality of signs. In "Strange Fits" the moon-sign is an omen, that is, it presages something greater (lesser) to come. Voice enters as voice when the omen rides the poet. The relation to voice is even stronger in "Three Years" where Nature takes over in *proprio sermone* at the very point at which children begin to speak articulately.[18] So that we hear Nature, and never Lucy: her life is tied to Nature's narrative. When Nature has finished speaking Lucy too is "finished". Nature's logos ("So Nature spoke, the work was done . . .") betrays. It promises life but produces death. Is the deeper thought here that speech always betrays – even this gentle, if still prophetic, mother-tongue?

The fully internalized speech of "A Slumber" does not cease to evoke a death, or the thought of a death. A representational element persists. Yet the poet's words neither anticipate a betrayal nor vicariously compensate for it. Their "pointed" or ominous quality is barely felt. There is no moon, no path, no precipitate symbol. They do not even give voice a chance to emerge as Voice.

We still feel, of course, how close the "idyll" of the first stanza is to a blind sublimity and the "elegy" of the second to a false sublimation. Yet they are shadows of moods only, reached through a purified form. The issue of loss and gain – of psychic balancing – has deepened measurably. If poetry still rises from loss, it has no magical (sublimating) or guilty (proleptic) relation to it. "A Slumber", a poem of enlightenment – and of the Enlightenment – removes superstition from poetic speech in a much deeper sense than expelling gaudy phrases and mythic personifications.

The melodious plot

Akenside's evening star lights him not to Olympia but from her tomb to Philomel's bower. One might take this as representing symbolically the very process of sublimation. A girl dies, song is born. The myth of Philomel already founded song on sorrow. Voice is intrinsically elegiac: Philomel's bower a melodious bier.

But this would simplify both the myth and Akenside's poem. The myth deals with loss of voice, not only with loss. A mutilated tongue speaks again through the cunning of art. In Akenside, moreover, the theme of voice precedes that of loss: if the "suppliant song" should fail, there would be no light for the poet. Loss of voice would mean loss of light. The lyrist skirts that darkening of the voice. Philomel is a symbol, primarily, for restored song rather than for restored love.

A "melodious plot", consequently, is both the aspired-to center of the poet's quest and the form of its path. The star must "suffer" the poet's song before it can grant a petition that allows song and loss to merge in the "green space" of memory. What moves us toward that full yet empty space, that para-paradise, is what we find when we get there: voice, our sense of its power and impotence. A memory-fiction of its starry influence survives together with an awareness of its present absence. This poet's poem helps us understand the forces of nostalgic lyricism Wordsworth overcame.

Voice is the only epiphany in Akenside's ode, but it reverberates in the confines of an operatic set. We hear a frozen music; such phrases as "the wakeful heifers gaze" are stagy orphisms. Nothing remains of the logos-power of the word, of its mimetic or re-creative virtue. What is evoked is a little moony world far tighter it would seem than that generous intercourse of gods and men suggested by the opening verses. How sterile this templar space when compared to the "wide quietness" of "To Psyche" or "murmurous haunt" of "To a Nightingale"! It is illumined by gaslight rather than by "a light in sound".[19] Voice, or poetry in general, is worshipped only as a fiction, as the fetish of a fiction even.

The tension between prophetic voice and fictive word becomes acute after Milton.[20] Not only is paradise understood to be lost (that is, understood to have been, or now always to be, a fiction) but the great voice seems lost that knew itself as logos: as participating in real influence. The *Philomel moment* of English poetry is therefore the post-prophetic moment,[21] when the theme of loss merges with that of voice – when, in fact, a "lost voice" becomes the subject or moving force of poetic song. "Shall we not hear thee in the storm? In the noise of the mountain stream? When the feeble sons of the wind come forth, and scarcely seen pass over the desert?"[22]

The Ossianic poems overhear these wind-notes that try to swell into a supreme fiction but remain curiously successive and apart, wreaths in the Gaelic night. Macpherson's melic vaporizer turns what light there is into motes of sound. One voice spells another in a supposedly epic chain which remains a composite lyric. The chain has no real continuity because what memories pass over Ossian, as over a wind-harp, are not ghosts of heroes so much as "sons of song". Their essence is vocative; their strength a fading power of vociferation. By a typical sublimation they die into song, or rather into the spectral, ominously heightened voice of nature. "When night comes on the hill; when the loud winds arise, my ghost shall stand in the blast, and mourn the death of my friends. The hunter shall hear from his booth. He shall fear but love my voice!" [23]

This melic undermining of the theme of succession – this substitution of voice for blood – is especially remarkable in the *Songs of Selma*. A hero's life flourishes as briefly there as the evening star, and with strange delight in its setting. The poem begins with Ossian's address to Hesperus: the "fair-hair'd angel", as Blake will call it, lifts its "unshorn head" from the cloud, to observe the scene but a moment and to depart. "The waves come with joy around thee: they bathe thy lovely hair. Farewell, thou silent beam!" It goes, as it came, in strength; from this, perhaps, the poet's delight in its setting, and the upswing of the ensuing movement: "Let the light of Ossian's soul arise!"

That light is memory, matrix of epic art. Ossian's soul lights up with memories of dead friends, the heroes and bards who used to gather annually in Selma. The evening star has led us not to the moon, its bright epiphany, but to memory – these dying voices from the past. We become aware of a reversal and a twofold sequence. The star's "silent beam" leads to memory by distancing the raging sounds of day ("The murmur of the torrent comes from afar. Roaring waves climb the distant rock"); memory, however, recovers an inconsolable sound. "Colma left alone on the hill with all her voice of song!"

The interlunar moment now repeats itself as Ossianic lover-hero-bard invokes the silence, or the hidden moon, or absent friend. "Rise, moon! from behind thy clouds. Stars of the night arise! Lead me, some light, to the place, where my love rests. . . . But here I must sit alone, by the rock of the mossy stream. The stream and the wind roar aloud. I hear not the voice of my love." These voices are like ghosts, doomed to wander about ravening and unsatisfied. They cannot center on anything because nothing abides their question. "Thou dost smile, and depart", as Ossian says of the evening star. The questioning voice alone, in its manifold, frustrated music of apostrophe, invocation, and exclamation, remains. This voice is heard as if afar, a passion to be memorialized but no longer owned. There is a kind of elegy in space itself, in our distance from the sublime of sound:

The sons of song are gone to rest. My voice remains, like a blast, that roars, lonely, on a sea-surrounded rock, after the winds are laid. The dark moss whistles there; the distant mariner sees the waving trees![24]

A voice without issue, a poetry without succession, is what meets us in the Ossianic fragments. They reflect the anxiety of English poetry as a whole. Macpherson's forgery is strangely true because the original voice he claimed to discover is so lonely, so discontinuous with the origin it posits. The poetry of this new Homer discloses "the westwardness of everything".[25] Deep no longer responds to deep and each hill repeats a lonely sound. The pseudo-psalmodic landscape before us actually spells the end of that "responsive" poetry Christopher Smart sought to revive at exactly the same historical moment.

Now too the poet's self-image changes radically. He sees himself as an aeolian harp, "self-sounding in the night".[26] Macpherson is acclaimed as a Northern Homer, an autochthonous poet springing from the peculiar genius of his region. Or, more sophisticated, poets understand that all origins are forged origins. For Blake they are part of the "mystery" caricatured in his mock-Eastern style, which multiplies births and creates an extraordinary *mélange* of genealogical fictions. The impossibility of succession leads to a clearer facing of the burden of originality on all poets, which a return to pseudo-origins evades. Blake's evening star, therefore, rises upon the twilight of English and classicizing poetry with the energy of dawn: it is, already, the morning star:

> Thou fair-hair'd angel of the evening,
> Now, while the sun rests on the mountains, light
> Thy bright torch of love; thy radiant crown
> Put on . . .

Coleridge and the morning star

> Tell also of the false Tongue!
>   vegetated
> Beneath your land of shadows, of its
>   sacrifices and
> Its offerings   Blake

My subject has not been a theme, or even thematics, but poetry – poetry as it impinges on those who seek to continue it. The drama begins, as always, in a darkling moment. There is the shadow of a prior greatness, or the discovery of a distance from a creating source. That shadow is always there, but the manifest voice of achievement from Spenser to Milton had made of England classic ground and put the glory on each successor poet.[27]

The burden of creativity became both ineluctable and as heavy as the pack Christian wore. After Milton, poetry joins or even rivals divinity in pressing its claim on the artist. Moreover, as soon as greatness is acknowledged, it raises the question of succession. A theological element enters; a reflection on who is – or could be – worthy to continue the line. In these circumstances literary criticism can take the form of a theologico-poetical examination of the pretender. Is he apostolic? The question need not be imposed from the outside: indeed, it generally comes from within the visionary poet, and leads to self-doubt as easily as to self-justification. The poet's struggle with his vocation is not always overt or dramatic; only with Collins, Smart, and the great Romantics does it become religious in intensity and direct their voice. What is at stake is, in fact, the erection of a voice. "Would to God all the Lord's people were prophets."[28]

Like drama generally, this one can have two endings: a happy and an unhappy. Keats's poetry is representative of the former. His "To a Nightingale", with its finely repeated darkling moment and green space, is a fulfillment of Akenside's "To the Evening Star". A belated poet rejoices in the symbols and accouterments of his tradition. They fill his verses with a presence rarely as frigid as Akenside's. But Coleridge is representative of the sadder ending. He is afflicted by secondariness as by a curse: his relation to writing of all kinds is more embarrassed than that of Keats and more devious than that of Akenside. His imagination sees itself as inherently "secondary" – not only because it follows great precursors in poetry or philosophy (though that is a factor) but chiefly because of the one precursor, the "primary Imagination . . . living power and prime agent of all human perception . . . repetition in the finite mind of the eternal act of creation in the infinite I AM". His religious sensibility, conspiring with a burdened personal situation, makes him feel at a hopeless remove from originality.

That Coleridge was deeply disturbed by the priority of others – and of the Other – is hardly in question. Too much in his life and writings reflects it. It can be argued that he was, in his way, as "counterfeit" a poet as Macpherson and Chatterton. He had done better, perhaps, to invent new origins, as they did, rather than to be echo and imitate imitations in a perverse sacrifice to divine primacy. His poetry shows to what extent he *shrinks* into creation, like Blake's Urizen.[29]

But we are not engaged here in a biography that would expose the *contre-faisant* to real creation Coleridge practiced. The one biographical detail relevant to this study is that he had to contend not only with an inherited sublime that "counterfeited infinity" (see "Religious Musings" and "The Destiny of Nations") but also with "sounds less deep and loud", with the new voice of feeling in Wordsworth. The latter meets him at the very threshold of his liberation from sublimity.

Some of his early poems – the "To the Nightingale" and "Aeolian Harp" of 1795 in particular – are clearly moving in a Wordsworthian direction, as is Southey in his "English Eclogues". But then "the giant Wordsworth – God bless him" preempts them all. Coleridge soon entails his portion of poetic genius on this contemporary giant. Though "Frost at Midnight" and "To the Nightingale" (the latter as revised for *Lyrical Ballads*) repay Wordsworth's influence by leading into "Tintern Abbey", such dialogue between the poets (Coleridge's truest "conversation") lasts but a year. It breaks off when the poets separate in Germany, with Coleridge going off to study at Göttingen. To the priority of Wordsworth, Germany eventually adds that of Kant, Schelling, and the Schlegels in philosophy and criticism.

Of course, such nova as "Kubla Khan" and "The Ancient Mariner" may make the question of originality seem a blind alley. It is true,

nevertheless, that the "Ancyent Marinere" was written "in imitation
of the *style* as well as of the spirit of the elder poets" and that the gloss
added by Coleridge at a later date antiques the poem even more as well
as putting its author at curious remove from his own work. The gloss
– that cool, continuous trot – frames a precipitous rime. The burden
of originality, in this original poem, is relieved by a (repeated) return
to fake eld.

A psychological analysis of the condition that removed Coleridge's
literary impotence is not our concern, however. Enough if we understand how problematic imaginative writing was for him. It was, at
once, inherently dependent or secondary, yet virtually primary or participating in the divine "I AM". His bravest poems tend to recant
themselves. The pattern is obvious in "The Aeolian Harp", yet elsewhere too, if more subtly, he worships the whirlwind or puts a finger
on his mouth like Job.

A test-case for this sacrificial or self-counterfeiting movement (when
originality was in his reach) is the "Hymn before Sunrise, in the Vale
of Chamouni". Coleridge falsifies his experience in two ways. He had
been on Scafell, not in Chamouny. This transposition to a traditionally
sublime spot occurred despite Wordsworth, or perhaps because of him.
It is difficult to work out the relation, but Coleridge, in this poem,
could have celebrated a native mountain in Wordsworthian style before
Wordsworth (*The Prelude*'s account of Snowdon was unwritten or still
in manuscript). There is also his notorious use of a minor German
poetess, Frederike Brun. He quietly incorporates essential lines from
her short "Chamonix beym Sonnenaufgang". This double shift, from
England to France in locality, and from English to German
(Klopstockian) verse in features of style and experience, is surely a kind
of flight from native origins, or from whatever Wordsworth
exemplified.[30]

Even were we to accept the Hymn's egregious sublimity, it would
remain a strange production. The style, as Wordsworth charged, is
"mock sublime", a turgid almost parodistic development of Miltonic
hymns to Creation. The impression is that Klopstock has been the
model rather than an English visionary. Add to this that the poem
turns on the old conceit of making silence speak – that its essential
subject is presence or absence of Voice – and you have a signal case
of Coleridge speaking with a tongue not his own, or adopting a
counterfeit logos. "Bowed low / In adoration" he ventriloquizes
nature, and sacrifices his genius and the *genius loci* to the tritest forms
of sublime ejaculation.

This is not the whole story, however. The poem's first section (to about line 37) bears traces of inward record and a powerful grasp of myth-making. The only conventional thing about it is the desensual-izing movement from visible to invisible. This is imposed on a remarkable *situation*. The poem begins with the near-mythic contrast of the "white" mountain (Blanc) shrouded in black, and the silent mountain rising from a sounding base. We feel the contending elements and approach Manichaeanism. For a moment only – but still for that moment – we understand Abel's cry in "The Wanderings of Cain": "The Lord is God of the living only, the dead have another God."

The Manichaean contrasts disappear into the conventional paradoxes of sublime rhetoric which characterize the later portions of the Hymn. (A "mighty voice" both calls the torrents "from night and utter death / From dark and icy caverns" and stops them "at once amid their mad-dest plunge", reverting them to "silent cataracts".) What does not disappear is the horror of stasis implicit in the opening moments. "Hast thou a charm to stay the morning-star . . . ?" Dread of stillness combines with dread of blackness. The mountain, co-herald of the dawn because of its snowy height, seems to be in league with darkness. It is a passing impression; yet that there was this *charm*, this bewitch-ment of time, is conveyed by a pattern of stills that, as in "The Ancient Mariner", can suddenly freeze the image of motion. It is as if time were subject to sudden arrest – to an embolism felt in the poem's develop-ment as a whole, which is really a non-development, or a passionate rhetorical goad to make the soul "rise" together with obstructed dawn.

In *this* darkling and enchanted moment it is morning that almost fails to rise. "Nightes dread" is now associated with dawn's delay. As a slowing of time it is, moreover, the opposite of erotic;[31] the "bald awful head", the "dread mountain form", etc., suggest if anything a scene of sacrifice. It is also significant that when the mountain is linked to the morning star a second time (lines 30 ff.), the diction swells distinctly toward the Miltonic and repeats the nightmare resonance of the opening verses. Is the mountain or the poet's soul the true subject of these lines?

> And thou, O silent Mountain, sole and bare
> O blacker than the darkness all the night   (original version)
>
> Thou first and chief, sole sovereign of the Vale!
> O struggling with the darkness all the night   (later version)

And who is being contended for in this cosmic battle?

> And visited all night by troops of stars
> Or when they climb the sky or when they sink . . .

This place, then, soul or mountain, is a virtual Prince of Darkness. The visiting "troops of stars" could be the Satanic "Stars of Night" (*Paradise Lost*, V. 745) or a sustaining, heavenly host.[32] We are on the verge of a "wild allegory";[33] but nothing really is clear except that the soul, in trying to "wake" or "rise", meets quasi-demonic forces. "Rising" gets confused with "rising up" – perhaps through a montage of the image of the morning star with the myth of Lucifer.

What more can be said? In this deeply religious, or mythopoeic, situation, continuity of self (in time) is threatened, and there is need for a rite, and specifically a rite of passage.[34] The morning star must be freed to continue its rising course: a progress leading toward dawn must be restored. The mountain too must "rise", for the sable charm invests it as well. But to free mountain or morning star is tantamount to finding some lost intermediary between darkness and dawn, some symbolic form, at least a voice. The darkness is a darkness of mediations. And in this darkness, even constituting it, is the poet's struggle to extricate a religious rather than demonic mediation. The image of Lucifer as Prince of the Air, Prince of Darkness, has merged with that of the mountain as "great hierarch" and "dread ambassador"; yet the image of Lucifer as morning star is also there, and blends with a mountain described as "Companion of the morning-star at dawn". The poet's soul, in this hymn, tries to call the one and not the other. "O which one, is it each one?"[35]

At the end, it is unsure who prevails. The mountain's mediation seems to lift the weight of that "dark, substantial, black" which oppressed air and soul in the beginning, but the supposed upward lumbering of its voice ("tell thou the silent sky", etc.) merely differentiates a silence which reaches, as in Pascal, the stars. Coleridge leaves us with a depressing sense of hierarchy, measured by the contrast between his bowed head and the "bald awful head" of "stupendous" Blanc. His "Instructions to a Mountain" would sound ludicrous if they were not despairing. They suggest the opposite of Shelley's "Thou hast a voice, great Mountain, to repeal / Large codes of fraud and woe", for they effectively make the mountain into the rock of institutionalized religion, complete with frigidly hieratic spheres. In a sense, then, the debased (Urizenic) Lucifer has triumphed because indistinguishable from the religious code. The true morning star never rises.[36]

Only at one point is there something like a genuine release from the "ebon mass". It is not unlike what the mariner feels after the spell begins to break and the albatross falls off; and it involves quiet gazing rather than rhetorical shouting. Struggling against the charm, the poet views the mountain as a wedge that pierces the surrounding blackness.

Then, as if recanting, he thinks the blackness away as a "crystal shrine" which is the mountain's home. Finally he desubstantializes it completely when through rapt gazing Mont Blanc vanishes from consciousness only to reappear blending subliminally – like a "beguiling melody" – into thought. Several stills, then, or re-visions relax the hold of a spell that almost paralyzed the soul. This spell becomes the "trance" of prayer and a "beguiling" thought-music. Its power continues to echo as the stills move quasi-cinematically into the unitive swell of mountain and mind.

The most curious of these still ecstasies[37] in Coleridge is also one of the earliest. A sonnet of 1790 shows the lover absorbed in the evening star:

> On thee full oft with fixed eye I gaze
> Till I, methinks, all spirit seem to grow.

By a sacrificial sleight of mind he then identifies the star with the beloved woman, so that, in effect, gazing is all there is – until his spirit should join her in the star's "kindred orb":

> Must she not be, as is thy placid sphere
> Serenely brilliant? Whilst to gaze a while
> Be all my wish 'mid Fancy's high career
> E'en till she quit this scene of earthly toil;
> Then Hope perchance might fondly sigh to join
> Her spirit in thy kindred orb, O Star benign!

I am not convinced of the star's benignity. Anti-erotic, it leads to death not love, or to a life beyond life. Nothing is lost by this sublimation except all. Having is replaced by hoping in a fatal movement that confirms Blake's "O Sunflower". Coleridge does not hope to have, he hopes that *then* he may hope. He does not seem to know his life has been stolen – as he knows, at least, in his mountain poem. There he recognizes the charm and tries to break a heliotropic (or melantropic) trance by recovering a sense of his own presence amid the ghostliness. But though he resists the charm it gets the better of him. The desire for sublimation is too strong and his soul passes into "the mighty Vision" and so "swells" to heaven. This dilation is sublimation still. The mountain's presence is no more benign than the star's.

"Ghost of a mountain – the forms seizing my Body as I passed & became realities – I, a Ghost, till I had reconquered my substance." This notebook entry, recorded first in November 1799, is repeated in September 1802, at the time, probably, of composing the "Hymn before Sunrise". The ghostliness he describes also befell the Ancient Mariner. It takes away the sense of easy personal presence while inten-

sifying the presence of otherness. Emptied of personality he must stand
on this very emptiness against impinging surreality. It is his only
"ground" (the question of ground being further subverted by locating
the action on a shifty sea). One can understand why the "coal-ridge"
of this massive mountain became a place for Coleridge's struggle to
ground the self. A late and beautiful letter recapitulates his whole
spiritual history as it impinges on the Hymn:

from my very childhood I have been accustomed to *abstract* and as it were
unrealize whatever of more than common interest my eyes dwelt on; and then
by a sort of transfusion and transmission of my consciousness to identify myself
with the Object – and I have often thought . . . that if ever I should feel once
again the genial warmth and stir of the poetic impulse, and refer to my own
experiences, I should venture on a yet stranger & wilder Allegory than of yore
– that I would *allegorize* myself, as a Rock with it's summit just raised above
the surface of some Bay or Strait in the Arctic Sea,

> While yet the stern and solitary Night
> Brook'd no alternate Sway –

all around me fixed and firm, methought as my own Substance, and near me
lofty Masses, that might have seemed to "hold the Moon and Stars in fee" and
often in such wild play with meteoric lights, or with the quiet Shine from above
. . . that it was a pride and a place of Healing to lie, as in an Apostle's Shadow,
within the Eclipse and deep substance-seeming Gloom of "these dread Am-
bassadors from Earth to Heaven, Great Hierarchs"! and tho' obscured yet to
think myself obscured by consubstantial Forms, based in the same Foundation
as my own. I grieved not to serve them – yea, lovingly and with gladsomeness
I abased myself in their presence: for they are my Brothers, I said.[38]

So the Valley of Chamouny is truly a "Valley of Wonders". But does
the poet succeed in "reconquering" his "substance" there? (How much
play with that grounding word in the above letter!) It is hard to say, from
the Hymn, whether loss of self or loss of voice was more important. Yet
writing the Hymn meant recovering a voice. In the Hymn as in the Rime,
release from the curse – that dread stillness, or paralysis of motion – is
obtained by the ability to pray. And prayer is interpreted in both poems
as praise:

> O happy living things! no tongue
> Their beauty might declare . . .

The weight of the Albatross (like the air's "ebon mass") is removed,
together with the stone from the tongue.

Yet voice remains uneasy, both in the Hymn and in the Rime. Praise
mutes itself in the act:

> O happy living things! *no tongue*
> Their beauty might declare:

> A spring of love gushed from my heart
> And I blessed them *unaware*

There is too great a contrast between the compulsive speech of the Mariner and this first, tongueless moment. The Hymn, similarly, is hardly an "unaware" blessing: its one moment of sweet unconsciousness (lines 17–23) does not compensate us for the forced sublimity of the rest.

Praise, according to the Psalmist, is a "sacrifice of thanksgiving". It substitutes for, or sublimates, the rite of blood-sacrifice. The Hymn on Mont Blanc is written against this background of sublimation. The exact pressure put on Coleridge – the offering demanded of him by the dread form – we shall never know. Coleridge's "Sca'fell Letter" shows him as "overawed", but there was nothing necessarily mysterious. He felt, that much is certain, a loss of substance, a passivity both shaming and sublime[39] – and he recovers himself, at least in the Hymn, by the will of his voice; more precisely, by the willed imitation of a sublime voice.

I will not deny that the inferred human situation is more impressive than the Hymn produced by it. But that is because, in Coleridge, poetry remains so closely linked to sublimation. Sublimation always sacrifices to an origin stronger than itself. If it did not cherish or dread this origin – this "hiding-place" of power – it would not shroud it from sight by displacement or falsification:

> Never mortal saw
> The cradle of the strong one,
> Never mortal heard
> The gathering of his voices;
> The deep-murmured charm.[40]

Such "wildly-silent" scenes[41] are not infrequent in Coleridge. He is often, in fancy, near an origin where a "great Spirit" with "plastic sweep" – the wind or voice of the opening of Genesis – moves on the still darkness. But he is, at the same time, so removed from this primal scene that it becomes a "stilly murmur" which "tells of silence". The voice redeeming that silence, or vexed into being by it, can be as cold as the eye of Ancient Mariner or moon. "Green vales and icy cliffs, all join my Hymn." Its "sunny domes" are accompanied by "caves of ice". In the end what predominates are the strange soteriological images, the "secret ministry of frost", the rock "in wild play . . . with the quiet Shine from above", or others calm yet glittering: the "mild splendor", for instance, of a "serenely brilliant" star, which summons the poet at evening to accept his death-in-life.

Afterthought

> The Imagination is always at the
> end of an era.   Wallace Stevens

These reflections must finally turn back on themselves. Is their objective really "objective"? Are we, should we be, aiming at positive literary history? Or have we found a kind of history-writing compatible with its subject-matter: poetry?

The theme of the evening star, as a point of departure, is not objective, but neither is it arbitrary. I have described elsewhere the idea of a Westering of the poetical spirit, and the fear of a decline in poetical energy which accompanied it. Others too have put forward a thesis on the belatedness of English poetry.[42] While it is notoriously difficult to explain the birth or rebirth of a symbol, I suspect that, after the Renaissance, the complex evening-consciousness of English poets reached toward the Hesper/Lucifer theme as toward a limit.

What was limited by the theme? The fear of discontinuity, of a break in personal or cultural development; but also a vatic overestimation of poetry which, putting too great a burden on the artist, made this break more likely. Vaticination remains in evening star poetry, yet is diminished in a special way. Symbol or substitute (Hesper/Philomel in Akenside) tends to become more important than the epiphanic source (the moon). A prophetic background supports a purely symbolic foreground. The aura of the symbol is reduced even as its autonomy is strengthened. It is ironic that, by the time of Stevens, "the philosophy of symbols" (as Yeats called it) confronts the poet with a new discontinuity: the symbols, or romantic relics, are so attenuated by common use that their ground (sky?) is lost. They become starry junk, and the poem is a device to dump them, to let the moon rise as moon, free of

> the moon and moon
> The yellow moon of words about the nightingale
> In measureless measures . . .[43]

Perhaps it was the masque, with its courtly center and operatic machinery, which first encouraged a translation of prophecy into "descendental" picture. Ben Jonson's masques, for instance, can be elaborate night-pieces converging on queen-moon or *roi-soleil*. Royal center, epiphanic allegory, and pictorial hinge go together.[44] A star-god or genius of some kind "descends" to point out his representative on earth, or do obeisance. In *Pleasure Reconciled to Virtue* (1619) the center explicitly descends westward: King James and Prince Charles are linked to the "bright race of Hesperus", which delimits their royal aura yet still discloses, epiphanically, an origin. To call James "the glory of the West" evokes a consciously Hesperian ideology with consequences for later English poetry.[45] In Hesperian verse, the epiphanic figure

> Sitting like a goddess bright
> In the center of her light[46]

diffuses into various, equally mortal or westering, presences:

> The Rainbow comes and goes,
> And lovely is the Rose,
> The Moon doth with delight
> Look round her when the heavens are bare;
> Waters on a starry night
> Are beautiful and fair;
> The sunshine is a glorious birth.[47]

From Ben Jonson to Wordsworth, and from masque to ode, is too abrupt a jump. But it illumines an important difference between epochs, bridged in part by our previous, historically oriented sketch: a difference in structure of sensibility or mode of representation. Wordsworth's mind, in the above stanza, loses itself only fractionally in the moon-moment. Its delight in other images is even more restrained: they remain as intransitive as the verbs, and alternate deliberately between sky and earth. Sight is segmented by them; and the serial impression they leave is of Wordsworth counting his blessings or storing them against the dying of all light. He is restrained because he is reflective; he is reflective because he is perplexed at nature's losing its immediacy. But the image of the moon challenges his restraint. With it the verses almost leap from perplexity into vision: the poet too would throw off all shadow, like heaven its clouds.

Yet the visionary personification that rises in him is simply the act of seeing – natural seeing – magnified. A personified moon makes the eyes of man personal again. Sight hovers on the edge of visionariness without passing over: "when the heavens are bare" is not an apocalyptic notation. Wordsworth's restraint is, as always, a restraint of vision. Though his eye leaps up, he subdues the star-symbol.

The evening star is, typically, like this Rainbow, Rose, Moon. A Hesperian image, it both rouses and chastens the prophetic soul. A fixed yet fugitive sign, its virtue is virtuality. It signals at most a continuation of the line. Through its binominal character, moreover, Hesper/Lucifer points at once beyond and toward itself. Always setting, yet always steadfast, it repeats in small the strange survival of poetry within the lights and shadows of historical circumstance.

Notes

1. This is the accepted date, though it is speculative. The poem first appeared in the posthumous edition of Akenside's *Poems* (1772).

2. See *The Greek Bucolic Poets*, ed. J. M. Edmonds, Loeb Classical Library (New York, 1928), pp. 410–13.

3. See *The Poems of Samuel Taylor Coleridge*, ed. E. H. Coleridge (Oxford: Oxford University Press, 1962), p. 16. In the 2nd (1797) edition of his *Poems on Various Subjects* Coleridge surmised that "if the Sonnet were comprized in less than fourteen lines, it would become a serious epigram".

4. The preposition "to" in st. 1 foregrounds itself so strongly that, to subordinate it, one is tempted to read it on the pattern of "tonight" (i.e. proclitically) and so bring it closer to the bonded preposition "sub" in *supply*, *suppliant* (a near pun, anticipating the reversal mentioned above) and even *suffer*. Compare the syntax of st. 6; also the "prefer" of line 19 which makes "vows" both its direct and indirect object. It draws attention once more not only to the prepositional but also to the syntactical bonding of one verse-line with another. All this fosters a sense of the discontinuous or precarious path followed by the verses' "feet". It is interesting that in Christopher Smart's *Song to David* (1763) the problem of hierarchy, subordination (hypotaxis), and prepositional-syntactical bonding reaches an acute stage.

5. Compare Tennyson, *In Memoriam*, 121, "Sweet Hesper-Phosphor, double name . . ."

6. See Blake, *Milton*, and Collins, "Ode on the Poetical Character".

7. Spenser, "Epithalamium", line 290.

8. Blake, "To the Evening Star". "Full soon" could mean both "very soon" and "soon full" (having reached its ripest or intensest point).

9. Shelley, "To a Skylark", lines 21–5. This describes the morning star; Shelley wrote an expressively bad poem to the evening star in 1811 (see *The Complete Works*, ed. T. Hutchinson [London: Oxford University Press, 1960], p. 870) and uses Plato's verses (cited above, p. 267) as an epigraph for "Adonais". His most famous evocation of Hesperus-Lucifer is in "The Triumph of Life", lines 412–20. On the importance to Shelley of the evening–morning star theme, see W. B. Yeats, "The Philosophy of Shelley's Poetry", in *Ideas of Good and Evil* (1903). To gain a complete "phenomenological thematics" it would be necessary, of course, to consider the evening star theme in relation to that of the moon, the night, other stars, birds (nightingale/lark), star flowers, the hymeneal theme (compare Catullus, "Vesper adest"), etc.

10. See the ending of "Night the Ninth" in the *Four Zoas*.

11. Like "golden", these lines were added in 1815. Compare "She Was a Phantom of Delight", whose first stanza is clearly indebted to the evening star motif, and whose rhythm is similar. For a large-scale speculation on sky–earth imagery in "Daffodils", see Frederick Garber, *Wordsworth and the Poetry of Encounter* (Urbana, Ill.: University of Illinois Press, 1971), pp. 152ff.

12. For an interpretation of Wordsworth's "middle-ground" parallel to mine, and to which I am indebted, see Paul de Man, "Symbolic Landscape in

Wordsworth and Yeats", in *In Defense of Reading*, eds. R. A. Brower and R. Poirier (New York: Oxford University Press, 1963).

13 "It Is No Spirit", lines 7–8.

14 Also perhaps Wordsworth's marital situation. He had gone to France to see Annette Vallon and his daughter prior to marrying Mary (in October 1802). There is also the poet's general sensitivity to "floating", or images of suspended animation, or even the word "hung".

15 For "race", a probable pun, see Psalms 19:5.

16 This and the following quotation are from *The Complete Poems of Emily Dickinson*, ed. T. H. Johnson (Boston: Little and Sons, 1960), poems 1135 and 1616. See also Eleanor Wilner, "The Poetics of Emily Dickinson", *English Literary History*, 38 (1971), 138–40.

17 Compare T. S. Eliot, *The Waste Land*, lines 97ff.

18 I am indebted for this insight to my student Frances Ferguson.

19 Coleridge, "The Aeolian Harp" (1795), line 28. The line was not in the original published version, but entered the text in 1828.

20 For the role Milton as Voice played in Wordsworth, and the Romantics generally, see Leslie Brisman, *Milton's Poetry of Choice and its Romantic Heirs* (Ithaca, N.Y.: Cornell University Press, 1973), ch. 5. For "Voice after Wordsworth", cf. Thomas Whitaker's "Voices in the Open" (lecture at the 1970 English Institute) and John Hollander's *Vision and Resonance: two senses of poetic form* (New York: Oxford University Press, 1975), as well as his essay "Wordsworth and the Music of Sound", in *New Perspectives on Coleridge and Wordsworth*, ed. Geoffrey Hartman (New York: Columbia University Press, 1972), pp. 41–84.

21 See Angus Fletcher, *The Prophetic Moment* (Chicago: University of Chicago Press, 1971).

22 "Fingal", in *The Poems of Ossian*, trans. by James Macpherson (Edinburgh: Patrick Geddes, 1896). Compare the role of voice (the wind's and that of – originally – Lucy Gray) in Coleridge's "Dejection: an Ode".

23 Macpherson, *Songs of Selma*.

24 Last lines of *Songs of Selma*.

25 Wallace Stevens, "Our Stars Come from Ireland", in *The Auroras of Autumn*.

26 Michael Bruce, "Lochleven", in *Poems on Several Occasions* (Edinburgh, 1782).

27 For the general thesis see Harold Bloom, "Coleridge: the Anxiety of Influence", in *New Perspectives on Coleridge and Wordsworth*, pp. 247–67; W. J. Bate, *The Burden of the Past and the English Poet* (Cambridge, Mass.: Harvard University Press, 1970); and G. H. Hartman, *Beyond Formalism* (New Haven: Yale University Press, 1970), pp. 270ff. and 367ff.

28 Numbers 11:29, and plate 1 of Blake's *Milton*.

29 Norman Fruman, in ch. 6 of *Coleridge, the Damaged Archangel* (London: Allen and Unwin, 1972), shows the young poet systematically "vamping" the mediocre poetry of his time. On this "substitution of conventionality for originality" and the closeness in Coleridge of "self-construction" and "self-annihilation", see M. G. Cooke, "Quisque Sui Faber: Coleridge in the *Biographia Literaria*", *Philological Quarterly*, 50 (1971), 208–29.

[30] The psychological background is extremely complex: he was deeply identified, by this time, with Wordsworth and indeed the entire Wordsworth "family", as the Verse Letter to Sara Hutchinson (later "Dejection") of the previous April shows. His Scafell experience was also recorded in (prose) letters to Sara. Bowles's "Coombe Ellen" and "Saint Michael's Mount" may have been in his mind, but in a negative way – his letter to Sotheby of 10 September 1802 leads into a mention of the Scafell–Chamouny Hymn via criticisms of Bowles's "second Volume" (*Poems*, by the Reverend Wm Lisle Bowles, vol. 2, 1801) which contained these poems.

[31] Fruman has interesting remarks on Coleridge's use of "hope" in an implicitly sexual sense (*Coleridge*, pp. 425ff.). Sara Hutchinson is always in his thought at this time (see note 30 above), and the attempt to "rise" out of a nightmare moment of trance or passivity could have involved sensual "Hopes & Fears".

[32] "Stay" in "Hast thou a charm to stay the morning star / In his steep course" could be ambiguous and reflect the double image of the mountain-darkness as (1) preventing and (2) supporting the star.

[33] See the letter quoted on p. 286.

[34] See Angus Fletcher on "liminal anxiety" in Coleridge, " 'Positive Negation': threshold, sequence, and personification in Coleridge", in *New Perspectives on Coleridge and Wordsworth*, pp. 133–64.

[35] G. M. Hopkins, "Carrion Comfort", line 13.

[36] Compare Harold Bloom, *Shelley's Mythmaking* (New Haven: Yale University Press, 1959), pp. 15–19.

[37] Compare "To the Nightingale", lines 12–14; "This Lime-Tree Bower My Prison", lines 38ff.; and passages mainly from the *Notebooks* which tell how gazing produced a "phantom-feeling" by abstracting or "unrealizing" objects. See *The Notebooks of Samuel Taylor Coleridge*, ed. Kathleen Coburn, 2 vols. (New York: Routledge, 1962), vol. 2: pp. 2495, 2546: also the letter quoted above, p. 286.

[38] *Collected Letters of Samuel Taylor Coleridge*, ed. E. L. Griggs (Oxford: Oxford University Press, 1956), vol. 4, pp. 974–5.

[39] There seem to have been two Scafell letters, now extant only in Sara Hutchinson's transcript (Griggs, *Collected Letters*, vol. 2, pp. 834–45). The second one (no. 451 in Griggs) begins strangely with Coleridge mentioning his "criminal" (for a family man) addiction to recklessness when descending mountains, then describing a narrow escape. "I lay in a state of almost prophetic Trance & Delight – & blessed God aloud, for the powers of Reason & the Will, which remaining no Danger can overpower us! O God, I exclaimed aloud – how calm, how blessed am I now / I know not how to proceed, how to return / but I am calm & fearless & confident / if this Reality were a Dream, if I were asleep, what agonies had I suffered! what screams! – When the Reason & the Will are away, what remains to us but Darkness & Dimness & bewildering Shame, and Pain that is utterly Lord over us, or fantastic Pleasure." This experience of mingled fear and exaltation may have something of the conventional "sublime" in it; but it confirms that there was a *trance* and a deep moment of wakeful, rather than sleep-bound, passivity. It also suggests that, however exalted the trance, Coleridge feared

it could lead (by the "streamy nature" of consciousness?) into painful sexual thoughts. The only explicit trace, in the Hymn, of this shame at passivity is its formal turn: "Awake my soul! not only passive praise / Thou owest . . ."

40 "On a Cataract. Improved from Stolberg" (1799?). Both of the F. L Stolberg lyrics translated by Coleridge – "Der Felsenstrom" and "Bei William Tell's Geburtsstätte" – are about places of origin.

41 The quotations in this paragraph come from "To the Rev. W. L. Bowles", "The Aeolian Harp", "Hymn before Sunrise, in the Vale of Chamouni", and "Kubla Khan".

42 That there may be a subjective or pseudohistorical element in the thesis does not disqualify it, unless we erect it into actual history: all art, it can be argued, seen from the point of view of "imagination", is a *second* rather than a *first* – haunted, that is, by being mere copy, re-creation, or afterglow. If poetry since the Renaissance (and at times in the Renaissance) felt itself approaching an evening stage, it could mean that poets judged work more absolutely: either as coinciding with, or failing, Imagination. For the thesis, see Bate, *The Burden of the Past and the English Poet*; Harold Bloom, *Yeats* (New York: Oxford University Press, 1970), and *The Anxiety of Influence: a theory of poetry* (New York: Oxford University Press, 1973); also G. H. Hartman, "Blake and the Progress of Poesy" and "Romantic Poetry and the Genius Loci", in *Beyond Formalism*.

43 Wallace Stevens, "Autumn Refrain". Compare "Man on the Dump".

44 On the relation between vision and representation in the masque, see Angus Fletcher, *The Transcendental Masque: an essay on Milton's Comus* (Ithaca: Cornell University Press, 1972), pp. 8–18.

45 Tudor myth, which exalted Elizabeth as "the bright *Occidental* star" (Dedicatory Epistle to the King James Bible) and compared James to "the radiant Cymbeline / Which shines here in the west" (*Cymbeline*, V.v.474–7), helped to convert the theme of a *translatio imperii* into that of a *translatio artis*.

46 Milton, "Arcades", lines 18–19. This queen-moon, it may be added, is also a "western star", since "Arcades" is based on the conceit of finding a new Arcady in the West – that is, in England. Keats's "Endymion" stands to the theme of the moon as Shelley's "Adonais" to that of the evening star: my essay breaks off before those luxurious revivals.

47 Wordsworth, "Ode, Intimations of Immortality", st. 2.

Ozone: an essay on Keats

RICHARD RAND

... car ce sont des mots inutiles, des mots d'arrière-garde ou d'avant-scène, des mots anachroniques en tout cas, tendus vers des tableaux muets, des mots destinés à s'effacer.   J. Derrida, *Droit de Regards*

In the dictionary, the one by Noah Webster, there is an anachronism of two senses: first, "an error in chronology, especially, a chronological misplacing of persons, events, objects, or customs in regard to each other"; and second, as "a person or a thing that is chronologically out of place, especially: one that belongs to a former age and is incongruous if found in the present". The two are independent, but they can also be linked, and the link concerns us here. If I assert, for example, that "John Keats took a lively interest in ozone", then I commit an anachronism in Webster's first sense, for ozone was first discovered in 1840 by the German chemist Christian Friedrich Schonbein, and Keats had already "checked out", as the current slang would have it, in February of 1821. And if I persist in my assertion − if I press the point that "John Keats took a lively interest in ozone" − then I run the risk of becoming an "anachronism" in Webster's second sense, "a person or thing that is chronologically out of place" − the place, in this instance, being the dominant academico-philological scientism of "today", the space of a certain discourse which would exclude the anachronic "misplacing" from its repertory of permissible utterances. In a word, if I insist that "John Keats took a lively interest in ozone", I will not be taken seriously as a scholar worth your while − a possibility which, all appearances to the contrary notwithstanding, I wish to defend myself against.

As a first defense − for I really do mean to carry forward in this matter of Keats and "ozone" − we could train the guns of science upon the guns of science itself. In conformity with conventional practice, for example, I have just referred to a dictionary and to the one conventionally referred to as "Webster's". It is notable that this dictionary offers a definition of "ozone", calling it an "allotropic triatomic form O_3 of oxygen that is normally a faintly blue irritating gas with a characteristic pungent odor, but at $-112°C$ condenses to a deep blue magnetic liquid". A passionate set of facts, and one which we shall soon return to, but not a set of facts that Webster (or Schonbein) could have known in 1840, no one at that time having discovered an "allotropic triatomic form" of anything, and no one having yet produced the temperature of $-112°C$. "Webster's Dictionary", indeed, stands self-accused of "anachronism", though another "science" can run to its rescue – the science, for example, of rhetoric, which hastens to find in the name and the work of "Webster's Dictionary" a trope, a rhetorical flower – a metonymy, if not a synecdoche, where the proper name of an author is made to serve as the proper name for a project that survives him. And rhetoric could do the same for a sentence, such as "John Keats took a lively interest in ozone", rescuing it from the status of an anachronic scandal by classifying it, if only to attack it, as a metaphor in doubtful taste.

Let us decline the support of rhetoric, and insist on the (anachronic) pertinence of "ozone" to the poetry of John Keats. For what *is* rhetoric, if not a version of ozone? Ozone, as we know, functions not only as an ambient gas in our own atmosphere, but also occupies a singular and strategically significant topos of its own: it forms the outer edge of the atmosphere, and protects us from the ultra-violet rays of the sun. It furnishes an analog to Freud's description of the stimulus barrier; thus analogized, it fulfills one of analogy's most exploited possibilities, that of a defensive barrier against the ultra-violet rays of nonsense, anachronistic nonsense included.

In refusing this support, even as we concede the (defensive) prominence of analogy in Keats's rhetoric, we only defer to Keats, or to Keats's own deference to "nonsense". For Keats knew the real: he knew, *inter alia*, the reality of ozone; he knew how fragile it is – how it has to be conserved, defended from aerosol cans that are powered by fluorocarbons, and from the easy overflights (the hyperboles) of Concordes. Certainly he knew that the ozone was blue – as blue as the "pure serene" of the sonnet on Chapman's Homer – just as he knew that ozone is produced by (sublime) lightning. Above all, he knew – by the reach of a really stupendous anachronism – the inner workings of its atomic structure; he knew that, as a volatile bi-atomic molecule, ozone is quickly split by electrical charges, leaving the single atoms of O to link up with the O_2 of oxygen, forming in the process the ozone of O_3, a fate that befalls the atmosphere with every flash of lightning, as happens to Keats's language when lightning strikes his verse. He knew, once again, that ozone has an odor of its own; it's almost as if he had invented the word himself: for the word does *not* derive from the "O" of oxygen, but from the present participle of the Greek word *ozein*, meaning "to smell". (Webster lets that odor waft, in a breezy cross-reference, to his entry under the word "odor".)

Am I serious? Or does the fear of anachronism make me hallucinate? Have I *really* forsaken the realm of metaphor, when I insist on the matter of the material? And the etymology – is there something perhaps a *little too familiar* about the resource to etymology? It recalls, however faintly and irritatingly, the color of someone else's prose, the stamp, already cancelled, of his postage. And if we hew too closely to that style, then we are trapped, really and truly, in the trap of anachronism. It is a trap that Harold Bloom loves to inspect, scornful as he is of the learning process when the teacher in question does not bear the proper name of Harold Bloom: "I don't", says Bloom, "find much pragmatic difference between the academic moldy figs who cry out slogans of ideas and meanings, and the augmenting textualists who parrot the new dogmas that there are only texts, that there is nothing outside the text . . ." To "parrot the new", of course, is to be "chronologically out of place"; it is to abuse the new, to fake the lightning flash of the new, to reduce it to an old, worn-out, worn-down *dogma*, long before that dogma has even found its way to the English language.

Let us try once more, before we bid it farewell. We are "always already" anachronistic, and never more so than when we say "always already". It is written into the language, into its etymology. Etymology itself is anachronism – it keeps the language on hold, it prevents it from saying what it ought to say, here and now. It is *untimely*, for instance, for "ozone" to derive from a smell.

It ought to derive from an atom or a *zone*, a place where the triatomic form of oxygen hangs out – that would be very up-to-date, certainly much more so than an odor, which would, in the current day and age, be promptly zapped by a deodorant spray from an aerosol can. But the etymon never leaves us alone; it is like an "anaglyph", that slightly raised inscription on a coin – *e pluribus unum*, for example – whose meaning has wandered so far from its first context that its very unfitness is lost on its users.

And poetry? Poetic language neither adds nor subtracts an etymon; it only aggravates anachronism as such. For all codes are antique markings, and the work that commences "once upon a time" is only being candid about the untimeliness of all work that commences. The point is banal, and I hesitate even to point it out; but there is *this* to be said about "Post-structuralism and English poetry": if the codes that we work with are antiquated, including the ones that would regulate our use of the anachronistic, it is a fact which has been called to our attention by those who work within those untimely codes. Operating within a set of codes – the codes and protocols of reading, academically received – post-structuralism is not only anachronistic, but also returns upon its codes and makes them anachronistic in a manner utterly unforeseen, unencoded, hence singular. Carrying the anachronism forward, they menace the totality of the code – first, by drawing forth from the code the set of laws that mark it off as a totality; and second, by putting that set of laws into the anachronic abyss of a singular critique. Post-structuralism never deserted the structuralism of which it is a post, but merely aggravated that set of codes, mining it from within, catastrophizing the code condensing it to the singularity of a pinpoint, to the singularity, indeed, of a single work composed by a single person bearing a single name. It exceeds the system from within, leaving it, as Keats would say, "o'er-brimm'd".

Falling in love

Keats took a lively interest in "o", in the "fifteenth letter of the alphabet", in "an instance of this letter printed, written, or otherwise represented", and in a "speech counterpart of the orthographic o" (Webster again). At a certain stage of his poetic activity – though the notion of stage is perhaps an anachronism at this stage of the game – at a certain stage, beginning with "Endymion" and ending with "The Fall of Hyperion" – a stage which I am tempted to call the "ozone" of his career, and which the academic tradition has tended to treat as the sum total of that career – Keats invested a truly remarkable degree of energy in "o" as a grapheme, in "o" as a phoneme, and in the virtual zone between and around the two terms. "O", in an infinity of manifestations, became the chief focus of his concern. I submit this point in the full knowledge that Keats himself would have questioned it; in the matter of vowels, he claimed to play the field. Thus, according to his friend, Benjamin Bailey:

One of Keats's favorite topics of discourse was the principle of melody in verse, upon which he had his own notions, particularly in the management of open and close vowels . . . Keat's theory was, that the vowels should be so managed as not to clash one with another so as to mar the melody – and yet that they should be interchanged, like differing notes of music to prevent monotony.

Such, in brief, was his *theory*: his practice, perhaps, was something else, at least for a while. It was a little like falling in love at first sight, which can only happen with one woman at a time. Or such, at least, is the experience of "Endymion". Endymion, we recall, falls in love, and does so in a dream; the object of his passion is an "o", sporting the alias of an "Oe" diphthong in the name of "Phoebe". The testimony of Endymion, who recounts his dream to his sister Peona – herself an inverted "oe" diphthong – does not provide us with the name of the lady he loves, but only a description of the apparition itself:

> And lo! from opening clouds, I saw emerge
> The loveliest moon, that ever silver'd o'er
> A shell for Neptune's goblet: she did soar
> So passionately bright, my dazzled soul
> Commingling with her argent spheres did roll
> Through clear and cloudy, even when she went
> At last into a dark and vapoury tent –
> Whereat, methought, the lidless-eyed train
> Of planets all were in the blue again.
> To commune with those orbs, once more I rais'd
> My sight right upward: but it was quite dazed
> By a bright something, sailing down apace,
> Making me quickly veil my eyes and face:
> Again I look'd, and, O ye deities!
> Who from Olympus watch our destinies!
> Whence that completed form of all completeness?
> Whence came that high perfection of all sweetness?

It is a moon, then, a full moon, that dazzles Endymion's soul, causing it to commingle with its "argent spheres" – eyes, to be sure, but also spheres: for there is more than one sphere in the word "moon", more than one "o", more than one "orb" in the orb known as the "moon". Endymion is possessed, enthralled by this "o" from the very first moment he sees "her" – just as Keats – or so he informs us – was possessed by a lady whom he saw for some few moments at Vauxhall.

To continue a little onward with the dream, Phoebe – she of the "pearl round ears, white neck and orbed brow", she of the "hovering feet" – descends to Endymion, then leads him skyward to a sort of zone, a bower full of "o's", audible "o's" that "arouse" him, erotically, so that he rises, as it were, even after "upmounting in that region / Where falling stars dart their artillery forth":

> Soon, it seemed, we left our journeying high,
> And straightway into frightful eddies sweep'd;
> Such as ay muster where grey time has scoop'd
> Huge dens and caverns in a mountain's side;
> There hollow sounds arous'd me, and I sigh'd
> To faint once more by looking on my bliss –

Before pursuing the course of this story still further, let us take note

of the following: Endymion tells the tale of a passion that *begins*: and
it begins, as every passion perhaps must, with a body, a body which
first excites the eye. It is a case of love, and of love at first *sight*, the
love of a "completed form of all completeness". This form is then to
be embraced in a world of *sound*, of "hollow sounds", of that "o"
sound; but the sounds do not come from the form itself that Endymion
embraces, for Phoebe herself doesn't make a sound. Endymion's first
act of love is an act of reading in the strictly visual sense. And, be it
mentioned in passing, this act of love, this primal scene, is itself read
by a third figure − a sort of peeping Tom, or Thomasina, a female.
As Endymion reports it, "once, above the edges of our nest, / An arch
face peep'd"; he goes on to construe that face, calling it "an Oread as
I guess". Let us grant that an *Oread* is a kind of nymph. You can also
read it, however − and we do so here and now − as the words "O
read". "O read", means the peeping Oread; and, when you do so,
"read O".

The rest consists of Endymion's quest for the lady of his dream, during which he runs into many things, but never the lady herself. There
are, indeed, other ladies: in particular, there is the famous Indian
Maiden of Book IV. Endymion falls in love with the Indian maiden,
a turn which troubles him, and which he is powerless to resist.

What is her power, and why does Endymion succumb? It is a matter
of love at first *sound*. Endymion comes upon the Indian maiden as she
"sings a song", a song that says, for ever and forever, "O sorrow, /
Why dost borrow / The mellow ditties from a mourning tongue?" The
Indian maid, of course, is very exciting. She is also almost invisible,
a dark object, to be heard and not seen. And she says, over and over
again, the sound of "o", an audible sequence of moans, groans, and
other sounds of woe, in a roundelay at least 140 lines in length, the
roundest roundelay in this or in any other language.

Hence the great affair, the great "betrayal", of Book IV, except that,
as we know, the betrayal is not a betrayal at all: loving the Indian
Maiden, Endymion betrays his fidelity to *Phoebe*, to the moon. This
becomes clear at the close of the poem, when Phoebe and the Indian
maiden, grapheme and phoneme, converge in a single speaking face,
at which point Endymion can go off with both women in one body −
their own:

> And as she *spake*, into her *face* there came
> Light, as reflected from a silver flame:
> Her *long* black hair swelled ampler, in display
> Full *golden*: in her *eyes* a brighter day
> Dawn'd *blue* and *full of love*.

I underscore "face", "full of golden", "eyes", "blue" and "full of
love", to signal the passage from "o" to "o", the chiasmus of the written and the spoken – at last, and thematically, achieved.

Let me insist at this point that I am not attempting to read "Endymion" merely to set out the premises from which a reading of that vast
and labyrinthine poem must start – with the body, as is true of any
passion, and with the body of the letter above all. The poem itself never
misses a chance to tell us so, over and over again. The assignment is
a formidable one, but not without its limits, and not without its laws.
In fact, these laws are spelled out in a book, or rather in two or three
different books. In "Book III", we encounter an old man who is really
a young man in disguise. His name is Glaucus. Glaucus himself
possesses a "book", which he has received from an old man, or, more
precisely, from the hand of an old man. Drowning in a shipwreck, the
old man passes the scroll, along with a slender wand, just before he
sinks below the brine, to the waiting Glaucus. Glaucus himself is weak,
and at one point he actually drops the book back into the ocean, but
then retrieves it, and "in the warming air / Part(s) its dripping leaves
with eager care". And what is the oceanic utterance of the dripping
leaves, the manuscript-in-a-bottle launched by the ocean itself? It is the
law of survival, of surviving the ocean, and of surviving as well the
oceanic utterance known as "Endymion". Anyone trying to read
"Endymion" will drown if he or she overlooks this critical utterance,
this *Guide Bleu*, this guide-book *en abyme*. I quote from the first ten and
a half lines, set off in italics from the main text. The passage begins
by stating the problem confronting Glaucus, Endymion, and all of us,
then offers a solution to that problem:

> In the wide sea there lives a forlorn wretch
> Doom'd with enfeebled carcase to outstretch
> His loath'd existence through ten centuries,
> And then to die alone. Who can devise
> A total opposition? No one. So
> One million times ocean must ebb and flow,
> And he oppressed.
>   Yet he shall not die,
> These things accomplished: – If he utterly
> Scans all the depths of magic, and expounds
> The meanings of all motions, shapes and sounds;
> If he explores all forms and substances
> Straight homeward to their symbol-essences;
> He shall not die.

If you, I, Glaucus or Endymion wish to "not die", we must undertake to do three things at once, three things which constitute the act

of reading. First, we must "scan the depths of magic", whether these depths be of heaven, hell or elsewhere. Second, we must "explore all forms and substances / Straight homeward to their symbol-essences". All forms being legible, they direct us to a home, to an essence which is itself a form or "symbol". Third, since the meaning of the legible form *is* that form itself, and since these meanings exist to be expounded, we must "expound / The meanings of all motions, shapes and sounds" – provided we wish (and really intend) not to die. We must, in a word, compose a work like "Endymion", expounding as it does the meaning, the motions, shapes and sounds, the forms and substances, the symbol-essences of that meaning, that motion, that shape, that sound, that form, that substance, that symbol-essence designated here as "o". The poem itself becomes, according to the abyssal logic of the "symbol-essence", a single enormous "O", a Grecian urn possessing more than one "leaf-fringed legend haunting about its shape".

Offspring

Now let us aggravate the ozone, or let the ozone aggravate *us* ("ozone is a faintly blue irritating gas . . ."), by dwelling just a bit further on the genetic privilege of the "o", which perhaps may account for its status as *primus inter pares* among the vowels. We find the point being made in a poem that tends to go unread:

> Two or three posies
> With two or three simples –
> Two or three noses
> With two or three pimples –
> Two or three wise men
> And two or three ninnies –
> Two or three purses
> And two or three guineas –
> Two or three raps
> At two or three doors –
> Two or three naps
> Of two or three hours –
> Two or three cats
> And two or three mice –
> Two or three sprats
> At a very great price –
> Two or three sandies
> And two or three tabbies –
> Two or three dandies
> And two Mrs — mum!

> Two or three smiles
> And two or three frowns −
> Two or three miles
> To two or three towns −
> Two or three pegs
> For two or three bonnets −
> Two or three dove's eggs
> To hatch into sonnets.

How, you may wonder, can "Two or three dove's eggs / hatch into sonnets"? They do so by expounding upon their symbol-essence, which is to say, by hatching into doves. A "dove", for Keats, is a sound as well as a bird: he tells us so from the very outset, in the poem called "Sleep and Poetry", where he exclaims that "Scarce can I scribble on: for lovely airs / Are fluttering around the room like doves in pairs." Earlier still, in the poem called "Calidore, A Fragment", Keats refers to "Delicious sounds: those bright-eyed things / That float about the air on azure wings". Doves are not the only winged creatures in the work of Keats, to be sure, but every winged creature − be it a gryphon, a fairy, an eagle or a nightingale − must at least begin as an egg. And an egg, according to Webster, is an "o": that branch of zoology which treats of eggs is denominated "oology", and the formation and maturation of an egg is called "oogenesis".

Well then: let us suppose that two or three dove's eggs can hatch into sonnets. What, you may ask, impatient in your common sense, does this actually mean? Are we seriously to reduce the meanings of all the motions, shapes and sounds that constitute a sonnet to a mere "o", to a dove's egg, or to two or three? One answer to this question − unavoidable, in fact, as a point of departure − is that we shall *indeed* reduce the meaning of a sonnet to the "o". But this is only to say that we haven't reduced it at all, we have only recognized the density, the semantic density, *in ovo*, of the "o". More than its sibling vowels, an "o" is already and variously meaningful, its meanings are hatched in advance. "O", says Webster, is an interjection "used to express various emotions (as astonishment, pain, or desire)." "O", says Webster again, is an interjection "used in direct address ('O Porter, come here please')". "O" is a meaningful statement, extending to an infinitely complex subject-matter, and attaining the dimensions of a genre − as of an elegy, a love poem, or an epic. As a form of address, "o" can hatch into an apostrophe, an ode. Thus the song of a nightingale hatches an ode, itself an egg which hatches the nightingale that sings a song forever in that ode.

Ozone

Keats himself was aware of a problem – of the disseminating potential of the "o", one which will eventually have to be checked or "quelled", as he would put it, by a kind of semantic birth-control. Thus, for example, Endymion compiles an endless list of meanings for the moon, addressing the moon:

> thou wast the deep glen;
> Thou wast the mountain-top – the sage's pen –
> The poet's harp – the voice of friends – the sun;
> Thou wast the river – thou wast glory won;
> Thou wast my clarion's blast – thou wast my steed –
> My goblet full of wine – my topmost deed; –
> Thou wast the charm of women, lovely moon:

So prolific is the "o", so productive and reproductive is its symbol-essence, that it really makes no sense to say that we *reduce* the meaning of a sonnet when we locate its genesis in the dove's egg of the ozone. Quite the reverse is true: for Keats, the composition of a sonnet not only hatches the "o"; it is also, at the same time, a way of reducing, controlling, quelling, and binding, as in a girdle, the polymorphous perversity of this letter. And it is here, in the stricture of poetic structure, that the situation of Keats most closely resembles that of the present-day structuralist on the point of becoming his own poet. Let me tarry for a moment, therefore, on the premises of a structuralism in Keats – a very rich structuralism, to be sure, but one which also became a stricture, a "zone" in the form of girdle, such as we find in the lines to "Fancy". There, you may remember, Keats compares the liberated Fancy to Proserpina in the days before she began to study under the tutelage of Pluto, "God of Torment", joying instead in the pleasures of letting her zone slip its golden clasp:

> Let, then, winged Fancy find
> Thee a mistress to thy mind:
> Dulcet eyed as Ceres' daughter,
> Ere the God of Torment taught her
> How to frown and how to chide;
> With a waist and with a side
> White as Hebe's, when her zone
> Slipt its golden clasp, and down
> Fell her kirtle to her feet,
> While she held the goblet sweet,
> And Jove grew languid. – Break the mesh
> Of the Fancy's silken leash;
> Quickly break her prison-string
> And such joys as these she'll bring.

What strictural structures do we have in mind, and how do you let them slip their golden clasps, especially when these strictures extend to every definition of poetic form, such as meter, as line, as stanza, as sonnet, as ode, as urn? When the egg of the dove is seen as a shell as well as an embryo? I have no intention of letting this brief meditation slip into the anachronistic rut of the *Well-Wrought Urn*, but I do insist that there is at least *one* kind of structure that ought to be mentioned here, however briefly, if only to point out one of the ways in which a post-structuralist reading of Keats can accomplish the necessary phase of delimiting the *totality* of a specific structure, or, which amounts to the same thing, of watching Keats perform this delimitation by functioning within its limits. I am referring to Keats's tropology, a classical labyrinth which is especially effective as a trap, because no one has hitherto noticed the thread which leads us beyond it.

To be crude, brutal and brief, let me simply announce that the thread in question is the number three. From "Endymion" onwards, Keats chooses to confine the semantic spread of giving word to three meanings; hence, the three apparitions of Phoebe in "Endymion"; hence Endymion's comment that he has a "triple soul"; hence that Homer, even in blindness, is "triple-sighted"; hence, the "casement high and triple-arch'd" of "The Eve of St Agnes"; and hence the threefold return of the "three figures" in the "Ode on Indolence".

Three is an excellent choice; it "hatches" the labyrinth from which we have yet to escape. It enables Keats to play out a semantic version of three-card monte, with a vengeance, underhanded, in ellipsis – it being a fact that we habitually, from Aristotle onward, think of metaphor as founded on two meanings – "tenor" and "vehicle", rather than three. Triadically, Keats can be explicit about the tenor and the vehicle of his metaphor, while keeping a third meaning up his sleeve – deploying it now and then with a lightning efficiency, even as he slips off one of the other two that are on the table.

In the sevice of brevity, three obvious instances of the triplicate metaphor:

(1) The moon: it is at once a woman, a celestial body, and a concentrated atom of language – an "o".

(2) A "vale". Not only a valley, it is also, as Robert Gittings has reported, a vagina – passionately, pervasively, inescapably, like a bower, a grotto, or a cave. Third, a vale is the place where everything happens, where the action of every text can be found. It is a page: when, in "The Fall of Hyperion", the poet asks Moneta ("The pale Omega of a withered race"), to "let me behold, according as thou sai'st / What in thy brain

so ferments to and fro", Moneta obliges by setting the poet
at her side in the midst of a *vale*: "No sooner had this con-
juration passed / My devout lips, than side by side we stood
. . . Deep in the shady sadness of a vale." There it is that the
history, the story of the fall of Saturn, is to be read.

(3) A "star". It is always, of course, a star. It is also a the penis,
one from which every reader of "The Eve of St Agnes"
seems to avert his or her gaze:

> Beyond a moral man impassion'ed far
> At these voluptuous accents, he arose,
> Ethereal, flushed, and like a throbbing star
> Seen mid the sapphire heaven's deep repose;
> Into her dream he melted, as the rose
> Blendeth its odour with the violet, –
> Solution sweet.

Third, a star is also a poet; Hermes, God of poets, is called the "star
of Lethe" in "Lamia"; and Apollo, in the first "Hyperion", seeks to
inhabit a star and make it sing: "Point me out the way / To any one
particular beauteous star, / And I will flit into it with my lyre, / And
make its silvery splendour pant with bliss."

You will notice that the erotic value of these words is and has been the
one most quickly occulted. And the cautionary point is that there can be
no effective psychoanalytic reading of Keats that does not work through
the three-fold value of the trope. Conversely, there can be no effective
reading of Keats's textual meditation *en abyme* which overlooks its implication, deliberate, complex, overdetermined, in the elaboration of a
sexual phantasm. Finally, the triple overdetermination of "natural" entities, such as valleys, stars, moons, and dove's eggs – is no excuse for
dismissing the fact that Keats really did write, in the idiom of the day,
about real scenes in nature. Which is to say, belaboring the obvious, that
Keats tells three stories *at once* – the story of sex, the story of language,
and the story of the story told. And, much as these stories intersect and
overdetermine each other, they are never integrated in a dialectical pattern: my point is not dogmatic, it is apodictically put, but it is nonetheless
true. Though the stories intersect and bind each other in surprising
ways, there is never a movement of negation and synthesis from one
story to the next. Rather, they ramify like branches. In the "Ode to
Psyche", Keats promises to "build a fane / In some untrodden region of
my mind, / Where branchèd thoughts, now grown with pleasant pain /
Instead of pines shall murmur in the wind". Out of the "branchèd
thoughts" of his triple figures, Keats will furnish the "wreathèd trellis of
a working brain". A trellis is hardly a dialectical construct.

More

Let us now draw toward a close by supposing an anachronism. Let us suppose that Gérard Genette has published a book on Keats, entitled *Mimologiques*, and that he did so in 1975. The book is one thousand pages long, and it tells us all there is to know about the ozone and the tropes of Keats. With his customary philological rigor, and with his exemplary patience and skill, Genette has traced out the neoclassical roots of the grand affair in the program set forward, or rather prescribed, by the great consortium of Jonson and Johnson (Ben and Sam). Let us imagine the most attentive reading that the most advanced and subtle structuralism can possibly devise – and let us be the first to admit our everlasting gratitude for the success of such a hazardous undertaking. Will Genette have done the job, whatever the job may be? The answer, I submit, is in the negative – and the reason I offer for saying so is that Keats looked upon the entire mimological program as a kind of extra-strength Tylenol, laced with the cyanide of utter stupefaction. Even as he subscribes to Jonson and Johnson's product, he also prescribes for himself an antidote, or several, one of which, if I may be permitted an inconsistency, was an overdose of the drug in question. Certain it is that the more loyal students of neoclassicism in his day were utterly appalled by the wreathèd trellis of Keats's working brain. Consider the following three compliments, compliments long since lost in the chorus of subsequent readers, from Tennyson and Hopkins and after, who perhaps developed a too-high tolerance for the neoclassical overdose.

The first compliment is from Byron; in a letter to Murray: "No more Keats, I entreat: – flay him alive; if some of you don't I must sakin him myself; there is no bearing the drivelling idiotism of the manikin."

The next is De Quincey's: "Upon this mother-tongue, upon this English language, has Keats trampled as with the hoofs of a buffalo. With its syntax, with its prosody, with its idiom, he has played such fantastic tricks as could enter only into the heart of a barbarian, and for which only the anarchy of Chaos could furnish a forgiving audience."

Last, and most suggestively, Poe: "[Keats] was the greatest poet of any of the English Poets of the same age, if not of any age. He was far in advance of the best of them, with the exception of Shelley, in the study of his themes. His principle fault is the grotesqueness of his abandon."

Keats, in a word, overdid it, and thereby did it *in*. By agitating, by aggravating the neoclassical program from within, Keats made the whole thing anachronistic. Not, perhaps, in the minds of his neoclassical readers, but in his *own* eyes, and in his *own* ears. And he tells us that he did so, expressly, in tales of violent death and overthrow. One such tale is "Lamia". Its heroine, an artist of the "o" (go look at the text yourself and you will see precisely what I mean; pay special attention to the passage describing her banquet-room (Part II, 173–190)) – is brought to a terrible end by Apollonius, who kills off her ozone with Keats's favorite fluorocarbon, the letter "e". ("Then Lamia breath'd death breath; the sophist's eye, / Like a sharp spear, went through her utterly, / Keen, cruel, perceant, stirring.")

More gently, but more thematically decisive, is the overthrow of Saturn in "The Fall of Hyperion", a poem which, as Paul de Man so keenly remarks, may very well be read as "The Fall of 'Hyperion'", of the poem entitled "Hyperion", perhaps the last of the great ozone poems. At the end of the first canto, the fallen Saturn has been moaning as he sits, fixed, beneath the sable trees. He moans by saying "Moan": ("Moan, brethren, moan . . . Moan and wail . . . Moan, brethren, moan; . . . moan, moan, / Moan, Cybele, moan . . . Moan, Brethren, moan . . ., the pain, the pain of feebleness. Moan, moan . . . Let me hear other groans . . .") It is a fact that the poet who attends this grotesque spectacle neither mourns nor bemoans:

> Methought I heard some old man of the earth
> Bewailing earthly loss; nor could my eyes
> And ears act with that pleasant unison of sense
> Which marries sweet sound with the grace of form,
> And dolorous accent from a tragic harp
> With large limb'd visions. More I scrutinized;
> . . . his awful presence there
> (Now all was silent) gave a deadly lie
> To what I erewhile heard; only his lips
> Trembled amid the white curls of his beard.

At this moment, it seems to me, the mimetic formalism of the ozone draws to its close, robbed of "that pleasant unison of sense / Which marries sweet sound with the grace of form". And here my paper must also come to a close.

But the work of Keats does not close off here. Keats, like Hyperion, "flares on", right on past the end – if an end there ever was – to yet another astonishing poem which nobody seems to read, entitled "The Jealousies . . ." As for why the "e's" should be jealous, and of *what*, in the work of a man whose first name was John and whose last name was Keats, I must leave to consider another time. I also defer the question of how this poem propels us forward into the worlds of Poe and Joyce, even as it draws upon the resources of Keats's *first love*, Edmund Spenser – of whom he wrote, in the volume of 1817, that "Spenserian vowels . . . elope with ease, / And float along like birds o'er summer seas."

Strategies of containment: Tennyson's *In Memoriam*

ROB JOHNSON

In defending his commentary on *In Memoriam* against readers of Tennyson who doubted the necessity or value of such an enterprise, A. C. Bradley declared: "We read for the most part half-asleep, but a poet writes wide-awake."[1] This remark sounds across eight decades with a curiously contemporary ring, closely paralleling Paul de Man's defence of deconstructionist reading against the charge that it is a gratuitous addition to the text: "by reading the text as we did we were only trying to come closer to being as rigorous a reader as the author had to be to write the sentence in the first place".[2]

The complex play of utterance that Bradley recognized in *In Memoriam* is often the result of a studiedly ambiguous rhetoric that may, for instance, deliberately exploit the element of difference in language, evoking significations of word or image incongruous with those ostensibly demanded by the argument. Or the syntax may distribute emphasis in ways that, while not destroying the ostensible meaning, make it appear more problematical than any prose paraphrase would suggest. Or the dividing line between elements of similarity and difference in a simile may be so blurred as to leave its interpretation more or less speculative. Or the speaker of the poem, constituted by rhetoric, may also be fragmented by it; so that "I" no longer signifies a unified subject but either of two "I"s, one of which regards the other's reactions with wonder, incredulity or dismay. All such play of utterance serves to dramatize a consciousness initially disoriented and dispersed by grief and at the end – taking its final state to be represented in the Prologue – still resorting to stratagem to assert one element of itself (faith) against another (doubt) that cannot be totally expelled but can only be confronted and contained.

The poem has not, indeed, always been read in this way. An eminently intelligent Victorian, the philosopher Henry Sidgwick, commented, for instance, that, in the Prologue, "Faith . . . is too completely triumphant . . . Faith must give the last word: but the last word is not the whole utterance of the truth: the whole truth is that assurance and doubt must alternate in the moral world in which we at present live, somewhat as night and day alternate in the physical world."[3] It is arguable, however, that Sidgwick's "whole truth" comes close to a fair summing-up of the situation actually presented in the Prologue – if, that is, the Prologue is read with due attention to its rhetorical emphases and setting-out. So read, the Prologue is an instance of how "difference" – used here in a very general sense to cover any discrepant and potentially disruptive element in personal consciousness, in society at large and in current perceptions of the cosmos – is contained but cannot be eradicated. What follows is an examination of *In Memoriam*'s rhetorical dramatization of difference – and of the stratagems by which the speaker of the poem seeks to contain it.

The opening stanza of the Prologue voices an ostensibly confident faith and strongly echoes the New Testament:

> Strong Son of God, immortal Love,
>   Whom we, that have not seen thy face,
>   By faith, and faith alone, embrace,
> Believing where we cannot prove.

There are several possible references here. The one mentioned by Tennyson himself[4] is 1 John 4:12: "No man hath seen God at any time. If we love one another God dwelleth in us." Another is the remark of the risen Christ to doubting Thomas: "Blessed are they who have not seen and have believed" (John 20:29). Yet another is 1 Peter 1:7,8: "Jesus Christ: whom having not seen ye love; in whom, though now ye see him not, yet believing, ye rejoice." All these are obviously relevant to the conjuncture in the Prologue of seeing and not seeing, believing (and, by implication, doubting) and loving. A more pointed comparison, however, is with another passage that expressly states what the others leave implicit – John 1:18: "No man hath seen God at any time; the only begotten Son . . . he hath declared him."

God has not been seen but the Son has. To some extent, therefore, the mystery of the Father has been dispelled by the Son in whose love God is manifest; but the odd thing about the being addressed in the Prologue as "Strong Son of God, immortal Love" is that, so far from dispelling the mystery of the Father, he seems fully to partake of it:

> Thine are these orbs of light and shade;
>   Thou madest Life in man and brute;
>   Thou madest Death; and lo, thy foot
> Is on the skull which thou hast made.
>
> Thou wilt not leave us in the dust:
>   Thou madest man, he knows not why,
>   He thinks he was not made to die;
> And thou hast made him: thou art just.

> Thou seemest human and divine,
>   The highest, holiest manhood, thou:
>   Our wills are ours, we know not how;
>   Our wills are ours, to make them thine.

Though hailed as "immortal Love", the Son is addressed first as the author of an ambiguous creation, responsible both for life and death, paralleled in the (literal and symbolic) "orbs of light and shade". The Son has his foot on the skull, traditionally a symbol of his triumph over death. But quite apart from the point that a skull, whatever its literary or graphic context, is inevitably a *memento mori*, the symbolism is slanted into ambiguity. The rather inexplicit "and lo", leading on from "Thou madest death", might convey that the placing of the Son's foot is a confirmation of what has just been said. Is this a triumph over death or over the dead? Is the Son only the triumphant New Testament redeemer? Does he not also suggest the enigmatic deity of Job? "The Lord gave and the Lord hath taken away". Certainly, in contrast with the New Testament passages, the Son's "declaration" of the Father seems to add remarkably little to what the Father has already, somewhat cryptically and ominously, declared on his own behalf. The text of creation, so far from being elucidated, seems to remain as the Father had left it.

We do gather in stanza four that the Son of God is to be identified with the incarnate Christ though the identification is oddly tentative. "Seemest" in "Thou seemest human and divine" (as if said by somebody encountering Christ – or the idea of Christ – for the first time) is, however, characteristic of *In Memoriam*. In this stanza we are confronted with two mysteries of faith: the combination of humanity and divinity in the Son and of free will and creaturely dependence ("Thou madest man") in ourselves. "Our wills are ours" but how can they be when we are "thine" through and through? The scope of free will is in any case limited. "To make them thine", echoing the three times repeated "thou madest", points a contrast as well as a parallel between the Son as maker of all things, including man, and man as (within limits) "maker" of himself. It is soon apparent, indeed, that the strength attributed to the Son of God in the opening line implies a proportionate weakness in the speaker. The repetition of "thine" and "thou", built up over twelve lines and locked, with the aid of a purely emphatic "thou", into the rhyme-scheme in the last four, brings home the Son's dominance of his creation and the consequent creaturely dependence of the speaker in common with all human beings. (And yet we have no assurance of the Son's strength other than "faith alone" – and what is the faith of such a weak creature worth?) This recognition of dependence is later explicitly extended to Hallam: "Forgive my grief for one removed, / Thy creature."

This is not the idealized Hallam in the later stanzas of the poem; though the Prologue, printed with the date 1849, is presumably delivered with retrospective awareness and with the force of the speaker's spiritual gains behind it. This reference is the first mention of the occasion for the poem and for much of the Prologue the speaker does not even use the first person singular. He shifts from "we", associating himself, presumably, with human beings in general, to "he", as if arrogating the stance of a detached, superior – even rather derisive – observer:

> Thou madest man, he knows not why,
> He thinks he was not made to die;
> And thou hast made him; thou art just.

There is a perfectly good argument here, if we waive the point that its premises are a matter of "faith alone". "God has made man. Man believes he has an immortal soul. God is just. God, being just, would not make a being that believed itself to have an immortal soul when in fact it did not. Therefore man has an immortal soul." There is a disparity, however, between the structure of the argument and its rhetorical setting-out that obscures its force and makes the conviction of immortality seem distinctly precarious. As in the symbol of Christ with his foot on the skull, connections are omitted or blurred. The metrical emphasis on "thinks", coming close on "he knows not why", makes the conviction seem, *not* what the argument requires it to be – some sort of innate idea of immortality proper to man as man – but merely what a manifestly fallible and ignorant creature "thinks". In the context, "thinks", like "feels" elsewhere in *In Memoriam*, carries a subversive implicit contrast with other expressions such as "knows" or "has good reason to believe" and a strong suggestion of its colloquial connotation: "but little does he know". Such suggestions could be carried further into an ironic reading of "thou art just" or a rueful unspoken parenthesis: "thou hadst better be!"

The intention in these remarks, as in previous remarks about Christ and the skull, is not simply to subvert the conventional reading. The passage "means" what the paraphrase of its argument represents it as meaning. But the setting out does suggest another and less reassuring perspective and at least an incipient alternative reading that cannot, once entertained, be dismissed. Hence the overtone of grimness and anxiety in what is, logically speaking, a positive argument. The effect resembles a version of *Hamlet* in which the Prince commands centre stage but Claudius is also always present, reminding the audience of another possible construction of events. It would obviously be perverse to deny the speaker's commitment to a belief in man's immortal soul; but it would equally obviously be naive to read that commitment as serenely untroubled.

To dismiss these two unlikely hypothetical readings is not, however, necessarily to point to any assured middle ground between them. Given that there is an interplay of faith and doubt in the Prologue, how are we to describe it? Faith desperately battling against a doubt that, in spite of all its efforts, keeps breaking through? Faith nobly confronting doubt and emerging from the struggle with head bloody but unbowed? Both these hypothetical readings could be supported by reference to the play of signifiers that constitutes "the text". Each might be described, in deconstructionist rhetoric, as a "misreading" in the sense that each is subject to correction by the other or by some further alternative reading that would still not be definitive. The Prologue presents faith and doubt as coexisting. But how do we describe that coexistence? Interplay? (As above.) Conflict? Challenge and response? Tremulous balance? Mutual deconstruction? The position taken here is not that the play of signifiers is simply "free". Within the limits set by "the text", different readings – different constructions of how faith and doubt interrelate – are, however, possible and any reading for which we settle will be haunted by our awareness of others.

Through his consciousness of other possible readings the reader constructs the haunted consciousness of the speaker in the Prologue. Arrived at a position of faith that reconciles him to his physical separation from the deceased, the speaker is still haunted by the earlier readings of himself and the world that form the substance of the narrative that follows. In the earliest phase of the poem[5] he was too disoriented by grief to be capable of reading himself at all. Bradley's citation of St Augustine in the *Confessions*, describing his state of mind after the death of a friend, is apt: "I became a great puzzle to myself, and asked my soul why she was so sad and why she so exceedingly disquieted me, but she knew not what to answer to me."[6] The analogy with *In Memoriam* is close, extending to the rhetoric, the subject being divided between the "I" that is puzzled and the "I" that puzzles, the self that interrogates and the soul that is unable to answer:

> O heart, how fares it with thee now,
>   That thou shouldst fail from thy desire,
>   Who scarcely darest to inquire,
> "What is it makes me beat so low?"   (IV)

The Speaker projects his grief as a feminized Sorrow:

> O Sorrow, cruel fellowship,
>   O Priestess in the vaults of Death,
>   O sweet and bitter in a breath,
> What whispers from thy lying lip?   (III)

What Sorrow whispers is that "the stars . . . blindly run", anticipating
a later reading of the experience of bereavement: that the world-process
does not favour the individual life, in which alone value resides, and
is therefore "meaningless". As a priestess, Sorrow is perverting her office, promoting not faith but faithlessness; so she presents a double
aspect – holy but deceptive. She is "cruel" but to renounce her would
be to renounce "fellowship" with the deceased. In his confusion, the
speaker is unable to confront the reading of life that Sorrow seems to
be proposing and dismisses her as simply lying. It is clear, however,
that this is merely an instance of one constituent of the "I" refusing
to acknowledge another. Apostrophe (the address to a personified component of consciousness or to an external object such as a house, a yew-
tree, the ship which is bringing back Hallam's body) is a device by
which the reader overhears the dialogue of the speaker's mind with
itself. *In Memoriam* is thus, in a sense, "confessional" poetry – but only at an obvious rhetorical remove.

Tennyson himself made the salutary point that in *In Memoriam*, " 'I'
is not always the author speaking of himself."[7] In the first phase of *In
Memoriam* the "I" is not even a coherent fictive presence. This difference of the "I" from itself is strikingly dramatized in the fantasy of
Lyric XIV, in which the ship bearing Hallam's corpse arrives and a living Hallam steps down the plank:

> And if along with these should come
>   The man I held as half-divine;
>   Should strike a sudden hand in mine,
> And ask a thousand things of home;
>
> And I should tell him all my pain,
>   And how my life had drooped of late,
>   And he should sorrow o'er my state
> And marvel what possessed my brain;
>
> And I perceived no touch of change,
>   No hint of death in all his frame,
>   But found him all in all the same,
> I should not feel it to be strange.

The effect lies in the build-up to the last line in which the "I" of the
preceding narrative is scrutinized by an implicit other "I" who finds

it strange that the first "I" finds nothing strange. The "I" is divided
in Antony Easthope's terms,[8] between the subject of the enunciation
(the previously concealed "I" in the final line) and the subject of the
enounced (the "I" of the preceding narrative.) The speaker of these
early lyrics is a stranger to himself, baffled by his own behaviour and
the feelings that prompt it:

> What words are these have fallen from me?
>   Can calm despair and wild unrest
>   Be tenants of a single breast,
> Or sorrow such a changeling be?   (XVI)

Here the speaker confronts two pervasive, ambivalent and troubling
aspects of the world: difference and change. His own consciousness is
as much a confusing prospect of shifting light and shade as external
nature is. He raises the possibility that Sorrow, in her "deep self", is
no "changeling" (XVI). But her "deep self" is perhaps unable to communicate: his words are "only words" and move "upon the topmost
froth of thought" (LII). He elsewhere refers to Sorrow as sporting with
words (XLVIII) and to grief as playing with "symbols" (LXXXV); and
he is quite clear that his "brief lays" are not to be read as offering
answers to serious philosophical questions:

> If these brief lays, of Sorrow born,
>   Were taken to be such as closed
>   Grave doubts and answers here proposed,
> Then these were such as men might scorn.   (XLVIII)

Rather, Sorrow "sports with words" and

>   loosens from the lip
>   Short swallow-flights of song, that dip
> Their wings in tears, and skim away.

This quality of sportiveness − "sportiveness" being arguably a
feature of all poetic utterance − is evident in the poem that alludes to
it. Is not "closed / Grave doubts", for instance, as much a play on
words as "I shall not murder / The mankind of her going with a grave
truth" in Dylan Thomas's "A Refusal to Mourn"? It may be supposed,
since he says as much, that the various forms of verbal play offer the
speaker at least "a doubtful gleam of solace" (XXXVIII) − an escape,
even, into a world where, as for Yeats's Happy Shepherd, "words alone
are certain good". But elsewhere words present him with a play of difference that accentuates life's uncertainties and apparent contradictions. Any solace the speaker could derive from such verbal play might
well be "doubtful" − at most, perhaps, the solace of imposing poetic

form on the constant slippage of meaning that words undergo in response to the fissile and volatile nature of consciousness, as in this echo of *Hamlet* I.ii ("Ay, madam, it is common"):

> One writes, that "Other friends remain",
>   That "Loss is common to the race" –
>   And common is the commonplace,
> And vacant chaff well meant for grain.
>
> That loss is common would not make
>   My own less bitter, rather more:
>   Too common! Never morning wore
> To evening, but some heart did break.   (VI)

"Common" slips, between the consoler and the inconsolable, from "common to the race – therefore you are not alone" through "commonplace – therefore not worth saying and, in the circumstances, merely offensive" to "too common – therefore suggesting a pessimistic view of the nature of things". The consoler thus merely reinforces the bereaved in his philosophical and religious anxieties. Also, the transitions from one implication of "common" to another and the derisory repetition of the word invite us to recall another sense: "common – and therefore not worth much". The speaker feels that Hallam and his grief at Hallam's death are being devalued.

Another instance is worth quoting in full:

> Calm is the morn without a sound,
>   Calm as to suit a calmer grief,
>   And only thro' the faded leaf
> The chestnut pattering to the ground:
>
> Calm and deep peace on this high wold,
>   And on these dews that drench the furze,
>   And all the silvery gossamers
> That twinkle into green and gold:
>
> Calm and still light on yon great plain
>   That sweeps with all its autumn bowers,
>   And crowded farms and lessening towers,
> To mingle with the bounding main:
>
> Calm and deep peace in this wide air,
>   These leaves that redden to the fall;
>   And in my heart, if calm at all,
> If any calm, a calm despair:
>
> Calm on the seas, and silver sleep,
>   And waves that sway themselves in rest,
>   And dead calm in that noble breast
> Which heaves but with the heaving deep.   (XI)

This lyric is the third in a series of nine in which the speaker follows in imagination the return of Hallam's body by sea. The maritime connotations of "calm" are thus strong, through not foregrounded until the sardonic last two lines. The lyric draws on pastoral and elegiac tradition but subverts the traditional expectations. Gray's "Elegy Written in a Country Churchyard" proceeds from "All the air a solemn stillness holds" to a correspondingly calm and solemn meditation on life. In Tennyson's poem we encounter a speaker who, far from being capable of general reflections on life, is not even wise to himself (and knows it). The suggestion of a correspondence between calm in nature and calm in the speaker's mind is evoked to be ironically dismissed. In any case, calm is no more a constant factor in human consciousness than is calm at sea, where it may be calm after or before a storm, calm that assists a ship's passage or that becalms it. It may be "calm of mind, all passion spent", philosophical calm or, explicitly here, the calm of somebody drained by despair. There is no precise and necessary link between "calm" and anything it signifies – nor between pastoral-elegiac signals and the sort of message they traditionally convey. The crucial element of difference is hinted at in the second line: not only is "calmer grief" ambiguous, as Bradley points out[9] ("calmer grief than mine" or "a grief grown calmer"?) but "as to suit" (as against "that suits") leaves it quite uncertain whether there is any reference to the speaker's actual state of mind or not. By the fourth stanza, he is in any case explicitly and emphatically uncertain about his own feelings: "if calm at all, / If any calm". The traditional "pathetic fallacy" is parodied in a parallel – that is also a contrast – between the "calm and deep peace" of the autumnal landscape and the speaker's (no more than possible) "calm despair". The speaker's calm ("if any calm") signifies difference from the calm of nature, not affinity with it. The notion of a spiritual affinity with nature is further parodied in another studiedly incongruous comparison between the calm (in motion) of the sea and the "dead calm" in the corpse's breast "which heaves but with the heaving deep". A similar effect of parody occurs at the end of the previous lyric where the speaker recoils from the thought that "hands so often clasped in mine, / Should toss with tangle and with shells". "Toss" and "heaves", both parodies of living movement, confront us with the brute physical reality in which alone, perhaps, our difference from the rest of the world will end. The conclusion is described by Bradley as "a transition of wonderful dignity and pathos".[10] It could also be read as overwrought feeling finding relief in something approaching black humour. "There may be a question whether I'm calm or not – but there's certainly no question in Arthur's case!" Is the "dead calm" of the corpse the only calm that is constant, unqualified and invulnerable?

The speaker of *In Memoriam* first confronts us as dismayed by the volatility and strangeness of his reactions: he wonders if his suffering is a dream (XIII) and his consciousness has the incoherence of delirium (XVI). He later sees a prospect of escape from this state of fragmented self-perception in an experience of apparent mystical communion in which, he believes, "what I am beheld again / What is, and no man understands" (CXXIV). What is constant in himself relates to a transcendental constant. For the present, however, the speaker can hope only that this volatility and seeming multiplicity of the self may offer the possibility of spiritual progress –

> That men may rise on stepping-stones
> Of their dead selves to higher things.   (I)

Foreshadowed here is the ambivalent attitude to change (which erodes values but may also consolidate and enrich them) and difference (which estranges but which is also the condition of fruitful relationship).

As consciousness is fluid, so are the terms in which we attempt to capture it. Faith, for instance, is not presented as a theological virtue, capable of clear definition. "Faith", as signifier, has no consistent and precise reference. It may signify faint trust (LV) defiant assertion (CXXIV) fearful, childlike dependence (ibid.) traditional "simple faith" (XXXII, XXXIII, XCVI) a rarefied, possibly pantheistic belief that "has centre everywhere" (XXXIII) a sheer determination to behave "as if" the object of faith existed –

> That we may raise from out of dust
> A voice as unto him that hears.   (CXXXI)

One phase of faith may rapidly pass into another (CXXIV). And faith may differ so much from one person to another – even when the object of faith is at least ostensibly the same – as to become unrecognizable. The faith that lies in "honest doubt" – and is thus defined in terms of what is commonly supposed to be its opposite – is unlikely to be recognized by the simple believer for whom "doubt is Devil-born" and whose faith is defined in terms of love: "I cannot understand; I love" (XCVII). It is the concept of love – identified with God and "Creation's finest law" (LVI) – that comes closest to being a constant in *In Memoriam* and a constant object of faith; though at one point even love is seen as capable of degenerating into unattractive forms that are none the less still forms of love – into "mere fellowship of sluggish moods" or, further, into "his coarsest Satyr-shape" (XXXV). The poem's settled concern is, however, with the threats to human love posed by death, the changes and chances of this mortal life and of the speculative hereafter and – with implicit reference to the speaker and Hallam – the necessary but hazardous element of difference between the parties.

The importance of "difference" in *In Memoriam* and in Tennyson's poetry generally can be brought home by the following, wrenched from its context in a much later poem, "The Ancient Sage":

> For Knowledge is the swallow on the lake
> That sees and stirs the surface-shadow there
> But never yet hath dipt into the abysm,
> The Abysm of all Abysms, beneath, within
> The blue of sky and sea, the green of earth,
> And in the million-millionth of a grain
> Which cleft and cleft again for evermore,
> And ever vanishing, never vanishes.

The infinite divisibility of matter was invoked by Tennyson, according to his son, as an argument against materialism: "Look at the mystery of a grain of sand; you can divide it for ever and ever. You cannot conceive anything material of which you cannot conceive the half."[11] ("Half', as K. W. Gransden has pointed out,[12] is a recurring word in Tennyson.) In "The Ancient Sage", as in *In Memoriam* decades earlier, "the Nameless", whatever transcends all change and division, is to be found not in external nature –

> I found Him not in world or sun
> Or eagle's wing or insect's eye –   (CXXIV)

but within the self. The defect of nature emphasized in the later poem is not, however, the amorality and random destructiveness of natural processes but nature's incorrigible plurality. A phenomenal world that differentiates itself *ad infinitum* provides no possible access to that which transcends all difference, the "One" towards which the speaker of *In Memoriam* gropes:

> He, They, One, All; within, without;
> The Power in darkness whom we guess.   (ibid.)

At the close of *In Memoriam* "one" is dominant:

> One God, one law, one element,
> And one far-off divine event,
> To which the whole creation moves.
>   (CXXXI [Epilogue])

Difference is cancelled, at least in prospect, and change contained as progress. Relationship (however conceived) to the "One" demands a "oneness" of the individual soul; but this unity of the self is frustrated by the diversity of the world and of our responses to it.

> O, tell me where the senses mix,
> O tell me where the passions meet,
>
> Whence radiate.   (LXXXVIII)

At such moments we are conscious of Tennyson's affinity with the French Symbolists and, at home, with Walter Pater in his quest for "the focus where the greatest number of vital forces unite in their purest energy".[13] Pater seeks to maintain this focus strictly within a world of flux in which forces are constantly being dispersed – hence, presumably, his paradoxical metaphor of the "hard gemlike flame". Tennyson's epiphanies have more in common with Eliot's "moment in and out of time", though he links his transcendentalism with a Victorian progressivist orientation towards the future: the "one far-off divine event". Progress thus becomes a collective movement in time towards what is eternally present but revealed to us now only in privileged moments that, however convincing at the time, are always vulnerable to retrospective doubt. Such a moment, towards the close of the poem, is the vision of Hallam "mix'd with God and Nature" (CXXX), hence eternal and omnipresent though still inexplicably an individual, the object of personal love. This vision, if only it could be maintained, would be a mystical union not only of two friends but of "Oneness" and difference.

Such a union would end the division by which the self is constituted in the first place. Self is initially defined by difference:

> The baby new to earth and sky,
>   What time his tender palm is prest
>   Against the circle of the breast,
> Has never thought that "this is I":
>
> But as he grows he gathers much,
>   And learns the use of "I", and "me",
>   And finds "I am not what I see,
> And other than the things I touch."
>
> So rounds he to a separate mind
>   From whence clear memory may begin,
>   As through the frame that binds him in
> His isolation grows defined.
>
> This use may lie in blood and breath,
>   Which else were fruitless of their due,

> Had man to learn himself anew
> Beyond the second birth of Death.   (XLV)

The child's progress is dramatized through a shift in signification from a
circle enclosing the world (the infantile world of which he, not yet
distinguished from the mother, is the circumference) to a circle whose circumference excludes him from a world now perceived as separate. It is a
progress that involves losses as well as gains: he "grows", "gathers",
"learns", "finds" but is in a sense dispossessed of what he "sees" and
"touches". He "rounds" – becomes complete in himself – but is
"separated" and "bound" (through a "frame" that constricts as well as
giving shape). The process that defines the self also defines its isolation.
(Compare Arnold's "Yes, in the sea of life enisled".) So ambiguous is the
process that its only conceivable use could be to ensure our spiritual progress beyond the grave.

   Under stress of grief, the speaker has a heightened sense of the difference
by which self is constituted. It is arguably as a stratagem to escape this sense
of estrangement that he pursues similarity in difference, devising similes
for himself and his situation out of the world from which he feels himself
excluded. He is like a happy lover who finds his beloved is not at home
(VIII); a bereaved husband (IX, XIII); the parents of a young girl on her
wedding day (XL); a poor girl hopelessly in love with a man of superior rank
(LX); the humble childhood friend of a great statesman (LXIV); the wife
in an intellectually unequal marriage (XCVII). In all these similes, of
course, Hallam plays the complementary role. Most of them present the
attentive reader with a question: just how "apt" is this simile supposed to
be? In one instance – the simile of the intellectually unequal marriage –
the reader is virtually warned off from pressing it too far: we are told that
the speaker's love, personified as the subject of the enounced, perceives
similarities that, like the spectre of the Brocken, are a hallucinatory projection of itself:

> My love has talk'd with rocks and trees;
>   He finds on misty mountain-ground
>   His own vast shadow glory-crown'd;
> He sees himself in all he sees.   (XCVII)

This mental process recalls the one described by Coleridge in "Frost at
Midnight": "the idling Spirit . . . everywhere / Echo or mirror seeking of
itself". In another instance the potentially consoling simile of the young
girl leaving home on her marriage is elaborated, with highly explicit
reference to Hallam, only to be immediately subverted:

> Ay me, the difference I discern!
>   How often shall her old fireside

> Be cheered with tidings of the bride,
> How often she herself return.   (XL)

The speaker's simile-hunting could be seen, in one aspect, as regressive behaviour: his adult self-concept in disarray, he reverts, in Lacanian terms, to the "mirror-stage" in which the child, growing towards a sense of separate identity, begins to find an image of himself in the "mirror" of other persons and objects. Regressiveness is, after all, something that the speaker – "an infant crying in the night" (LIV) – virtually attributes to himself.

When we come to particular similes, it is often very much up to the reader to determine their precise rhetorical force. What, in a given instance, is the proportionate importance of similarity and of difference? Thus the speaker's comparison of himself to "some poor girl" in love with a man hopelessly beyond her reach (LX) occurs in the first of a series of poems which, Bradley remarks, "are criticised by some readers on the ground that they are written in a tone of excessive and unnatural humility"[14] – as perhaps in the conclusion of this poem:

> At night she weeps, "How vain am I!
> How should he love a thing so low?"   (LX)

Much depends on how closely we assimilate "she" to the speaker. Clearly, if the comparison is to have any point, he must see himself as sharing some of the girl's abjectness. But the effect is also to differentiate him from her; his ability to see himself as "some poor girl" implies a degree of detachment. He is not wallowing in the abjectness of his grief: it might be truer to say that he is wondering at it. He is, to recall the passage from St Augustine, a puzzle to himself. Taken aback by his grief – and perhaps feeling himself unmanned by it – he projects it, in feminine form, as other.

The same sort of question is presented by a later simile in which the departed Hallam is compared to "some divinely gifted man" of humble birth who rises to become "the pillar of a people's hope" and the speaker to a childhood friend

> Who ploughs with pain his native lea
> And reaps the labour of his hands,
> Or in the furrow musing stands:
> "Does my old friend remember me?"   (LXIV)

This simile does more than underline the speculative question: supposing that personality does survive death, how can we be sure that the departed will remember the people they knew in this life? It could be read as conveying the sense of desertion that is a common component of grief. The speaker is less obviously distant from the humble childhood friend than from the "poor girl" in the earlier lyric. Any disparity is rather between Hallam, passively elevated by death, and the upwardly mobile politician, born "on a simple village green",

> Who breaks his birth's invidious bar,
>   And grasps the skirts of happy chance,
>   And breasts the blows of circumstance,
> And grapples with his evil star;
>
> Who makes by force his merit known
>   And lives to clutch the golden keys,
>   To mould a mighty state's decrees,
> And shape the whisper of the throne;
>
> And moving up from high to higher,
>   Becomes on Fortune's crowning slope
>   The pillar of a people's hope,
> The centre of a world's desire.   (LXIV)

Such aggressive and insidious energy, evoked particularly in the verbs, might suggest, among other possible literary precedents, Marlowe's Tamburlaine or at least Dryden's Achitophel. If we seriously press the analogy between Hallam and this lively exponent of the career open to the talents, we may begin to ask what sort of Hallam we are seeing. The answer could be a less innocuous figure than the Hallam that the speaker seems generally concerned to promote. Does the simile open up a further dimension of ambiguity in the speaker's feelings? It admits a variety of readings, all defensible and none definitive.

Both the similes just considered postulate difference between the speaker and the departed Hallam; but difference also characterized their relationship in life. It was indeed the enabling condition of their friendship: "his unlikeness fitted mine" (LXXIX). Not much is ever said of this unlikeness, though it has been hinted at earlier:

> So many worlds, so much to do,
>   So little done, such things to be,
>   How know I what had need of thee,
> For thou wert strong as thou wert true?   (LXXIII)

Hallam's death occurred because his strength was needed elsewhere in a universe imagined as containing many inhabited worlds. "Strong" – like "Strong Son of God" in the Prologue – might also imply a contrast with the speaker. "We are both 'true' but you are 'strong' as well – which is why you are gone elsewhere and I sit lingering here." But Hallam's strength could also conceivably have separated him from the speaker in this world. "Strong" and "true" do not denote incompatible qualities; but there is a suggestion that in practice these qualities could pull in different directions, an intimation of something volatile and uncertain in the relationship. "Unlikeness" between persons, like other forms of difference, has both positive and negative aspects.

It is therefore important that difference should be contained so that it may enrich, not disrupt, a relationship. The value of "unlikeness" is explained in a lyric addressed to Charles Tennyson, that opens by echoing a much earlier one (IX) in which there is a stark opposition between the speaker's love of the deceased and his love for his brothers:

> "More than my brothers are to me," –
> Let this not vex thee, noble heart!
> I know thee of what force thou art
> To hold the costliest love in fee.
>
> But thou and I are one in kind,
>   As moulded like in Nature's mint;
>   And hill and wood and field did print
> The same sweet forms in either mind.
>
> For us the same cold streamlet curled
>   Through all his eddying coves, the same
>   All winds that roam the twilight came
> In whispers of the beauteous world.
>
> At one dear knee we proffered vows,
>   One lesson from one book we learned,
>   Ere childhood's flaxen ringlet turned
> To black and brown on kindred brows.
>
> And so my wealth resembles thine,
>   But he was rich where I was poor,
>   And he supplied my want the more
> As his unlikeness fitted mine.   (LXXIX)

The monetary imagery is appropriate to the quite matter-of-fact appraisal of the two relationships. The speaker and his brother belong to the same currency, "printed" off the same plate, the common experience of natural sights and sounds and of family life. Hallam, however, provided something else that the speaker had come to need: not more of the same but foreign exchange. The fact that this explanation is now possible confirms what the preceding lyric, describing the second Christmas in the narrative sequence, had already indicated: difference, the disruptive element, has been contained.

The second Christmas lyric follows a series of lyrics (LXXIII–LXXVII) which dwell on the destructiveness of change and the ephemerality of fame, particularly poetic fame. The speaker eventually arrives at an implied assurance that, whatever else may yield to change, his love and grief are constant. Or are they? Can there be a last state of grief that is worse than the first?

> O sorrow, then can sorrow wane?
> O grief, can grief be changed to less?

> O last regret, regret can die!　　　　　(LXXVIII)

This fear – that he may lose his hold even on the grief with which he has come to identify himself – is prompted by the contrast with the first Christmas following Hallam's death which had been dominated by "an awful sense / Of one mute Shadow watching all" (XXX). This earlier Christmas is described as an occasion of cruel irony: "The time draws near the birth of Christ" (XXVIII) but Christ, it seems, is stillborn:

> Yet go, and while the holly boughs
> 　Entwine the cold baptismal font,
> 　Make one wreath more for Use and Wont,
> That guard the portals of the house;

> Old sisters of a day gone by,
> 　Gray nurses, loving nothing new;
> 　Why should they miss their yearly due
> Before their time? They too will die.　　　　　(XXIX)

These two quasi-mythological figures, for all their grimness, are guardians of the household, conservative presences that will let nothing threaten its continuity and stability – including the inhibiting effect of Hallam's memory ("How dare we keep our Christmas Eve?"). Under their influence, the family simulates enough Christmas cheer to raise a song proclaiming the faith that the dead do not "lose their mortal sympathy, / Nor change to us, although they change" (XXX). The song is less an expression of faith than a foreshadowing of a faith that will be achieved later. The speaker himself can raise only hope – or, more precisely, a prayer that hope may be possible:

> O Father, touch the east, and light
> 　The light that shone when Hope was born.　　　　　(XXX)

A year later the situation has changed. There are no overt signs of grief and this suggests a new source of grief: the death of grief. But the speaker quickly reassures himself:

> O last regret, regret can die!
> 　No – mixt with all this mystic frame,
> 　Her deep relations are the same,
> But with long use her tears are dry.　　　　　(LXXVIII)

It is quite appropriate that the reassuring address to the speaker's brother should immediately follow this realization. Hallam has now been assimilated into "the mystic frame", the structuring of the self, the pattern of personal thought and feeling as moulded, in part at least, by experience – much of it, in this instance, the experience of family and countryside that the two brothers have shared. "The mystic frame", as its previous use indicates, is also the level of spiritual perception where "truths . . . darkly join" (XXXVI). In the present context it could also be taken to mean the framework of religious custom to which the family conforms, especially at Christmas, and with which the memory of Hallam is now intimately linked. The self is not now seen as structured independently of others and of the (structured) experience it shares with them; so that "the mystic frame" is not limited by the individual's conscious "isolation" (XLV). Or as Tennyson once engagingly put it: "every human being is a vanful of human beings, of those who have gone before him, and of those who form part of his life".[15]

The speaker can now acknowledge to his brother the value of Hallam's "unlikeness" because it is no longer seen as a threat. Difference has been contained. The point is brought out quite explicitly later when the speaker, about to lose his childhood home, is split between "two spirits of a diverse love" – love for the home of his childhood and love for the same place as associated with Hallam. These two loves are both so deeply incorporated into the mystic frame that they "will not yield each other way". As he leaves, however, "They mix in one another's arms / To one pure image of regret" (CII). Hallam has been domesticated – received into the mystic frame as he was received into the family, when alive, as a house guest. Indeed Hallam is constantly a visitor, whether alive or dead, physical or spiritual, actual or imagined – right up to the Epilogue where he is a conjectured "stiller guest" at the wedding. He is recalled as a "welcome guest" at the Christmas before his death (XXIX); he is a shadowy and disturbing guest at the Christmas following (XXX). He is recalled later as coming down as a visitor from London, on which occasion

> He brought an eye for all he saw;
> He mixt in all our simple sports.   (LXXXIX)

And why not? we may ask. But this participation by Hallam, now a sophisticated visitor from the city, is significant as (presumably needed) evidence that he is still one of "us". The awaited arrival of Hallam's corpse is a parody of his visits in life. The role of visitor is also at times assumed by the speaker. Creeping "like a guilty thing" to the door of

Hallam's old home, he is virtually a visitor turned away (VII). He imagines himself as "an honoured guest" in the household of a Hallam still alive and married into the family (LXXXIV). His later mystical (or imagined) encounters with the departed (XCV and CXXX) are still visits – or visitations – by Hallam.

The most distinguished visitor in the poem is, however, Christ in the house of Mary after the raising of Lazarus (XXXII). Mary's eyes on this occasion are "homes of silent prayer", a domestic metaphor paralleled in "household fountains never dry" (CIX) for the inner sources of Hallam's conversation, and, less unusually, "the household jar within" (XCIV) for emotional disturbance. Such images exemplify the status of domesticity in *In Memoriam*. Visits are important because the household is important. It is important that Hallam's body be brought home to England if only because it "flatters . . . home-bred fancies" (X). In contrast is the homelessness of the dead sailor whose "heavy-shotted hammock-shroud / Drops in his vast and wandering grave" (VI). The value of home is evident in the address to Charles Tennyson, as it is – negatively – in the third Christmas lyric when the family has moved from the home of the speaker's childhood and of Hallam's visits to "new unhallowed ground" (CIV). Home, by implication, is consecrated ground and virtually becomes so in the Christmas lyrics. Christ can be seen as the archetypal visitor, and the Incarnation as the domestication of divinity itself.

"Oneness", in this poem, begins, humanly speaking, at home. Home is the locus of value within the social order and, for humanity in its present state, within the cosmic order. The political standpoint of *In Memoriam* derives, directly or not, from Edmund Burke, the Burke of *Reflections on the Revolution in France* (1790). For Burke continuity and stability are assured by an entrenched landed aristocracy and gentry. Tennyson's social perspective has shifted into a lower key: in *In Memoriam*, it is the ordinary household, rather than the large country seat, that ensures the unity and continuity of the national life. The perspective is middle-class and domestic. The preoccupations, however, are very much the same as Burke's. When the newly wedded girl leaves her parents' home

> She enters other realms of love;
>
> Her office there to rear, to teach,
>   Becoming as is meet and fit
>   A link among the days, to knit
> The generations each with each.   (XL)

Denied public distinction, the wife and mother – "the angel in the house" – has nevertheless a crucial role in the body politic: to foster the continuity that, amid the spectacular transformations overtaking modern England, was so much the concern of writers and political thinkers from Scott and Burke onwards. Continuity – "oneness" as it embraces the generations – also begins at home.

The restraining and stabilizing influence of domesticity, institutionalized in marriage, is assumed in a metaphorical address to Sorrow:

> O Sorrow, wilt thou live with me
> No casual mistress, but a wife,
> My bosom-friend and half of life;
> As I confess it needs must be?
>
> O Sorrow, wilt thou rule my blood,
> Be sometimes lovely like a bride,
> And put thy harsher moods aside,
> If thou wilt have me wise and good?
>
> My centred passion cannot move,
> Nor will it lessen from to-day;
> But I'll have leave at times to play
> As with the creature of my love;
>
> And set thee forth, for thou art mine,
> With so much hope for years to come,
> That, howsoe'er I know thee, some
> Could hardly tell what name were thine.   (LIX)

The analogy is here quite close and detailed. The "wife", as her part in a stratagem for keeping the husband "wise and good", is clearly meant to have some of the attributes of the mistress from whom she is distinguished. The stratagem by which the speaker hopes to come to terms with his grief is analogous to marriage as a stratagem for containing male sexuality. And grief is analogous to sexual appetite in so far as grief is a potentially subversive and destructive emotion. The metaphor can be read as very pointedly sustained in the last stanza: "I shall lavish so much adornment on you that people will wonder if you are a respectable married woman at all." Here, as elsewhere, the "I" rhetorically confronts, as other, a divisive element within itself in the hope of containing it.

The speaker's most ambitious stratagem for containing difference and achieving "oneness" is attained in lyric CXXX:

> Thy voice is on the rolling air;
> I hear thee where the waters run;
> Thou standest in the rising sun,
> And in the setting thou art fair.

What art thou then? I cannot guess;
  But tho' I seem in star and flower
  To feel thee some diffusive power,
I do not therefore love thee less:

My love involves the love before;
  My love is vaster passion now;
  Tho' mix'd with God and Nature thou,
I seem to love thee more and more.

Far off thou art, but ever nigh;
  I have thee still, and I rejoice;
  I prosper, circled with thy voice;
I shall not lose thee though I die.   (CXXX)

The cosmic perspective is assimilated. Hallam stands, like a figure from Revelation,[16] in the rising sun. Love and "vastness" are coextensive. Though Hallam is differentiated from nothing – not even clearly from the speaker who feels him as a "diffusive power" – he is none the less still conceived as a distinct object of love. Though he no longer has an individual body, he is none the less "heard" and "felt". The stratagem is highly effective – at least if we suppose the speaker to be entirely convinced of its validity. Difference is banished. Since Hallam is not differentiated from anything, nothing can estrange the speaker from Hallam; equally, Hallam cannot estrange the speaker from anything else. "Oneness" prevails; but relationship (implying difference) somehow remains possible. The speaker, apparently, has it all ways. How much we concern ourselves with the credibility – or intelligibility – of this mystical perspective may depend on how far the text seems to invite us to consider it as the final outcome of the speaker's struggles. If the speaker's final state is not here at all but in the Prologue, then there is no reason to suppose that the experience described is any more a permanent and comprehensive answer to life's problems than are most Romantic epiphanies. This vision of the cosmic Hallam is introduced at the end of the previous lyric:

Behold, I dream a dream of good,
  And mingle all the world with thee.   (CXXIX)

"A dream of good" may be contrasted with another sort of dream:

Are God and Nature then at strife,
  That Nature lends such evil dreams? –   (LV)

"Nature" here being a rather feverish construction of Lyall's *Principles of Geology* and Chambers's *Vestiges of Creation*. The implication could be that since we have no certain knowledge of the nature of things but only "dreams", it is wise to settle for "good" dreams as against "evil" ones. Again, it is the dreamer, the subject of the verb, who mingles Hallam and the world – they do not mingle of their own accord. "Behold, I dream" has the force of "See what I'm doing." Faith is not here a gift of God passively received but an act of will, of that "living will that shalt endure" (CXXXI). To put it in Romantic literary terms, faith here has less in common with Wordsworthian "wise passiveness" than with active Coleridgean imagination, "the shaping spirit".

The actual existence of the object of faith is by no means unhesitatingly maintained, for all the speaker's visionary fervour. The characteristic "seem" occurs in two crucial places. And in the following lyric the "living will" is invoked

> That we may lift from out of dust
>   A voice as unto him that hears –   (CXXXI)

a turn of phrase ("*as* unto") by no means indicating total intellectual confidence that there is indeed "one who hears". Faith is a matter of will, of still trusting, even though less "faintly" than before, the larger hope. The nearest the speaker ever comes to a passive, unsolicited encounter with an independently existing spiritual presence is in the earlier experience when he reads the dead man's letters in the garden at night:

> So word by word and line by line,
>   The dead man touched me from the past,
>   And all at once it seemed at last
> The living soul was flashed on mine.   (XCV)

There is nothing particularly mystical about the initial effect of reading the letters: the dead man "touches" the living through the material signs that trigger memories of his former presence. "Flashed" is certainly a metaphor for some sort of immediate non-physical contact; but it is characteristically qualified by "seemed" and a few lines later we read: "At length my trance / Was cancelled, stricken through with doubt." Furthermore, although it is the speaker who is "touched" and "flashed on", his experience is not entirely passive: it is invited by his act of reading the letters, an act motivated by his "hunger" for the dead man's presence. So even here there is an element of purposive action; and in the end there is no assurance that the invited response, though forthcoming and in excess of what was anticipated, is anything more than an echo of the invitation itself. The experience (*as* experience) is not open to question; its significance, in retrospect, is. Are we to suppose that the "dream" of the cosmic Hallam – rhetorically, far more overtly staged and perhaps far more consciously and deliberately induced – is any less open to retrospective questioning? Not if the Prologue is to be taken, as presumably it is, as evidence of the speaker's final standpoint. There Hallam is no longer a "diffusive power", scarcely distinguishable from Christ as omnipresent Logos. He is unambiguously restored to creaturely status. "He lives in thee" may recall the subsequently described but chronologically earlier vision; but it has quite different implications. Hallam is no longer omnipresent – that is, always "here", always heard, seen and felt throughout nature: he is now "there" – "and there / I find him worthier to be loved". Hallam is still loved but safely distanced – a new stratagem and one perhaps easier to maintain in the teeth of experience and adverse criticism.

The speaker never escapes from "the dialogue of the mind with itself".[17] Difference is never conclusively banished. No "dream of good" is more than one alternative, haunted by the possibility of other dreams. The "living will" – described by Tennyson elsewhere as "that which we know as Free-will, the higher and enduring part of man"[18] – would have no *raison d'être* at all, except in a world of difference where alternatives constantly confront us and rejected alternatives stubbornly refuse to quit the field. In the Prologue faith asserts itself in an indefinitely continuing confrontation with doubt and through a rhetoric that dramatizes the confrontation. It is an act of will that involves an act of the imagination, a choice of "dreams". But imagination remains susceptible to the dream that faith rejects.

Notes

[1] A. C. Bradley, *A Commentary on Tennyson's In Memoriam*, 3rd ed. (London: Macmillan, 1910), p. xii.

[2] Paul de Man, *Allegories of Reading: figural language in Rousseau, Nietzche, Rilke and Proust* (New Haven and London: Yale University Press, 1979), p. 17.

[3] Hallam Tennyson, *Alfred Lord Tennyson, A Memoir*, 2 vols. (London: Macmillan, 1897), vol. 1, p. 304. All subsequent references to the *Memoir* are to the first volume.

[4] Hallam Tennyson, *Tennyson*, p. 312n.

[5] That is, up to and including lyric XXVII. (Corresponding to Part I in Bradley's division of the poem. See Bradley, *In Memoriam*, p. 30.)

[6] Augustine, *Confessions*, IV, 4. Quoted Bradley, *In Memoriam*, p. 86.

[7] Hallam Tennyson, *Tennyson*, p. 305.

[8] Anthony Easthope, *Poetry and Discourse* (London: Methuen [New Accents], 1983) pp. 42–3.

[9] Bradley, *In Memoriam*, p. 93.

[10] Ibid.

[11] Hallam Tennyson, *Tennyson*, p. 319n.

[12] K. W. Gransden, *Tennyson: In Memoriam*, Studies in English Literature No. 22 (London: Edward Arnold, 1964), p. 25.

[13] Walter Pater, *The Renaissance* (New York: New American Library, 1959), Conclusion.

[14] Bradley, *In Memoriam*, p. 157.

[15] Hallam Tennyson, *Tennyson*, p. 323n.

[16] Revelation 19:17. See *The Poems of Tennyson*, ed. Christopher Ricks, Longmans' Annotated English Poets (London, 1969), p. 979n.

[17] Matthew Arnold, Preface to the first Edition of *Poems*, 1853.

[18] Hallam Tennyson, *Tennyson*, p. 319.

Topography and tropography in Thomas Hardy's "In Front of the Landscape"

J. HILLIS MILLER

Take, as an example, Thomas Hardy's poem, "In Front of the Landscape". This is put as the opening text in *Satires of Circumstance* (1914). What is its identity as a text? If this identity arises from relations to previous and later texts and readers, among the most important of these relations are those to other poems by Hardy, for example to the other poems in Hardy's volume of 1914, or, more broadly, to all the poems taken together in *The Complete Poems of Thomas Hardy*. To call "In Front of the Landscape" an example of Hardy's poetry is an example of the falsification involved in assuming that Thomas Hardy is a single person or that his poems taken together form a coherent whole. The differences of "In Front of the Landscape" from any other poem by Hardy are more important, it may be, than any similarities. The poem tells the reader things about "Hardy" she or he can learn only from this poem. If "Wessex Heights" dramatizes the relation the speaker has to the swarm of ghosts from the past when he sees them from the relative detachment of the hilltop, "In Front of the Landscape" describes what it is like, for Hardy, down there in the lowlands.

What is "in front of the landscape" for the speaker of this poem is a great "tide of visions", memories of this or that person from his past. This so overwhelms and drowns him with its immediacy that it almost hides the scene behind. What should be there in the present is rendered ghostlike and insubstantial, as though the landscape were the mist and the mist the substantial reality. Scenes, objects, and persons from the past, "miscalled of the bygone", have more presence and solidity than anything present in the present. It is the presence and force of a great flood ramping over the land and sinking it:

> Plunging and labouring on in a tide of visions,
>   Dolorous and dear,
> Forward I pushed my way as amid waste waters
>   Stretching around,
> Through whose eddies there glimmered the customed landscape
>   Yonder and near.

Blotted to feeble mist. And the coomb and the upland
  Coppice-crowned,
Ancient chalk-pit, milestone, rills in the grass-flat
  Stroked by the light,
Seemed but a ghost-like gauze, and no substantial
  Meadow or mound.[1]

"In Front of the Landscape" is one of Hardy's most grandly rhythmical poems. It is unusually open in its expression of emotion. For once the meter does not seem an arbitrary framework into which certain material is pushed, trimmed to shape. The dactylic meter fits the thematic mood and the organizing figure affirming that memories are like the inundating waters of great sea-swells, wave after wave. The reader will feel the swing and rise of the lines. This rhythm is punctuated by the rhyming of the last line of each stanza with the second line. Each stanza is like a wave finally breaking and crashing. The alternate long and short lines within each stanza give the rhythm of waters moving across a shallow tideland, building up in a slow mounting like a long indrawing breath: "Plunging and labouring on in a tide of visions", and then more rapidly dropping as it is exhaled: "Dolorous and dear". Within the complex wave movement of each stanza a new wave is preparing in the end-word of each fourth line: "Stretching around", "Stroked by the light". These have no rhymes within their own stanzas but hang there in the air, so to speak. They are responded to finally by the first and last short lines in the next stanza. The poem proceeds by way of a braided effect, in a complex rhythm of one wave which completes itself but always contains within itself the doubling or crossing rhythm of the next preparing wave. This interweaving is reinforced by frequent grammatical enjambment from one stanza to the next, as in the two stanzas quoted above. In the last stanza of all the last two short lines rhyme: "Round him that looms"; "Save a few tombs?"

I have said that the poem is unusual among Hardy's in its rhythmical majesty. It is like some grand organ fugue. The poem is unusual also in its match of rhythm and theme, its frank yielding to the fallacy of imitative form. The rhythm is not only obviously meant to mime the movement of tidal waves but is also meant to mime what the figure mimes: the inundation of the poet by waves or visionary memories. There is no actual water named anywhere in the poem, only the figure of water introduced in the initial phrase "tide of visions". This is then made explicitly figurative in a simile later in the poem: " – Yea, *as* the rhyme / Sung by the sea-swell, so in their pleading dumbness / Captured me these" (my italics). To put this another way, the words of the poem are themselves the incarnation of the tide of visions. The poem is a repetition once more, after the fact (since the poem is in the past tense), of what was itself a repetition of those earlier scenes. The figure of the waves is an element in a series projected backward from the present attempt to give experience form in poetry toward the past moment when the poet took his walk. It is as true to say that the figure of the waves names the musical, rhythmical, rhyming form of the poem itself as that it names the form the experience intrinsically had when it occurred.

In Hardy's poetry, even in this one, more obviously in many others, there is always more or less discrepancy between the rigid stanzaic pattern and the material put into it. Once the pattern is set up it goes on repeating itself from stanza to stanza, coercing whatever it is Hardy wants to say into taking that shape. The past experience is repeated in a new form which has its own intrinsic power of replication. This occurs for example whenever the poem is re-read and its form takes shape once more in the mind of the reader. What "In Front of the Landscape" communicates is not the "original original" experiences to which it refers and not the repetitions of those in the "original" experience when the speaker took his walk and confronted his tide of visions. What the poem communicates is itself, its own form. The figure of the waves names that form.

The signs of this "present" activity, the craftsmanship involved in the writing of the poem, include the artifice of the difficult stanza pattern and rhyme scheme. These are evidence of present choice and deliberate work to make the words fit. Another sign of poetic work, often present in Hardy's poetry, is a slowing down of the forward rhythmic movement of the poem in the counter-movement of a careful choice, one by one, so it seems, of words or phrases. Many of these seem slightly odd, unexpected, or out of place. The reader, if he is a teacher, may have a subliminal desire to write "dic." in the margin, until he has thought more about the lines and comes to see how right the word or phrase is: "brinily trundled"; "harrowed"; "unreason"; "wryness"; "misprision"; "corporate"; "frilled"; "scantly"; "perambulates". It is a feature of Hardy's poetry that he gets away with or even admirably exploits words which hardly any other poet would dare use at all. Often these words are harsh monosyllables slowing the line down almost to a halt, as word follows word: "Cheeks that were fair in their flush-time, ash now with anguish." Or the words may be polysyllables full of clogged consonants, technical or archaic words, words not in everyone's vocabulary, like "brinily" or "misprision". This slowing down by word choice is a counter-pointed rhythm fighting against the swelling forward wave-like movement. The reader can see the poet feeling his way along the line, choosing word after word carefully, after much thought. He chooses each word not only for its more exact correspondence to the experience in the past he wants the poem to duplicate but for its creation of an integument of signs, there on the page. These will have a coercive power over the reader, as the notation of musical sounds in a score, when played aloud again, will, to borrow a formulation from *Tess of the d'Urbervilles*, "lead" the listener "through sequences of emotion, which [the composer] alone had felt at first" (ch. 13). It is impossible to tell whether these sequences of emotion were intrinsic to the original experience which the poem records or whether they are created by the formal properties of the poem as Hardy has happened to compose it. The reader has access only to the poem. We cannot compare it with anything which it might seem to copy.

The great tide of visions of which the poem speaks is made of scenes, such as the "headland of hoary aspect / Gnawed by the tide", or of objects, for example "Instruments of strings with the tenderest passion / Vibrant, beside / Lamps long extinguished, robes", but most of all of persons with whom the poet had once been associated over the various times of his past life. These are, to borrow some fine phrases from "Wessex Heights", "shadows of beings who fellowed with myself of earlier days" (CP, p. 319). The sequence from musical instruments to lamps and robes continues with the fine irony of "cheeks, eyes with the earth's crust / Now corporate". The poet detaches parts of the bodies of those he has known and lists them as vanished objects like the rest. He thinks of them now as parts of the vast corporate body of the earth. Of that body we will all one day be members. These persons are now apparently all buried in the graveyard which is the goal of his long walk through the Wessex countryside:

> So did beset me scenes, miscalled of the bygone,
>   Over the leaze,
> Past the clump, and down to where lay the beheld ones.

It has been suggested by Hermann Lea that the scene of the poem is "Came Down near Culliver Tree", about three miles south of Dorchester. J. O. Bailey has observed that there is a chalk-pit nearby to match the one mentioned in stanza two of the poem, as well as many burial tumuli "scattered in all directions from this point".[2] The latter may be referred to in the last lines. Those lines imagine passers-by wondering who this dull perambulating form is who walks where there is nothing to see "save a few tombs". But the phrase, "where lay

the beheld ones", must refer to a modern burial ground, perhaps
the one southward in Weymouth, perhaps the ones northward in
Dorchester or in Stinsford. Though all these old associates are now
dead, this does not keep them from appearing before the poet as
"infinite spectacles", "speechful faces, gazing insistent". These walking ghosts have so much solidity that they are "hindering [him] to
discern [his] paced advancement / Lengthening to miles". The ghosts
of the old associates apparently do not speak (though in one place he
says he can "hear them"), but they have "speechful faces". Their
"dumb pleading" is a double reproach. It is a reproach to the speaker
for not having appreciated them sufficiently when they were alive and
it is a reproach for his having in any case later on betrayed them. On
the one hand:

> For, their lost revisiting manifestations
>   In their live time
> Much had I slighted, caring not for their purport,
>   Seeing behind
> Things more coveted, reckoned the better worth calling
>   Sweet, sad, sublime.

It appears to be a law, in this poem, if not necessarily always in
Hardy, that what you have in the present as an actual physical presence
you do not really have. The fact that something is there and that you
possess it makes it seem worthless. It also makes it impossible to
understand its "purport". The mind and feelings always look beyond
or behind what is possessed now to what is not possessed. Those always
seem more desirable, more valuable. What you have you do not have.
You do not have it in the sense of neither understanding it nor valuing
it. What you have and understand in the sense of "reckoning" it as this
or as that, "sweet", "sad", or "sublime", you do not have. Only later
on, when they come back "before the intenser stare of the mind", intenser, that is, than the look of his "bypast / Body-borne eyes", intenser than any real stare at what is physically present, only when they
come back as avenging ghosts, are they comprehended. Only then are
they read, interpreted, deciphered, "with fuller translation than rested
upon them / As living kind".

The irony of "In Front of the Landscape" is that the speaker is
recalling a walk in which he committed again the crime he deplores.
The real landscape is scarcely seen by the walker and not valued by
him. His eyes, his attention, his feelings are all intensely focussed on
what in this case is not behind what is immediately present but in front
of it, between him and it. He sees only what is not any longer the
desired and as yet unpossessed future but the betrayed past. In either

case, however, in either desire or regret, the detachment from what is actually there is almost total. It is as though Hardy goes through the world always out of phase. He dwells in anticipation or in memory. He never lives in other than a false appearance of the present. He always lags behind in his efforts to "translate" the people and places he encounters. This anachronism can never by any means be put back into harmonious chiming. There is always a delay before the feedback, and the feedback always comes too late. While he is occupied in "reckoning" at last the worth and purport of something he once had but undervalued, misread, he is already confronting a new scene which his preoccupation is leading him once more to misvalue and misread. He is thereby storing up for himself yet further times in the future when he will suffer again the pangs of retrospective understanding. It will then once more be too late. The effort of retrospection will then once more put swarms of ghosts like an almost impenetrable fog or like an obliterating flood between him and the real scene, the real present. That present he will once more misvalue.

On the one hand, then, the ghosts reproach him for not having understood and valued them when they were alive and bodily present, before his body-borne eyes. On the other hand they also reproach him for having in any case betrayed them thereafter. The lines stating this are central to the poem. Their difficulty calls for commentary:

> O they were speechful faces, gazing insistent,
>   Some as with smiles,
> Some as with slow-born tears that brinily trundled
>   Over the wrecked
> Cheeks that were fair in their flush-time, ash now with anguish,
>   Harrowed by wiles.

The faces of the phantoms pass him in a beseeching procession, some "as with" smiles, some "as with" tears. The repeated "as with" is odd. Does the poet mean that the ghosts do not not really either smile or cry? Or does he mean that he could not quite make out their features? Or does he mean, as perhaps is most probable, that the speech of these "speechful faces, gazing insistent" is the expressiveness of their features, so that it is as if they were speaking to him with their smiles or with their tears? The puzzle is a good example of the grammatical, syntactical, and lexical difficulty of Hardy's poetry. Overwhelmed by the great flood of their abundance, the reader hurries on from poem to poem, moving toward those generalizations which will allow him to encompass the whole. If he is at all a "good" reader, he will nevertheless constantly be slowed down or even stopped by local difficulties.

These must be brooded on and meditated over. They must be teased for their just meaning before the reader can proceed even to the next lines, much less to all the other poems.

If the faces of the ghosts are "speechful" because they speak to him "as with" their smiles or their tears, when the poet says in the next stanza that he can "hear them" he may mean that he reads their legible features as though they were audible sounds, not that the ghosts actually speak aloud. The lines of the smiles and the wrinkles that have been carved into the cheeks of the ghosts by their suffering, "Harrowed" by "wiles" in the literal sense of being trenched out, as well as in the figurative sense of "worn by fear or anxiety", are deciphered as speaking signs. They are interpreted as "insistent" messages of reproach, "pleading dumbness", beseeching demands for response from the poet whom they haunt. The pervasive image of the waves of waste waters is obliquely present in the image of the tears that "brinily trundled / Over the wrecked / Cheeks". It is as though the faces were battered ships aground in a storm dripping with salt water cascading down from the last wave which has just washed over them. If the poet is overwhelmed by a tide of visions, each separate ghost too swims bathed in the universal medium of the total simultaneous presence of all the scenes, places, objects, and persons from the poet's past. There is a congruence between the form of a book of Hardy's poems, or the whole volume of them taken together in *The Complete Poems*, and the poet's mind as he presents it in "Wessex Heights", or, in a different way, in "In Front of the Landscape". Both book and mind are capacious spaces filled pellmell in profusion with an incoherent multitude of persons, scenes, and actions all going on at once side by side, without touching and without connection. Each is a detached fragment of a life story missing its context before and after.

If the stanza quoted above contains puzzles which slow down the reader or ought to slow him down, this is even more true of the following stanza:

> Yes, I could see them, feel them, hear them, address them –
> Halo-bedecked –
> And, alas, onwards, shaken by fierce unreason,
> Rigid in hate,
> Smitten by years-long wryness born of misprision,
> Dreaded, suspect.

If the reader can guess what the poet means by saying he can "hear" the ghosts when they do not speak, what is he to make of the claim that he can also "feel" the ghosts? A ghost by definition is impalpable, and yet somehow the word seems right for the coercive intimacy, like an urgent touch, with which the phantoms appeal to him and "capture" him in their "pleading dumbness". A formulation by Jacques Derrida in "Télépathie"[3] is strangely apposite here. It is as though, by a species of telepathy, Derrida has written his sentence with this line of Hardy (which he has never read) in mind. He seems to have had a premonition of a critic's need, at some point in the future, to account for the strange presence of "feel them" in Hardy's sequence. This is an example of the theme of Derrida's essay, which I have elsewhere discussed more fully in its relation to Hardy's poetry.[4] "Before 'seeing' or 'hearing'," says Derrida, "touch, put your fingertips there, or [it seems] that seeing and hearing amount to touching at a distance – a very old idea, but it requires the archaic to deal with the archaic."[5]

The poet can see the ghosts, hear them in their pleading dumbness. He can even (therefore) feel them, as though seeing and hearing were touching at a distance, in this case a distance of years, or as if he were doubting Thomas palping the wound in the side of the resurrected "halo-bedecked" Christ, or as if the ghosts were putting an importunate insistent hand on his arm. He can also "address them", presumably to plead with them in justification of his past actions toward them. The four lines which conclude the stanza are fundamentally ambiguous. It is impossible to be sure whether the "onwards", and all that grammatically hangs from it, the series of four participles, "shaken", "smitten", "dreaded", "suspect", apply to the ghosts, as is most probably the case, or, as would be an equally possible reading of the syntax, whether the "onwards" applies to the poet, the "I" which is the "subject" of the sentence:

> And, alas, onwards, shaken by fierce unreason,
>> Rigid in hate,
> Smitten by years-long wryness born of misprision,
>> Dreaded, suspect.

This can either mean that the procession of ghosts passes majestically and silently on, unappeased by the poet's appeal, unforgiving, or that the poet himself moves "onwards", as in fact he does, shaken, smitten, and twisted to wryness by the ghosts' misunderstanding of him. Even though the former is more likely, the latter remains hovering as a possibility for the reader (for this reader at least) as he tries to identify the reference of "shaken", smitten", "dreaded", "suspect". Even if a decision is made about that, if the reader decides, for example, that it must be the ghosts who move onwards, the participles in all their violence remain undecidable in meaning. They oscillate between active

and passive possibilities. Are the ghosts "rigid in hate" because they
are shaken by the "fierce unreason" of the speaker who has taken them
wrongly, twisted them to a "years-long wryness" by his "misprision"
of them, or is their refusal to accept the explanation offered by the
speaker's address to them a case of "fierce unreason", a taking wrongly
of the speaker's treatment of them? It cannot be decided which. The
power of the lines is the way they vibrate, affirming both possibilities,
and neither unequivocally. Are the ghosts "dreaded" by the speaker,
"suspected" by him, because they are so fiercely unreasonable and
so bent on taking revenge? They would then take revenge by continuously haunting him, showing "hourly before the intenser stare of
the mind / As they were ghosts avenging their slights by my bypast /
Body-borne eyes". Or is it the speaker who is "dreaded" and "suspect"
in the sense that the ghosts abhor him without reason, unreasonably
blaming him for having taken them wrongly?

There is no way to tell, nor is there any way to tell whether the
"misprision" in question is the mistaking of the ghosts by the speaker,
who took them wrongly in the sense of misprizing them when they
were alive, "caring not for their purport", or whether the ghosts are
twisted into wryness by *their* misprision of the speaker's attitude
toward them. "Misprision" – the word means etymologically "take
wrongly", from late Latin *minusprehendere*, from Latin, *minus*, less,
plus *prehendere*, to take. "Misprision" has lately been restored by
Harold Bloom to its now archaic meaning of "mistake" by being used
to name the misinterpretation of the writings of an earlier writer by a
later who is influenced by that earlier writer. Hardy too uses the word
here to name a misreading of one person by another. Misprision is a
misinterpretation of the signs presented by the faces and features of
others, whether fair in their flush-time or marked by lines of care and
smitten to wryness. Misprision also has an overtone of "misprizing".
Its strict modern meaning is a double one. It means either the miscon-
duct or neglect of duty of a public official, for example in wrongfully
appropriating public funds, or "misprision of felony (or treason)". The
latter is a term used in common law to define the offense of concealing
knowledge of a felony or treason by one who has not participated in
it. Both these meanings resonate in Hardy's line. The ghosts may be
smitten to wryness by having been misappropriated by the speaker or
by others, taken wrongly, or there may be some crime somewhere,
some treasonous betrayal, either on their part or on the part of the
speaker, which they have wrongly concealed or which they have suffered for because it has been wrongly concealed by others. In any case,
there is a lot of guilt around somewhere. It is a guilt born of betrayal

of trust. Both the ghosts and the speaker are suffering intensely for it. Exactly what betrayal is in question for each of the ghosts the reader is not told. He knows only that they were once fair and happy and that the speaker "fellowed" with them. Later they were betrayed by him or by others, or thought they were betrayed. They suffered intensely for this, so intensely as to be left, even after death, with a fierce, implacable, unreasonable desire for revenge. No reason is given for these betrayals nor for these misprisions. They just happened. By the time the speaker is able to appreciate the "purport" of these persons now dead and enghosted, it is too late. Not only are they dead. They are wholly unforgiving, rigid in hate of him.

The phrase "fierce unreason" may be given a wide application as an accurate description of many aspects of Hardy's poetry. "Unreason": the word suggests an absence of *logos* in all its senses of reason, meaning, word, mind, measure, or ground. The word "fierce" is as important as the word "unreason". It names the psychic and spiritual violence of Hardy's experience and of the experience the poems inflict on the reader. The relation between one person and another in Hardy's poetry, or in this poem at least, is the fierce unreason of a multiple betrayal. This betrayal has no reason and leads to a hatred exceeding reason. The poet himself is the victim of a fierce unreason which makes it impossible for him to remain of one mind long enough to be a single continuous self. At the same time he is unable to escape enough from his earlier selves to avoid being unreasonably persecuted by ghosts remaining in his mind from the acts of those earlier selves. He can neither be continuous with those earlier selves nor discontinuous enough to free himself from himself, and so he suffers from the fierce unreason of this anomaly. What David Hume describes objectively enough as a lack of substance and consistency in the self,[6] Hardy experiences as intense suffering born of the co-presence of continuity and discontinuity. He has the continuity of an elephant's memory and the discontinuity of a butterfly's inability to remain the same self for longer than the duration of a brief episode in his life. This inability has no reason or is given no reason. It is an unreasonable fact.

Fierce unreason defines well enough, finally, the local lack of reason, in the sense of single determinate meaning, in the verbal texture of Hardy's verse, however straightforward in meaning that verse first appears to be. The unreadable oscillations in meaning I have identified are born of syntactical, grammatical, and lexical ambiguities. They impose on the reader a sense of fierce unreason, the lack of a firm ground in a single meaning, as he struggles to make univocal sense of what Hardy is saying. This local ambiguity is matched on a larger scale by

the "unreason" of the poems' inconsistency with one another, if Hardy
is right (and he is) in what he repeatedly says, in his prefaces to individual books of poems, of his poems' lack of a coherent philosophy.
They cannot be made to hang together, neither individually nor collectively. The poems too are cases of "fierce unreason". They respond to
the reader's search for a comprehensive logic with a violence of
repudiation undoing all his attempts to "translate" them into an order
satisfying to the mind.

Hardy's use of the word "translate" must be scrutinized more
carefully as a translation to the last step in my interpretation of "In
Front of the Landscape". The word appears in the last line of the next-
to-last stanza. The phantoms who haunt the intenser stare of the poet's
mind, almost blotting out the real landscape behind, now "Show, too,
with fuller translation than rested upon them / As living kind". This
leads to the last stanza, with its altered rhyme scheme of closure and
with its shift to an imagining of what the speaker must look like to
others who see him on such walks and of what they must say of him:

> Hence wag the tongues of the passing people, saying
>   In their surmise,
> "Ah – whose is this dull form that perambulates, seeing nought
>   Round him that looms
> Whithersoever his footsteps turn in his farings,
>   Save a few tombs?"

"In Front of the Landscape" seems in many ways compatible with
"Wessex Heights". Both are poems in which the speaker confronts
swarms of ghosts from his past. He confronts also his own past selves
and experiences the pain of being neither wholly different nor wholly
the same, neither wholly continuous nor wholly discontinuous with
himself. In "Wessex Heights", however, the act of physically climbing
the heights gives the speaker at least a partial detachment from those
past selves and those past relationships. He knows "some liberty" (*CP*,
320), a liberty like that of being not yet born or already dead and a
revisiting ghost haunting others. "In Front of the Landscape", on the
contrary, offers no hope of liberation. The poet remains in the
lowlands, haunted by implacable avenging phantoms. Neither the poet
nor the poem get anywhere, in spite of the poet's movement across the
landscape. They get nowhere but perhaps to a better understanding of
where he is. The poet remains in the same situation at the end as he
was in the beginning. The poem can end only with a shift to the different perspective of the imagined watchers of his "perambulations".
The poem does not record a movement toward liberation. It iterates
rather the fact that no liberty is possible.

Something has happened in the poem, however. The poem itself has got written. This act is the covert dramatic action of the poem. This action is a shift from passive suffering to verbal praxis. This is the linguistic moment in this poem. The shift from "experience" to "language" is covertly signalled in the shift from the past to the present tense at the beginning of the penultimate stanza: "Thus do they now show hourly before the intenser / Stare of the mind". The stanzas until then are in the past tense. They record something which occurred to the poet at some time in the past, something he suffered. With the change to the present tense pathos becomes action. This action is within the poem. It is performed by its words. What takes place takes place within the space of the poem. It is translated there, carried over into the pages of a book.

This "translation" is a successful defense. It is an impressive act of will to power over the ghosts. In the poem the ghosts are no longer intense presences which can almost palpably be felt. They are now no more than words. Though, for Hardy, ghosts in their literal form have power to hurt even more than sticks and stones, when they are turned into words, "translated", they will never hurt him. One motivation driving Hardy to write so many poems and to derive such satisfaction from it[7] is that the writing functions as a successful "trope of defense" against all those reproaching and beseeching phantoms from his past. Writing is a "trope" in the literal sense of turning, displacement, or transformation. "Translation" – the word translates *translatio*. The latter is a traditional rhetorical term in Latin, for example in Quintilian's *Institutio Oratorio*. *Translatio* translates the Greek *metaphora*, "metaphor". The linguistic moment in this poem is a triple act of translation: the translation of the phantoms the poet's mind beholds into words; the translation of the phantoms into metaphor, the metaphor of the tide of visions which underlies and pervades all this poem; the translation or transportation of the phantoms into the formal order of the poem. They are transposed not just into words, but into words architecturally or musically ordered. Within this order all those ghosts and the scenes, objects, episodes which are their contexts can exist side by side, just as all Hardy's poems, in spite of their discord, exist side by side in Hardy's *The Complete Poems*. This complex act of translation is not, as it first seems, a seeing clearly for the first time these people and their true "purport". It is a metaphorical transformation. It is a misreading or distortion, as all translation, for example from one language to another, necessarily is. In the act of defending himself from the reproach the phantoms make that they have not been seen clearly, that they have been misprized, Hardy commits again the crime of misprision from which he would defend himself. He commits it blatantly, out there in the open, on the page, where all who read may see. Therefore another poem in self-defense must be written. This commits the crime once more, and so yet another is necessary, *ad infinitum*. The poet never has a chance to catch up with his past transgressions. He cannot compensate for them, do justice to his past at last, pay off his debt to himself and to others, and wipe his slate clean. The act of compensation, the plea of innocence in response to the phantoms' recriminations, always turns into another act of self-incrimination.

This failure is also the triumph of the poetry. It is only by this constantly repeated act of misprision that Hardy can successfully defend himself and maintain his integrity. It is the integrity not of a self but of a grammatical function producing ultimately that disharmony of *The Complete Poems* Hardy so insists on in the prefaces. The individual acts of defense, turning perception into language, are more important than their hanging together.

It would appear at first that "In Front of the Landscape" depends on the experience of disjunction between the actual landscape and those mental visions which intervene for the speaker between his eye and the scene, blotting it to feeble mist. The poem, it seems, exemplifies that law of Hardy's experience which says you never have or prize what "is" in the present, but always look before and after, and pine for what is not. The fundamental categories of the poem, it seems, are perception and interpersonal relations. The poem has to do with seeing and not seeing, and with struggles for power, by way of appropriation and misappropriation, between one person and another. The speaker cannot see the landscape because its place has been taken by the phantoms who exercise a coercive power over him, captivating him: "so in their pleading dumbness / Captured me these".

Is this in fact the case? If the full implications of the word "translation" are accepted, the word "misprision" is tipped toward that secondary meaning it can have of mistaking or misreading rather than of simply misappropriating. The speaker's original misprision of the phantoms was a mistaken interpretation of the signs they displayed, their "purport", what they said and what their features showed as legible tokens. The activity the poem first records as having taken place in the past and then, with the shift to the present tense, enacts within itself, is also an activity of "translation". This means it is mistranslation or misreading, a doing violence to the signs he sees. The signs now misread, however, are not merely, or not originally, those internal ones of memory. They are the tombs scattered around the landscape, perhaps initially the many prehistoric tumuli which dot the region where Hardy was walking, but also the graves of the dead friends, lovers, and relatives whose ghosts Hardy sees. He looks across the scene and then walks "Over the leaze, / Past the clump, and down to where lay the beheld ones". The passers-by who see him out walking know that he "sees nought", wherever his footsteps take him, "save a few tombs". The poet transforms those tombs. He translates them into the tide of visions the poem so eloquently names. Far from being detached from the landscape, the speaker's linguistic activity in the poem, like the past crimes of misprision he deplores, is based on taking features of the visual scene, in this case not faces but tombs, as signs, not merely as perceptual objects, as they are for the passers-by. These signs are then translated. This activity transforms the neutral notation of topographical description into what might be called a tropography. This tropography is the mapping of an act of figuration which is both Hardy's crime and his defense.

The poem, words on the page, is the monument or tomb of this act. The linguistic act of "translation" is not a figure for perception. Perception is translation. This means the writing of the poem is not the record of the appearance of the ghosts. The writing is the act which raises the ghosts by turning dead signs into beseeching phantoms. The poem in turn, as the remnant of its writing, becomes dead letters once more waiting for some reader to "translate" it again and to raise again the ghosts which inhabit it. In doing so the reader commits in his turn the crime of misprision which the poem both regrets and commits. In this case too, the linguistic moment has a momentum which leads to its repetition time after time, without hope of ever laying the ghosts once and for all.

Once again, as in passages by Wordsworth I have elsewhere discussed, but also in passages in Hegel and in Baudelaire,[8] among many others, in a tradition already present in the Greek pun on *soma/sema* (body/sign), the relation between a dead body and the mound or tomb above it, or between the corpse and the inscription on the tombstone above it, figures the complex relation between perception and language, or between language and its necessary material substrate – the stone, paper, or modulated air on which it is inscribed. The passers-by see the tombs as tombs, as harmless and insignificant matter. Hardy tells the reader in "In Front of the Landscape" that the robes, cheeks, and eyes of those he once loved are "with the earth's crust / Now corporate", and that others who "had shared in the dramas" are now "clay cadavers". The dead are not just dead. They are turned to earth, incorporated in it, dispersed into the landscape. To see that landscape is to see the dead, or it is to see what they now are, harmless mounds on the earth. The "intenser stare" of Hardy's mind resurrects those clay cadavers. It translates them back into what they were. It then transforms them into a "tide". This activity at first seems to be one of perception ("stare"). It then emerges as in fact an act of writing ("translation"). This act of translation is the writing of the poem itself. The poem is written as it were on or over those mounds, tombs, clay cadavers. The poem is a species of epitaph, an inscription on a tombstone, *sema* over *soma*.

There is more to be said of this act of inscription.[9] It is, as all epitaphs tend to be, also an act of invocation, an apostrophe or prosopopoeia addressing the absent, the dead, and thereby raising the ghosts of the dead. Though prosopopoeia overlaps with catachresis, as is evident from the way so many catachreses are personifications or anthropomorphisms, e.g. face of a mountain, leg of a chair, prosopopoeia differs fundamentally from catachresis in a curious way. Though, as the word prosopopoeia suggests (*prosopon* is "mask" in Greek), personification gives a face to what no longer has one or never had one, it is at the same time an act of effacement or defacement, while catachresis makes things appear by naming them. Catachresis has to do with the phenomenal, the visible, the aesthetic in the Hegelian sense of "shining forth". Prosopopoeia, on the other hand, always buries what it evokes in the apostrophic praise, like Antony speaking over the dead body of Caesar. Prosopopoeia effaces what it gives a face to by making it vanish into the earth and become "a body wholly body",[10] *soma* without *sema*, or *soma* coming into the open as the material base of *sema*, as no longer overt personification but now effaced catachresis become mere literal name, like a tombstone with the letters worn away or a coin rubbed smooth, "effaced".

Hardy in "In Front of the Landscape" raises the dead from their tombs, where they have become "clay cadavers", their "eyes with the earth's crust / Now corporate". He is confronted and indicted for his betrayals by those "speechful faces gazing insistent", "halo-bedecked". At the same time this drama of personification has been dispersed unostentatiously or in effaced form throughout the whole landscape or in the literal words the poet uses to name the aspects of that landscape. The upland is "Coppice-crowned", as though it were a king's head, the light "strokes" the landscape, and if one of the images from the past which rises to haunt the poet is "the one of the broad brow", the cliffs by the sea are named as "a headland of hoary aspect / Gnawed by the tide, / Frilled by the nimb of the morning". "Headland" is not metaphor. It is the "proper" name for this topographical feature, though of course a cliff by the sea is not properly speaking a head. It is another personifying catachresis, and the reader may not even notice, so effaced is the linguistic action, so easy to take for granted, that the lines project into the landscape exactly the same image of a halo-fringed head, in this case that of an old man ("of hoary aspect") that the reader has already encountered in the description of the ghosts the speaker confronts as he advances through his tide of visions. These ghosts are no more than the embodiment or bringing into the open, like a photograph being developed, or an inscription in invisible ink being made to appear, of something already dispersed everywhere in the landscape in the ordinary language anyone could use to name it. To recognize this turns the ghosts back into language or disperses them back into the earth's crust. They are no more than a trick of words, and to see this is to lay the ghosts and to confront mere earth.

Moreover, the two lovers who once stood on the headland "touched by the fringe of an ecstasy / Scantly descried" should have taken warning from the scene around them, for what is going on there is a grotesque horrible Dantesque scene of a halo-nimbed head being gnawed by some remorseless creature, apparently another head, as in Ugolino's gnawing of Ruggierri's nape in Inferno XXXII and XXXIII. If the sea can chew, it must have teeth, a mouth, eyes, a face, though the prosopopoeia is evanescent, latent, once more effaced. This horrible drama proleptically figures the relation of mutual paingiving which all human love, for Hardy, comes to in the end, even love like that between the two guilelessly glad friends who stood there on the headland touched by the fringe of an ecstasy. The image of the sea wearing away the land, as one head might gnaw at another, also figures the ultimate engulfment of each distinct shape or form, for example each living human body, by the shapeless matter which will eventually reincorporate it, as a cadaver is consumed, decomposes, and disperses into the earth. The figure, finally, figures the activity it itself manifests in effaced or scarcely manifested form, namely the effacement of the inaugural figures by which man takes possession of nature. These figures vanish into the innocently "literal" language whereby, for example, we call a cliff by the sea a "headland". If "In Front of the Landscape" brings those "dead metaphors" back to life, it also kills them again by exposing their base in baseless habits of language, projecting life where there is none. These habits no one, not even the greatest poet, with his matchless mastery of language, can either fully efface or fully control. He can neither do without that form of translation called prosopopoeia, nor can he safely manipulate it for his own ends.

"In Front of the Landscape" develops a tropographical ratio: as the perception transfiguring the landscape is to that landscape as it is in itself, neutral and harmless earth, so the poem as language is to its material base, the indifferent body which in one way or another is necessary to support any inscription, for example the paper on which Hardy's poems are printed. This ratio is a false or misleading one, since what appears to be the literal base of the metaphorical transposition, "perception", does not, it turns out, exist as such for Hardy at all. Perception is the figure and reading is the literal activity, in more senses than one, "lettering" and "real" at once, of which perception is the figure. Perception for Hardy does not literally exist. It is always already translation. It is an activity that posits, reading, misreading, transposing, dead earth as signs. For Hardy, the identity of the literary text is this proliferating act of translation. This act repeats itself before and behind within the poem. It is again repeated again whenever you or I or another read the poem.

Notes

[1] Thomas Hardy, *The Complete Poems*, New Wessex edition, ed. James Gibson (London: Macmillan, 1976), p. 303, hereafter referred to as *CP*.

[2] J. O. Bailey, *The Poetry of Thomas Hardy: a handbook and commentary* (Chapel Hill, North Carolina: The University of North Carolina Press, 1970), pp. 261–2.

[3] Jacques Derrida, "Télépathie", *Furor*, 2 (1981), 5–41.

[4] In an essay on Hardy's poem "The Torn Letter", "'Jacques Derrida and the 'Dislocation of Souls'", in *Taking Chances: Derrida, psychoanalysis and literature*, ed. Joseph H. Smith and William Kerrigan (Baltimore and London: Johns Hopkins University Press, 1984), pp. 134–45.

[5] Derrida, "Télépathie", pp. 15–16, my translation.

[6] In "Of Personal Identity", section 6 of Book I, Part IV of *A Treatise of Human Nature* (1739).

[7] The poet's second wife noted that her husband was never so happy as when he had finished writing another gloomy poem.

[8] In "The Stone and the Shell: Wordsworth's dream of the Arab", *Moments Premiers* (Paris: Corti, 1973), pp. 125–47. Paul de Man discusses related passages from Hegel and Baudelaire in an essay on Michael Riffaterre, forthcoming in *The Resistance to Theory* (Minneapolis: University of Minnesota Press, 1986).

[9] I am indebted here to astute comments made orally by Patricia Parker when an earlier version of this essay was presented as a lecture at the University of Toronto.

[10] Wallace Stevens, "The Idea of Order at Key West", *The Collected Poems* (New York: Alfred A. Knopf, 1954), p. 128.

Yeats in theory

DANIEL O'HARA

One of the more remarked but less closely pondered aspects of American critical theory over the last four or so decades is the persistent centrality of Yeats to its development.[1] I can think of no other modern literary figure, with the possible exceptions of Stevens or Joyce, whose work has been so seminally influential. The major critical movements from the 1940s to the 1970s – New Criticism, archetypal and phenomenological criticism, and a variety of post-structuralist discourses (revisionary psychoanalytic criticism, dialectical hermeneutics, and deconstruction) all owe a considerable debt to Yeats.[2] Whether as sublime master of the concrete universal, demonic adversary of genuine Romantic visionaries, or seductive forerunner of the vertiginous interplay of self-subverting tropes, Yeats has repeatedly appeared as a representative case in point.

Belated ironic modernist or last decadent romantic: the course of Yeats's reputation has run between these extreme positions. But in the different quests to know their own "Yeats" for theoretical purposes, his American metacritics, in so far as they appear to have even partially succeeded in this endeavor, have suffered strange fates. Their imaginations, whether they are of the systematic kind or not, have been brought face to face with the poverty of their own inventiveness, in a manner that resembles nothing so much as the climactic expressions of those few more sensitive protagonists in Joyce's *Dubliners*. As they finally confront the deadly if curiously alluring work of the spiritual paralysis then afflicting Irish culture, they become affecting instances of what they dread to behold all around them – transparent figures of paralysis fixed fast in a profound and permanent attitude of imaginative defeat, caught within the prison of the very discourses their author has devised for their epiphanic educations in the (admittedly bitter) self-knowledge of internal exile. For, in attempting to comprehend and use Yeats, his American theoretical heirs conceive designs which paralyze their imaginative developments, even as they disseminate and so perpetuate the error of proposing such undertakings as exemplary. Rather than authoring "Yeats", then, their chosen poet has authored and – paradoxically if not perversely – authorized them.

Before going on to justify this apparently extravagant claim, I want to air a suspicion that critical theorists today are perhaps turning more systematically away from literature and toward other forms of discourse for intellectual and methodological inspiration not simply as a rebellious act against their literary origins, but also, given this cautionary example of a previous theoretical generation or two, as a necessary defensive maneuver in the endless struggle for psychic survival. Quite simply – and perhaps all too simply – I think "literature", as represented by the visionary tradition which culminates ironically in Yeats, constitutes for current theorists the uncanny, the ever-imminent return of the repressed, which must be repeatedly repressed anew by way of fresh imaginings of other, fabulously traumatic origins entirely of their own production, if the catastrophe of theoretical creation is to occur over the course of their careers in manageable forms. In short, what I'm pointing out in American critical theory is the rationalization and professionalization – the modernization – of the sublime: what I am more euphemistically calling here the profession of the sublime.

Now, I'm not trying to claim that no other literary figures, modern or not, could be similarly adduced as plausible candidates for such ironic centrality. Besides Yeats: Milton, Rousseau, Wordsworth, Emerson, and Mallarmé immediately spring to mind for the honor. Nor am I making the claim that all significant American theorists are essentially Yeatsians; it seems only the major ones are. Finally, however, I *am* claiming that it is because these theorists do confront the question of literature's status and effect, however problematically, that they will remain major figures in their own right. For such critics as R. P. Blackmur, Northrop Frye, Harold Bloom, and Paul de Man (among others) attempt to theorize that allusive power of intertextuality which has traditionally defined the literary and which has traditionally been defined as the sublime – that diversely characterized, awe-inspiring alien force which emerges in the act of reading trailing the impressive (and hence repressive) aura of innumerable echoes. Such a force often subverts and problematizes the systematic intentions of even the most self-aware and talented of critical interpreters with a persuasive vision of genius. That is, the sublime is a vision of power, individual or communal, affirmative or demonic in nature, which can inform various critical projects. In classic terms of individual morality, this vision is of a monumental nobility or heroism. In romantic terms of natural processes and objects, it is a vision of apocalyptically self-delighting energy. And in the modern or contemporary terms of rhetorical criticism (paradox, tension, irony, corrosive figurative disjunctions and logical aporias), this vision is one which inspires and privileges notions of deconstructive analysis, revisionary repression, or even, on occasion, genealogical research into discursive formations.[3]

R. P. Blackmur's criticism seems a far cry from the sublime in most of these ethical, therapeutic, epistemological or "strategic" senses. Yet his two earliest essays on Yeats, "The Later Poetry of W. B. Yeats" (1936) and "W. B. Yeats: Between Myth and Philosophy" (1942), both of which are collected in *Language As Gesture* (1952), do indeed circulate conceptually around a largely unnamed but clearly revised formalist notion of the sublime. Blackmur's focus – the semantic status of the poetic image in Yeats's doctrinal poems written in the light cast by *A Vision* (1925; 1937) – establishes the sublime in New Critical terms as a powerful imagistic mediation of the conflict between common emotional experience sanctioned by literary tradition or philosophic precedent and private mythology – the latter, for Blackmur, being a personal discipline or convention of occult meaning which transforms Yeats from one of many "magicians in the dark" into a forceful inventor of dramatic lyrics that successfully cast their spell.

No poet in recent times, for example, has seemed to base his work on a system, quasi-philosophical, partly historical, and largely allegorical, both so complicated and so esoteric, as the system which Yeats worked out in the two versions of *A Vision* . . . The point is that the reader has a richer poem if he can substitute the manipulative force of Yeats's specific conventions for the general literary conventions. Belief or imaginative assent is no more difficult for either set. It is the emotion that counts . . . The terror [of this assent] is in the recognition, the strength in the image which compels assent.[4]

Blackmur's own diction in these passages is used to articulate the motif of voyaging through a poet's oeuvre which structures these two essays on Yeats (and a good deal of the rest of the volume as well). It approaches the intensity and scope of the classic expressions of the sublime found in Longinus, Edmund Burke, and even Kant. The terror of assent – of assenting to an inspiring, endlessly reverberating image like that of the lightning flash – characterizes the formulations of the sublime experience, even as the explanations for and interpretations of its causes and significances strongly diverge.[5] In assenting to the sublime figure, one permits one's psyche to be re-configured, much as the poet in the Longinian conception has permitted his or her psyche to be so revised by the inspiring work of prior poets. But, of course, the sublime is not really a matter of choice. It is the form of compulsion *par excellence*, for the creator and especially for the reader, no matter how imperious or tyrannical. As Longinus advises, "a figure is at its best when the very fact it is a figure escapes attention . . . by the very excess of light. For just as all dim lights are extinguished in the blaze of the sun, so do the artifices of rhetoric fade from view when bathed in the pervading splendor of sublimity."[6] The famous classical and neoclassical canon that the best art hides its artifice thus tallies well with more sinister forms of deception such as seduction and self-betrayal.

Blackmur, in effect, is arguing that Yeats through his invention of a private mythology has usurped the place of literary tradition with its public conventions, and thereby imposes himself and his meaning upon his readers with a force unequalled in lyric poetry since the seventeenth century (a time for Blackmur more conducive to poetry) and rivals, if clearly falling short of, the epic achievements of Milton, not to mention those of Dante and Homer.[7] The point is not the accuracy of Blackmur's historical comparisons but the power of the conviction informing them; it testifies to Yeats's sublime mastery in our time, and it inspires Blackmur's own critically equivalent project of formalist usurpation of general literary convention by imposing an array of terms and distinctions – a theory of poetic language as the body's gesturing toward thought – which compel our assent by way of an intense pre-occupation, even obsession, with the literary image. This process finally amounts to that critical form of terrorization known as the sublime. Blackmur's criticism, in consequence, even when later in his career he turns to the social dimensions of literature and literary study, remains partially haunted and somewhat deformed by the specter of this essentially Yeatsian and visionary aesthetic project of imposing a systematic viewpoint of one's own. Like Yeats's later poetry written in the shadow of *A Vision*, it forces a recognition of that terror which compels assent to an image not one's own and sanctioned by no general cultural conventions of meaning-production but only by the portable "self-culture" barbarously culled from the underside of the Western mind.

Blackmur's situation is thus representative of the New Criticism, and especially I think of the criticism of such arch-New Critics as Cleanth Brooks and Allen Tate.[8] Even T. S. Eliot, the apparent god in the New Critical machine of interpretation, is haunted by Yeats's achievement, as his commentary in the "familiar compound ghost" passage from "Little Gidding" bears striking witness.[9] My point is not that there are no other haunting presences in Blackmur and the rest, only that he and they owe their influential understanding of the aesthetic dimensions of the theoretical enterprise to Yeats's imposing example.

For the New Critics, theory defines a field of methodological reflection upon the unique impositions of private mythologies or personal conventions by individual poets, and, as such, theory in their hands is always "modern" or belated. In their hands, that is, it becomes an academically regularized discipline for the establishment of an ideology of professionalization organized around a rationally articulated technique of imagistic analysis. Such a methodological focus on poetic and critical practices insures a minimally effective consensus and constitutes the critical version of the sublime as practiced by an elite group of experts who impress the recognition of their own terrified assent given to the entire corpus of literature upon the most receptive of student minds.

The finest of the New Critics, in some of their most memorable performances, like Blackmur here on Yeats, become unexpected celebrants of the power of passion due to what they claim is a virtually perfect appropriation and orchestration of formal devices on the part of an arch-artificer. That is, such critics, even as they gesture forth their privileged theories of paradoxical aesthetic resolutions, resemble Gabriel Conroy at the end of "The Dead" (an ending which alludes to that of Yeats's "Ross Alchemica"). Gabriel, you will recall, finally realizes passion's glory at the very moment when he must recognize his near total incapacity for it – an annihilating dénouement ironically arranged for him by his most hospitable Irish author from his place of exile. The New Critics, in short, convince us primarily of their own enthrallment to a sublime mastery they lack individually but achieve institutionally.

With the criticism of Northrop Frye and Harold Bloom, however, one begins to see a disciplining of the sublime, an assimilation of it by an ever-elaborating theoretical apparatus which schematizes and conventionalizes individual authors, reducing them to replaceable and recirculating "types" and "topoi" either in an ostensibly Christian humanistic vision of the verbal universe or in a self-confessed Jewish Gnostic's revisionary map of the literary unconscious. Frye and Bloom are more like, respectively, the Joyce behind *Ulysses* and the Yeats behind *A Vision* than they are like any of the New Critics who, neither gifted anatomists nor maddened pedants, approach those masterful images which compel assent upon their knees as if they were themselves the unwitting creations of the author they would understand. And yet, despite this success by Frye and Bloom in producing their own enormously influential private mythologies, it is achieved at a considerable cost. Both critics create systems of Ptolemaic complexity which, in the final analysis and after many years of "field testing", tend to inhibit the very thing both claim they desire the most for their work: general educational efficacy.[10] Moreover, in their interpretations of Yeats, one can see how this scapegoat for all that they would and do not avoid also functions as their ironic muse, prophetically remembering what they do not want to and surely do become: inventors of private mythologies which have been perversely adopted by subsequent generations of theorists as an esoteric ideology of resentful professionalization. In this sense, Yeats appears to be playing Molly to two of her would-be lords and masters – with predictable results: "As well him as another", and all that.

Frye and Bloom, antipathetic in style and tone, do indeed share, however, a common point of intellectual departure with Yeats, viz., a fiercely ascetic anti-naturalism which ironically manifests itself in the critics as a defensive attack on the poet for distorting the authentic humanistic vision of his romantic ancestors in the tradition of prophecy, Blake and Shelley. That is, Frye and Bloom not only do unto Yeats what they accuse him of doing unto his precursors but they do so in the name of their own more original realization of the antithetical intention inherent in that apocalyptic humanism which goes back through Milton to *The Bible* and its orthodox and heretical commentators, and which authorizes the assimilation of all obstacles to vision under a composite trope for fallen nature: the Great Whore of Babylon, Vala, the Covering Cherub, and so on. It is as if Yeats's influence as the culminating moment in the poetic line of vision can be met only by critically transforming him into the theoretical equivalent of Joyce's Molly: fecund abyss of the vision – of a rival – out of which, nevertheless, a new heterocosm will arise. In sum, then, Frye and Bloom would usurp Yeats's position in the tradition of vision with their schematic systematic speculations by using him much as Satan uses Sin in *Paradise Lost* as the primordial occasion for bearing original witness to a perverse sublimity all their own.

More particularly, Frye in "Yeats and The Language of Symbolism" (1947) clearly prepares for the development of his own system in *Anatomy of Criticism* (1957), even as he also articulates here what is left implicit regarding Yeats in *Fearly Symmetry* (1947).[11] For Frye, Yeats's need for his own visionary system accurately reflects the failure of nineteenth-century criticism to provide its poets with a comprehensive "grammar" of poetic symbolism which would do for them what the visionary and allegorical traditions do for Spenser and Milton, namely, grant them a visionary mode of apprehension freed from specific or, at times, specifiable doctrinal content for individual emblems. Frye argues that not only does Yeats have to create his own symbolic grammar in *A Vision* but he must worry over the question of belief down to the most minute particular because the system's broad outlines emerge out of debased, rightly marginalized and so unauthorized occult and aesthetic traditions. Unlike his own system to be, Frye implicitly suggests, history in *A Vision* and in the major poetry written under its influence is nothing more than "a Kilkenny cat-fight" and man is nothing more than the tragic human embodiment of the dying-god Dionysus whose death provides an amusing spectacle for woman (conceived as a "malignant grinning female") whose courtier-priest is the poet (conceived as "a walking crystal set") tuned to the channel of the dead, a medium whose message is the triumph of the demonic over the still living.[12] Frye concludes that Yeats "best" fulfills the tragic impulses in the Romantic tradition: "In searching for a new language of symbols, then, Yeats was to a great extent simply fulfilling the Romantic tradition from which he had started, his final position being simply a more systematic expression of the romanticism of Nietzsche and Lawrence."[13] According to Frye, therefore, Yeats produces a proto-fascist vision of "imaginative nihilism" all too appropriate for our time. Enamoured, like Narcissus, with "the reflecting illusion of his own mask",[14] Yeats transforms himself into a site for the production of the sublime as the dead's tragically spiteful jealousy for all that lives:

Yeats began his career with a set of romantic values and an intuition, recorded on the first page of his *Collected Poems*, that "Words alone are certain good." As he went on, his romantic values consolidated into a tragic mask, through which we hear voices full of terror, cruelty, and a dreadful beauty, voices of the malignant ghosts of the dead repeating their passionate crimes. No one can deny that a tragic and terrible mask is the obvious reflection of our age; nor is it an easy mask to wear, since it is not for those who take refuge either in moral outrage or in facile bravado. But as it begins to settle on the creator of lovely and fragile Victorian poetry a new exuberance comes into the voice. In Yeats's early poems we find neither youth nor age, but an after-dinner dream of both; in the *Last Poems* the lusts of youth break out beside the "old man's eagle mind" flying far above the conflicts of illusion. For while illusion enslaves, vision emancipates, and even the thought of death in a dying world seems a buoyant thought, a defiant upstream leap of the elderly salmon returning to the place of seed . . . the poet does not want mere equality with others; he wants to be recognized as himself the true kind, the creator of social values whose praise of gold inspires others to strut about under gold crowns. Like Milton's Samson, or Jesus of whom Samson was a prototype, he is a tragic hero to his followers and the buffoon of a Philistine carnival; yet the tragedy ends in triumph and the carnival in confusion.[15]

Frye's final remarks here allude to the situation in Yeats's early play *The King's Threshold* in which a poet goes on "a hunger strike at a king's court because he is excluded from the high table where the bishops and councillors sit".[16] To clinch his judgment of Yeats, Frye concludes with a sublime passage from the play that survives its different versions in which first the poet and then the king are the ultimate victors:

> And I would have all know that when all falls
> In ruin, poetry calls out in joy,
> Being the scattering hand, the bursting pod,
> The victim's joy among the holy flame,
> God's laughter at the shattering of the world.[17]

Trashing Yeats's imaginative origins in this fashion prepares the ground for replacing them with origins of Frye's own invention which would be more capacious and "pure", or more "conventional" in some "genuine" sense of the word which he will define in *Anatomy of Criticism*.

I have quoted Frye's conclusion at length, however, not only because it demonstrates how the critic uses the poet's supposed failure to justify an emerging visionary project for theory, but because it also suggests in the final lines that Frye here betrays the original tragic enchantment with Yeats, the virtual sexual fascination for the spectacle of his "imaginative nihilism" which informs Frye's creation of the critical image of Yeats as the decadent Samson of the visionary temple, an image that haunts the critic's career and re-emerges at the conclusion of *The Great Code: The Bible and literature*.[18] Even more significantly for my argument, Frye in this passage also prophesies his own imaginative fate as a producer of the sublime for the coming generation of speculative critics he is to sire: "As he went on, his romantic values consolidated into a . . . terrible mask . . . the obvious reflection of our age."[19]

In a sense, Harold Bloom's position on Yeats articulated in a five-hundred-page tome *Yeats* (1970) and then substantially revised in an essay from *Poetry and Repression* (1976) entitled "Yeats, Gnosticism, and the sacred void" constitutes a theoretical elaboration of Frye's relationship to Yeats and a generalization of such internecine psychic wars for imaginative space and revisionary authority into a system of his own and into a methodological principle of reading which he applies to literary and cultural history from Milton on. Bloom's theory of revisionary interpretation as animated by the anxiety of influence owes as much to Yeats's own example, of course, as it seems to do to the positions of Pater, Nietzsche, Freud and occult thinkers whose presences haunt the margins of the *Yeats* volume and who are to muscle their way into the body of Bloom's text with a vengeance in subsequent books.[20]

Perhaps the finest, most accessible version of Bloom's theory, free
of what one of his ablest critics nicely calls the "baroque encrusta-
tions"[21] of its later developments, occurs early in *Yeats*:

Poetic influence, as I conceive it, is a variety of melancholy or an anxiety-
principle. It concerns the poet's sense of his precursors, and of his own achievement in relation to theirs. Have they left him room enough, or has their priority
cost him his art? More crucially, where did they go wrong, so as to make it
possible for him to go right? In this revisionary sense, in which the poet creates
his own precursors by necessarily misinterpreting them, poetic influence forms
and malforms new poets, and aids their art at the cost of increasing, finally,
their already acute sense of isolation. Critics of a Platonizing kind (in a broad
sense, which would include such splendid critics as Borges, Frye, Wilson
Knight) refuse to see poetic influence as anxiety because they believe in different versions of what Frye calls the Myth of Concern: "We belong to
something before we are anything, nor does growing in being diminish the link
of belonging." So, a poet's reputation and influence, that is, what others think
he is, is his real self. Milton is what he creates and gives. I urge the contrary
view, for the melancholy only the strongest of poets overcome is that they too
must belong to something before they are anything, and the link is never
diminished. As scholars we can accept what grieves us as isolate egos, but poets
do not exist to accept griefs. Freud thought all men unconsciously wished to
beget themselves, to be their own fathers in place of their phallic fathers, and
so "rescue" their mothers from erotic degradation. It may not be true of all
men, but it seems to be definitive of poets *as poets*. The poet, if he could, would
be his own precursor, and so rescue the Muse from her degradation. In this
sense, poetic influence is analogous to Romantic love; both processes are il-
luminated by Patmore's egregious remark: "What a Lover sees in the Beloved
is the projected shadow of his own potential beauty in the eyes of God." This
is certainly what the ephebe or potential poet sees in his precursor, and is akin
to Valéry's observations: "One reads well when one reads with some quite personal goal in mind. It may be to acquire some power. It can be out of hatred
for the author."[22]

If Blackmur reduces the sublime as represented by Yeats to a formalist
conception of New Critical paradox and irony (language as gestural
body); and Frye impersonalizes the Yeatsian sublime to the level of
disposable cultural archetypes (Kilkenny cat-fights, malignant grinning
females, and walking crystal sets); then Bloom personalizes the archetypes of Frye's universe (in a phantasmagorical rather than literally
biographical manner) and so exposes the psychic undercurrents of the
critical quest to know and master an author, or rather stages them as
if they were the stuff of Wagnerian opera.

For my purposes, the later essay, which revises Bloom's essentially
Frye-like critique of Yeats's poetry for failing to measure up to the
visionary humanism of his Romantic fathers, occupies an even more
important place in Bloom's theoretical career than the massive book,

since it correctly accepts Yeats's prominence in the tradition and, more tellingly, embraces now what Bloom had formerly scorned as Yeats's inhumane aestheticism, seeing it instead as the terrible psychic cost of all authentic imaginative careers. Following Yeats's lead, Bloom accepts, for example, the poet's identification of the Muse-principle with "the principle of self-destruction" in poets, that instinct for their own imaginative deaths which lures them on with an impossible vision of sublimity until the inevitable disaster.

The sublime, in this light, becomes wholly demonic, a desperate "evasion of dying" in a quest for symbolic immortality that must compulsively court the catastrophe of creative death in an obsessive pattern of demonic repetition, in which "awareness of the precursor", "the presence of the Muse", and the theme of sexual love[23] compose one complex structure in a career of systematic misreading of self and other. Like a blind aerialist who must practice his art in the open air without a net, the visionary, for Bloom, can only create when at mortal risk. For only the "absolute completion" in the imagination of "every human impulse, however destructive", grants Yeats a sense of "freedom" which is, Bloom claims, akin to the Gnostic "liberation" from the coils of the world.[24] But this "freedom" is finally a delusion, of course, a monumental lie against time and process, for the quest can never be completed as envisioned; it can only be completed by an imaginative or literal act of dying. In fact, the "freedom" of such completion can only be bought by psychic burnout, madness or suicide. "Like the Valentinian entity called Error, Yeats elaborated his own matter in the void, and like his masters Pater and Nietzsche, he came to regard that void as being itself sacred."[25]

Consequently, Bloom concludes (as Frye does) that Yeats completes his Romantic heritage as a kind of decadent or demonic Samson by defensively misreading it in such a way as to bring what Pater calls "the House Beautiful" crashing down all around us. For Yeats's "demonic Gnosticism", Bloom suggests, is "his repressive defense against the anxiety of influence, and in particular against the composite Romantic precursor he had formed out of Shelley, Blake and Pater". The "Yeatsian Sublime" is then representative, in its "triumph (however equivocal)", of every belated Romantic quester's wish "to achieve a victory over and against the enormous pressures of poetic anteriority". Yeats's "poetic variety of Gnosticism" thus represents "his own wilful misprision of Romantic tradition".[26] That Bloom originally casts these reflexive conclusions in a series of rhetorical questions only heightens their penetrating power. The terror of assent, which arises from the self-conscious recognition of the compelling nature of another's images, becomes a critical method of close reading with Blackmur, inspires with Frye a theoretical system and an ideology of careerism, and in Bloom crystallizes into an occult justification of imaginative existence itself, an admittedly self-defeating aesthetic metaphysics.

This happens, I dare to speculate, because the sublime, the terror in assenting to an alien authority experienced as desired for and as the self, when methodized, regulated, systematized, and acted out as a career – in short, professionalized into modern discursive practices – ultimately subverts the very categories and discipline designed to assimilate and contain the sublime, before dwindling into some new kind of domesticity, or all too familiar critical mode. Whether conceived as moral genius, natural spectacle, category mistake, hyperbole (and catachresis), or as a primal repression constitutive of the self on the model of the catastrophe of creation in Gnostic myth, the sublime exceeds and at the same time conventionalizes its own formulations, authorizes and transgresses all authority structures including those of the sublime experience itself. The sublime, in short, cannot finally be distinguished from the principle of change itself, however vainly one attempts to conceptualize the latter.

Consequently, the sublime discloses the essential nature of all literary ideas – their fundamental groundlessness that makes every effort to theorize on their basis in the manner of academic philosophy a ridiculous enterprise at worst and at best a diverting work of literary art. The end of all theorizing the sublime always reveals a scene of instruction, personal or communal in scope, like that which concludes Joyce's major texts. An elaborate literary artifice produces an apocalyptically ironic vision destructive of all device as its own irrational self-representation as rhetoric. What else could result from this comically hollow affirmation of an annihilating prospect of descent to first principles but such a "purely" literary conception of the sublime? The sublime, in short, constitutes an empty theoretical category for referring to the death of the critical imagination in its own vastly allusive capacities.

With this curious notion of reflexively allegorizing the impossibility of critical thinking in a climactically self-subverting trope, we approach the end of our quest to articulate Yeats's presence in American literary theory over the last forty years or so as the principle of the sublime which inspires, sustains, and finally destroys the imaginative developments of the critics it also fosters. That is, we have at last reached the late Paul de Man.

De Man discusses Yeats throughout his career. The poet is the focus of de Man's most original thinking in the 1962 New Critically styled essay "Symbolic Landscape in Wordsworth and Yeats". Yeats also plays a significant role in clarifying de Man's conceptions of "modernism" in the phenomenologically based interpretations of "Lyric and Modernity" in *Blindness and Insight* (1971). Most memorably, perhaps, Yeats provides a major example for de Man's devilishly clever analysis of rhetorical questions in the opening essay of *Allegories of Reading* (1979). (See: "How can we know the dancer from the dance?" from *Among School Children*.) Thanks to its inclusion in Josué Harari's anthology of post-structuralist criticism, *Textual Strategies*, this essay, "Semiology and Rhetoric", has become a classic of American deconstruction. At each stage of de Man's career, therefore, Yeats has conjured forth the appropriate occasion for theoretical speculation and transformation. With the posthumous publication, in *The Rhetoric of Romanticism* (1984), of a generous selection from the Yeats sections of de Man's previously unavailable 1960 Harvard dissertation on "Mallarmé, Yeats, and the Post-Romantic Predicament", we can see that what appears to have been pragmatic opportunism in de Man's periodic use of Yeats is actually the deceptively piecemeal manifestation of a permanent structural category in the critic's thinking that amounts in retrospect at least to an intellectual passion. "Image and Emblem in Yeats", I dare say, composes now not only a "prophetic" overview of de Man's career to come, but, as well, that of American literary theory.

The most succinct formulation of the theoretical problem de Man wrestles with in "Image and Emblem" occurs in the slightly later essay on "Symbolic Landscape in Wordsworth and Yeats" written for his mentor Reuben Brower and included in the the latter's collection *In Defense of Reading* (1962). In analyzing Yeats's later poetry, de Man discovers that "two distinct readings . . . become apparent". "They do not", he goes on to say, "necessarily cancel each other out, but represent very different attitudes toward a common situation." It seems that each of the readings depends on "altogether divergent uses of imagery", that of natural analogues for mental processes and of "an emblematic key" to otherwise esoteric allegorical or occult significances. While both kinds of symbolic imagery "lead from material to spiritual insights", emblematic imagery "originates from experiences without earthly equivalence". At this point let me quote at greater length from de Man for discussion's sake:

The texture [of Yeats's] language, in the poetry written after 1900, thus depends on an altogether composite style, held together by almost miraculous skill. On the one hand, the poems seduce by the sensuous "loveliness" of their natural landscapes and images, while gaining their deeper structural unity and most of their intellectual content from nonnatural or even antinatural uses of language. The juxtaposition of two truly incompatible conceptions of style is . . . precarious. In Yeats, the imagination . . . scorns any delicate balance between perception and imagination . . . in fact scorns the perception, but seems unable to do without it; stripped of its natural attributes [Yeats's poetry] would become a lifeless skeleton. The result, in Yeats's masterful hands, can be intensely dramatic, but it could certainly never end . . . in a promise of "tranquility".[27]

Like Blackmur in "Between Myth and Philosophy", de Man takes Yeats's systematic conviction seriously and so finds a conflict between the common inherited conventions of poetic language and Yeats's personal convention of occult significance. But whereas Blackmur argues that Yeats finally reconciles these opposing dimensions of his poetic style in sublime images that compel assent, de Man, granting the same mastery, suspects its seductive balance of so-called natural and constitutive symbols. For such a balance, scorned by the very imagination so dependent on it for self-expression, suggests to de Man a possibility, which he asserts by denying, of mutual cancellation of meaning, rather than a synthetic stucture of resolution. This unstable ironic hovering between antinomies points, paradoxically enough, not to the gestural semantics of the body but to a fundamental privileging of the antinatural imagination, invoked most fully at the conclusion of the 1960 essay "Intentional Structure of the Romantic Image", which compulsively creates and consumes all oppositions as a gesture of earthly transcendence: "But this 'imagination' has little in common", de Man claims there, "with the faculty that produces natural images born 'as flowers originate'. It marks instead a possibility for consciousness to exist entirely by and for itself, independently of all relationship with the outside world, without being moved by an intent aimed at a part of this world."[28] The early Sartrean notion of Being as a being in and for itself alone certainly informs, as Frank Lentricchia suggests,[29] de Man's conception of this antinatural imagination. As we shall see, however, Yeats's own poetic practice, as much as Sartre's or Hegel's philosophy for that matter, shapes de Man's prophetic utterance.

De Man's position on Yeats in his dissertation arises from a distinction, drawn from Yeats's *Autobiographies*, between two different versions of Romantic quest, the Faustian, which consumes experience in pursuit of greater knowledge and self-determination, only to end in a baleful recognition of the quest's failure to achieve either aim; and the Quixotic, which begins with the knowledge of the impossibility of the quest and inevitable defeat, and so becomes more a test than a quest,

a trial, however deranged, of "loyalty and perseverance". In this manner, de Man questions Frye's facile assimilation of Yeats's career to the
convention of tragic romance, even as he anticipates in outline the
Gnostic and nihilistic dimensions of Bloom's conclusions.

De Man then discusses the development of Yeats's style, which apparently shifts abruptly from vague *symboliste* word-painting to hard
and realistic concreteness. De Man changes focus suddenly to relate the
themes of Romantic passion and what he terms apocalyptic death to the
self-defeating logic of the visionary imagination as exemplified in
Yeats's composite style. I cite now a cento of passages from "Image and
Emblem" to give the full argument most economically:

> the images have given up all pretense at being natural objects and have become
> something else. They are taken from the literary tradition and receive their
> meaning from traditional or personal, but not from natural associations – in
> the same way that the colors of a national banner are determined, not by
> analogy with nature, but by the decree of an independent will... Yeats's entire
> effect is calculated to seduce the reader by the apparent realism of his narration
> . . . A definite stylistic pattern thus begins to appear: the poem uses natural
> imagery and gains its immediate appeal and effectiveness from this
> imagery; the true meaning, however, is only revealed if the "images" are read
> as emblems, and one is led to believe that [the poem] consists of emblems mas-
> querading as images rather than the opposite . . . But when nature itself is thus
> considered a mere sign, or a mouthpiece without actual substance, then one has
> left the mainstream of the tradition [in Western poetry and philosophy] and
> embarked on "strange seas of thought" . . . If this rhetoric is able to deceive
> the reader, it can never deceive the author, whose fundamental bewilderment
> is bound to emerge sooner or later . . . Why is it then that the poetry . . . is
> a poetry of terror and annihilation, apocalyptic rather than eschatological? It
> can only be because Yeats still experiences the Annunciation . . . the advent
> of the emblem . . . as an intolerable destruction of nature . . . Yeats ends
> . . . in utter mockery . . . The failure of the emblem [to transform] . . . the utterly
> worthless content of reality . . . amounts to total nihilism. Yeats [however] has
> burned his bridges, and there is no return out of his exploded paradise of emblems
> back to a wasted earth. Those who look to Yeats for reassurance from the anxieties
> of our post-romantic predicament, or for relief from the paralysis of nihilism, will
> not find it in his conception of the emblem. He cautions instead against the danger
> of unwarranted hopeful solutions, and thus accomplishes all that the highest
> forms of language can for the moment accomplish.[30]

Unfortunately, I cannot here explore the de Manian archive disclosed
in these passages, which forecast so accurately the themes, major
tropes, and philosophical turns that are to come in American theory,
even the linguistic turn as suggested by de Man's analogy with the
national banner. All I can do is recall that two major books in critical
theory (besides de Man's own *Blindness and Insight*) to survive the

nineteen-sixties are Hartman's *Wordsworth's Poetry* (1964), which argues a case for this poet remarkably similar to that argued for Yeats here by de Man; and Bloom's *Yeats*, which, as we saw, equates (and laments) Yeats's equation of Romantic passion, apocalyptic death, and the anxiety of influence in a way that reminds one of de Man's similar formula, which itself subsumes all potential psychological categories in a *symboliste* problematic of the antinatural or antithetical imagination.[31]

But let us return more directly to these passages. What de Man terms "gnostic eros" – lovers who embrace so as to exhaust their passion and destroy each other – and "apocalyptic death" – a pursuit of annihilation as the ultimate provocation to vision – are two of Yeats's major themes, which use the rhetoric of the Decadence to represent the post-Romantic predicament operative primarily on the level of style. The strategic use of natural imagery to insinuate the truth formerly conveyed by emblematic (or what Benjamin calls allegorical) imagery ironically confesses, in de Man's view, that modern literature necessarily implies a visionary aesthetics which subverts the very possibility of aesthetic vision. With this conclusion, de Man envisions his own end as "the dancing invalid"[32] of a deconstructive puppet-play which endlessly re-enacts a transcendental linguistic process of signification without significance. For, as de Man concludes in "Shelley Disfigured" (1979), his climactically corrosive statement on self-deconstruction texts, "to read is to understand, to question, to know, to forget, to erase, to deface, to repeat – that is to say, the endless prosopopoeia by which the dead are made to have a face and a voice which tells the allegory of their demise and allows us to apostrophize them in our turn. No degree of knowledge can ever stop this madness, for it is the madness of words."[33]

In sum, then, Yeats's "visionary madness", which inspires the "revisionary madness" of Frye and Bloom,[34] becomes in de Man what it always already is in theory as far as he is here finally able to say: "the madness of words". I am reminded in this context of Joyce's remark in a letter to his son Giorgio – originally written in Italian – which expresses his poignant response both to the prospects of the newest global war interfering with the reception of that seventeen-year epic of self-punishment, *Finnegans Wake*; and to the latest prognosis for his favorite child's clearly incurable insanity: "Here I conclude. My eyes are tired. For over half a century they have gazed into nullity (*nulla*), where they have found a most lovely nothing (*un bellissimo niente*)."[35] Could it be that American literary theory, largely written under Yeats's influence and over nearly a similar period of catastrophes, should elicit from its would-be critical historians a more Joycean kind of response? This seems especially apropos now as it appears likely that it has been de Man on Yeats, both officially and covertly, who has specifically shaped the critical developments of so many, in order thereby to seductively replicate in the emerging theoretical practice in the profession the intellectual impasse that, in his passion for Yeats, had haunted him from the first. Perhaps, Joyce should become our muse?

In conclusion, I want to examine a short lyric by Yeats, written at the height of his imaginative powers, dealing with a tragic theme in his familiar archetypal manner, and clearly conceived in the light of a lifelong obsession with the paradoxical interaction of love and vision, or what I call, when referring to the problematic informing both *Per Amica Silentia Lunae* (1917) and *A Vision*, the poetics of loss. Yeats originally composed "Her Vison in The Wood" in 1926 and later included it in the sequence "A Woman Young and Old", which concludes *The Winding Stair and Other Poems* (1933) and which complements the concluding sequence of *The Tower* (1928), "A Man Young and Old".

Given the elaborate Chinese-box effects involved in reading a poem that is part of a sequence which climaxes one volume and that is intended to be read as paralleling another sequence climaxing another, earlier volume – even though the author composed both sequences at the same time in the context of the recently completed first version of his "system" in *A Vision* (1925) – given such an ever-spiraling labyrinth of possible interpretive perspectives which could paralyze the critical mind even before it begins to understand, I will simply give my interpretation of the poem as an allegory of vision, whose implications for theory admittedly seem central – probably due to this hermeneutic fiat. But first, of course, the poem itself:

> Dry timber under that rich foliage,
> At wine-dark midnight in the sacred wood,
> Too old for a man's love I stood in rage
> Imagining men. Imagining that I could
> A greater with a lesser pang assuage
> Or but to find if withered vein ran blood,
> I tore my body that its wine might cover
> Whatever could recall the lip of lover.
>
> And after that I held my fingers up,
> Stared at the wine-dark nail, or dark that ran
> Down every withered finger from the top;
> But the dark changed to red, and torches shone,

And deafening music shook the leaves; a troop
Shouldered a litter with wounded man,
Or smote upon the string and to the sound
Sang of the beast that gave the fatal wound.

All stately women moving to a song
With loosened hair or foreheads grief-distraught,
It seemed a Quattrocento painter's throng,
A thoughtless image of Mantegna's thought –
Why should they think that are for ever young?
Till suddenly in grief's contagion caught,
I stared upon his blood-bedabbled breast
And sang my malediction with the rest.

That thing all blood and mire, that beast-torn wreck,
Half turned and fixed a glazing eye on mine,
And, though love's bitter-sweet had all come back,
Those bodies from a picture or a coin
Nor saw my body fall nor heard it shriek,
Nor knew, drunken with singing as with wine,
That they had brought no fabulous symbol there
But my heart's victim and its torturer.[36]

The first stanza of the poem dramatizes how vision arises out of a catastrophic act of creation which tears the self asunder, sometimes in an all-too literal manner, as a terrible form of imaginative compensation for an enraging loss of youthful desire. The second stanza shows vision becoming actualized or embodied by archetypal presences, the perception of which clearly is mad and maddening. Caught up in the thoughtless eternity of newly envisioned passion, the self momentarily merges with the company of archetypes, represented as a chorus of tragic revellers, reenacting the ritual of the dying god. Whether one identifies this latter figure as Dionysus, Adonis, or Diarmuid of Irish myth matters less than the recognition of the timeless pattern of tragic romance. Finally in the last stanza, the fallen sublime figure or hero resists with his accusing "glazing eye" the transformation into a thoughtless image of the speaker's desire for visionary thought and so, suddenly, this sublime figure blocks or represses access to the symbolic immortality of eternal youth in the heaven of archetypes in which the speaker for a moment envisages residing. Yet, in the very instant when she admits defeat by recognizing that the troops of women mourning the god-man's fatal wound brought "no fabulous symbol" there but rather her "heart's victim and its torturer", Yeats's female persona, in denying reality to this entire tragic visionary spectacle, becomes herself, precisely because of her occult alliance with the deadly beast,

an embodied emblem of vision which passionately enacts the reality of
loss primordially constituting the Venus and Adonis myth, especially
as it can be imagined by Yeats from the goddess-muse's side. That is,
the speaker becomes divine due to the failure of vision.

Yeats, therefore, imagines in this poem his Maud Gonne-based
Muse-figure imagining those conditions of creative possibility which
delimit and empower his tragic quest for vision. Our author, who
would know himself, in other words, is in the same position of the
theoretical reader who would know him, because neither can do so except through the mediating agency of a figure designed to inspire and
doomed to fail in the quest, and, in sublimely doing so, to succeed all
the more deceptively. That is, just as Yeats creates his scapegoat muse
here, so his theorists recreate him as their scapegoat muse, much as
Joyce invents Molly Bloom's unfaithful mothering mind in which to
place the Homeric climax of his modern epic set in the least likely of
European capitals, Yeats's Dublin.

The Gnostic Sophia in the Valentinian Speculation is one of the last
emanations of the Alien God, that unknown and unknowable Fore-
Father and Fore-Mother, that Abysmal Ground of All. She desires, as
do the other emanations, to know the Father, and decides to do so by
emulating his solitary self-creation. In the attempt, she conceives and
gives birth to an abortion, the Demiurge or God of this fallen world
of nature and mutability. Until a redeemer comes to remind her (and
us, her offspring) that all we can ever know, with respect to the Father,
is that we cannot know him ever, and so should not attempt such a vain
quest, cosmic ignorance must and will proliferate. An American critical
theorist, in order to know the Sublime, tries to produce it by
elaborating his system, with Yeats as the scapegoat muse of the project,
his rival theorists as the last incarnations of the Demiurge, and himself,
of course, as the Alien God's authentic representative. As such, one
could conclude that, thanks to Yeats, critical theory in America, that
profession of the sublime, has for nearly half a century been essentially
a cult affair or even an occult enterprise, or, rather, such *has become*
the fate of one American specialty: Occult criticism – Yeats in theory
indeed.[37]

Notes

[1] See Frank Lentricchia, *After The New Criticism* (Chicago: The University
of Chicago Press, 1979).
[2] See, for instance, the survey of critical positions in my "Self-Born

Mockery" chapter in *Tragic Knowledge: Yeats's autobiography and hermeneutics* (New York: Columbia University Press, 1981).

3 For an example of both such turning from "literature" and continued use of the sublime for research purposes, see Paul Bové, *Intellectuals In Power: a genealogy of critical humanism* (New York: Columbia University Press, 1986).

4 R. P. Blackmur, *Language As Gesture: essays in poetry* (New York: Columbia University Press, 1981), pp. 85, 101, 121.

5 For the best current study of the theory of the sublime (it even supersedes Thomas Weiskel's brilliant *The Romantic Sublime*), see Neil Hertz's *The End of The Line* (New York: Columbia University Press, 1985).

6 Hazard Adams (ed.), *Critical Theory since Plato* (New York: Harcourt Brace, 1976), p. 89. Donald Pease's "Sublime Politics" (in *boundary 2*, 12.3; 13.1, Spring/Fall 1984, pp. 259–79) is the finest analysis of the professionalization of the sublime.

7 For the ironic placement of Blackmur in critical history, see Paul Bové's forthcoming volume in the University of Wisconsin series on American Writers being edited by Frank Lentricchia, *The Politics Of The New Criticism*.

8 See Bové, *The Politics Of The New Criticism*.

9 See Ronald Bush, *T. S. Eliot: a study in character and style* (New York: Oxford University Press, 1984), pp. 231–6.

10 The difference between Frye and Bloom lies in their different conceptions of the nature of such efficacy. Frye wishes to liberate the repressed imaginative forces of us all, while Bloom, especially in *A Map of Misreading*, argues for the useful repressive power of a monumentally conceived tradition, since such a notion of tradition weeds out the weak imaginations from those strong enough to measure up.

11 For more on this topic, see my "Against Nature: on Northrop Frye and critical romance", in *The Romance of Interpretation: visionary criticism from Pater to de Man* (New York: Columbia University Press, 1985).

12 Northrop Frye, *Fables of Identity: studies in poetic mythology* (New York: Harcourt Brace, 1963), p. 230.

13 Frye, *Fables*, p. 226.

14 Ibid., p. 235.

15 Ibid., pp. 236–7.

16 Ibid., p. 237.

17 As quoted in Frye, *Fables*, p. 237.

18 See my "Against Nature", in *The Romance of Interpretation*.

19 Frye, *Fables*, p. 236.

20 See my "The Genius of Irony: Nietzsche in Bloom", in *The Romance of Interpretation*.

21 Paul Bové, *Destructive Poetics* (New York: Columbia University Press, 1980), p. 23.

22 *Yeats*, p. 5.

23 *Poetry and Repression: revisionism from Blake to Stevens* (New Haven: Yale University Press, 1976), p. 208.

24 Ibid., p. 215.

368   DANIEL O'HARA

25 Ibid., p. 212.
26 Ibid., p. 216.
27 Paul de Man, "Symbolic Landscape in Wordsworth and Yeats", in *The Rhetoric of Romanticism* (New York: Columbia University Press, 1984), p. 143.
28 de Man, "Symbolic Landscape", p. 16.
29 See the chapter on de Man, "The Rhetoric of Authority", in Lentricchia's *After The New Criticism* and the latter's remarks on de Man in *Criticism and Social Change* (Chicago: The University of Chicago Press, 1983).
30 de Man, "Symbolic Landscape", pp. 146, 165, 179, 194, 168, 177, 220, 238.
31 See my "Nietzsche's Teacher: Paul de Man", in *The Romance of Interpretation*.
32 de Man, "Symbolic Landscape", p. 287.
33 Ibid., p. 122.
34 The phrase "visionary madness", originally coined by Reuben Brower, derives from Yeats's "the madness of vision" found in a letter to Dorothy Wellesley sent just after the completion of the revisions of *A Vision* (1937). See Blackmur, *Language as Gesture*, p. 113. The phrase refers to Yeats's conviction that only via insanity may the highest inspiration come. My own phrase "revisionary madness" refers to the strange practices of current theorists. See my "Revisionary Madness: the prospects of American critical theory at the present time" in W. T. J. Mitchell (ed.), *Against Theory: literary study and the new pragmatism* (Chicago: The University of Chicago Press, 1985).
35 As quoted in Lionel Trilling, "James Joyce in His Letter", *The Last Decade: essays and reviews, 1965–75*, ed. Diana Trilling (New York: Harcourt Brace, 1979), p. 24.
36 *The Poems of W. B. Yeats: a new edition*, ed. Richard J. Finneran (New York: Macmillan, 1983), pp. 273–4.
37 In retelling and applying this myth to the predicament of American critical theorists today, I am clearly indebted to Harold Bloom's work in general and in particular to Hans Jonas's *The Gnostic Religion: the message of the alien God and the beginnings of Christianity*, 2nd, enlarged edition (Boston: Beacon Press, 1958). In addition, for extremely clarifying discussions of Paul de Man's position on the Kantian sublime in "The Epistemology of Metaphor", *Critical Inquiry*, 5, 1 (Autumn), 11–28, I wish to thank Robin Nilon of Temple University.

The spider and the weevil:
self and writing in Eliot's early poetry

MAUD ELLMANN

I "I who am here dissembled"

In Book III of Ovid's *Metamorphoses*, Liriope, the nymph, is ravished by the river-god, Cephisus, and she gives birth to a child of unearthly beauty named Narcissus.[1] But Tiresias, the prophet, threatens that the child will only live to a ripe age "If he ne'er know himself" (III.348). Narcissus grows more beautiful with every year, and as a youth he fascinates young women and young men alike, but he spurns all their loves. One day, when he is hunting in the woods, Echo the nymph catches sight of him and is instantly inflamed with love. Doomed by Juno never to originate but only to repeat the words of others, she tempts Narcissus by returning his own speech, as if she knew that he could only love the echo of his own desire. As soon as she reveals herself to him, he recognizes her as other and reviles her. Consumed with love, her flesh decays until there is nothing left but voice and bones, and when her bones have turned to rock she dwindles to a hollow repetition.

At last, taking pity on his disappointed lovers, the goddess Nemesis draws Narcissus to a hidden pool, where he falls in love with his own shimmering image. This spatial, visionary double now avenges Echo, the dilatory double of his speech. Just as Echo's bones had turned to rock, he stares in wonder at his beauty, "like a statue carved from Parian marble" (III.419). In a capture too complete, a reciprocity too perfect, his image woos him, smiles with him, weeps with him. "What I desire I have", he moans, in the anguish of his own satiety: "strange prayer for a lover, I would that my love were absent from me" (III.466–8). Echo pities his woe and reiterates his last farewell to his delusion. And just as Echo is unselfed by her own voice, so Narcissus dies into the insubstantial image that he worships, transfixed by the shadow of his shadow in the Stygian flood (III.504–5).

Narcissus rejects Echo because repetition threatens subjectivity, when his own voice returns to him as other: but he escapes the temporal difference in the voice to be trapped into the spatial repetition

of the gaze. Since he only knows himself through doubling, selfhood
originates in its own rupture, glacified by its own effigies. But John
Brenkman has pointed out that it is when the silent image mimes his
speech, as the dead letter mocks the living voice, that Narcissus can
misrecognize the shadow as himself, and die. For this reason,
Brenkman argues that the mirror image is a kind of writing, "a non-
living representation of the voice", and that the "drama of Narcissus
. . . read as a drama of the self − puts the self in primordial relation
to its other, to spatiality, to death, to 'writing'."[2] In Ovid, Narcissus
can accede to selfhood only in the face of writing, where death solicits
him in mute ventriloquy.

When Eliot completed "The Death of Saint Narcissus" in 1915, it
is as if he had canonized Narcissus as the patron saint of
autobiographers, and prefaced all his future speculations on himself
with Ovid's fable.[3] For the autobiographer surrenders self to language
even as he woos his images, and the search for self conceals his
jouissance in self-perdition. As Narcissus knows, to love oneself is to
dream oneself away: "I would that my love were absent from me." To
write is to inscribe one's absence from oneself: temporal division, for
the self that was eludes the self that is, while the written and the
writing selves can never coincide; spatial division, for writing exter-
nalizes memory and halts the flux of subjectivity. This is why Narcissus turns to Parian marble when he is confronted with the writing
of himself, transformed into the tomb of his own image. This chapter
will explore three early works of Eliot, three different kinds of failure
of identity. Serial and aleatory, Saint Narcissus drifts from form to
form, in a dreamy oscillation with his image. But Prufrock's subjectivity is all too fixed, "pinned and wriggling" in a paranoic opposition to
the other. Finally, "Gerontion" breaks Narcissus's looking-glass into
a "wilderness of mirrors", and the mansion of the self is blasted by the
winds of otherness.

II Diabolical mysticism

The Death of Saint Narcissus

Come under the shadow of this gray rock −
Come in under the shadow of this gray rock,
And I will show you something different from either
Your shadow sprawling over the sand at daybreak, or
Your shadow leaping behind the fire against the red rock:
I will show you his bloody cloth and limbs
And the gray shadow on his lips.

He walked once between the sea and the high cliffs
When the wind made him aware of his limbs smoothly
  passing each other
And of his arms crossed over his breast.
When he walked over the meadows
He was stifled and soothed by his own rhythm.
By the river
His eyes were aware of the pointed corners of his eyes
And his hands aware of the pointed tips of his fingers.

    Struck down by such knowledge
He could not live men's ways, but became a dancer before God.
If he walked in city streets
He seemed to tread on faces, convulsive thighs and knees.
So he came out under the rock.

    First he was sure that he had been a tree,
Twisting its branches among each other
And tangling its roots among each other.

    Then he knew that he had been a fish
With slippery white belly held tight in his own fingers,
Writhing in his own clutch, his ancient beauty
Caught fast in the pink tips of his new beauty.

    Then he had been a young girl
Caught in the woods by a drunken old man
Knowing at the end the taste of his own whiteness
The horror of his own smoothness,
And he felt drunken and old.

    So he became a dancer to God.
Because his flesh was in love with the burning arrows
He danced on the hot sand
Until the arrows came.
As he embraced them his white skin surrendered itself to
  the redness of blood, and satisfied him.
Now he is green, dry and stained
With the shadow in his mouth.

"The Death of Saint Narcissus" had a hard time being born. Pound
submitted the poem to Harriet Monroe's magazine, *Poetry*, in 1915,
but Eliot promptly withdrew the text from publication. The surviving
galley proof is "scored through by hand with the manuscript directive
'Kill' (i.e. suppress) in the margin of each section", as if to emulate its
suicidal hero.[4] Lyndall Gordon speculates that Eliot may have
thought the poem too personal:[5] and it would be fitting if the text

were put to death for its self-revelations, since it is such a failure to ex-
tinguish personality that condemns Narcissus to embrace his death.
Furthermore, the poem is still dying in the silence of its critics. Hived
off into the *Poems Written in Early Youth*, "Narcissus" has fallen to
the ranks of juvenilia, and both its author and its readers treat the poem
as a "quarry" for *The Waste Land*.[6] Slightly altered, the first stanza
reappears in "The Burial of the Dead": and Phlebas the Phoenician
supersedes Narcissus, who also "passed the stages of his age and
youth" in fluid metamorphoses.[7] Yet "The Death of Saint Narcissus"
deserves an independent reading, as Eliot's most fierce, yet most ambivalent attack on personality.

Its ambiguities begin with its title, and particularly with the name
of its protagonist. Narcissus, Bishop of Jerusalem, escaped into the
desert in the second century A.D., falsely accused of "a certain grave
slander to his hurt".[8] Eliot's Narcissus flees into the desert, too, but
his name conflates this hounded bishop with Narcissus of the pagan
legend, and also with the persecuted Saint Sebastian. During his travels
through Belgium and Italy in the summer of 1914, Eliot saw three
paintings of St Sebastian, by Mantegna, Hans Memling, and Antonello
da Messina, and was struck by the eroticism of the images – though
he was hasty to insist that a female saint would be more titillating.[9]
Bound and helpless, his firm flesh flayed with arrows, it is his terrible
beauty that unites Sebastian with Narcissus. Both these allusions suggest that the poem is exploring the perversions of mysticism, which
had intrigued Eliot since 1907. In his notes on philosophy at Harvard,
he describes delusional insanity as "a diabolical mysticism, mys. upside
down"; and he also observes that the sexual element is "very promi-
nent" in religious disorders.[10] Indeed, it is the erotic element that
warps the martyrdom of Saint Narcissus, who immolates himself in
onanistic ecstasy: "Because his flesh was in love with the burning
arrows . . . "(34). The poem also seems to mock its author's future
doctrine of impersonality, as if there were a masochistic pay-off for the
artist in his "continual extinction" in his work.[11] In "Narcissus",
self-destruction and self-love enmesh themselves with one another like
the tree: "Twisting its branches among each other / And tangling its
roots among each other" (22–3).

In *The Picture of Dorian Gray*, Wilde uses narcissism to disguise
homoeroticism, and Eliot may unconsciously be copying this subter-
fuge when he screens Sebastian, the homosexual icon, with Narcissus,
who can only love his likenesses.[12] Indeed, the poem never settles for
a single consciousness or two. The narrator begins his tale outside the
cave, and seems to stand outside Narcissus's mind: but he is gradually

confounded with the hero, as if Narcissus were divulging his own secrets in the third person. What is more, the "death" of Saint Narcissus turns out to be the story of his lives, or of his lives and deaths in love with one another. The text begins and ends with an invocation of the tomb; between, he flits through wanton metamorphoses. Each stanza, almost every line, creates the self anew, like a phenomenological assembly-line. The moment he beholds himself, Narcissus slips out of his own clutches, only to take form again in some new beauty radically other than the old. As a tree, he is twisted in his own branches; as a fish he writhes in his own grasp: "his ancient beauty / Caught fast in the pink tips of his new beauty" (26–7). He becomes a young girl, violated by a drunken old man, who is just another incarnation of himself: "he felt drunken and old" (32). Here, self-consciousness compels the rape of self by self, in a whole chain of erotic violence, as doubles proliferate with each embrace. The arrows which assail him are the piercing corners of his flesh, and his own body is the wound that goads him into exile:

> By the river
> His eyes were aware of the pointed corners of his eyes
> And his hands aware of the pointed tips of his fingers.
>
> Struck down by such knowledge
> He could not live men's ways, but became a dancer before God.
>
> (13–17)

Man or woman, fish or tree, each death engenders a new life, as if Narcissus were creating the world anew in his own image. But the dancer and the tree are also typical Romantic images, and the corpse which withers in the tomb may represent the undead narcissism of Romanticism, which Eliot will never quite succeed in burying.[13]

In this protean world, there is no memory but frantic clutching, as each embodiment dissolves, followed by a stranger beauty and a further evanescence. Consciousness "watches its successive modes of existence pass, one after another, and escape it", as Georges Poulet has written in another context. "To feel oneself live is to feel oneself leave behind, in every instant, an instant which *was* the very self."[14] "The Death of Saint Narcissus" is investigating time – autobiographical time – in which the present folds back narcissistically upon the past, to seize the fading image of the self. Like the autobiographer, the narcissist longs to expunge the temporal and spatial difference that separates him from his image – yet he can only love himself because that self is severed from within. Time frustrates narcissism but sustains it, too, for the

time in which the narcissist eludes his own embrace is the time which
perpetuates desire.

Shadows tend to stand for time in Eliot, and "The Death of Saint
Narcissus" is a maze of shadows. The shadow in "The Hollow Men"
marks the delay that separates conception from creation:

> Between the idea
> And the reality
> Between the motion
> And the act
> Falls the shadow (V, 5–9)

In *The Waste Land*, the shadows of the morning and the evening represent the time before and after that eclipses the present, and taunts the
subject with his difference from himself. Indeed, all these shadows
menace *presence*, and for this reason they foreshadow death. It is with
the shadow under the red rock that the speakers of "Narcissus" and
The Waste Land lure their people and the reader to the tomb:[15]

> There is shadow under this red rock,
> (Come in under the shadow of this red rock),
> And I will show you something different from either
> Your shadow at morning striding behind you
> Or your shadow at evening rising to meet you;
> I will show you fear in a handful of dust.

"Narcissus" begins by coaxing us to the shadows, indicating that to
come into the poem is to come under the shadow: to watch the shadows
play upon the tomb, as they played upon the walls of Plato's cave –
another fable of the love of sunless simulacra.[16] In Ovid, the tale of
Echo frames Narcissus's tragedy; and Eliot frames his "Narcissus" in
the tomb where it began, to make the text itself an echo-chamber. For
narcissism is not only the hero's malady, but a diagnosis of the *text*,
its own perverse self-referentiality. Mallarmé dreamed of the poem as
a grotto where language narcissistically reflects itself;[17] and the echoes
that rebound across "The Death of Saint Narcissus" whisper that the
poem has encrypted reference, so that its words can only whisper of
themselves. Claustral, circular, the poem's repetitions gesture
backwards to enfold its own ancient beauty in its new. The "convulsive
thighs and knees" (19) of the third stanza are remembered in the sixth,
when the old man assaults the young girl: and the victim and the
violator oscillate in pseudo-symmetry, as if brutality and suffering were
mirror-images of one another. As motifs repeat themselves, they alter,
for it is difference that elicits repetition, and nothing can be doubled
unless it has already double-crossed its self-identity. If reference

perishes with Saint Narcissus, the flux of figuration takes its place, promiscuous as his posthumous metamorphoses. Within the first stanza, the rock changes from grey to red, for the day has worn its course from dawn to dusk, and time is the accomplice to alterity. The colour of Narcissus turns from grey to green (7, 38). The last line of the poem echoes the last line of the first stanza, but the shadow that was "on his lips" (7) has entered "in his mouth" (39). This change from "on" to "in" summarizes the interiorizing movement of the poem as a whole, for in the last line, the text embraces its own image in a final circularity in which it, too, falls silent in its self-satiety.

Lyndall Gordon argues that "where Narcissus differs from *The Waste Land* pilgrim is in his failure to receive a sign".[18] But his beauty is itself a sign that marks him off: "he could not live men's ways . . . " (17). To be a dancer before God is to make oneself into a sign, directed by the most inscrutable of choreographers. And in the end, Narcissus dies into a trace, forfeiting his being to the "sign of blood":[19]

> He danced on the hot sand
> Until the arrows came.
> As he embraced them his white skin surrendered itself to
>   the redness of blood, and satisfied him.
> Now he is green, dry and stained
> With the shadow in his mouth.   (35–9)

In *Dorian Gray*, the image thrives at the expense of self, the self at the expense of image, and Narcissus seems to be obeying a similar economy: for at the end, his body turns from grey to green as if his lost unliving image had begun to stir, and the whole cycle of self-love and self-oblivion had recommenced.[20] The text invites the reader to the tomb, in order to reactivate the corpse of speech, a sign from which all selfhood has departed. While the shadow stains Narcissus's lips with his forbidden pleasures, it also represents the shadow of his voice: like writing, it traces a lost speech.

In Ovid, Narcissus confronts the silent traces of his living voice, and knows himself as relic, simulacrum. Being written, he is already mostly dead. His death is implicated in his doubling, as Freud links death to the compulsion to repeat, and as the tomb, in Eliot, reverberates with doubles, shadows, repetitions.[21] Like Narcissus, the autobiographer sacrifices self to writing, in his compulsion to repeat his life; but Eliot's laconic allegory implicates the reader, too. To seek one's image in the play of its reflections is to face one's death foreshadowed in the crypt of textuality.

III Prufrock's fixation

Freud argues that a narcissist may love:

(1) what he himself is (i.e. himself),
(2) what he himself was,
(3) what he himself would like to be,
(4) someone who was once part of himself.[22]

This list reveals that narcissism is an epistemological position, as well as an erotic one, because the self can only love the self by disavowing time. The narcissist denies the difference between what he was, what he is, and what he might have come to be, coercing all his past and future selves into the delusion of the present. In Ovid, Narcissus never "is", for his presence is founded on its representation, and his identity is just the phantom of his own imago. Likewise, Eliot's Narcissus can only love a self that has already slipped away, for there is no present tense in narcissistic time. His world consists of his discarded incarnations, too other to be integrated in the self, and yet too similar to break his solipsism.

"The Love Song of J. Alfred Prufrock" was written earlier than "Saint Narcissus", but the crypt of narcissism has already been shattered, for the subject is patrolled at every moment, positioned by a gaze he cannot tame.[23] While Narcissus makes himself his object, and generates his doubles from the split, Prufrock sees himself being seen: and he no longer loves himself but the look that constitutes his being from beyond. "The eyes that fix you in a formulated phrase" (56) fix the self in language and in space, estranging it to two exteriorities: and Prufrock owes his selfhood to the other as he owes his face to the faces that he meets. The rhythm of the poem is convulsive, for the other always takes the subject by surprise, and the moment of subjection is abrupt and ineluctable. Even the title, "Love Song", appeals to the other, but instead of a specific being, a general unease of otherness surrounds him like the yellow fog, remorseless and impersonal. Often, Prufrock acts as his own other, pinned and wriggling under his own pitiless gaze. Although he sees himself being seen, this is rather how he would be seen – were anybody really looking. We are not in Merleau-Ponty's world, which reciprocates the gaze of its spectator, but in the realm of Lacan's gaze, which *overlooks* the subject and sees *through* subjectivity to death: "as if a magic lantern threw the nerves in patterns on a screen" (105).[24] Here, paranoia is the least of all delusions, much less deceitful than the ego that fancies itself master of the visible. The other is neither an external presence nor a mere hallucination of the self, for the gaze transpierces the interiority on which the very fiction of the self depends. Maurice Blanchot describes this sense of otherness in terms which could have been an afterthought to "Prufrock":

When I am alone . . . I am not alone, but am already returning to myself in the form of Someone. Someone is there, where I am alone. The fact of being alone is that I belong to this dead time that is not my time, nor yours, nor common time, but the time of Someone. Someone is what is still present when no one is there. In the place where I am alone, I am not there, there is no one there, but the impersonal is there: the outside as that which anticipates, precedes, dissolves all possibility of personal relationship . . . Then fascination reigns.[25]

Though Blanchot is considering the loneliness of writing, this broken solitude also captures the ambience of "Prufrock". Moreover, it evokes the claustrophobia of the psychoanalytic transference: and "The Love Song" belongs to the same tradition as the transference, for both derive from courtly love, which in Lacan's words is a refined way of "making up for the absence of sexual relation by pretending that it is we who put an obstacle to it".[26] A detour through Freud's theory of the transference will show how "Prufrock" shatters the dyadic world of narcissism, and institutes the drama of revision in its stead.

The word "transference" has two meanings in Freud, as if it were infected by the ambivalence that it describes: and both these meanings appertain to "Prufrock". Transference, in the singular, refers to the romance of therapy, in which the patient projects her archaic fantasies on to the analyst, and casts him in the script of a forgotten love. Like Hamlet, both must stage a play within a play, where they compulsively repeat another scene, with ghosts for audience. But Freud first used "transference" to mean displacement, as in the chimeras of a dream, where wishes slide from sign to sign. François Roustang has pointed out that these two meanings are continuous, because the transference in treatment is the detour through which love must lose its way, as wishes err through the displacements of the dream or death divaricates through life.[27] When Freud speaks of transferences in the plural, he usually means displacement – but just as the transference gains centre stage in therapy, engulfing every other aspect of the treatment, so the singular form absorbs the plural, and the circulation of desire congeals into a single love, a stark subjection.[28] These two meanings also correspond to two forms of magic which Freud discusses in *Totem and Taboo*, a work which is in many ways an allegory of the transference. Contagious magic operates through contiguity, and thus compares to metonymy and synecdoche, while imitative magic works through similarity, disregarding distance like a metaphor.[29] To cast a spell on someone through contagious magic, the witch must steal his hair, his garments, or his name, and this part will yield the power of the whole. Imitative magic, on the other hand, demands the manufacture of an effigy. "Whatever is then done to the effigy", writes Freud, "the same thing happens to the detested original . . . "(SE, vol. 13, p. 79). In treatment, the analyst plays effigy in order to ensnare the patient's love and conjure up the spirits of the dead, to whom all love in Freud eventually returns. "To urge the patient to suppress her love", he argues, "would be just as though, after summoning up a spirit from the underworld by cunning spells, one were to send him down again without having asked him a single question" (SE vol. 12, p. 164). Dangerous as it is to call upon these demons, for all the wonders that they tell, Freud assures us that "when all is said and done, it is impossible to destroy anyone *in absentia* or *in effigie*" (SE, vol. 12, p. 108). It seems the transference has now become the scene to murder, rather than the theatre of desire. Why "destroy"?

Because it represents an absence, the effigy belongs to death, and death can only manifest itself in simulacra. It is death that necessitates the spectacle "without the repetition of which we could remain foreign to and ignorant of . . . the fiction, more or less removed from reality, of death", in Bataille's words.[30] In *Totem and Taboo*, Freud argues that primitive man first acknowledged death when he staged it in the form of ghosts, but this is also when he first defied it, for the belief in ghosts discredits death's finality.[31] This duplicity extends to all representations – gods and demons, effigies and fetishes – which deny the absence and the truancy of their originals, as spectres disavow the death they figure forth. Furthermore, Freud's theory implies that the very notion of the other originates in the belief in spirits, and the being that I constitute as "someone else" is merely the ghost of a ghost, a demon in ruins. It follows that the analyst, as effigy, must occupy the place of death, while the patient, like the primitive, submits to the supremacy of death in the same gesture with which he seems to be denying it (SE, vol.13, p.93). For death is implicated in the effigy itself, in the very act of theatralization.

This may be the reason why Hamlet exults in the success of the play within the play as if he had already wreaked revenge by staging it:[32] and psychoanalysis confuses world with stage as profoundly as Hamlet does. For instance, when the transference first makes itself felt, Freud says there is "a complete *change of scene*" (my italics):

it is as though some piece of make-believe had been stopped by the sudden irruption of reality – as when, for instance, a cry of fire is raised during a theatrical performance. No doctor who experiences this for the first time will find it easy to retain his grasp on the analytic situation and to keep clear of the illusion that the treatment is really at an end. (SE, vol. 12, p. 162)

It is only later that he finds that the fire and the cry are just the greatest masquerade of all. As "Prufrock" will reveal, every struggle to escape the theatre merely forges a new mask, another effigy. The drama is a struggle to the death, where no one can be finally killed, because nothing real takes place; and the transference fizzles into silence. For it is when the patient says "nothing" that Freud detects the signs of transference-love, and argues that every thought connected to the analyst has been replaced by silence (SE, vol. 12, p. 138). The theory of the transference is therefore the nothing that comes of nothing, a romance to dispel the silence that descends when the patient names the nothing of desire. This may be why Freud finds transference funny, where love no longer touches and death no longer kills, and neither actor knows his lines, since both are dummies of a blind ventriloquism: and both play out a comedy of errors in which inside and outside, self and other, theatre and reality, hatred and desire are confounded in the laughter of the dead.[33] To extend Freud's metaphor, transference is all smoke and no fire; or better, a fire drill, rehearsing a catastrophe which has always already occurred and yet could never come to pass.

Distemporal, ectopic, the transference abolishes the history it repeats, but it divides the present from itself with an indelible anteriority. As Freud writes, "The patient does not remember anything of what he has forgotten or repressed, but *acts* it out . . . He *repeats* it, without . . . knowing that he is repeating it" (SE, vol. 12, p. 150). Through repetition, the transference creates the simulacrum of a present in which no presence can be realized. But it is love which compels the patient to repeat, and to create the theatre of his own malaise, a love which Freud repeatedly identifies with writing. To the well-educated layman, he suggests, "things that have to do with love are incommensurable with everything else; they are, as it were, written on a special page on which no other writing is tolerated" (SE, vol. 12, p. 160). For Freud, however, the page of Love is never clean, and every passion reinscribes a palimpsest. The accidents of early years predetermine one's capacity to love, and they produce "what might be described as a stereotype plate (or several such), which is constantly repeated – constantly reprinted afresh – in the course of the person's life . . ." (SE, vol. 12, pp. 99–100). Two years later, in 1914, he reiterates that love consists of "new editions of old traits" (SE, vol. 12, p. 168). The reprints and the re-editions of this very metaphor reveal a printerly obsession in Freud's writing, a scriptural tic that leads Derrida to describe psychoanalysis as a "writing-machine".[34] But it is a love-machine by the same token, for love in Freud consists of the tragicomic drama of revision. Like transference, revision has no present tense, for it can either mean a second, after vision, or a preparation endlessly prolonged: in Eliot's words, "the waste sad time / Stretching before and after".[35] Furthermore, the transference casts the patient as a revisionary poet, in Harold Bloom's sense of the term: for in the process of rewriting the text of her desire she must struggle with the dead, in a battle for mastery or annihilation.[36]

J. Alfred Prufrock is a revisionary, too, much as he would like to be a visionary, and it is the impossibility of sexual relation that enables him to stage his love: a staging which in Freud is just another kind of writing. In "Prufrock", love compels revision, repetition, acting-out: and it encompasses both moments of the transference, the circulation of metonymies, the frozen effigies. The following analysis will show how "The Love Song" is structured like the transference, just as the transference is fraught with poetry in Freud.

Hugh Kenner says that "J. Alfred Prufrock is a name plus a voice."[37] This is a useful formula, for it avoids mistaking Prufrock for a real person, and treats him as an artifact of language: but it fails to register the tension between the name and the voices of the text. There is a sharp disjunction between the poem and its title; between the love song we expect, and the monologue we hear; between the speaker and his name. Like a letter without an address, Prufrock's love song returns to sender. From the first line, when Prufrock beckons to a nameless other, the poem puts its persons and positions into jeopardy: "Let us go then, you and I." Is the you, here, male or female, dead or alive? A lover or a friend? An *alter ego* or an effigy? Most critics think that Prufrock is addressing his divided self, and Robert Langbaum even argues that "we all" agree upon this reading.[38] Although Eliot himself suggested that the "you" stood for an "unidentified male companion", most readers have ignored the hint, perhaps because it whispers of a homosexual attachment – though Eliot also protested that the second person has "no emotional content whatever".[39] If the "you" is part of Prufrock, even an estranged, dissociated part, it does not threaten the decorum of the text nor endanger the monopoly of subjectivity. When the critics sense a split in Prufrock's *personality*, however, they have really made a diagnosis of the *text*, for its broken idioms belie the singularity of voice and proper name. Traces of a prolonged incubation, these incongruities have disconcerted many readers: Ezra Pound urged Eliot to cut the Hamlet passage, which he had composed in 1910 at Harvard; C. K. Stead could have wished he had removed the fog.[40] But the meaning of the text depends upon the fissures of its discourse, for they dramatize the speaker's dislocation from himself, misfitted in the language which bespeaks him.

Kristian Smidt argues that the "you" invokes the reader – perhaps unwittingly suggesting that the poem is a love-song to its own interpreter.[41] This is less improbable than it might seem, for Prufrock seeks a lover's understanding from the reader, and it is impossible to separate the sexual from the textual flirtation. "Speaking of love is in itself a *jouissance*", writes Jacques Lacan: and in "Prufrock", the act of speech *becomes* the act of love, in the moment that they both become impossible.[42] As its title intimates, "Prufrock" is exploring love *and* song, the articulation of language and desire, and the digressions that divert them both from satisfaction. The speaker never makes his declaration, any more than he consummates his love, but the ruses which defer his union with the object of his ardour serve the purpose of sustaining the desire of desire. For Prufrock is in love with language, with fetishes and decoys and deflections, with all the signs that separate him from his dream of total revelation, yet also keep that dream tormentingly alive. It is unclear from the title whether Prufrock writes the love song or the song writes him, whether it is *by* him or *about* him. But the rhetorical obsessionality suggests that the subject is enslaved to his own discourse like an actor imprisoned in a script, or an analyst conscripted in the transference. His poem is in love with the process of its composition, even as it courts the other in its longing for a reference beyond itself. Though it may address a lover, the reader, or the self, it is primarily a love song to a love song: a song of longing for the power, shared by all the greatest bards, to sing of love.[43] Moreover, it is a song-in-progress, beset by all the wishes and frustrations that attend upon the act of writing as they dog the enterprises of desire. Prufrock despairs of his prowess in the language, even more than in the act, of love, deprived of both performance and performative: "And how should I begin?" "So how should I presume?" (68, 54).

All Prufrock's actions can be understood in terms of language or desire, and his whole universe trembles between word and flesh. His noctambulations represent his verbal cruising, while the streets he wanders trace discursive stratagems: "a tedious argument / Of insidious intent" (8–9). The steps he climbs are "stops and steps of the mind", and of the poem's own decisions and revisions (48).[44] The constant repetitions – "There will be time, there will be time" (26) – do not mean that there is time for everything, but that the poem is beginning and beginning, unable to decide on one line and discard another. It is writing as it might be raining, and the subject is enslaved to an autonomous compulsion to revise:

> There will be time to murder and create . . .
> And time yet for a hundred indecisions,
> And for a hundred visions and revisions,
> Before the taking of a toast and tea.   (28–34)

With a kind of inky Midas touch, hands "lift and drop a *question* on your plate" (30); eyes "fix you in a formulated *phrase*" (56); and the sea is where one drowns in *voices* rather than in foam:

> We have lingered in the chambers of the sea
> By sea-girls wreathed with seaweed red and brown
> Till human voices wake us, and we drown.   (129–31)

Prufrock hesitates, digresses, deferring both his amorous and his discursive realizations. Like the act of love, the act of writing is continually suspended in a kind of *scriptus interruptus*.

If he could confess his love, Prufrock dreams that he could know himself. "I shall tell you all!" (95), he cries: and yet the very processes of narrative reduce his history to synecdochic smithereens: "Then how should I begin / To spit out all the butt-ends of my days and ways?" (59–60). Remembering becomes dismembering, as all his memories and fantasies disintegrate into the butt-ends of impossible totalities. Prufrock is himself a moving fragmentation, and the reader is obliged to conjure him out a bald spot, a morning coat, a simple pin, some arms and legs, all casually thrown together. When he says, "I should have been a pair of ragged claws" (73), even the claws are decomposing, let alone the lobster. He sees his "head (grown slightly bald) brought in upon a platter" (82), decapitated before he ever had a chance to prophesy from empty cisterns or exhausted wells.[45] The city, too, consists of broken tortuosities: its hotels are reduced to oyster-shells, and even the fog descends like the muzzle and the tongue of some lost Cheshire cat. Meanwhile, the female body is disorganized into an inventory of its parts and its associated bric-à-brac: hands, faces, voices, eyes, arms, teacups, and the skirts that trail across the floor. Prufrock never speaks *about* his love, for he is subjected to his own desire, which circulates through objects and part-objects: "Arms that are braceleted and white and bare / (But in the lamplight, downed with light brown hair!). . . . Arms that lie along a table, or wrap about a shawl" (64–7). Dismembered, fetishized, these lovely arms reveal that it is the phantasmal fragmentations of synecdoche that liberate the body for desire. In Freud, the fetish occupies the place of lack, in the same way that the analyst occupies the place of death, and in both cases the absence of an object institutes displacement, with its contagious magic of synecdoche.[46] Desire circumambulates through orts and fragments, eroding any bodily *Gestalt*, and love is the unfamiliar name that "Prufrock" gives this skittish deconstruction.

One of Eliot's first readers, the anonymous reviewer for *The Times Literary Supplement*, glimpsed the disintegration of his rhetoric more clearly than his later, friendlier critics:

> Mr Eliot's notion of poetry – he calls the "observations" poems – seems to be a purely analytical treatment, verging sometimes on the catalogue, of personal relations and environments, uninspired by any glimpse beyond them and untouched by any genuine rush of feeling . . . Among other reminiscences which pass through the rhapsodist's mind and which he thinks the public should know about are dust in crevices, smells of chestnuts in the streets, and female smells in cluttered rooms, and cigarettes in corridors, and cocktail smells in bars.
>
> The fact that these things occurred to the mind of Mr Eliot is surely of the smallest importance to any one – even to himself. They certainly have no relation to "poetry" . . .[47]

As far as this critic is concerned, everything that poetry had formerly excluded as eccentric now returns impertinently to the light. In "Prufrock", these fragments form a kind of switchboard for the transmigrations of desire, subversive of the very notion of totality. Through their sheer itemization, the objects in the poem overwhelm the self, and do Prufrock's experiencing for him. For example, the evening etherized upon a table transfers the speaker's anaesthesia to the atmosphere: but the image seems to etherize – or otherize – the subject in return, to bleed him of his body and his consciousness. Indeed, the ether is the least fragmented body in the poem, and the only body that enjoys its sensuality. It is the fog that "licks" and "rubs", the air that indulges in caresses:

> And the afternoon, the evening, sleeps so peacefully!
> Smoothed by long fingers,
> Asleep . . . tired . . . or it malingers,
> Stretched on the floor, here beside you and me.   (75–8)

Here, Prufrock's love is staged "beside" him, in the empty air. But it is important that the air is associated with the afternoon or evening, for Prufrock is etherized by *time*. This is the time that separates desire from fulfillment, motive from execution, thought from speech: in Eliot's words, "the awful separation between potential passion and any actualization possible in life".[48] Time defers.

The way that time defers is through revision. Time itself becomes the object of revision, for the whole poem frets over the problems of writing about time. The incessant repetition of "There will be time" is itself a way of losing time, as Nancy K. Gish suggests;[49] but also a way of gaining it, to prolong the re-editions of desire. "Stretched . . . beside you and me", time deflects Prufrock's ardour from his lover, but time, in the form of the voluptuous evening, has itself become the object of desire. Indeed, he addresses time so constantly, in every tone of envy, rage, pain, impatience, longing, humour, flattery, seduction, that he can only be in love with time. Revisionary time: because revision has no present tense, and "The Love Song" hesitates between anticipation and regret for missed appointments with the self, the other or the muse. It begins in the future tense ("there will be time . . ." [23ff.]); shifts into the perfect ("For I have known . . ." [50ff.]); and finally subsides into the past conditional, the tense of wishful thinking: "I should have been . . . " (73). Presence would mean speech, apocalypse, so Prufrock only pauses in the present tense to say what he is not – "No, I am not Prince Hamlet!" (a negation, by the way, that conjures up the effigy that it denies, since Hamlet is the very spirit of theatricality). The poem concludes dreaming the future, faithful if only to its hopeless passion for postponement: "Till human voices wake us, and we drown." Prufrock feels the need to speak as a proof of his identity and as a rock to give him anchorage: yet speech would also mean his end, for voices are waters in which Prufrocks drown.

Through time, all Prufrock's aims have turned awry. His passion and his speech have lost themselves in detours, never to achieve satiety. Love becomes desire – tormenting, inexhaustible – while speech and revelation have surrendered to writing and revision, to the digressions which prolong his dalliance with time. Time is the greatest fetish of them all, the mother of all fetishes, since it is through time that all aims turn aside to revel in the detours of the transference. Like Freud, Prufrock believes that speech alone could transform repetition into memory. What talking *cures* is writing, for illness lies in the compulsive re-editions of the text of love.[50] But Prufrock's very histrionics show he is condemned to re-enactment, to forget what he repeats in a script that restlessly obliterates its history. By refusing to declare his love, or pop the overwhelming question, Prufrock renounces the position of the speaking subject, but he instigates the drama of revision in its stead. And it is by refusing sexual relation that he conjures up the theatre of desire. The love song Prufrock could not *sing* has been *writing* itself all the time, and the love that could not speak its name has been roving among all the fetishes his rhetoric has liberated to desire. We had the love song, even if we missed the meaning.

IV   "Gull against the wind"

It was not, we remember, the "immense spaces" themselves but their *eternal silence* that terrified Pascal.   T. S. Eliot[51]

Here I am.

So speaks Gerontion – or the voice suspended from his title – or the writings that his name does not entitle us to read as his. Does "Gerontion" designate the speaker? Or does it name the house he does not own? The battle he did not fight? The thoughts he cannot choose but think? As soon as speech begins, the "I" begins to lose itself in the giddy nowness of a discourse without a source, the abyss of a "here" without a name. The gap between Gerontion's name and his "I am" is the first of many "windy spaces" (16) in the text: *brisures* where the bond between the speaker and his voice is welded in its own dissolve, immuring him into a prisonhouse of language.[52] For the house in which the speaker stiffens is built out of the words he frames around his own vacuity. Here I am, in a language which I only rent and do not own, a house whose fissures threaten all propriety of discourse.

All is "hidden when we would backward see from what region of remoteness the whatness of our whoness hath fetched its whenceness", writes Joyce in "The Oxen of the Sun".[53] Identity, or "whoness", depends upon "whenceness", upon a date of birth, a locus of origination. But Gerontion has no origin. All he has is the "dead present" of his house, whose landlord is a parody of whenceness:[54]

> And the Jew squats on the window sill, the owner,
> Spawned in some estaminet of Antwerp,
> Blistered in Brussels, patched and peeled in London.   (8–10)

In this fascistic image, the Jew reduces history to vagrancy, contagion, and miscegenation rather than the revelation of the spirit. Under his dominion, Gerontion forfeits his own past:

> I was neither at the hot gates
> Nor fought in the warm rain
> Nor knee deep in the salt marsh, heaving a cutlass,
> Bitten by flies, fought.   (3–6)

In *The Dry Salvages* (II, 40), Eliot rejects "superficial notions of evolution", and it could be said that evolution denies history, in that it denies dissemination, difference, waste, and loss.[55] "Gerontion", on the other hand, conceives of history as a bad investment, a pointless avarice. "Since what is kept must be adulterated" (58), to preserve the past is merely to corrupt it; and this is why the withered stumps of time lie strewn about, sterile and illegible: "Rocks, moss, stonecrop, iron, merds" (12). Stubborn in their negativity, these vestiges deface their history; and the very words have been reduced to "stonecrop", too – traces without syntax, memory, relations. Thus, it is no accident that critics restore meaning to the poem by restoring history to its words. In the face of Gerontion's oblivion, or history's vicious coquetry (33–43), Frye speaks of the "mnemonic adhesiveness" of the language, Pearson of "association", and Kenner (after Empson) of the "echoes and recesses" of the words.[56] These readings reverse the poem's strategies, replenishing its broken images with memory and sense; they shut away, as best they can, the infinite spaces and their eternal silence which terrify Gerontion as they terrified Pascal. For the text has less to do with time than space, less to do with history than amnesia. Evolution gives way to repetition, and Gerontion's monologue retraces its own steps, as if iteration were itself a science of forgetting.

The poem begins with Gerontion thinking in his house, but ends with his dry thoughts rattling in his brain: and the verbal echo identifies the house as his own consciousness, its tenants as the figments of his reverie. The image of the house, in its very spatiality, casts suspicion on the myth of unextended mind. But this draughty dwelling also represents the words which house the speaker, and the text which drives the reader down the same blind discursive corridors. To read "Gerontion" is to tenant it: to "squat", in the poem's idiom, with no defense against eviction. Like the speaker, the reader raids this house for meaning, for both "would see a sign", and to reinvest Gerontion's words with history is to take signs for wonders (17). Yet its cunning passages all lead to the silence that the text is built upon: "The word within a word, unable to speak a word, / Swaddled with darkness" (18–19). Here one can tunnel no further; and when "The tiger springs in the new year" (49), the text itself unravels like a spring: a spring about to snap and break into a demonic repetition of the *cogito*. "I am a thing that thinks", wrote Descartes in the Third Meditation: "I shall now close my eyes, I shall stop my ears, I shall call away all my senses, I shall efface even from my thoughts all the images of corporeal things . . ."[57] "I have lost my sight, smell, hearing, taste and touch" (60), Gerontion echoes. But the trouble with the *cogito* is that the self confirms its own existence only in the instant of self-consciousness, and therefore to stop thinking is to cease to be. This is why Gerontion obsessively repeats, "Think now . . . Think now . . . Think . . . Think at last . . . Think at last . . ." (34, 37, 44, 49, 51).

The second half of the poem unwinds the first, as the devouring are devoured, and Gerontion reiterates his already forgotten monologue. Mr Silvero, Madame de Tornquist, Fraulein von Kulp, who partook of their unspeakable communion in the first juvescence of the text, are now to be consumed, as the poem and the year turn back again, and the tiger resurges like a scar: "Us he devours" (51). As in "Prufrock", speech alone can transform repetition into memory: but Gerontion rebegins at every turn, as if each speech act dispossessed its antecedents. To repeat is to forget, but also to retrace an "absolute past", a past that never was a present: a reading that was always already a reading and never an originary utterance.[58] "Being read to by a boy" (2), Gerontion's meditation is immured within the iteration of another text, and his own identity dissolves into the writing of the other.

"Gerontion" is "about" writing, though the poem does not use that word, for it figures writing as repetition and forgetting, and finally as the desiccation of the speaking subject. Gerontion dies into an echo – "Thoughts of a dry brain in a dry season" (76) – as Ovid's Echo dried to voice and bones. The echo in the text suggests that writing, like history, no longer moves in a straight line. Derrida argues that the notion of the line, whether straight or circular, has exercised a secret tyranny on Western thought, shaping all conceptions of language and temporality. But "Gerontion" stands in what he calls "the suspense between two ages of writing": between the myth of linearity and another order, imaginable only as the fission of the old.[59] In the Epicurean fallout that concludes the poem, the line collapses into "fractured atoms" (70) hurled through space, while another writing issues forth, in the form of a fortuitous dissemination.[60] This writing erases history, if history is understood as the progressive revelation of the truth, rather than the traces of alterity.

Eliot argues elsewhere that writing brings forgetfulness, because it usurps the power to preserve the past, and forces memory to sink into desuetude. By extending memory, writing wrenches history from consciousness, and enslaves the subject to a supplement.[61] Rather than the master of its mansion, the ego turns into the tenant of a rented house. Selfhood can no longer hold itself intact, any more than Gerontion can seal his house against the wind, for writing threatens the interiority on which the very fiction of the self depends. In "Gerontion", the "windy spaces" are the index of an irreducible extension: they mean that identity can never close upon itself, on the inside of its own interiority.[62] They designate a *movement*, a spacing rather than a space, for every effort to subdue the wind displaces it, and opens up another hole, another draught. Space is not a place but a contagion, that rushes through the corridors of history, whistles through the cracks under the door, and blows through every fissure of the house, the brain, the text, into the cunning passages between the words.[63] It even insinuates itself into the sneeze. This wind no longer breathes divine afflatus – there is no blessing in this breeze – for it was woven in the "vacant shuttles" (30) of a writing that is the forgetting of the spirit, a writing that is spacing.[64]

Mallarmé imagined the heavens as a page turned inside out: the white stars on the night sky shadowed forth in negative the white page spangled with the darkness of the word. "Tu remarquas on n'écrit pas, lumineusement, sur champ obscur, l'alphabet des astres . . . l'homme poursuit noir sur blanc."[65] *L'alphabet des astres* – astral and disastrous – both sense of "des astres" suit Gerontion's alphabet. But "noir sur blanc" surrenders in the end to "blanc sur blanc", for discourse perishes beneath the blizzard of its blanks, as the "Gull against the wind" descends into white feathers on a whiter snow:

> De Bailhache, Fresca, Mrs. Cammel, whirled
> Beyond the circuit of the shuddering Bear
> In fractured atoms. Gull against the wind, in the windy straits
> Of Belle Isle, or running on the Horn,
> White feathers in the snow, the Gulf claims,
> And an old man driven by the Trades
> To a sleepy corner.   (68–74)

And could these feathers be the pens of a writing that is spacing, a white ink that erases its own trace?

"Gerontion" ends in disaster. The tenants of his house are disengorged and whirled among the interstellar winds. The spacing that inhabits writing as its other takes command, as if the Trades, the Gulf winds, and the windy straits had swept away the last saving darkness of the word. The whole text stutters on the *cogito*, to intimate that Descartes could not shut extension out: interiority is howling with the winds of space, the "chilled delirium" (63) of exteriority. This violence is reinscribed in windstorms, windy spaces, vacant shuttles, snow, the whitenesses bespattered through the text; together with the mazy vacancies of history, the spider's web and the corrosive writings of the weevil: all those figures with which the poem meditates its own spacing, its own exploding interior.[66] Household pests, the spider and the weevil sculpture space into the very architecture of interiority, and it is impossible to fumigate the prisonhouse of language, to rid it of these stealthy artisans of negativity. The poem ends in fractured atoms, for its thoughts no longer have an I to think them, nor a house to shelter them against the storms of snow.

V The backward devils

In"Saint Narcissus", "Prufrock", and "Gerontion", Eliot creates three paradigms of subjectivity, all of which confound the notion of a unified integral self. The series opens ominously with Saint Narcissus, who courts his death in his infatuation with himself. The world of "Narcissus" is a world in flux, where the hero slips through his own fingers, driven as relentlessly through incarnations as the poem drives the reader through *non sequiturs*. It is such a world that Eliot resists in a letter to Bonamy Dobrée in 1927, where he complains that "if there is no fixed truth, there is no fixed object for the will to tend to. If truth is always changing, there is nothing to do but sit down and watch the pictures."[67] Prufrock, on the other hand, would like to fix himself, but instead he is fixated in and by the other, and he dwells in a revisionary time, trapped between nostalgia and suspense for a self-coincidence which never can occur. While Kant determines time to be the "inner sense", and Heidegger perceives it as "the essence of autosolicitation", Prufrock's time consists in the delay, which separates the subject from himself.[68] Gerontion, too, complains that history "gives too late" (40) or "gives too soon" (42), eroding the present and the presence of the self. In this poem, inside and outside, self and other, time and space invade each other: as if the weevil, in its restless deconstruction, had consumed the walls that hold antitheses apart.

Framed within the repetition of another text, Gerontion turns into the reader of his own discourse, a fate which Eliot foretells for every poet. In a lecture on "The Varieties of Metaphysical Poetry", he declares that the poet "is not necessarily aware of all the implications of his own work. Indeed he had better not be occupied with general questions at all. He is an accident, & should behave as such."[69] (Since writing is disaster in "Gerontion", the writer is as accidental as could be, the helpless agent of his own dissemination.) If the writer cannot *own* his work, all he can do is *read* it: "in the course of time a poet may become merely a reader in respect of his own works, forgetting his original meaning . . ." At this stage, "what a poem means is as much what it means to others as what it means to the author . . ."[70] But now the author is an other too, and he has as much or as little right as any *hypocrite lecteur* to shrug aside the poem's embryology. However, if Gerontion is a model, reading must imply the loss of self, rather than the mastery of meaning. The reader is "fundamentally anonymous", as Blanchot writes: "he is any reader, unique but transparent. Instead of adding his name to the book . . . he rather erases all names by his nameless presence . . ."[71] The act of reading is an act of dispossession, as violent as the explosion of Gerontion's house, and the reading subject is a moving cancellation, driven by his own forgetfulness.

In *On Poetry and Poets*, Eliot argues that speech, at its most fundamental level, means "one person talking to another", and therefore presupposes a community. On the other hand, we read and write alone: and Eliot laments that "most poetry today is written to be read in solitude". What unites Narcissus, Prufrock, and Gerontion is their solitude, which is beyond bereavement, eviction, or senility, beyond the pain and the absurdity of sex: theirs is that solitude beyond the very possibility of integration that Eliot associates with reading and with writing.[72] Saint Narcissus never speaks at all, but retreats into the desert of his self-delight; and Prufrock only writes because he is convinced that he cannot be heard, like Guido in the poem's epigraph, who speaks because he knows that he is dead. Gerontion is not a "character", but a dull head among windy spaces, a space where reading and rewriting recommence, evacuating every interlocutor. Tongued with flame beyond the language of the living, all three of these personae are telling us that they cannot be told, for they are paralysed in the necessity and the impossibility of speech: "And how should I begin?"

Notes

[1] Ovid, *Metamorphoses*, trans. Frank Justus Miller (London: Heinemann; Loeb Classical Library, 1936), vol. I, bk. III, pp. 148–61, lines 339–510. Book and line numbers henceforth given in text.

[2] John Brenkman, "Narcissus in the Text", *Georgia Review*, 30 (1976), 320. Compare Plato, who argues that painted images resemble writing in that both maintain a "most majestic silence" (Plato, *Phaedrus*, trans. R. Hackworth [Cambridge: Cambridge University Press, 1952], ch. XXV, p. 158).

[3] T. S. Eliot, *Poems Written in Early Youth* (London: Faber, 1967), pp. 34–5; all quotations from the poem come from *The Complete Poems and Plays of T. S. Eliot* (London: Faber, 1969): henceforth cited as *CPP*. Line numbers to Eliot's poems henceforth given in text.

[4] See *Poems Written in Early Youth*, p. 42.

[5] L. Gordon, *Eliot's Early Years* (Oxford and New York: Oxford University Press, 1977), p. 94.

[6] See, *inter alia*, Marianne Thormählen, *The Waste Land: a fragmentary wholeness* (Lund: CWK Gleerup, 1978), p. 11.

[7] *The Waste Land*, I, 25–9; IV, 318.

[8] See Eusebius, *The Ecclesiastical History and the Martyrs of Palestine*, trans. Lawlor and Oulton (London: Macmillan, 1927), vol. I, bk. VI, 9, pp. 184–5; see also Gordon, *Eliot's Early Years*, pp. 91, 58; and Nancy K. Gish, *Time in the Poetry of T. S. Eliot* (London and Basingstoke: Macmillan, 1981), pp. 51–2.

⁹ See Gordon, *Eliot's Early Years*, pp. 61–2; 61n.

¹⁰ Eliot, Notes on Philosophy, MS., Houghton Library, Cambridge, Massachussetts, b.MS.Am 1691 (130). See also Gordon, *Eliot's Early Years*, p. 70; and pp. 141–2, for a bibliography of Eliot's reading in mysticism, 1908–14.

¹¹ I am alluding to Eliot's "Tradition and the Individual Talent", *Selected Essays* (1932; 3rd ed. London: Faber, 1951), p. 17.

¹² I owe this insight to Eve Kosofsky Sedgwick: see her *Between Men: English Literature and Male Homosocial Desire* (New York: Columbia, 1985), for similar ruses in nineteenth-century literature. Like Narcissus, Dorian needs the picture to recognize his own beauty (Oscar Wilde, *The Picture of Dorian Gray*, in *Complete Writings* [New York: Nottingham Society, 1909], Vol.X, p. 30), but the artist, Basil Hallward, also feels the picture is the mirror of his soul (138). Thus, the images of the artist and his subject overlap in a homoerotic union, like the mirror in Joyce's Circe, where Bloom and Stephen superimpose their images on Shakespeare's horned, ataxic, beardless face (James Joyce, *Ulysses* [Harmondsworth: Penguin, 1969], p. 508).

¹³ A further possibility is that Eliot borrowed the transformations of Narcissus from the fragments of Empedocles, which he would have read in John Burnet's *Early Greek Philosophy* at Harvard. Empedocles claims to be an exiled divinity, condemned by a decree of Necessity to "wander thrice ten thousand years from the abodes of the blessed, being born throughout the time in all manners of mortal forms . . . I have been ere now a boy and a girl, a bush and a bird and a dumb fish in the sea", he laments. And now that these wandering spirits are ensepulchred in flesh, he mourns that "We have come under this roofed-in cave" (Empedocles, *Purifications*, in John Burnet, *Early Greek Philosophy* [London: Adam and Charles Black, 1908], Fragments 115, 117, 120, pp. 256–7). Though the transmigrations and the cave resemble Eliot's, they prove that the poem is polymorphously allusive, rather than exhausting its prefigurements: for the hero's metamorphoses continue in the work of hermeneutics long after the last shadow has descended in the text.

¹⁴ Georges Poulet, *Studies in Human Time*, trans. Elliot Coleman (Baltimore: Johns Hopkins University Press, 1956), p. 16.

¹⁵ *The Waste Land*, I, 25–30.

¹⁶ See Plato, *The Republic* (London: Dent, 1906), bk. VII, pp. 220ff.

¹⁷ See Mallarmé, *Oeuvres complètes*, ed. Henri Mondor and G. Jean-Aubry (Paris: Gallimard, 1945), p. 851; and Jacques Derrida, "The Double Session", in *Dissemination*, trans. Barbara Johnson (Chicago: Chicago University Press, 1981), pp. 210ff.

¹⁸ *Eliot's Early Years*, p. 91.

¹⁹ See *Murder in the Cathedral*, CPP, pp. 274–5.

²⁰ Eusebius writes, "Narcissus appeared from somewhere, as if come to life again", after his exile among the rocks (Eusebius, *Ecclesiastical History*, vol. I, bk. VI, 9, p. 185).

²¹ See Freud, *Beyond the Pleasure Principle*, in *The Complete Psychological Works*, trans. James Strachey (London: Hogarth, 1953–74), vol. 18, pp. 1–64. Henceforth cited as SE (Standard Edition).

22 Freud, "On Narcissism: An Introduction", vol. 14, p. 90.

23 Gordon says that "Prufrock" was completed in July–August, 1911 (*Eliot's Early Years*, p. 45); and Eliot, in a letter to John C. Pope, stated that the poem was conceived in 1910. See J. C. Pope, "Prufrock and Raskolnikov Again: a letter from Eliot", *American Literature*, 18 (1947), 319–21. "Prufrock" was first published in *Poetry*, 6 (1915), 130–5.

24 See Maurice Merleau-Ponty, *The Visible and the Invisible*, trans. Alphonso Lingis (Evanston: Northwestern University Press, 1968), p. 139; Jacques Lacan, "Of the Gaze as Objet Petit a'", in *The Four Fundamental Concepts of Psycho-Analysis* (London: Hogarth, 1977).

25 *The Gaze of Orpheus*, p. 74.

26 See *Feminine Sexuality: Jacques Lacan and the école freudienne*, ed. Juliet Mitchell and Jacqueline Rose (New York: Norton, 1982), p. 141.

27 See Roustang, *Psychoanalysis Never Lets Go*, trans. Ned Lukacher (Baltimore: Johns Hopkins University Press, 1980), pp. 66–7; see also Freud, *Beyond the Pleasure Principle*, SE, vol. 18, pp. 1–64.

28 See SE, vol. 12, p. 104.

29 Freud, *Totem and Taboo*, SE, vol. 13, p. 81.

30 Quoted in Jacques Derrida, "From Restricted to General Economy: A Hegelianism without Reserve", in *Writing and Difference* (Chicago: University of Chicago Press, 1978), p. 258.

31 See also "The 'Uncanny'", where Freud speaks of the double as at once the "assurance of immortality" and the "uncanny harbinger of death" (SE, vol. 17, p. 235).

32 See Ernest Jones, *Hamlet and Oedipus* (1949; New York: Norton, 1976), p. 89: the idea is Otto Rank's.

33 See SE, vol. 12, p. 159.

34 See Derrida, "Freud and the Scene of Writing", in *Writing and Difference*, pp. 227ff.

35 "Burnt Norton", V, 38–9.

36 See Harold Bloom, *Poetry and Repression: Revisionism from Blake to Stevens* (New Haven: Yale University Press, 1976), esp. ch.1.

37 *The Invisible Poet: T. S. Eliot* (1959; rpt. London: Methuen, 1979), p. 35. On p. 3, Kenner argues that the name was an unconscious reminiscence of "Prufrock-Littau, furniture wholesalers".

38 See Robert Langbaum, "New Modes of Characterization in *The Waste Land*", in *T. S. Eliot in his Time: essays on the occasion of the fiftieth anniversary of The Waste Land*, ed. A. Walton Litz (Princeton: Princeton University Press, 1973), p. 98. For critics who agree with Langbaum, see, for instance, George Williamson, *A Reader's Guide to T. S. Eliot: a poem-by-poem analysis* (New York: H. Woolf, 1953), pp. 59, 65; Elizabeth Schneider, "Prufrock and After: the theme of change", *Publications of the Modern Language Association of America*, 87 (1972), 1104; C. K. Stead, *The New Poetic: Yeats to Eliot* (London: Hutchinson, 1964), pp. 149, 152, 154; see also Robert Langbaum, *The Poetry of Experience: The Dramatic Monologue in Modern Literary Tradition* (New York: Norton, 1957), p. 190. My own view is closer to Robert M. Adams, who sees Prufrock as "a set of quasi-persons", in "Precipitating Eliot", in Litz (ed.), *Eliot in his Time*, p. 148.

[39] Quoted from a letter to Kristian Smidt in his *Poetry and Belief in the Work of T. S. Eliot* (1949; rpt. London: Routledge and Kegan Paul, 1961), p. 85.

[40] *The Letters of Ezra Pound: 1907–41*, ed. D. D. Paige (1950; rpt. New York: New Directions, 1971), p. 153; Stead, p. 153.

[41] *Poetry and Belief*, p. 85.

[42] Lacan, *Feminine Sexuality*, p. 154.

[43] This is John E. Jackson's idea, in *La Question du moi: un aspect de la modernité poétique européenne: T. S. Eliot – Paul Célan – Yves Bonnefoy* (Neuchatel: Editions de la Baconnière, 1978), p. 50.

[44] See "Ash Wednesday", III, 19, *CPP*, p. 93.

[45] See *The Waste Land*, V, 385, *CPP*, p. 73.

[46] See Freud, "On Fetishism", SE, vol. 21, pp. 149–57. In "The 'Uncanny' " (1919), Freud makes the link explicit, when he compares the double, which represents the "energetic denial of the power of death", to the multiplication of phallic symbols in dreams, which represent the denial of castration (SE, vol. 18, p. 235).

[47] Anon., rev. of *Prufrock and Other Observations*, *Times Literary Supplement*, 805 (1917), 299. For a similar view in an early reviewer see anon., rev. of *Ara Vos Prec*, *Times Literary Supplement*, 948 (1920), 184. Terry Eagleton also mentions the fetishistic aspect of "Prufrock" in *Exiles and Emigrés* (London: Chatto and Windus, 1970), p. 143.

[48] Eliot, "Beyle and Balzac", rev. of *History of the French Novel, to the Close of the Nineteenth Century*, 2, by George Saintsbury, *Atheneum*, 464 (1919), 392–3.

[49] *Time in the Poetry of T. S. Eliot* New Jersey: Barnes and Noble, 1981), pp. 15–16.

[50] It was Josef Breuer's patient "Anna O." who coined the phrase "the talking cure" for psychoanalysis: see Breuer and Freud, *Studies on Hysteria*, SE, vol. 2, p. 30.

[51] *The Use of Poetry and the Use of Criticism* (1933; rpt. London: Faber, 1964), p. 133.

[52] See Jacques Derrida, *Of Grammatology*, trans. Gayatri Chakravorty Spivak (Baltimore and London: Johns Hopkins University Press, 1976), p. 65. See also Friedrich Nietzsche, *Der Wille Zur Macht, Gesammelte Werke* (Munchen: Musarion Verlag, 1922), vol. 19, no. 522, p. 34.

[53] James Joyce, *Ulysses* (Harmondsworth: Penguin, 1969), p. 391.

[54] See Blanchot, *The Gaze of Orpheus*, p. 74.

[55] See Georges Bataille, *Visions of Excess: Selected Writings, 1927–1939*, trans. Allan Stoekl, *Theory and History of Literature*, Vol. 14 (Minneapolis: University of Minnesota Press, 1985), Pt. II; and Derrida, "From Restricted to General Economy: a Hegelianism without reserve", in *Writing and Difference*, trans. Alan Bass (London: Routledge, 1978), p. 257.

[56] Northrop Frye, *T. S. Eliot* (Edinburgh and London: Oliver and Boyd, 1963), p. 84; Gabriel Pearson, "Eliot: An American Use of Symbolism", in *Eliot in Perspective: A Symposium*, ed. Graham Martin (London: Macmillan, 1970), pp. 85–6; Hugh Kenner, *The Invisible Poet*, p. 116. For speculations on the influence of Henry Adams on Eliot's view of history, see Harvey Gross, " 'Gerontion' and the Meaning of History", *Publications of the Modern Language Association of America*, 73 (1958), 299–304.

[57] René Descartes, *Philosophical Works*, trans. Haldane and Ross (1911; rpt. New York: Dover, 1931), p. 157.

[58] See Derrida, *Of Grammatology*, p. 66.

[59] Ibid., p. 87.

[60] See Epicurus, Letter to Herodotus, II, in *Letters, Principle Doctrines, and Vatican Sayings*, trans. Russell M. Geer (Indianapolis and New York: Bobbs-Merrill, 1964), pp. 12–13; see also Jacques Derrida, "My Chances/*Mes Chances*: a rendezvous with some Epicurean stereophonies", in *Taking Chances: Derrida, Psychoanalysis, and Literature*, ed. Joseph H. Smith and William Kerrigan (Baltimore and London: Johns Hopkins University Press, 1984), pp. 1–32.

[61] See T. S. Eliot, *On Poetry and Poets* (London: Faber, 1957), p. 16, where he argues that "before the use of written language . . . the memory of the primitive bards, story-tellers and scholars must have been prodigious". In this prejudice he follows Plato (*Phaedrus*, ch. 25, p. 157): "If men learn [writing], it will implant forgetfulness in their souls: they will cease to exercise memory because they rely on that which is written, calling things to remembrance no longer from within themselves, but by means of external marks . . ." See Derrida, *Of Grammatology*, p. 24, for a discussion of this passage.

[62] See Derrida, *Positions*, trans. Alan Bass (Chicago: University of Chicago Press, 1982), pp. 81, 94.

[63] Derrida (*Positions*, p. 81) stresses that spacing must be conceived of as a *movement*.

[64] See Derrida, *Grammatology*, p. 24.

[65] Mallarmé, "Quant au livre", in *Oeuvres complètes*, p. 370.

[66] See Derrida, "The Double Session" in *Dissemination*, pp. 175–286, for a similar analysis of the play of "les blancs" in Mallarmé.

[67] See Bonamy Dobrée, "T. S. Eliot: a personal reminiscence", in *T. S. Eliot: The Man and his Work*, ed. Allen Tate (New York: Dell, 1966), p. 78.

[68] See I. Kant, *Critique of Pure Reason*, trans. Norman Kemp Smith (New York: St Martin's, 1965), pp. 65–6; M. Heidegger, *Kant and the Problem of Metaphysics* (Bloomington: Indiana University Press, 1962), p. 194. See also John Brenkman's fuller discussion of these passages in "Narcissus in the Text", p. 314.

[69] The Varieties of Metaphysical Poetry III, Three Lectures delivered at Johns Hopkins University, January, 1933: The Turnbull Lectures, MS. Houghton Library, Cambridge, Massachusetts, b.MS.Am 1261.

[70] *The Use of Poetry*, p. 130.

[71] *The Gaze of Orpheus*, p. 93.

[72] *On Poetry and Poets*, pp. 31, 17.

Frost's thanatography

WALLACE MARTIN

Unaffected by the contentions of critical theorists during the past two decades, Frost's admirers have been struggling with problems imposed upon them by traditional criticism and scholarship. One of these emerged from analysis of his poems. The new critics assumed that the ambiguity, paradox, tension, and irony uncovered during explication could be subsumed in a unifying attitude authorized by the dramatic speaker. Explication of Frost's poems revealed that often they do not conform to this model – not because it is difficult to envision a plausible speaker, but because diverse speakers, and hence disparate interpretations, can be educed from a single poem. The new critical fiction that separates the speaker from the writer cannot be sustained in the face of a suspicion that we, the readers, are being gulled by the writer's crafty evasions. Hence we are driven to seek the person behind the persona. And it has been biography, that final, factual ground for the unification of meaning, reference, self, and art, that has cast a pall over Frost's literary stature in the eyes of his admirers.

Since 1966, Lawrance Thompson's biography (the last volume of which appeared ten years later) has been the skeleton in the closet of Frost studies. Weak critics have repeatedly claimed there is no skeleton, but the figure they parade in its place, decked with the wry humor, geniality, and sustaining wisdom they learned to love, is obviously a scarecrow. Strong critics – David Bromwich and Helen Vendler – admit that they have seen a genuine skeleton (their ontology certifying its authenticity), and face the destructive consequences of this revelation. Thompson's scrupulously documented picture of the poet shows us a selfish, egotistical, cunning, paranoid, manic depressive, anatomized in the index, as Pritchard notes, in headings such as: anti-intellectual, brute, cowardice, depression, escapist, fear, hate, insanity, jealousy, prophet, puritan, rage, rebel, revenge. Here is a man who, as baffler–teaser–deceiver, charlatan, myth-maker, and pretender in pursuit of the ideal (among other headings) could indeed produce the public figure and poetic personae that readers learned to love, and that discerning critics always distrusted.

Despite their commitment to fact and reference, traditional critics have seldom subjected their literary judgments entirely to biography. In the end, they are concerned not with the flesh-and-blood writer but with the author, who unites personae and person, texts and acts. Frank Lentricchia provides one explanation of how this inner unity differs from its outward manifestations: "because consciousness is continuous, the self maintains its identity through time, thereby insuring that the individual poems in the Frost canon, though spread out through the poet's private and public history, are enveloped by a guiding presence which guarantees the wholeness of the poetic corpus" (pp. 14–15; page numbers refer to works cited on page 405). Poirier subscribes to a similar view: "the biographical material does not tell us as much about the man as the poetry does . . . The kind of poetry he wrote, and the kind of experiences to which he was susceptible, emerge from the same configuration in him, prior to his poems or to his experiences" (pp. 63–4).

This view allows the critic to rescue the poet from his life and lesser poetry. Hence Lentricchia can distinguish Frost's "redemptive imagination" from those "terrible moments when, impelled by a disturbed psyche, it shapes out a 'lesser' (not a 'better') world destructive of the self" (p. 12). Hence Poirier can blame Frost's association with "second-rate literary minds" and "people ignorant of social theory" for some of his shortcomings, in order to preserve his "best self" from his weaker performances and disreputable ironies (pp. 237, 242). What seems most remarkable, a decade after the publication of their books on Frost, is that they represented him as a tough-minded pragmatist, opposed to the idealism of Kantian aesthetics and the commitment to imagination characteristic of Emerson and Stevens – yet failed to recognize that their position was based on an internalization of idealism in their conception of the "self".

Another way to preserve Frost from his biography is to argue that the self is unknowable, and that the life of the poet requires a special kind of interpretation. This is the method of William Pritchard: "My decision to write a 'literary life' of Frost came out of the belief that whatever he did, for better or worse, was done poetically, was performed in a style which must not be pushed out of the way in order to get at the 'real' or 'deeper' motives that supposedly underlay it . . . My procedure is to move back and forth between life and art, often blurring the distinctions in the interest of telling a story of a literary life" (pp. xvi–xvii). Uncertainty about Frost's life results in part from the fact that he often gave Thompson different accounts of a single incident (Sutton). Pritchard suggests a literary explanation: "It might be that with sufficient play of mind – sufficient unto the needs of a poet – any significant choice can and must be imagined and successively reimagined . . . to tell a story about the self which stays fresh" (pp. 3–4). As responsible biographer, Thompson was constrained to choose between these stories; as sympathetic critic, Pritchard is forced to accept them all, because poets may become stale if they don't blur fact and fiction. Driven to such extremes of undecidability, traditional criticism seems scarcely distinguishable from its post-structuralist alternatives.

Rather than deliberately blurring life and art, the critic might better seek some pattern in the literary life as such, on the assumption that art, rather than adding style to a life that would otherwise be intelligible, shapes an artistic career in ways that remain unnoticed by most biographers. Such is Lawrence Lipking's thesis in *The Life of the Poet*. The first decisive moment in the poet's career is that of initiation:

When Robert Frost, for instance, reread his best early poem, 'The Tuft of Flowers', sixteen years later [1913], something about its happy message and pretty language . . . must have struck him as facile . . . Frost's soliloquy changed to a debate. *North of Boston*, the book that resulted, opens with an explicit statement of intentions, on the page after the table of contents: "*Mending Wall* takes up the theme where A Tuft of Flowers in *A Boy's Will* laid it down".
. . . A harder, broken speech replaces the language of the flowers. And through that act of reinterpretation Frost becomes Frost. That is the way that a poet comes into his own.   (p. 10)

In annotating this paragraph, Lipking mars its exemplary force by remarking that it was the mixed critical reception of *A Boy's Will* as well as solitary musing that "provoked" Frost into the change of style from soliloquy to debate and dialogue. But at least two of the dialogue poems in *North of Boston* had been written before 1912, and others, according to Thompson (vol. 1, p. 428), were written that year. What then is the biographical basis for this description of the moment of initiation in 1913 when Frost reread "A Tuft of Flowers"? There is none; Lipking has imagined it. Yet it is necessary to posit such moments to make the life of the poet intelligible, in traditional terms.

It was Frost who, through a prefatory note, provided the basis for Lipking's genetic account of the relationship between the first and second books. As Lipking says, "great poets forge their own identities" (p. 4). Frost admitted that his was a forgery in a letter written to Untermeyer in 1916:

The poet in me died nearly ten years ago. Fortunately he had run through several phases, four to be exact, all well-defined, before he went. The calf I was in the nineties I merely take to market. I am become my own salesman. Two of my phases you have been so – what shall I say – as to like. Take care that you don't get your mouth set to declare the other two (as I release them) a falling off of power . . . since they were almost inextricably mixed with the first two in the writing and only my sagacity has separated or sorted them in the afterthought for putting on the market.   (*Letters*, p. 201)

This letter has troubled Frost's critics, and one might have expected it to trouble Lipking: the pattern which he discerns in the lives of the poets is one they may have contrived to plant there, knowing critics want to unearth it. Though the hard-headed among them may be able to swallow or discount Frost's claim that he stages his own "development", they reject the assertion that "the poet" in him died nearly ten years before 1916, as well as the following passage:

The day I did The Trial by Existence (*Boy's Will*) says I to myself, this is the way of all flesh. I was not much over twenty, but I was wise for my years . . . I must get as much done as possible before thirty. I tell you, Louis, it's all over at thirty. . . I took measures accordingly. And now my time is my own. I have myself all in a strong box where I can unfold as a personality at discretion.   (*Letters*, p. 202)

Poirier: "Quantitatively the claim is absurd that in 1916 he had all the poems that were subsequently to appear . . . Control and management of the self is expressed in a fantasy that depends on holding back something that he had in store, and for which an imagined trunk full of completed poems is only a metaphor" (pp. 78–9). Thompson says the letter was written in a "gloomy, self-lacerating mood" (vol. 2, p. 539); Pritchard characterizes it as "playful" and remarks that "the fantasy" of the strong box "deliberately exaggerates the facts" (pp. 133–4). How can Frost be saved from his fantasies? First, by placing his "strong box" in the historical context he shared with Untermeyer, one preserved in Bartlett's *Familiar Quotations*, which contains a poem by Bertha Adams Backus famous in its time ("Then Laugh", 1911):

> Build for yourself a strong-box
> Fashion each part with care
> When it's strong as your hand can make it,
> Put all your troubles there;
> Hide there all thought of your failures . . .

But what are we to make of the egotistical, self-pitying claim that the poet in him died around 1906 ("it's all over at thirty"), about the time that he completed "The Trial by Existence"?

That poem contains one of Frost's revisionary readings of Shelley ("The light of heaven falls whole and white / And is not shattered into dyes"). In the context of the letter, this reworking of "Adonais" can be understood as an identification with the fate of Shelley and Keats. Frost's lie to himself may be more outrageous than the one Poirier and Pritchard impute to him. To convince himself that he was as great as those poets, Frost may have inferred that his achievements, at thirty, should equal theirs. Having failed to equal them, he claims to Untermeyer that the poems to appear in the future have either been written or stored internally, before the poet's death, whence the "self" can "unfold" them as "personality".

Given the incoherence of traditional readings of Frost, which would save him by explaining his "fantasies", endowing him with a "self" separated from his acts and texts, and trimming his literary corpus to fit the fashions sanctioned by one or another mode of traditional criticism, one might try to take him at his word, wherever it may lead. His remark about "the way of all flesh" leads toward Paul de Man's assertion that literature "originates in the void that separates intent from reality. The imagination takes its flight only after the void, the inauthenticity of the existential project has been revealed; literature begins where the existential demystification ends" (pp. 34–5). Frost dates his consciousness of death, when he "did" "The Trial by Existence", in the mid 1890s (Thompson says the first draft was written in 1892); the poem was completed in 1906, at about which time Frost claims that he died as a poet. While the connection de Man posits between the birth of the imagination and a consciousness of death may explain Frost's coming-of-age as a poet, it does nothing to explain either the purported death of "the poet in me" about ten years later or the poetic productivity of the following years.

Loss of faith in one's imaginative gift is a topos that Bloom, following the Romantic poets, has explored at length. The consciousness of utter poverty, of having nothing to say that has not already been said, is a feeling which most of us who write about literature have not (for better or worse) experienced. It can drive the poet to the extremes of revisionism that Bloom discusses – writing becomes an aggressive rewriting – and essays that apply this insight to Frost remain to be written. But Bloom, like de Man, tells only part of the story. The inauthenticity of the existential project and the death of the imagination are incorporated or encrypted in the living tomb of the poet who, ironically, has survived to remember these events. Yet he cannot, properly speaking, remember them, except as a negation: they can be voluntarily recalled only as that which does not exist.

Only by accident is the poet given access to the forgotten resources that were stored, unconsciously, during the days of his power. In "The Figure a Poem Makes", Frost describes the experience:

For me the initial delight is in the surprise of remembering something I didn't know I knew. I am in a place, in a situation, as if I had materialized from cloud or risen out of the ground. There is a glad recognition of the long lost and the rest follows. Step by step the wonder and unexpected supply keeps growing. The impressions most useful to my purpose seem always those I was unaware of and so made no note of at the time when taken, and the conclusion is come to that like giants we are always hurling experience ahead of us to pave the future with against the day when we may want to strike a line of purpose across it for somewhere.

The cloud and giant are parsed, with a difference, elsewhere in Frost's prose. Fourteen years earlier, in the introduction to an anthology of poems from Dartmouth College, he said that

a poet's germination is less like that of a bean in the ground than of a waterspout at sea. He has to begin as a cloud of all the other poets he ever read . . . The base of water he picks up from below is of course all the life he ever lived outside of books.

The mature poet differs from the novice only in his ability to draw the waters of experience up toward the cloud of past poems, so that the two join "to roll as one pillar between heaven and earth". The figure of the giant reappears in "The Constant Symbol" (1946):

The mind is a baby giant who, more provident in the cradle than he knows, has hurled his paths in life all round ahead of him like playthings given – data so-called. They are vocabulary, grammar, prosody, and diary, and it will go hard if he can't find stepping stones of them for his feet wherever he wants to go.

The poem, in Frost's view, is for its maker always a double reading (of past experience, and of other texts) and hence always a double repetition. The poet is thanatographer, perpetually rediscovering a dead self and finding that it provided for a future – the "now" of its verbal memorial. Aside from the emphasis on verbal experience, the structure Frost describes is of course that of what M. H. Abrams calls "the greater Romantic lyric": "it begins with a description of the peaceful outer scene, this . . . calls forth a recollection in tranquillity of earlier experiences in the same setting and leads to a sequence of reflections" (p. 80). We tend to associate this pattern with its reassuring exemplars, which according to Abrams attain a fusion of subject and object or provide providential solace for the future. But Abrams points out that in many such poems the subject is "a recurrent state often called by the specialised term 'dejection' " (p. 104). If Frost had written a poem on the subject (as did Coleridge, Wordsworth, and Shelley) rather than telling Untermeyer about it in a letter, his critics might take more kindly to the death of the poet in him.

Frost used this pattern throughout his life and repeatedly referred to it in his prose, despite the fact that it was seldom the structuring principle of the later poems. It presupposes an unreflective confidence in the possibility of moving back and forth across the cut separating the imaginary from the symbolic, stitching the two together along the way, and an equal confidence in the reader who will witness the process. If the reader draws back to judge the persona who thus relaxes conscious control, the poet may be hurt; if the poet draws back from the persona to represent dramatically the self-mystification that the process can entail, the reader may misunderstand, experiencing a sympathetic identification when the writer intended to depict an error. In one of the few valuable essays on Frost published during the past decade, David Wyatt describes a common form of this error: "the fictions of order a self projects back onto experience, even while that experience is still to be completed . . . supplant the moment it actually lived" (p. 135).

Reviewers of Frost's first two books led him to realize that his personae were being mistaken for himself and that the person he ventured to expose was subject to unthinking, callous judgment. His defenses against such misunderstanding included a toughening of the personae (leading toward irony and humor) and, more subtly and perhaps vengefully, the creation of poems so beautiful and non-committal that they would be imputed to varied personae. For example, distinguished critics have characterized "Neither Out Far Nor In Deep" as profound, tender and terrible, "a neatly turned piece of entertainment", and as a "freakish" representation of "ordinary folk". In such cases, as Wyatt remarks, "the reader is the figure a Frost poem makes" – a conclusion underwritten in Frost's late poem "Iota Subscript".

More important, given the rapidity of his rise to fame and the literary contentions into which his notoriety thrust him, he had to develop a persona of his own. To chart its development, one would need to trace critical responses to his work, identifying the persona that reviewers, at each stage, thrust upon him, and then to note how he tried to reinforce or alter that image in his succeeding poems. In response to reviewers of *North of Boston* (including Amy Lowell) who represented him as a grim, humourless recorder of the decay of New England, he produced the comic and satirical poems in *Mountain Interval* and *New Hampshire*. At first troubled by the ways in which he was being associated with the New Humanism of Irving Babbitt, and then hurt by the hostile fire from the political left which resulted from that association, he produced a persona in the poems of *A Further Range* that, after the fact, justified the earlier attacks. To say that "he became his admirers" is to point out one lamentable aspect of poetic fame; far worse is the poet's fate or choice to become the persona that has been imagined by his enemies.

On occasion, Frost attempted to explain this progression. In "The Constant Symbol", he described two exemplary careers (those of a minister and an American President) to show how choices that early in life seem inconsequential can lead to "alien entanglements" that pervert the intentions and ideals of youth. These paragraphs stick out from the surrounding text, leading one to infer that Frost wanted their message applied to himself. Quite apart from the usefulness of such evidence for those interested in the career of the poet and Frost's view of himself, it could be argued that the interpretation of many of Frost's later poems turns on assumptions about the relationships between his persona, his audiences (there were several), and the public images that mediated between them. Recent studies of autobiography contribute to an understanding of these relationships, which are most concisely adumbrated in "Borges and I".

Necessary as it is for an understanding of the bulk of Frost's poetry, reception study should not divert attention from the strict logic which leads from the moments of joyful reminiscence in the early lyrics to the unconsoling ontology of some late poems. Thus to "stage" a progression from early to late is to create a misleading story, but a necessary one, since narration is the method, subject, and theme of the texts involved.

Distracted by the necessity to deal with Frost's critics, as he himself was, I neglected to explore the implications of his description of poetic creation. A moment of consciousness or forgetfulness brings back an earlier experience, sensory or verbal, from the crypt of the poet who has died. A sense of repetition suggests the possibility of discovering the real. In creating a path between the past and the present, the poem reveals a teleology – the earlier of the two incidents seems to have existed so that it could find its fulfilment in the later one – yet the former, as it turns out, is one that had no particular significance when it occurred. As Frost remarks, "the logic is backward, in retrospect, after the act". The past moment from which creation springs must be unknowing; it cannot entail intentionality or purpose. Poetic creation can serve as a paradigm for the interpretation of other phenomena, since all theories, no matter what their scientific pretensions, are in Frost's view ultimately metaphors. Evolution, which is a form of creation, might then have proceeded not as a mere adaptation to circumstance, or a fortuitous collocation of accidents, but as a series of unknowing events that could find their purpose only in later consciousness. This view underlies a number of poems Frost wrote in the 1930s.

Another corollary of this view is that no intentional act can be performed with knowledge of its consequences. We know, fully, only in retrospect, when a moment of unanticipated recollection reveals what we unwittingly laid in wait for our future. Used as a metaphor in interpreting politics, this view leads to the conclusion that a government which intervenes in the lives of its citizens acts blindly. Since the ultimate effect of an action is likely to be different from the one it was intended to produce, a government that acts with good intentions is likely to produce harmful results. The implications of the theory for the individual are equally harsh. We never really know what we do.

Balanced against the heartening assertion that we are like giants, hurling experience ahead of us to pave the future, is this sentence, written in 1892: "For those who fix today a point through which from earlier years they draw a line of life projected far into the future, this hour is of a deep significance." They act in blindness. The alternative is to yield to accident and whim, as Frost's sterner critics have pointed out. They would probably condemn Kierkegaard's irony on the same grounds. Given our ignorance of the present and the future, we should await understanding, rather than looking for information that will allay our bewilderment. Frost's fullest justification of this conclusion in prose can be found in "The Prerequisites".

These forms of unknowing can be as destructive as Frost's critics think they are. Knowledge is always undercut by narrative. And the narrative we construct in retrospect, by backward logic, has no stability because the future will reveal another "present" that will alter our configuration of the past. That is why the story of one's life keeps changing. Where critics find a stable self, Frost asks: "Who in Hell are we? That is the question for all over seventy-five" (Sergeant, p. xvi). Occasionally Frost states the deconstructive basis of his thought, as in "Carpe Diem": "But bid life seize the present? / It lives less in the present / Than in the future always, / And less in both together / Than in the past. The present / Is too much for the senses." Such passages drive his admirers to gentle correction or stern admonition.

Given these premises, no attempt to extract a message from his works, based on a stable relationship between signifiers and signifieds, can possibly succeed. He himself was not content with this perpetually shifting system, and attempted, in some poems, to cut through it, to uncover what we have learned to call its ontological basis. It is this aspect of his thought that connects him with Heidegger (a relationship that Joseph Riddel will discuss in a forthcoming publication). His allegorical poems, although no less ambiguous than the lyrics that lead gently from experience to symbol, allow less latitude for humanistic recuperation.

"Beech", the first poem in *A Witness Tree*, is one such allegory. A forester marks off a right-angled line in a forest (not at its edge). Actually, he does not mark it; he imagines it, after placing "an iron spine / And pile of rocks" as a reference-point from which it is projected. No plot is thus marked − enclosure would require another line − and in any case the forester, unlike the farmer, has no use for an act of appropriation in the middle of a wood.

The forester intends not to claim ownership, but to establish "truth", the truth of his being "not unbounded". In keeping with the conventions employed to ensure the validity of such actions, there must be a witness to certify the signature of the one who asserts or appropriates. The witness in this case is a tree, and the signature takes the form of a cut, a slash on the witness.

The first, imaginary line, marking off nothing from nothing, was not enough to establish the difference, the appropriation necessary to create truth. It must be guaranteed by a second mark, not imaginary but real − a form of violence against nature. Things must be forced to remember, to bear witness to our appropriation. They must be wounded. ("A thing is branded on the memory to make it stay there; only what goes on hurting will stick." *The Genealogy of Morals*, II, iii.) Then when we look at things, they confirm the division we have made to establish meaning by returning to us testimony of the endurance of our division.

These acts are "circumstanced with dark and doubt". The witness tree is circum-stanced by other trees (which create the dark surrounding it); the doubt they cannot experience is supplied by the forester. What is doubtful is not some particular truth about man or nature, but the act of establishing truth by imagining a line and making a scar, a cut that when healed is only a trace that may appear to be natural. Without the lines, no truth, and no doubt. With them comes truth that is undecidable (not bounded, not unbounded). No dark for birch, before its grey bark is scored. Present to be witness, the birch survives as testament of a primal writing that as yet says nothing; but even that nothing is already doubtful.

In a later poem, "In Winter in the Woods Alone", there is no attempt to sort out the duplicities attendant on the act of doubly dividing and signing to create meaning. The persona enters a wood, marks a tree, chops it down, and retreats to prepare "another blow". This pointless violence is an attempt to cut through to "the thing". "The thing is not an object; it cannot become one." At the same time, self and other, human and inhuman, are reversible terms. We are all marked men. "By means of [his attack] he seizes himself, cuts into